A History of France

from the Earliest Times to the Treaty of Versailles

William Stearns Davis

Must Have Books
503 Deerfield Place
Victoria, BC
V9B 6G5
Canada
trava2911@gmail.com

ISBN: 9781773236780

Copyright 2021 – Must Have Books

All rights reserved in accordance with international law. No part of this book may be reproduced or transmitted in any form or by any means, electronic or mechanical, including photocopying, recording, or by any information storage or retrieval system, except in the case of excerpts by a reviewer who may quote brief passages in an article or review, without written permission from the publisher.

TO THE MEMORY OF
HARRY DEIMAN
CHAPLAIN 354TH UNITED STATES INFANTRY
KILLED IN ACTION IN FRANCE
FIGHTING FOR THE CAUSE OF LIBERTY
SEPTEMBER 29, 1918

NAPOLEON I

PREFACE

THIS book was originally intended for members of the American army who naturally would desire to know something of the past of the great French nation on whose soil they expected to do battle for Liberty. The happy but abrupt close of the war vitiated this purpose, but the volume was continued and was extended on a somewhat more ambitious scale to assist in making intelligent Americans in general acquainted with the history of a country with which we have established an ever-deepening friendship.

During the war period, when this task was begun, it seemed possible at first to take some elementary history of France in the French language, translate the same, and present it to new readers in a suitable American dress. This soon appeared impracticable, but certain French manuals were extremely helpful in preparing this work. This is true of the well-known *Histoire de la civilisation française* by M. Alfred Rambaud, and even more particularly of the three admirable volumes of M. Albert Malet's *Histoire de France*, which, taken consecutively, form a national history for use in secondary schools superior possibly to any similar books wherein English or American students learn the story of their own respective countries. Very specific acknowledgment must be made of M. Malet's work for material used in Chapters IX, XIII, and XVIII, which utilization in some cases almost amounts to a free translation. The same is true also of the supplemental matter on the acquisition of the French Colonies (Chapter XXV). Of course every competent scholar of French history will recognize the well-known books in the English language which have been frequently laid under contribution. They are listed with other important volumes in

PREFACE

the bibliography of works on French history in English, given in the appendix. Certain sections relating to the Frankish kings, and to life in the Middle Ages, have also been adapted from the present author's own short *History of Mediæval and Modern Europe* (Boston, 1914).

To readers interested in the present-day problems of Europe (and what Americans are not?) the reforms of Napoleon are likely to seem more important than those of Charlemagne, and the policy of Thiers and Gambetta than that of Philip Augustus. The story of France is an extremely long one, and inevitably the narrative is obliged to begin with only a jejune outline, but this has been gradually allowed to broaden and deepen, so that the major fraction of the entire book is devoted to the period since 1789; and the story of the "New Régime," of its sorrows, reverses, and final vindication and victory in 1918, is told with considerable detail, and one may hope with corresponding clarity and helpfulness.

One limitation must be stated very frankly. No other *one* nation of Europe has touched so many outside factors as France. A complete history of France would make an almost equally complete history of nearly all the great wars and major diplomatic intrigues that have agitated Europe. To write a short history, therefore, that was not simply to degenerate into a dry epitome, *military and diplomatic annals have perforce been cut to the bone*. The story has been the story of the French people, its progress, setbacks, trials, and victories, and only so far as foreign or military events have contributed to that story have they been mentioned.

Very hearty recognition and thanks are due to my assistant, Miss Gertrude A. Jacobsen, A.M., Fellow in History in the University of Minnesota, who redacted the entire text of this volume, prepared the maps, compiled the chronological and bibliographical tables as well as the appendix on the "States General," and also did a large amount of the necessary translating. Without her faithful and highly scholarly and efficient

PREFACE

aid, the successful completion of the book would have been wellnigh impossible. Warm thanks also are due to my colleagues Dean Guy S. Ford and Professors M. W. Tyler and A. C. Krey, of the History Department of this university, for careful reading of the manuscript, and for many valuable suggestions and corrections.

W. S. D.

The University of Minnesota
Minneapolis, Minn.

CONTENTS

I. The Land of the Gauls and the French	1
II. The Roman Province and the Frankish Kingdom	9
III. From Franks to Frenchmen	29
IV. The Golden Age of Feudalism (996–1270)	42
V. Life in the Feudal Ages	64
VI. The Dawn of the Modern Era (1270–1483)	81
VII. The Turbulent Sixteenth Century (1483–1610)	107
VIII. The Great Cardinal and his Successor	132
IX. Louis XIV, the Sun King: His Work in France	152
X. Louis XIV, Dominator of Europe	170
XI. The Wane of the Old Monarchy	196
XII. France, the Homeland of New Ideas	214
XIII. Old France on the Eve of the Revolution	243
XIV. The Fiery Coming of the New Régime (1789–92)	268
XV. The Years of Blood and Wrath (1792–95)	299
XVI. Napoleon Bonaparte, as Master of Europe	330
XVII. The Napoleonic Régime in France: The Consulate and the Empire	349
XVIII. "Glory and Madness" — Moscow, Leipzig, and Waterloo	381
XIX. The Restored Bourbons and their Exit	395

CONTENTS

XX. The "Citizen-King" and the Rule of the Bourgeois 418

    Aspects of French Life under the Restored Monarchy (1814–48)   439

XXI. Radical Outbreaks and the Reaction to Cæsarism: The Second Republic (1848–51)   453

XXII. Napoleon the Little: His Prosperity and Decadence   472

XXIII. The Crucifixion by Prussia (1870–71)   496

ILLUSTRATIONS

Napoleon I	*Frontispiece*
Merovingian Manor House	24
From Garnier and Ammann's *Histoire de l'Habitation humaine*	
The Louvre of Philip Augustus	58
After Hoffbauer's restoration	
Castle of Coucy (restored): Erected A.D. 1225–1230	64
This castle, one of the great historic monuments of France, was completely destroyed by the Germans in their retreat to the "Hindenburg Line" in March, 1917	
A Battle in the Fifteenth Century	92
After a drawing in a fifteenth-century manuscript of the *Chroniques de Froissart*. The battle portrayed is that of Auray (1364) but the armament is that of the fifteenth century and the landscape entirely conventional	
Attack and Defense of a City in the Fifteenth Century	92
After a drawing in a fifteenth-century manuscript of the *Chroniques de Froissart*. It figures the siege of Aubenton by the Comte de Hainault in 1340, with the equipment and architecture of the fifteenth century	
The Tournament at which Henry II was Mortally Wounded, June 19, 1559	114
After an engraving in the collection of Perdrissin and Tortorel, published in 1570	
Louis XI	118
Catherine de' Medici	118
Henry IV	118
Maximilien, Duke of Sully	118

ILLUSTRATIONS

Consecration of Louis XIV at Reims	146
After an engraving on copper by Lepautre	
Louis XIV	152
Cardinal Richelieu	152
Jean-Baptiste Colbert	152
Mme. de Pompadour	152
The Château of Versailles before the End of the Seventeenth Century	184
After an engraving on copper by G. Pérelle	
Voltaire	228
Jean-Jacques Rousseau	228
Mirabeau	228
Louis XVI	228
The Constituent Assembly at Versailles on the Night of August 4, 1789	276
From an engraving on copper by Helman after a design by Monnet	
Marie Antoinette	288
Robespierre	288
Marat	288
Danton	288
Napoleon in Bivouac in the Valley of the Grand-Saint-Bernard	334
After a design by Thévenin in the Museum of Versailles	
Louis-Philippe	424
Napoleon III	424
Adolphe Thiers	424

ILLUSTRATIONS

Léon Gambetta	424
Marshal Foch saluting the Statue of General Kléber after the Entry of the French into Strasbourg in 1918	600

    From a photograph copyrighted by Underwood & Underwood, New York

    With the exception of the portraits and the view of Marshal Foch at Strasbourg, the illustrations are reproduced from cuts in A. Parmentier's *Album Historique*, published in four volumes in Paris, 1896-1907.

MAPS

France, showing Provinces as existing in 1789 (*colored*)	
France, showing Places and Geographical Features mentioned in Chapter I	2
The Monarchy of the Franks	18
Charlemagne's Empire	34
France at the Accession of Philip Augustus, 1180	54
France about 1453	98
France, 1461-1492, under Louis XI and Charles of Burgundy	104
France, 1610-1715	132
Europe in 1810, showing Napoleon's Power at its Height	346
The French Empire in Africa, 1914	568
Indo-China and the French Possessions, 1914	574
France in Departments, 1871-1914 (*colored*)	602

A HISTORY OF FRANCE

CHAPTER I

THE LAND OF THE GAULS AND THE FRENCH

In 1869 a distinguished Frenchman, an ex-prime minister, began a long history of his nation with these words, "France inhabits a country, long ago civilized and Christianized, where despite much imperfection and much social misery, thirty-eight millions of men live in security and peace, under laws equal for all and efficiently upheld."[1] This statement was all the more true on the eve of the Great War in 1914. To understand the history of any country, however, it is absolutely necessary to understand something of its geography, and geographical factors have influenced the history of France certainly as much as that of any great nation of the Old World save possibly in the case of England.

Of the larger or more famous countries of Europe, Russia, the Scandinavian lands, Germany, Holland, and Belgium assuredly belong to the North, with its severe winters and the changes in civilization inevitable in a severe climate. Great Britain and Ireland are also Northern lands, but with their national life profoundly modified through encirclement by the sea. Greece, Italy, and Spain look out upon the blue Mediterranean. They are Southern lands — of the olive, the vine, and the luxurious forests. They receive the hot winds of Africa, and they have enjoyed direct contact with the older civilizations of the East. There is one land, however, that is both Southern and Northern, both of Southern wine and Northern corn; and whose southern shores have been trodden by the old Greeks and Phœnicians, while from her northern headlands can be seen the cliffs of

[1] Guizot.

southern England. That country is France, "the mediating land" (as has been well said) between ancient and modern civilization, and between southern and northern Europe.

France thus lies most decidedly in the cross-roads of world events. It is better to study her annals than those of any other *one* country in Europe, if the reader would get a general view of universal history. France has been a participant in, or interested spectator of, nearly every great war or diplomatic contest for over a thousand years; and a very great proportion of all the religious, intellectual, social, and economic movements which have affected the world either began in France or were speedily caught up and acted upon by Frenchmen soon after they had commenced their working elsewhere.

Nevertheless, geographically France is a highly separate and an economically independent nation. In 1914 she was probably less dependent on imported commodities and foreign commerce for her prosperous life than any other country in western Europe. She came far nearer to feeding herself than either England or Germany. Better than any other great power, saving the United States, she could have endured complete isolation and blockade provided she could have held intact her boundaries.[1] France is decidedly separated from her neighbors by great natural barriers. Her coast-line is longer than her land frontiers: there being 395 miles of water along the Mediterranean shores, 572 on the North Sea and the British Channel, and 584 on the open Atlantic and the stormy Bay of Biscay. To the south, the lofty Pyrenees form a barrier against Spain, which permitted France to feel very secure even in the days when Spain was formidable. Towards Italy and Switzerland, the Alps and their cousins the Jura are a still more reliable bulwark. Before 1870 the Rhine was a protection against Germany and, after the loss of Alsace-Lorraine, the Vosges Mountains were still a difficult problem for

[1] Of course very early in the war of 1914 the Germans seized the district of coal and iron mines in the northeast of France, thus putting the latter under a heavy handicap until relieved by England and America.

armies. Only towards the northwest, the Belgian boundary ran across fields arbitrarily marked off without natural limits, and here alone neither mountains nor rivers could come to the aid of French generals defending their homeland. It is not surprising, therefore, that it was across Belgium that in 1914 Prussian militarism attempted to "hack its way" to Paris, discarding neutral rights and plighted word.

As Old-World countries go, France has a large territory. Only Russia is essentially larger. As the crow flies it is 606 miles from north to south, 675 miles from northwest to southwest (the longest diagonal), and 556 miles from west to east. The total area in 1914 (before the recovery of Alsace-Lorraine) was about 200,700 square miles, now restored by the victory over Germany to about 206,300. Corsica, which is Italian in location though completely French in loyalty, added about 3375 more. France is thus somewhat smaller than Texas, the largest American federal state. She is much larger than California, the second in size. Her boundaries are ample to contain great diversities in customs, products, and scenery.

Although France does not possess the deeply indented coast of Britain, Greece, and Norway, she is provided with ample outlets for a great commerce and easy intercourse with distant nations. On the Mediterranean lie Marseilles, the most active harbor upon that "Great Sea," and Toulon, the chief French naval post. On Biscay are Bordeaux, La Rochelle, and Saint-Nazaire, the harbor-town for Nantes. On the Breton and Channel Coasts are Brest, Cherbourg, and especially Le Havre (which is peculiarly the port of Paris), and also Boulogne, Calais, and Dunkirk — the last three mainly important for their communications with England.

When one turns away from the seacoast, the whole bulk of French territory roughly distributes itself into three great sections — the Highlands, the Great Plateau, and the River Systems.

The Highlands are, of course, in the south and southeast only, where the national boundaries run up to the summits of the Pyrenees and the Alps. These districts are picturesque and interesting, but not large enough to contribute much to the general life of the nation.

The Great Central Plateau covers nearly half of the southern section of France, but it is cut off from the Alps by the broad, deep valley of the Rhone. Many parts of this plateau are comparatively level and without striking scenery: but nearly one seventh of the entire area of France is embraced in the great "Massif Central" radiating around Auvergne, which rises sometimes to a height of 3300 to 4000 feet, throwing up sharp mountains to over 6000 feet high. The upper parts of this plateau are rather barren, and raise only scanty crops for a correspondingly sparse population. On the southern side of the Plateau, cutting off warm Languedoc and the plains of the lower Rhone from the more barren plains of Rouergue, the Cévennes rise, as very respectable mountains, to over 5000 feet. Other parts of the Great Plateau are Limousin and Marche, where heights of 3300 feet are reached. On the northeast towards Germany, the Ardennes (between the Meuse and the Moselle) form another plateau 1600 to 2400 feet high in places, covered with forests, and broken by many marshy depressions, ravines, and fertile valleys. Since the Ardennes lie very directly on the route of armies passing between France and Germany, their position has served to determine the lines of march and location of many famous campaigns and battles.

But more Frenchmen by far live in the long river valleys than on the Great Central Plateau. There are over 4300 miles of navigable rivers in the country, besides nearly 200 miles more that have been converted into canals. The country also has adapted itself easily to the building of ordinary canals, of which there are more than 2000 miles. The rivers and the canals combined make inland navigation far more important in France than in almost any other European nation. Long before the days of railroads, the canal and river systems rendered it relatively easy to move heavy freight from one end to the other of the country, giving a great impetus toward national unity not enjoyed by lands more dependent for communications on carts and packhorses: and even now in the days of railroads the river barge has been a serious competitor to the freight train.

Making the circuit of the French coasts one finds a succession of important rivers, and along the banks of each thereof lie numerous famous cities and millions of prosperous people. Without the men of the river valleys there would be no France.

Beginning in the southwest there is the Garonne. It really begins in the Spanish Pyrenees, but it receives many affluents from the Massif Central. Its 346 miles of current drain an area of 22,080 square miles before it is joined by the slightly weaker Dordogne (305 miles) which rises in the height of land in Auvergne. The Dordogne digs its course into the plateau and wanders through a beautiful vineyard country, which is continued when this river (blending with the Garonne) continues as the more famous Gironde. This last is really a maritime estuary: fifteen miles from its mouth lies Bordeaux, one of the great ports of France, and its banks are lined with some of the most famous wine-lands in the world, producing the renowned vintage of Médoc.

From the mouth of the Gironde northward for some distance no stream of importance enters the Bay of Biscay; then is discovered the capital river of the nation, the Loire, undoubtedly the chief artery of France: 670 miles long, it winds from the mountains well over to the eastern side of the country. It drains 46,750 square miles and in this large area live 7,000,000 Frenchmen. It starts in the uplands a little to the west of the lower course of its chief rival, the Rhone. It swings northward and comes within 70 miles of Paris, then takes a great bend westward near Orléans. Whereupon, rapid and strong, fed by dozens of rich affluents, it sets out unweariedly for the Atlantic. Along its banks lie the regions which are the real heart of France: the Orléannais, Touraine, Anjou, and in confines of its wider valley

Berri, Maine, and Poitou — names graven upon French annals. In its wide valley lies a bright, thriving corn and wine country dotted with famous châteaux — Blois, Amboise, Chinon, Loches, to name only a very few: and among the equally famous cities touched by its swift current it is enough to name Orléans, Tours, Saumur, Angers, and Nantes.

North of the Loire flows the second river peculiarly dear to Frenchmen. The Seine is undoubtedly the smaller stream. It is only 485 miles long, draining 30,030 square miles. But it has been favored like the Tiber, the Thames, and the Hudson by the fame and historical greatness of the cities upon its banks. On its affluent, the Marne (its own name stamped upon history), lies Châlons where the hordes of Attila were turned away: and upon the Vesle lies Reims of immortal and melancholy memory. The Seine flows directly across Normandy and there on its banks stands Rouen, the stately Norman capital: while at its mouth is Le Havre, the thriving seaport: but of course the chief distinction of the Seine is that it is the river of Paris, where so often has seemed to throb the life of France.

In the extreme north of the country, the land tapers off towards Flanders and is very little above the level of the sea. The rivers are unimportant, sluggish, and frequently are made over into canals. This land of Picardy, Artois, and French Flanders is fertile, if somewhat monotonous, and contains the most important coal-fields in the nation, while Lille and Amiens are important and enterprising cities; but there is little distinctive in this region which belongs neither to the Great Plateau nor the Great Valleys.

There is still another mighty river in France, although it has played a less part in the national history than the Seine, the Loire, or even the Garonne-Gironde. The Rhone is 507 miles long and drains 38,180 square miles, but one tenth of this area is in Switzerland. It rises really in the St. Gothard Alps and issues from Lake Geneva. At Lyons (the second city of France) it is joined by the long and powerful Saone coming down from the

FERTILITY OF THE COUNTRY

north; then the united current advances southward through another rich vineyard-lined valley until, after a long course, at Avignon its banks suddenly become far less fertile and attractive, and the end of a stream, that has rushed down from the clear Alpine glaciers, is a muddy, sandy delta beside the Mediterranean.

The climate of the large country served by these great rivers obviously is extremely varied. On the whole it is one of the best climates in the world, "not so continental as Central Europe, and not so maritime as that of England." The coldest region is naturally the Great Central Plateau where the winters are frequently severe, although followed (American fashion) by decidedly hot summers. The northeast parts of the Plateau, Champagne, Lorraine, and the Vosges region, have a "continental" climate much like that of Germany and Austria. The frosts average 85 days per winter, although there is seldom much snow lingering upon the plains. The river valleys are milder. In Paris the frosts average only 56 days per year. The rains indeed average no less than 154 days per year, but the rainy spells are seldom extremely long, and the total rainfall is only 20 inches per annum. Brittany, a great buttress thrown out into the tumbling Atlantic, has a moist maritime climate very like that of the southwest of England. The Biscay-Garonne region is decidedly warm and dry. As for the southeastern region south of the mountains, Languedoc-Provence, this would have a really torrid climate except for the terrible and frequent *mistral*, a powerful wind which, rushing down from the Cévennes, purifies the air and throws back the moisture upon the sea, leaving these provinces so dry that Marseilles has only 55 rainy days per year.

Such a country is bound to have an abundant natural flora and fauna with corresponding cultivated products. Southern France is the land of the olive, the vine, and the mulberry. Northern France raises corn, and orchard and garden products like England and Germany. There are wide stretches of the open country which, except for the architecture of the farms and villages, look decidedly familiar to citizens of the Eastern States of America. There is still (considering the length of human habitation in the region) a surprising amount of forest land, carefully tended, but of unspoiled natural beauty. On the eve of the Great War, the state of the local communes owned over 10,000 square miles of forest land, and wide stretches beyond this were private property. These forests not merely added to the public wealth, but served to keep France an unartificialized nation, with verdant nature not too severely thrust into the background by "civilization."

To conclude this glance at the physical home of the ancient Gaul and the modern Frenchman — France is a region which, by geographical location and size, by the majesty of her rivers, and by the diversity of her scenery and mountains, is admirably fitted to be the home of a mighty nation.

CHAPTER II
THE ROMAN PROVINCE AND THE FRANKISH KINGDOM

IN some year about 600 B.C. a small fleet of galleys from the Asiatic Greek city of Phocæa ploughed its way boldly into the western Mediterranean, effected a landing at the harbor now known as Marseilles, coerced or cajoled the native chiefs into allowing the shipmen to make a settlement, "to found a colony" as the Greeks said, and presently the newcomers established a town with the temples, market-place, walls, magistrates, and general customs of a genuine Hellenic city. These bold settlers were far indeed from their old home by the Ægean "under the blue Ionian weather," but those were the days of Greek maritime enterprise, when its mariners were exploring all the nooks of the Mediterranean just as later the Spaniards searched out the Golden Indies. The Phœnicians, already commercial monopolists in these seas, frowned on the intruders and did their best to fight them away. This opposition was vain. The settlement became rooted, prospered, and defied its foes, although it was the most distant of all the Greek colonies. With this foundation of "Massalia" begins the history of the country later ages were to call "France." Hitherto it had been merely the home of savage tribes. Now it becomes linked to civilization.

The tribesmen with whom the Greeks of Massalia chaffered and bartered are ordinarily named "Gauls." They had probably been in the region a considerable time, having ousted some older and still more primitive folk. These Gauls were mainly Celts, members of a great race that was spreading over most of western Europe save only southern and central Italy. Their kinsfolk were penetrating into Spain and Britain, and even to-day there are many pure-blooded Celts in Scotland, Wales, and Ireland.[1]

[1] And of course the pronounced Celtic element in French Brittany is very noticeable.

When the Greeks first met them, they were decidedly untamed savages, red-headed, heavy-fisted, and with many of the general customs, virtues, and vices of Iroquois Indians. Contact with the Greeks, however, taught them much. They improved their weapons, learned to live more or less in towns, and consolidated their petty clans into greater tribes under kings or an oligarchy of chieftains. They also developed a peculiar type of worship. We know very little about the precise religious beliefs taught by the famous "Druids," for they served their uncouth gods with strictly mysterious rites when they met under their "sacred oaks," probably to offer human sacrifices; but we do know that they constituted an arrogant priestly caste something like the Hindoo Brahmins and the Egyptian priesthoods, and that they exercised a formidable political power over their awestricken laity. As for the rest of the Gauls, they were gradually struggling upward from savagery to barbarism. Usually they dwelt in tribes each under its elected or hereditary chief, with his Druids for advisers or spiritual masters, and his body of warriors who chose or confirmed him and then fought his battles. Below the warriors was a less honorable company of the servile men and of the women who performed the inglorious works of peace, tilled the fields, pounded the grain, and reared the children, while their lords lolled on their bearskins, drank much home-brewed liquor or choicer wines from Greek traders, gambled, quarreled, hunted, and waited a summons to battle. Each clan had ordinarily its own central "town" of circular wattled huts, and if the clan were powerful it probably occupied a hilltop enclosed by rude but often formidable timber and earthworks; or perhaps entrenched itself in a hold amid the dark recesses of wood and marsh.

Before the Romans entered the land there were already signs of a higher order of things. Clans were merging into confederacies covering considerable districts. Certain chiefs and tribes were striking coins with crude legends in the Greek alphabet. Traders from Massalia or from Italy were bringing in various Southern hardwares and fabrics as well as liquors to exchange for furs, skins, and other crude natural products. Left to themselves, in other words, these "Gallic" sections of the Celts might have evolved a real civilization in a few hundred years longer — if they had been let alone.

They were not to be let alone. Already by about 122 B.C. the Romans in their resistless expansion had occupied the extreme southeast of the country along the Mediterranean, the later Provence (that is, the Roman "Province" as contrasted with the rest of Gaul); but this was not a very large district, and for two generations the great Italian conquerors contented themselves with what was little more than a series of forts to command the important and strategic highroad from Italy into Spain. Still, Roman influence crept imperceptibly northward. In nearly every clan and tribal confederacy there would be a pro-Roman party among the chiefs, which held that Roman advance was inevitable and had better be welcomed and not resisted, and an anti-Roman "patriotic" party, crying out against southern encroachments, and almost always stoutly supported in its views by the Druids. Then, in 58 B.C., Gaul was entered by the greatest secular figure in ancient history: possibly by the greatest secular figure in all history — Gaius Julius Cæsar himself.

Cæsar wished to conquer Gaul, partly because he needed the glory and wealth flowing from such a victory to increase his chances of becoming monarch of Rome on the ruins of the tottering Roman Republic, partly because the security of the ancient world genuinely demanded that Gaul should be plucked from barbarian turbulence and set in an orderly place in civilization. He had plenty of excuses for intervention. Formidable German tribes (more barbarous and warlike than the Gauls themselves) were threatening to cross the Rhine and conquer the whole land. Many Gallic chieftains and factions, growing anxious, were ready to call in the Romans. Other chieftains were promptly won over by the master-politician's ready tact and persuasiveness. Cæsar had seldom the use of more than 50,000

Italian troops at any time during his nine years of campaigning, but they were legionaries of the best Roman discipline and led by an incomparable commander. The invaders thus were able to overrun and to subjugate nearly the whole land before the Gauls, realizing slowly that the Romans had come to stay, could begin to drop their feuds and organize resistance. Then it was too late. Cæsar had grasped the points of vantage and penetrated deep into the country. The Gauls found indeed an able and inspiring chief in Vercingetorix, who rose to the level of a true national hero. He fired nearly the whole land so that it blazed up against Cæsar in desperate revolt, but his hundreds of thousands of ill-disciplined levies were no match for the legionaries' javelins and short swords. Cæsar presently drove him into the stronghold of Alesia (not far from Dijon), beat back all attempts to throw in succor and starved him into surrender. That act practically ended the story of pre-Roman Gaul. By 50 B.C. the country was completely submissive, so submissive in fact that a little later Cæsar could call off nearly all his troops to follow him over the Rubicon for his march into Italy to found the Roman Empire.

The conqueror had been ruthless in his slaughter of enemies and his confiscations of their wealth. But when the brutal work had once been done, it was followed by an era of benevolence and conciliation. First, the Gauls were taught that it was hopeless to resist Rome; then, secondly, that it was not at all disagreeable to be her subjects. Taxes were reasonable. Law and order took the place of outrageous tribal oppressions. The Druids with their human sacrifices were suppressed. Gallic nobles were flattered with Roman citizenship. If they were really prominent nobles they might presently hope to become Roman senators. The recruiting masters for the legions enrolled thousands of Gallic youth, promising them all the pay, booty, privileges, and hopes of promotion which were ordinarily offered in the imperial armies.

Since the Gauls were themselves without a well-developed

civilization, they, like most barbarians under similar pressure, easily adopted the superior usages of their masters. It was easy to rename their crude gods "Jupiter" or "Mercury" or "Juno." The provincial governors took the young chieftains into their palaces at once as guests and hostages and not merely taught them Latin, but also gave them a taste for Virgil and Cicero, as well as a great delight in Roman clothes, Roman social customs, and Roman institutions. Especially did the imperial government favor the founding and building of cities. The old Græco-Roman civilization was essentially a *city* civilization, as contrasted with a society based upon rural settlements. The Romans therefore promoted the building of cities as a prime step to Latinization. Sometimes old Celtic communities were recast in a Roman mould. More often new "colonies" or "municipia" were created outright, and the natives induced to settle therein. Very many of the most famous cities of France are thus of a direct Roman foundation. Among these (to name a few from many) are Limoges, Tours, and Soissons.[1] Each of these cities had its own special charter (often from the Emperor direct) authorizing its citizens to elect their own magistrates, pass local laws, and enjoy very large autonomy so long as the taxes went in promptly to the imperial "fiscus." Each city also would have its temples to the usual Roman gods, its public baths, its amphitheater for the wild-beast fights and gladiators quite in Italian fashion, its circus for the horse-races, its forum for trade and public meetings, its "curia" for the gatherings of the local senate, its theater for Latin comedies, its schools for Latin oratory — in short, all the paraphernalia of a "little Rome" wherein the citizens called themselves Julius and Fabius and Claudius, wore long togas and tried hard to forget that their grandfathers had carried their spears behind Vercingetorix.

[1] Paris (oldest name *Lutetia*) was a very insignificant stronghold on an island in the Seine when the Romans took it in 52 A.D. By 100 A.D. under Roman rule it had begun to develop as a sizable provincial town, and was started on its advance to greatness.

As for the general administration of the land, Gaul was for a long time divided into six rather large Roman provinces,[1] with the proconsuls mainly occupied with checking up the tax accounts of the various cities and acting as judges on appeal in important litigation. So submissive was the whole country that the imperial government seldom found it necessary to station a single large garrison in many very wide regions. The decrees of the Cæsars could usually be enforced by mere constables, although all men knew that close to the Rhine there always lay several reliable legions, whose prime business indeed was to keep the Germanic tribes from penetrating westward into the Empire, but which could be readily ordered about to snuff out any disorder in Gaul, should insurrection threaten.

The Gallic provinces thus became one of the most prosperous, peaceful, and important parts of the Roman Empire. Thanks to their possession the Cæsars were able to establish contact with more distant lands: with Britain (which they conquered in the first century of our era) and with Germany, which they indeed failed to conquer, but which they repeatedly invaded.

The Romans even gave to the Gauls a national capital. Lugdunum (modern Lyons) became an elegant city with magnificent public buildings comparable to those by the Tiber. Here, once a year, assembled the deputies of all the Gallic cities to celebrate elaborate sacrifices in honor of the "Sacred Emperor" to whom they owed their prosperity, and also (an important political privilege) to petition the Cæsars for redress of grievances, especially against evil governors. The results of all this Romanization were manifold. The Gauls became among the most loyal

[1] These provinces were:
      I. Narbonensis (the old province before Cæsar).
      II. Aquitania.
      III. Lugdunensis.
      IV. Belgica.
      V. Lower Germany.
      VI. Upper Germany.

The last three included considerable territories not ordinarily reckoned now as part of France.

and devoted subjects of the Empire. Their old Celtic tongue was largely lost, at least by the upper classes, and the old tribal laws and customs equally perished. Some of the most distinguished poets and orators of the later Latin literature were born in the land we now call France. The Rhone, the Loire, and especially the Moselle were lined with cities and splendid villas that barely differed from those in Italy. Rome had made here one of her fairest conquests. First she had conquered by the sword: then more worthily by her superior civilization.

For nearly three hundred years after the days of Julius Cæsar the Gallic lands have no important history save as a part of the great Roman Empire. After the edict of Caracalla (213 A.D.?) all their free inhabitants had become Roman citizens — legally the equals of the original ruling race. As the Empire declined, thanks to gross mismanagement by the Cæsars, the degeneracy of the army and the fundamental defects of the ancient social system which rested in slavery, the Gauls of course had their share of the world's sorrow. Beginning about 250 A.D. and for the next forty-odd years this part of the Empire was exposed to devastating raids by the Germanic tribes from across the Rhine, raids which the now demoralized legionaries failed to repel. Many Gallic cities were thus desolated. The survivors protected themselves with new walls, often erected in frantic haste, as existing archæological remains often testify. The old Roman society was apparently drifting on the rocks, but by about 300 A.D. the catastrophe seemed averted when a new succession of able emperors seized the helm of state, and by drastic reforms insured temporary safety. The Roman Empire, and Gaul with it, received another hundred years' respite.

During these silent years a new force was penetrating Gaul as everywhere else in the Empire. Soon after 100 A.D. Christianity begins to show itself in these provinces. About 170 A.D. there were enough Christians in Lyons to warrant a wholesale persecution by the pagan priests and governor. Presently we hear of churches in Autun, Dijon, and Besançon. About 251 one meets traces of Christianity in Limoges, Tours, and even Paris (still a second-class city). The early annals of the Gallic Church are not very clear. Probably here, as elsewhere, the cities were Christianized long before the rural communities ceased their superstitious worship of the old gods: and the pagans were probably in a decided majority everywhere until after about 350 A.D., when a great apostle of the Western Church, St. Martin of Tours, went up and down the land converting whole districts to the new faith. Still it is certain that when Constantine the Great (306-337) and his successors showed Christianity indulgence and then made it the official religion of the Roman Empire, the Gallic lands accepted the change fairly readily. By 400 A.D. Gaul was officially "Christian." What is more it was "Catholic" and "Orthodox" Christian: that is to say, the bulk of its people accepted the famous Nicene Creed and the forms of belief supported by the Church of Rome and the other great centers of theological leadership. The formidable un-orthodox "Arian" (Unitarian) heresy, although it had followers in the region, had gained no general footing. This was a very important fact, for it prevented Gaul from being isolated from the rest of the world's thought at the moment the Roman Empire was dissolving before the Goths and Vandals.

About 375 A.D. the Germanic tribes began to penetrate again into the decadent Empire, and the legions soon proved too feeble to turn them out. But the first barbarian attacks were mainly upon the Balkan lands, and not till about 400 A.D. were the Rhine barriers forced and the "Romans" (as the Gauls now gladly called themselves) trembled at the sight of their burning villages while the invaders drew nigh.

Rome had not been built in a day, Roman Gaul was not conquered in a day. Some parts were quickly overrun by the barbarians; some resisted stoutly; some temporarily expelled the first conquerors; some compounded with the invaders on terms that allowed German and Gallo-Roman to settle down rather comfortably together. It was of course a miserable time, when the old civilization was painfully dying, and when the newer civilization was anything but safely born. The liberal arts seemed sterile or dead. Cities were decaying, if they were not devastated outright by the invader; the magnificent Roman road system, which had covered Gaul like a network of modern railways, was degenerating; commerce and all but the most necessary industries were nigh perishing. The only reliable law was that of the strongest. Alone in the Church and especially in the monks' and nuns' cloisters seemed there any sure refuge for peace-loving men and delicate women. Nevertheless, the age of the Germanic invasions was not one of unmitigated destruction and misery. The invaders were well aware that the invaded were their superiors in everything but warfare. The barbarian chiefs were prompt to adopt not merely Roman dresses, table manners, and court ceremonial, but also to make Gallo-Roman noblemen their ministers and officials to control the great population of provincials which the Germans knew how to conquer, but afterward did not know how to govern. Much of the old Roman law survived, along with many features of the old tax system. It was an era of twilight, but not of absolute darkness.

When the Roman Empire of the West finally went under, in 476 A.D., the greater part of Gaul was already in German hands. Since 412 the formidable Visigoths had held sway in nearly all of the south with their capital at Bordeaux. Nearer the Rhine, in the east center, the Burgundians were in control. In the north (quite isolated from Italy, curiously enough) the Roman power was making its last stand, under the "Patrician" Syagrius. The Visigoths and Burgundians had gone through the forms of professing Christianity, but it was of the unorthodox Arian type — hence they were in very bad odor with the native clergy and native population, which were mostly Catholics devoted to the Nicene Creed.

Conditions therefore were anything but static, when a new

power began asserting itself in the north and speedily overshadowed all Gaul. The Franks had been a loose confederacy of Germanic tribes on the right bank of the Rhine since the third century. They had occasionally fought against the Romans; more often they had been their well-paid allies and had sent their warriors into the Cæsars' armies. For a long time they showed no great wish to invade Gaul. Then in the fifth century they gradually followed the example of their fellow Germans and began to spread into what is now the extreme north of France. It was a slow, somewhat hesitant invasion, for the Franks were sadly disunited. Salians, Ripuarians, and other tribes of their confederacy whetted their weapons to fight against one another even more than against Syagrius. They were fierce, untamed warriors in any case — not even Arians, but downright heathen: cruel in customs and very willing to settle all issues by appeal to their "franciskas" — their great battle-axes, which possibly gave them their tribal name. In 481 the chief of the Salian Franks, Hilderic, died, and passed on his stormy authority to his fifteen-year-old son Clovis. A bad man, but a mighty ruler, had thrust himself into history.

Clovis was of execrable morality even in an age of perfidy and blood. The most that can be said is that the evils of the times demanded sharp surgery if civilization was not to end in anarchy, and Clovis assuredly never declined to use the scalpel. A man of daring courage, indomitable energy, and inexhaustible resource as well as completely lacking pity or scruple, he must have won the absolute devotion of his host of hardy warriors from the day when they lifted him on their shields as their king, and thundered their deep "Aye! Aye!" while he flourished his sword and announced he would rule over them. In 486 near Soissons he defeated and completely overthrew Syagrius, the last champion of the Roman power. Northern Gaul was in his hands — at least as soon as he could conquer or assassinate all the other lesser Frankish chiefs who might try to defy his mandates.

His methods smote the imaginations as well as the fears of

THE MONARCHY OF THE FRANKS

CLOVIS AND CHRISTIANITY 19

the bands which followed him. The King had once claimed as his booty a beautiful bowl, when a certain unruly soldier, jealous of an attempt to take apparently more than the royal share, deliberately shivered the vessel with his battle-axe, crying, "Naught shalt thou have, beyond whatever the [customary] lot may give thee!" The King dissembled. He had overstepped his technical rights: but a year later at a review of his men-at-arms he found the offending warrior standing with his weapons for inspection. "No man has arms so ill cared for as thou!" declared the King, and contemptuously flung the man's hatchet on the ground. As the other stooped to pick it up, Clovis instantly raised his own axe and buried it in the wretch's skull — "Thus didst thou," he announced, "to that bowl!" Such methods are admirably calculated to win the implicit obedience of a certain type of warriors, the more so as nearly all such robust deeds justified themselves by their complete success.

Clovis, as intimated, had been a pagan. Probably for long he had been impressed by the splendid liturgy and ceremonial of the Gallo-Roman churches as well as by the political advantages of being in religious adjustment with his new non-Germanic subjects. That he ever understood the least thing about the spiritual teachings of Christianity we cannot imagine. What *did* appeal to him, however, was that the "White Christ" of the priests seemed to be a very powerful god with "good magic," and quite likely, if respectfully treated, to help against the King's enemies. Clovis presently married a Burgundian princess, Clotilda, who was a Catholic Christian, although most of her family were Arians. The King did not at once embrace his wife's religion, but he listened to her arguments with deepening courtesy. At last, in 496, he found himself in mortal battle with a rival tribe, the Alemanni. The fight was going sore against Clovis. His stoutest axemen were giving way. The old Frankish pagan gods proffered no help. It was time for desperate expedients. "O Lord Jesus Christ," prayed the King, "whom Clotilda worships; if Thou wilt now grant me victory, I will believe in

Thee, and be baptized with Thy name." And lo! the tide of battle turned: the Alemanni fled: Clovis marched home victorious.

The King had every reason for keeping his bargain and vow. Such a God was certainly the one for him to champion. Clovis was baptized with magnificent ceremony at Reims (doubtless in the church that preceded the later famous Gothic cathedral) by the venerable Bishop St. Remigius, who devised a great procession and religious festival when Clovis and three thousand of his mighty men all marched up to the font together. "Bow thy head meekly," commanded the bishop when the fierce young warrior approached for baptism; "adore what thou hast once burned: burn that which thou once adored!" It was a happy day for the bishop. The King of all North Gaul had been won for Christianity, and that, too, luckily enough, the highly orthodox type of Catholicism. He was thus placed on extremely friendly relations with the powerful and numerous Gallo-Roman clergy. He had all the zeal of a new convert: and in the rest of Gaul the Catholic Gallo-Romans were ready to welcome his sway, in place of that of the Arian kings of the other Germanic invaders.

Clovis the Christian soon proved himself even more of a conqueror than Clovis the Pagan. In 500 A.D. he subjugated the Burgundians. In 507 A.D. he said to his lords, "It goes much against my grain that these Arian heretics [the Visigoths] should hold any part of Gaul. Let us go forth with the help of the Lord and overthrow them and make their land our own"! — and once more the Saints blessed his lancers and his axemen. Nearly the whole of southern Gaul was conquered, barring only a strip close to the Pyrenees. At last in 511 A.D. this treacherous and bloodthirsty king died after having smitten down practically every foe — foreign or domestic — who opposed him. He had displayed *one* enormous virtue, however, in the eyes of the churchmen who wrote our chronicles — he had been the unrelenting champion of orthodoxy from the day of his conversion. "Therefore," it was written by the pious historian Gregory of Tours, "every day God cast down his enemies and added increase to his kingdom, because he walked before Him with upright heart, and did that which was pleasing in His eyes."

Clovis left his heirs a fairly well-compacted dominion, embracing nearly all of modern France and a considerable slice also of western Germany. Frankish law, however, made it hard to keep a kingdom together. There was no right of primogeniture. Each of Clovis's four sons claimed his share of the kingdom, and soon the process of division and subdivision brought on a whole devil's dance of civil wars between bloody and self-seeking men. There was no guiding principle in these wars of the "Merovingian" kings (so called from Merovius, an ancestor of Clovis). The subject population was the helpless victim of the devastating conflicts of rival kings and of their equally turbulent warriors. Sometimes the realm, which we can now call "Frankland," was divided into more than four unhappy contending kingdoms, divided and subdivided like so many farms between litigious heirs. Sometimes a single masterful scion of Clovis was lucky enough to eliminate all his brothers or nephews and reign for a few years alone.

Clovis's sons had inherited a really formidable royal power from their great if evil father. Under the grandsons, however, the kingly authority was obviously shrinking before that of the *leudes*, the Frankish upper-warriors, who were demanding offices, honors, and lands in payment for support through the incessant wars. Under the great-grandsons, although the country sometimes again was nominally united under one king, it was evident the monarchs were becoming more and more the puppets of certain great ministers, especially of that very arrogant official who called himself the "Mayor of the Palace" (*Major Domus*). Frankland also showed signs of splitting up into three great units along somewhat natural and therefore fairly enduring lines — Neustria (virtually most of northern France), Austrasia (east of Neustria and including the extreme east of present-day France and the west of modern Germany), and Aquitania (the bulk of

France south of the Loire). Dagobert (628-38) was the last Merovingian king who exercised any real personal authority. After him the main power in Frankland lay really with the masterful Major Domus, who continually waxed as his royal "sovereign" waned.

Unfortunately for the peace of the realm there was no orderly line of succession to this position of supreme uncrowned ruler of Frankland. To become Major Domus implied conciliating the interests of whatever was the dominant faction of Frankish *leudes* (mighty men) supplemented as these usually were by the old landed aristocracy which claimed descent from the Gallo-Romans. The Church, with its puissant and often very "secular" bishops, had also to be propitiated. All this meant a new series of schisms, conspiracies and wars frequently very bloody and very personal. The Mayor (Major Domus) of Austrasia fought against his rival of Neustria; while Aquitaine under a semi-independent Duke (=*Dux*, in origin simply "leader") would defy them both. Meantime in the seventh, even as in the sixth century, civilization seemed ever more steadily on the defensive. Then at last came a turn for the better. A great official family came forward. After various vicissitudes his dynasty, later famous as the "Carolingian" (from Charlemagne, its most distinguished member), began to supply Mayors of the Palace who ruled both Neustria and Austrasia simultaneously in a kind of hereditary succession. Rivals were put down: disorderly elements quelled by a heavy hand. It was the rare good fortune of this dynasty to supply *four* rulers in direct sequence from father to great-grandson who were all men of first-class ability, neither tyrants nor weaklings, neither sordid politicians nor reckless idealists, men who knew how to fight and how to spare, how to regulate and how to let alone: — four men, in short, who did very much to shape the entire history of Europe.

The story of the Carolingian house involves much more than the history of France. It is the story of early mediæval Germany, and the same of Italy. It touches deeply on the history of the

THE MOSLEM INVASION

rise of the Papacy, and even affects the annals of Spain. To us, whose main interest is in France, it is sufficient to state certain prime facts, but to ignore most of the non-French elements in these great rulers' annals. We may outline the careers of these four princes thus.

Pepin of Heristal was the first of the family who exercised what may be called systematic and solidly founded authority. He was in power from 679 to 714. In his days public affairs were in such chaos that successful fighting was practically all that could be asked of him. Pepin discharged his full duty in this matter. Most of his rivals perished and the rest submitted. There was again something like law and order in the land. The great Mayor not merely won victories over rebels, but reorganized the Frankish army so that it became again a real fighting machine, formidable to its foreign enemies. There was soon to be need for this army.

Pepin was followed by his illegitimate son Charles Martel (714-41), who only gained power after another period of bloody confusion, but who then showed himself alike as heavy-handed and as worldly-wise as his father. His first exploits were against the various German tribes to the east of Austrasia — only half Christianized as yet and still utterly barbarous. Saxons, Bavarians, and Alemans all alike fled before him. He also made head against the malcontent Dukes of Aquitaine who, ruling over a population of almost strictly "Roman" descent, were ill-disposed to brook Northern authority.

The issue with Aquitaine had been by no means settled when its Duke Odo suddenly changed from a defiant enemy to trembling suppliant. A terrible danger was threatening not merely Aquitaine but Frankland itself and indeed all Christendom. Over a hundred years had elapsed since Mohammed the Arabian had founded his religion of Islam — of the One Allah and his prophet, with the choice of accepting the same or the sword. In the interval the fanatical Moslems had overrun Persia, Syria, Egypt, and all North Africa, sweeping the native populations away from their old faiths and accumulating belligerent converts as a rolling snowball gathers size. Early in the eighth century their hosts had crossed into Spain, snuffed out the decadent Visigothic dynasts, and rendered nearly the entire peninsula the mere emirate of the distant Kalif of Damascus. But the conquering hordes of Arabs, Moors, and Greek and Spanish renegades had no intention of stopping in Spain. Had not Allah promised the whole world to the disciples of the Koran? In 730, after some earlier reverses, the Moslem bands began pouring through the passes of the Pyrenees and into smiling Aquitania. The Moorish riders, on their wiry desert steeds, worked rapidly upward, pillaging, carrying captive, and ruthlessly burning churches and convents. Duke Odo strove to fight them off. His strength was vain. After a brave resistance the Arab Emir Abd-Rahman took Bordeaux, the richest city possibly then in old Gaul, and distributed an enormous booty among his greedy followers.

Bordeaux was not the last Christian city to suffer. The Moslem horsemen were forcing their way northward and eastward into the Loire valley and ravaging clear into Burgundy as far as Autun and Sens. Odo cried lustily to Charles for aid, and it could not be denied. If Aquitaine was conquered to-day, Frankland proper would be in flames to-morrow. The great Mayor called out his full levy of Northern axemen. In September or October, 732, Charles led his host to face the Arab Emir in one of the plains near Tours on the Loire.[1] Probably neither Christians not Moslems realized that here was to be fought out one of the world's decisive battles, which, according to many later opinions, was to settle whether the civilized world was to read the Bible or the Koran. One thing is certain. If Charles the Frank had been badly defeated, there was no other Christian leader in all western Europe with military power enough to curb the Islamites.[2]

[1] The exact position of the battle is uncertain, possibly it was nearer Poitiers than Tours.
[2] Of course Leo the Isaurian, Emperor of Constantinople, had inflicted a great defeat on the Arabs when they attacked his capital in 717, but that would not have saved Western Christendom.

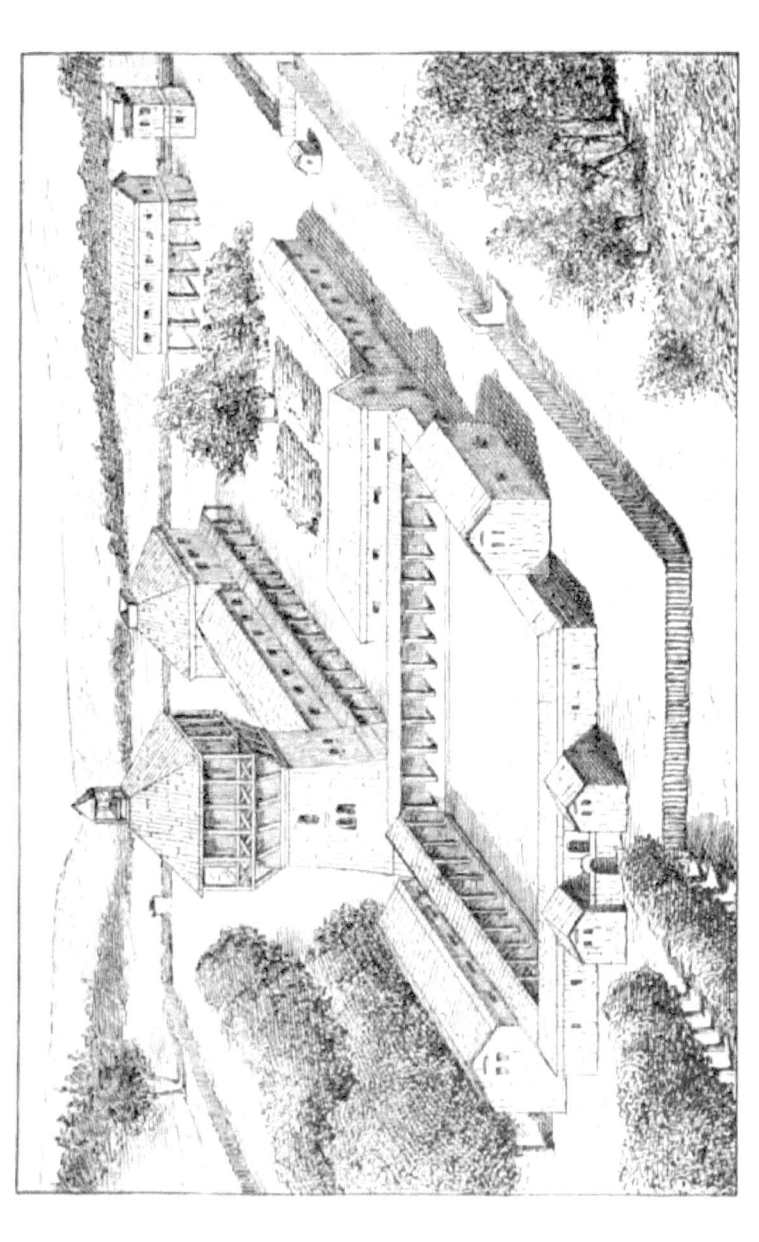

MEROVINGIAN MANOR HOUSE

Restored. Notice the great court surrounded by dwelling-rooms and a portico. A palisade encircles the whole, and a huge wooden tower for defense rises in the center. In the background are the farm buildings. (*After Garnier and Ammann: Histoire de l'habitation humaine*)

For several days the armies confronted, then Abd-Rahman flung his magnificent Moorish cavalry on the Frankish battle-lines. But the Northern infantry, standing in dense array "like solid walls or icebergs," as says the old chronicler, smote back the plunging lancers with terrible loss. Presently the Christians took the offensive, and began hewing their way into the Infidels' camp. Abd-Rahman was slain. His motley host fell into confusion. Night descended before the rout was complete, but under cover of the darkness the Moslems fled in panic southward, leaving their tents crammed with spoil for the victors. A great battle had been won, and Charles was henceforth Charles "Martel" ("The Hammer").

It took several years more of hard fighting to clear the Arab-Moors out of certain strongholds they had seized in South Gaul, but the Infidels never came back for a large-scale invasion. Their spell of victory had been broken, Allah had turned against them. Why struggle against Fate! Their conqueror, of course, reaped vast glory from his victory, as well as greatly strengthening his grip upon all Frankland.

The victor at Tours was succeeded by his son Pepin "the Short" (741–68), a leader who inherited so firm an authority from his father that he could devote some of his energies to the doings of peace as well as to those of war. In 752 he felt such confidence that he disposed of the absurd Merovingian "sluggard king" Childeric, the last of the nominal dynasty, who had lived in perpetual retirement, and whose power had dwindled to the shadow of a shade. Pepin was emboldened to take the royal title himself (a step which might have been opposed by certain Frankish noblemen) by the formal consent of the Pope of Rome. The Papacy was developing its temporal power in Italy, was in considerable fear of the attacks of the intractable Lombards, and was very anxious to stand favorably with the greatest ruler beyond the Alps. King Pepin duly repaid this favor in 753 by marching with full force into Italy and forcing the King of the Lombards to promise to let the Popes alone in their government in Rome. Thus then began those intimate dealings between the rulers of Frankland, or France, and the Papacy, which led to one working alliance or agreement after another, and were only ended in the twentieth century in the absolute divorce of Church and State by the Third Republic of our day.

Pepin left a royal title, a firm understanding with the greatest spiritual power in Christendom, a powerful army, and a loyal aristocracy and people to his son Charles, soon to be enrolled in universal history as Charlemagne (Charles, or Karl the Great, Carolus Magnus). The new ruler, of course, profited largely by the successes of his predecessors, but it is undeniable that he was by far the ablest of all the highly talented four. His reign (768–814) forms one of the turning-points in French as well as in German, Italian, and ecclesiastical history.

The Frankland of Charlemagne was very different from the Frankland of Clovis. Many of the relics of the old Roman culture had been lost. The Gallo-Roman cities had often dwindled now to starving villages, or had perished outright. The once teeming commerce of the ancient Empire had been nearly obliterated. Every little region and manor lived for itself and by itself, supplying its own economic needs and cheerfully going without any but a very few imported articles. The incessant wars and ravagings had destroyed many of the arts of peace and blighted still more of those surviving. Even the Church had been too often monopolized by worldly prelates, and the convents had become the refuge for the idle as well as for the pious and quiet-minded. The Merovingian period and that of the Mayors of the Palace had thus been often a time of cultural retrogression and destruction, melancholy to record. But not all elements had been destructive. Along with all the rack and ruin certain great facts stand out, which were to mean very much in the history of the New France yet-to-be.

1. Between 500 and 800 the process of race consolidation was fairly completed. The Franks and the Gallo-Romans had been

shaken down together; intermarriage and constant contact had largely destroyed the barriers between them. There was obviously a greater Germanic element in the North (and especially the Northeast) than in the South, where Aquitaine continued predominantly Gallo-Roman; but nowhere were the racial lines now very deliberately drawn. There were assuredly serfs and great lords — but many of the serfs were doubtless descended from Clovis's warriors, and many of the lords boasted Gallo-Roman ancestors. The French people was thus being created, a people Celtic in its main origins, but stamped with the language, laws, and culture of Imperial Rome, and later still given a strong infusion of Northern firmness and virility by the Teutonic invaders. We have thus what is essentially a mixed nation, both in its race and in its culture, and history proves that it is ordinarily the mixed nations which inherit the earth. Celtic brilliancy, Italian finesse, and Northern steadfastness were to meet together in France.

2. During the Merovingian period we find shaping itself the economic and political unit which is characteristic of France all through the Middle Ages and down to the very edge of recent times. This is the great lord's manor. Under later Roman conditions, when the cities were declining, and the poorer population was always tending to fall under the power of the wealthy, it became more and more normal to be either the owner or the dependent of a great estate (a *fundus*). In this the humbler members were simply serfs, though not absolutely slaves, and were permitted to till and occupy a little parcel of ground, but were unable to leave the estate without their master's permission and were subject to many other harsh restraints. In Frankish days these great estates had continued to multiply. There were still a few free peasants, self-respecting owners of petty farms, but they tended ever to diminish, and the government being very weak and the age very lawless, a poor man could seldom protect his rights unless he "commended himself" (that is, became the dependent) to some great landowner who could afford him

decent protection. Not merely the king, his favored warriors, and the descendants of the Gallo-Roman nobility could possess these huge serf-populated estates: they were often held by the powerful and wealthy bishops and abbots of the Church, who thus (besides their spiritual cares) were in a very temporal sense the masters of some hundreds or thousands of peasants, ruling them through their overseers and bailiffs. This was not strictly feudalism, but it was a very great step towards that feudalism which was now speedily to develop through western Europe.

When Charlemagne was at the height of his power (about 800) the territories of modern France made up nearly half of his entire dominions. They were already distinguishing themselves from his other lands (Germany and Italy) by very marked characteristics. Germany was too remote in the North to be genuinely Latinized: Italy was too Southern to borrow much from Germany: The French lands, the heart of the old Frankish kingdom, had drawn strength alike from the North and from the South.

CHAPTER III
FROM FRANKS TO FRENCHMEN

IN 768 Pepin the Short, the great King of the Franks, passed away to make room for his greater son, whom the common usage of history knows in Latin as Carolus Magnus, or, to use the familiar French form, Charlemagne. The new monarch may be considered, on the whole, as the most important personage in mediæval history. His reign marked an epoch between the ancient world and the modern, and his commanding personality stamped its impress deeply upon his own age and cast its shadow over several subsequent centuries.

An intimate companion, Einhard, who wrote a biography of Charlemagne far superior to the run of mediæval literary efforts, has left us a well-rounded picture of this truly remarkable man. We are told that he was "large and robust, and of commanding stature and excellent proportions. The top of his head was round, his eyes large and animated, his nose somewhat long. He had a fine head of gray hair, and his face was bright and pleasant: so that whether sitting or standing he showed great presence and dignity. His walk was firm and the whole carriage of his body manly. His voice was clear, but not so strong as his frame might have led one to expect." [1]

We are also told of his simple habits as to dress, his temperance in eating and drinking: his delight in riding and hunting, and in manly sports. "He was ready and fluent in speaking, and able to express himself with great clearness. He took pains to learn foreign languages, gaining such a mastery of Latin that he could make an address in that tongue as well as in his own (Frankish language), while Greek he could understand rather

---

[1] A mosaic portrait, fairly authentic, of Charlemagne at St. John Lateran, in Rome, shows that he wore a heavy mustache, not the famous "long beard" which figured so much in later minstrelsy and legend.

than speak." When at table, he delighted in music or in listening to the reading of pious books or histories. He was fond, too, of attending the lectures on grammar, logic, and astronomy of the learned men of his day. One must not exaggerate the profundity of this royal scholar, however. With all his genuine love of letters he never really learned how to write.

In his temperament Charlemagne had indeed many human infirmities; he could be cruel, and perpetrate acts of manifest tyranny, yet considering his epoch he may be called just, magnanimous, and far-sighted. From his father he inherited an effective war-power, and none of the neighbors of the Franks could match him in arms. He had a high regard for the old Roman civilization, as he understood it, and throughout his reign labored earnestly and intelligently to increase the knowledge and influence the morals of his people. Beginning his career simply as a powerful Germanic king, as he discovered his dominions swelling into a veritable Western Empire he allowed his imagination to lead his ambition to a loftier title. The ruler who began as King of the Franks ended as a Roman Emperor, claiming all the power of the old Cæsars.

It is practically impossible to discuss this great ruler, and to confine the narrative to simply those things which took place on the territory that was to be the later-day France. Almost all that he did outside of the old Gaulish lands rebounded upon their local fortunes, and particularly he engaged in a long series of wars which were destined to react upon France by determining the religion and culture of its eastern neighbors down to the present day. When Charlemagne came to the throne a large fraction of modern Germany was not merely independent of the Frankish kings, but was heathen and savage. Especially behind their swamps and forests the Saxons had resisted every attempt at their conversion and civilization. Many years of Charlemagne's reign (772 to 804, with considerable intermissions) were consumed in the attempt to bring this fierce, untamed people under the yoke of Western culture as it then existed.

THE CAMPAIGNS IN SAXONY

Modern ethics does not commend the propagation of Christianity and civilization by the sword, yet the fact remains that if the Saxons had been let alone they would probably have remained for centuries in pagan squalor and degradation. Campaign after campaign Charlemagne directed into their country. Usually the Frankish host invaded the swampy Saxon land in the springtime and remained for the summer, chasing the enemy into the fens and forests, taking hostages, bribing or browbeating the prisoners into accepting baptism, and finally erecting a few fortresses in which were left garrisons. Then the invaders would retire; the Saxons would emerge from the greenwood, many of the new converts would solemnly "scrape off" the waters of baptism, and lapse back to their old gods; some of the Frankish fortresses would be stormed and taken, the rest would be besieged. The next spring would bring anew the invading host and the former process would be repeated: each campaign, however, would fasten the Frankish yoke a little more firmly, and would leave the pagan party a little weaker. With the host of Charlemagne would go another host of priests and monks, "so that this race" (says the mediæval chronicler), "which from the beginning of the world had been bound by the chain of demons, might bow to the yoke of the sweet and gentle Christ." Whenever conditions admitted, churches and monasteries were built, bishoprics established, and the *whole* population duly baptized — usually under sore compulsion, with Frankish men-at-arms pointing out with their spears the nearest way to the font.

It was a weary, uneventful war. There were no great battles. The contest was almost entirely of the guerrilla order: petty skirmishes, raids, and sieges. In 785 Wittekind, the most formidable Saxon chief, made his submission: but many of his followers held out till 804. Then at last came peace to the exhausted land. But the war had not been waged in vain. Mediæval civilization (such as it then was) took root in Saxony with surprising rapidity. Within a century the region was reckoned among the most progressive and civilized lands in western Europe, although by that time Charlemagne's empire was rapidly breaking to pieces, and Saxony and France were parting company forever.

The great King inherited from his father a close alliance with the Papacy. The standing dread of the Popes was the seizure of Rome by the Lombards, then dominating northern Italy, and threatening in turn to seize the remainder of the peninsula. Already on their part the Popes were claiming the "secular power" over the city of Rome, and were resentful of any formidable neighbor. If they were to have any overlord in temporal matters it was far better to have one like the Frankish king — too distant to be constantly meddling. In 773 Desiderius, the ambitious King of the Lombards, pressed Rome so hard, the Pope issued an earnest plea to Frankland for help, and he did not cry in vain. With an overpowering host the great King of the North swept through the Alpine passes. Desiderius shut himself up, terror-stricken, in his capital of Pavia, where he was duly blockaded, starved out, and compelled to surrender in 774. Meantime the victor proceeded in person to Rome where the grateful Pope received him with great splendor and rewarded him with the title of "Patrician" (that is, High Protector) of the Holy and Eternal City. As for the Lombard Kingdom it was simply suppressed now in Charlemagne's favor. He called himself "King of Italy" and actually dominated nearly all of that peninsula save the extreme south where the Greeks of Constantinople still held many districts.

As years went on and the Frankish monarchy grew not merely by these conquests, but by the subjection of the Germanic King of Bavaria, and of the barbarous princes of the Avars (in modern Austria-Hungary), and as its ruler grew ever more irresistible in war, ever more indefatigable in spreading the works of peace, the conviction doubtless became very general that here was a sovereign and a dominion for which the old names and titles of a Northern kingdom were totally inadequate. Hitherto, although in practice the power of the old Roman Emperors had absolutely ceased in western Europe, men, even in Frankland, admitted that *in theory* the Greek-speaking Emperors of Constantinople were the successors of the ancient Cæsars, and were therefore entitled to the highest technical rank among all monarchs. But the Popes had quarreled with these rulers on many theological points and were almost inclined to brand them as schismatics. They were also very anxious to prove their own independence of any secular control, by affecting, as direct successors of St. Peter, to have the right to give the power "in this world" to whomsoever they might choose to honor.

In 800 matters came to a climax. The power of Charlemagne was clearly too great to consider him merely an ordinary "king" (*rex*). Pope Leo on his part was very anxious to show the marked gratitude of the Roman See to the ruler who had released it from the fear of the Lombards, and rendered many other great favors. He was also desirous of showing his independence of the Greek rulers of Constantinople. If it was said there could be only one true "Emperor" in the world, the answer came conveniently to hand that for the moment at Constantinople ruled only an Empress, Irene, a most unworthy woman who had gained the power by blinding and deposing her own son. All things thus conjoined to promote one of the great spectacular acts of history.

In 800 Charlemagne found himself in Rome to quell certain local disturbances. It was Christmas Day. A brilliant company had gathered in the magnificent Basilica of St. Peter.[1] The King was praying at the great altar. One can imagine the impressive ceremonial: the incense smoke, the chanting choir, the splendidly arrayed courtiers in the nave, the still more splendidly vested ecclesiastics nearer the altar. Suddenly Pope Leo approached the kneeling monarch and placed on his head a glittering crown. Catching the meaning instantly, the populace made the great church quiver with the shout: "*To Charles the Mighty, great and pacific Emperor of the Romans*, crowned of God — be long life and victory!"

[1] Not the present church of St. Peter, but its predecessor on the same site. Probably in some respects a finer building.

Whether Charlemagne was Emperor because the Roman people (decadent successors of the departed empire-builders) had acclaimed him as their monarch, or because the Pope as God's direct deputy had crowned him, or because he had already won the right to the title by his own mighty deeds, no man then really stopped to inquire. The answer was to be fought out in blood during the next centuries, but the problem, as it developed, concerned German rather than French history. In any case, for the next fourteen years, the one-time "king" is "Carolus Augustus," in his proclamations, claiming to inherit all the titles, honors, and power of the original Cæsars. From this time onward also Charlemagne consciously tried to centralize his authority. He never became ashamed of his Frankish traditions and institutions: he never played the tyrant; nevertheless, the world saw something very different from the old Frankish monarchy. The "Holy Roman Empire" was born — an attempt to refound the old Roman Empire of the West, but on a strictly Christian basis. The lands of France were soon to be severed from this pretentious but unstable structure, but in Germany and in the later Austria it was to exist, first as a considerable power and then as a splendid shadow merely, down to the days when Napoleon Bonaparte ground up so much of the venerable rubbish of mediæval Europe (1806).

This Empire of 800 embraced all of modern France, Belgium, Holland, and Switzerland. It also contained the greater part of modern Germany and Italy, and had some hold on the western portion of Austria-Hungary and the extreme northeast corner of Spain. It was a huge, ill-compacted monarchy, held together really only by the terror of the Frankish arms and the remarkable genius of Charlemagne. While he lived, however, such was his personal ability that it really seemed as if the nations were about to be fused together.

To govern his vast dominions he used no intricate machinery. At his court (usually held at Aachen, or Aix-la-Chapelle, in the extreme west of modern Germany) were a few high officers, and

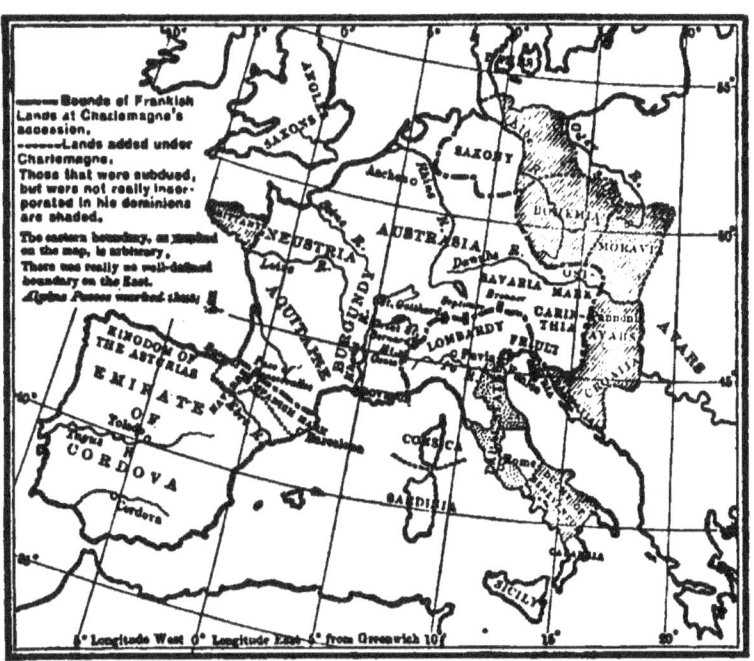

CHARLEMAGNE'S EMPIRE

a council of worldly-wise bishops and battle-loving noblemen. In the various districts were "counts"[1] to enforce justice and lead the provincial militia. Over the various frontier districts, or *marks*, were *markgrafs* (marquises), usually well-tried military men. To keep these officials in order there were constantly going about "imperial messengers" (*missi dominici*) to check up injustice, and to make frequent report of local conditions to the sovereign. This system worked admirably so long as Charlemagne lived to cover its defects by his personal genius. The moment he was gone it was to break down almost completely.

But Charlemagne gave more than firm government with law and order (things scarce enough, be it noted, since the fall of old Rome!). Under his fostering there took place a real revival of learning and letters. Literature and mere literacy were at a very low ebb even in the Church when he became king, and he devoted himself with genuine enthusiasm to combating these evils. To aid him in the task he summoned from Anglo-Saxon England a distinguished scholar, Alcuin, who became master of the palace school — a sort of model academy maintained at court and frequented by youths of noble family. The bishops and abbots throughout the Empire were required to establish similar schools for their localities, while earnestly did Charlemagne attack the deplorably prevalent notion that ignorance was compatible with genuine piety. "Let schools be established in each monastery or bishopric" (ran his mandate) "in which boys may learn to read, and to correct carefully the Psalms, the signs in writing, the songs, the calendar, and the grammar, because often men desire to pray to God properly, but they pray badly because of the incorrect books."

Under Alcuin's guidance there was a widespread revival of interest in the old Latin classics. Cicero, Horace, Virgil, and Seneca were copied and studied in numerous monasteries; and their style was imitated in poems, histories, and essays. There was very little originality in these literary attempts — usually

[1] Literally *comites* — "companions" of the king or emperor.

merely a slavish rehandling of ideas that had been new eight centuries earlier: but it was a great thing that the wisdom of the ancients ("lost pagans" as the pious often branded them!) should be held in honor, and that a mighty ruler exalted the scholar as well as the warrior.

How Charlemagne disciplined unworthy ecclesiastics, reorganized the Frankish Church, established just systems of laws, promoted skillful agriculture — there is no space here to tell. In 814 the great Emperor died, at the height of his prosperity. Few rulers had seemed so successful as he. Particularly in the old Gallic lands thoughtful men doubtless blessed their days, and said that now Gallo-Roman and German had been welded together as members of a new and better Western Empire, and that the end of the centuries of confusion, following the fall of Rome, had surely come.

The reign of Charlemagne was thus a delightful burst of sunlight in an epoch when there was a sad excess of twilight if not of gross darkness. It was too blessed to last. The forces of lawlessness had been only temporarily checked, and the infirmities of the organization of the Frankish Empire had been too great to be overcome by any but a very great monarch. Four times the Carolingian line had provided such a ruler, but a fifth was not to be forthcoming. Charlemagne handed over an undivided empire to his amiable, but not forceful or especially intelligent, son, Louis the Pious (814–40). The only hope of perpetuating the unwieldy empire lay in a policy of wise, firm consolidation and centralization which would fuse the Gallic, Germanic, and Italian peoples into a single contented nationality. No such highly difficult performance was to be expected of Louis. For a few years his father's old example and his old officers held the Empire tolerably together, then centrifugal influences burst loose.

The wedge was first driven in the Emperor's own household. Louis had been an only surviving son, but his own sons —

DIVISION OF THE EMPIRE

Lothair, Louis, and Charles "the Bald" — soon reached out greedy hands, even in their father's lifetime, for their own selfish share in the government. Never was the absence of genuine primogeniture more to be deplored in a monarchy than in the Frankish Empire of the ninth century. The three unscrupulous brothers quarreled and fought among themselves, deposed their father when he would not divide the inheritance to suit the stronger of them, then reinstated him again — at every turn weakening the imperial power, and strengthening the ever-assertive nobles by greater concessions of the government domain lands, wealth, and authority. Louis died in 840 with his realm already on the point of flying to pieces.

Lothair, the eldest of these unfilial sons, claimed the title of "Emperor," and this his brothers were willing to concede him. But over the boundaries of their personal dominions there was bloody war. In 841 at Fontenay (near Troyes) was a battle of large importance. Lothair was defeated by Louis and Charles the Bald and presently was forced to make peace on their terms. In 843 came the once famous "Treaty of Verdun" which was practically the end of the Frankish Empire. Louis received substantially all of Germany; Lothair a long, narrow strip from the North Sea along the west of the Rhine and clear into Italy (hence the name of "Lothair's Land" — "Lorraine" — for the debatable territory between France and Germany); and Charles the Bald took the remainder of the distracted Frankish Empire — virtually the whole of France. The shares of Louis and Charles were along genuine geographical and national lines and were destined to endure. That of Lothair was a mere artificial block of territory without fixed national antecedents, a veritable apple of discord between France and Germany as each power developed. In 843 began this question of a debatable land, and in 1914 the Alsace-Lorraine question was still troubling the peace of Europe.

The Treaty of Verdun was, of course, a mere breathing-spell between new wars. Lothair presently died and his sons and their unfriendly uncles soon quarreled over his dominions. Once or twice the Empire of Charlemagne was nearly united, not thanks to the capacity of any one prince, but because of the elimination or dying off of nearly all the other candidates. Some of the later Carolingians were men of fair ability, but many were only a grade better than the Merovingian sluggards whom their grandfathers had supplanted. In 884 for the last time the Frankish Empire seemed united under the Emperor Charles "the Fat" — incapable and lazy, with undoubted imperial blood as his chief if not sole asset.

By this time, not pitiful Charles the Fat, but Charles the Great himself might have been sorely taxed to put health into the vast, unwieldy realm. Not merely were the local counts (the ordinary imperial governors) showing more and more of "feudal" independence and playing the part of petty kings, not merely were the monarch's domain lands nearly all granted away to grasping noblemen while his mandates were ever less respected, but a serious foreign danger was afflicting the whole empire — particularly the part soon to be known as France. All through this sorrowful ninth century, from the Scandinavian fiords the pagan Northmen were descending in their dragon ships to harry the Frankish coasts. Year by year they would ascend the French rivers for many miles, burn, pillage, and carry captive; defeat the local levies mustered against them, and quickly make off with their spoil when at last a regular army had been gathered. These "vikings" were first-class fighting men, able to outmatch almost any equal number, and directed by chiefs possessed alike of valor and of skill. Many famous Frankish towns were devastated by them, and finally in 885–86 they ascended the Seine and laid systematic siege to Paris.

Paris was already a town of increasing importance: now it won a lasting name for itself in history by the valiant defense put up by its brave Bishop Gozlin and its secular chief Count Eudes against the destroying pagans. The capture of Paris (in the then demoralized state of the region) would probably have been followed by the permanent conquest by the vikings of all northern France, just as their comrades mastered Anglo-Saxon England. But Paris held out. The city was still not much more than the island in the Seine whereon stands to-day Notre Dame, and the main fighting was for the possession of the bridges connecting the city with the mainland. The pagans were able to capture one of these bridges, but not the other. The siege was long and desperate. Count Eudes left the city to urge the Emperor to hasten with succor, but presently he valiantly returned with a small band, cutting his way through the Northmen with his battle-axe, and heartening the defenders. At last Charles the Fat appeared with a huge relieving army, but the degenerate Emperor lacked the courage to put it to the touch with a decisive battle. He shamefully ransomed Paris by a heavy payment, and by allowing the repulsed vikings to depart to ravage Burgundy "because the inhabitants thereof obeyed not the Emperor."

This caitiff deed was almost the last important act by a ruler of the entire Frankish Empire. In 887 Charles the Fat was deposed by his high nobles, but his dominions were not passed on undivided to a rival. A bastard Carolingian reigned in Germany: in the present southeast of France there soon appeared a "King of Burgundy," and in France proper (as we may now call old Frankish "Neustria"), after some pretenders and contentions, a legitimate Carolingian, Charles "the Simple," continued in nominal power (893-923).[1]

It was a very nominal "power" indeed which this representative of a mighty name (not quite so "simple" as his name implied) could exercise. The "Holy Roman Empire" was now in complete abeyance. When it was to be revived it was to be in Germany and Italy, and was never really to include France. The feudal system[2] was now in full process of development, and every gain for the warlike barons was a corresponding

[1] Eudes, the brave Count of Paris, was pretty generally acknowledged as King of "France" after 888 and down to his death in 898. After that Charles the Simple's claims were generally accepted.

[2] See chap. IV.

loss of authority for their monarch. Because the feudal system of vassals and suzerains needed an apex no one thought of abolishing the kingship, and for a long time it was easier for the great lords to unite on a Caroling to enjoy the honor, than to confer it on a rival nobleman of non-royal lineage.

Charles the Simple thus reigned in name, at least, in about a fourth of his famous ancestor's one-time dominions. One important act he ratified which was pregnant for the future. The Northmen were becoming somewhat tamer, thanks to steady contact with the Christians, but they were becoming anxious for a permanent settlement. Charles bargained therefore with Rollo, the master of a strong fleet of dragon ships. The Frankish King would grant Rollo a broad strip of land along the Channel, including the important city of Rouen. This territory was to become a feudal principality, and Rollo its new duke would marry Charles's daughter and "do homage" to him for his fief. The viking chief and his best sword-hands were also to become Christians and to adopt civilized customs. The bargain was made and honestly carried out in 912. The Northmen speedily became "Normans" in their land of "Normandy." Their rude Scandinavian speech soon was merged as a mere dialect of what was now clearly "French." Rollo, who had duly renamed himself Robert, and all his chief warriors soon took on the standard virtues and vices of feudal barons. On the whole, Normandy was speedily better governed, more devoted to the arts of peace, more clearly the home of chivalrous knighthood (as that institution developed) than almost any other part of France. The last great racial contribution had been made to the French people — to the Celt, the Latin, the German, had now come the Scandinavian, bringing all the vigor of the extreme North, a strengthening and not a weakening of the new nation.

The Carolingian kings of this survival of old Frankland lasted till 987. Their power had ever dwindled, despite vigorous attempts of a few of these princes to reassert it. "Kings of Laon" they were sarcastically called, from the only city — in the wide lands of their great barons — where they seemed to have actual authority. At last in 987 the dynasty had nearly died out. Its only real representative was still another Charles, Duke of Lorraine. It was alleged that this man was really a vassal of the German Emperor. He was otherwise very obnoxious to the western barons, and an eager candidate from another line came forward. Hugh Capet, "Duke of France" (that is, the region then centering around Paris), was a descendant of the brave Count Eudes, who had defended the city against the vikings. He was wealthy, ambitious, tactful, and above all was supported by the great influence of the Church. Thanks to bribing the other great nobles by heavy gifts out of his possessions, and therefore compromising his future authority, he gained their consent so that on July 1, 987, he was solemnly crowned in Reims as "King of the Gauls, the Bretons, the Normans, the Aquitanians, the Goths, and the Gascons."

This new power of Hugh Capet did not seem very well assured. Doubtless many of the dukes and counts who did homage to him at Reims, silently expected that the new dynasty would soon perish as had that of other upstarts. If they imagined this, however, they were wrong. Hugh Capet was founding a dynasty which in one or another of its branches was to reign uninterruptedly until 1792.[1] With his coming we can justly say that "Frankland" had perished, "France" was fairly upon the scene.

[1] Of course there are still in the twentieth century persons descended from this Capetian line, who would have good claims to the crown of France, by hereditary succession, if the Third Republic were to be changed again into a monarchy. In a certain sense, therefore, the dynasty of Hugh Capet exists even to-day, as a traceable family.

CHAPTER IV
THE GOLDEN AGE OF FEUDALISM: 996-1270

WHEN Hugh Capet became king, the "feudal system" was already in full being and enjoying a healthy life — full of danger for the royal power. Too often the "Feudal Age" is used as a term as if it were synonymous with the "Middle Ages." As a matter of fact it includes only about the years between 900 to 1300, during which time the authority of the kings and of the "nation" was weak and what we call the "feudal nobility" was strong. After that, feudalism decidedly waned, or lived on mainly for the sake of its social trappings, and the kingship ever more steadily gained the upper hand. In the days of its prosperity feudalism was by no means confined to France; Germany, Italy, Spain, and, after the Norman Conquest (1066), England, all had their share of the system. At the same time feudalism had its most complete and characteristic growth in France, and when we use the word we instinctively describe it in French terms, just as in philosophy and art one is always tempted to turn to Greek schools, types, or models.

The origins of feudalism can be traced back to old Roman and Germanic times even before the great invasions. There were plenty of tokens of "feudal conditions" in Charlemagne's day. But what really brought the feudal régime to pass was the direful weakening of the government under his very unhappy successors, and the compelling need men felt for *some* system of society which would guard against the worst forms of anarchy.

By 900 even, the power of the kings who inherited the fragments of the Frankish Empire, had sunk low indeed. Even if they had been wise and vigorous monarchs the whole spirit of the age was undermining their authority. Many causes, long operating, were tending to upset what we may call the normal

THE FIEF AND MILITARY SERVICE

political society, in which all men are fellow members of an extensive nation, and replace it with a new order. This "feudalism" is extremely difficult to describe in a few words, but perhaps it is correct to say that it is a condition in which lawful authority is not based on the common allegiance of everybody to a central "government," but on a great number of special compacts, each between two persons, whereby the greater "lord" becomes at once a kind of landlord, and also a high magistrate and war-chief over the lesser "vassal." In the feudal period the question would not be so much, "Of what nation are you?" as, "Of what lord do you hold your lands?" The manner in which this question was answered, settled the social and political status of an individual.

Of all the causes contributing to the growth of feudalism the most general was the fact that kings and other magnates would grant away the lands whereof they were possessed in return for military service.[1] At first this "leasing" (as modern men would say) was only temporary; it ceased when the very peculiar "rent" (military service plus certain financial assistance) was not duly paid, and in any case when either the "landlord" (suzerain) or "tenant" (vassal) died. But when the king's power weakened, and inasmuch as long occupancy of a "fief" (feudal holding) made the tenant feel that the possession thereof was his *right*, not his privilege, the status of "vassalage" became ever more permanent. The king could not recall the fief except in extreme cases. He was also bound to confirm it to his late vassal's son, or sons, or if there was no son, to his daughter, or even his indirect heirs. By 900 the great vassals of kingdoms were forgetting all but their most formal duties to their nominal overlord. They became independent princes in all but name, and seldom enough did their "liege lord the king" have power to coerce them.

[1] Along with the mere private control of the land would usually go various kinds of "immunity"; for example, exemption from royal jurisdiction over the land and from royal taxes. The new "vassal" would thus be high-judge himself over the lands granted him, and would collect his own taxes.

The greater vassals, however, were in turn compelled to parcel out their own dominions among lesser princelets still, and these again might have dependent on them a swarm of petty nobles each possessing perhaps only a fortified tower and a few bare acres. The feudal system indeed caught in its tentacles practically the entire social fabric of France. The bishops and abbots of the Church were too frequently feudal lords, with all the political and military rights and duties (except that of personally swinging the sword)[1] of a lay nobleman. Between one fifth and one fourth of the entire territory of France is estimated to have belonged to these wealthy and sometimes direfully "secular" great churchmen.

Naturally enough the miserable lower classes, who had been held in various degrees of bondage during the Roman and Frankish periods, became adjuncts to the feudal system, as mere villeins to the lords: the humble and necessary supporters (serfs or not much better) of the dominant nobility. Their exact condition will be made clearer a little later.[2]

In this feudal régime there was no essential order or system. Theoretically every nobleman[3] owed allegiance to some overlord, and he to some higher overlord, and so on in ascending order up to the king. Actually there was every kind of confusion. "Organized anarchy," so feudalism has been justly called by a despairing scholar. Still, despite the confusion, there are a few lines of demarcation which simplify certain feudal institutions and conditions. The following points may be helpful:

1. In the first place, as a rule the lowest feudal noblemen ranked as mere "seigneurs" or "sires" ("lords"), possessors of

---

[1] It was charged that churchmen often evaded the ecclesiastical prohibition of priests "using the sword" by carrying huge weighted *maces* (that is, war-clubs) that smote out the enemy's brains without actually "shedding his blood." A good many of these militant clergymen seem to pass across French history.

[2] See p. 75.

[3] That is, every man who "held land" or had fair claims to hold it as a regular vassal: in other words, about every person who was a stout fighter, was not the son of a villein, did not live by handicraft or agriculture or trade, and had not entered the Church.

a small castle. Above these would follow, in a kind of order, barons, viscounts, counts, marquises, and dukes: and at the head of all the king. A great abbot of the Church might rank up with a viscount, a prince-bishop as a count or even higher. However, there were no fixed usages. In France certain counts were every whit as powerful as certain dukes,[1] while other counts might be "doing homage" for some of their lands to a viscount or even baron. And there were certain noblemen of still lower nominal rank, who held up their heads arrogantly with the best; for example, the lord of a great castle in Picardy, the famous relics whereof were wantonly destroyed by the Germans in 1917, made following proud boast in his family motto:

"No king am I, prince, duke, nor count,
I'm just the *Sire* of Coucy!"

2. In the next particular should be observed the ordinary obligations of a nobleman to his suzerain. These were before all "homage," the duty of kneeling down before the overlord on proper occasions and swearing to execute the feudal duties, and to do the lord no injury. The main fulfillment of homage, of course, came in the obligation to fight against the suzerain's enemies, to give him good counsel, especially to aid him in awarding and enforcing justice, and on certain rather rare occasions (ransom from captivity, dowry for eldest daughter, etc.) to supply him with money. In return the suzerain would owe his "vassal" military protection against *his* enemies, and fair play in any lawsuit, and must also see to it that his children were not cheated out of their father's inheritance.

3. Finally, we observe that the center of all feudal life and action was ordinarily the nobleman's castle. Every full-fledged fief possessed at least one, sometimes an elaborate fortress, sometimes merely a petty tower.[2] Even with the smallest castle, how-

[1] In the later days of French royalty at least, the brothers and younger sons of the king would often have the title of "counts," and yet of course take precedence at court before practically all "dukes."

[2] Of course, a fief (feudal holding) could consist of a mere grant, say of market dues or hunting privileges in a forest; but normally it involved a land grant.

ever, the capture thereof (before the coming of gunpowder) was a slow and bloody business. Behind his good walls and with a few trusty retainers and a good supply of bread and beer, even a very feeble baron could often "make good his rights" against his suzerain. These castles had been multiplied particularly to check the ravages of the Northmen and other raiders: but everywhere they sprang up and became so many centers for political disintegration. Only tedious blockade and starvation could ordinarily reduce them, and their masters comported themselves like so many petty kings. They exercised powers of "pit and gallows" (life and death) over their peasants; coined money in their own name; and waged bloody warfare against their neighbors in the next castle, or perhaps against the prince-abbot of the neighboring monastery. A rude sense of honor usually compelled them to execute their bare pledge to their suzerain, especially by giving the stipulated number of days of military service; but if an overlord was a wise man, he did not interfere in the internal management of his vassals' fiefs nor in their private quarrels. The suzerain's hold also upon the dependents of his own liegemen was at best precarious. "The vassal of my vassal is *not* my vassal" ran the old saying. It was enough if the lesser nobles did their sworn duty by their lord, and did not involve him in war with his neighbors; while he in turn (unless he were the actual king) was probably full of distrust towards *his* suzerain.

This then was the setting of French mediæval society — the masses of toiling peasantry, without political rights or standing; the barons in armor, riding roughshod over the unprivileged, unarmed multitude; and the enfeebled king, often trembling before his own "vassals." Only for the terrible thunders of the Church had these feudal lords genuine awe.[1]

For two hundred years after the Archbishop of Reims (the first churchman of the land) put the crown on the head of Hugh Capet, the new kingdom of France had a struggling and often

[1] For a clearer picture of life in the feudal ages, see pp. 64–80.

precarious existence, and the royal crown must often have seemed to be made indeed of mere tinsel. To buy the support of the nobles who had assented to his coronation, Hugh had been forced to make almost ruinous concessions of land and authority. Nowhere seemed the "organized anarchy" of feudalism more triumphant than in France just before 1000. In theory Hugh had taken over the vast powers of Charlemagne, minus only the imperial title; practically he was only the most honored among several hundred barons, who called him "fair sire" more because each man desired a check upon his own unfriendly neighbors than because he wished to have any effective king over him.

Hugh indeed possessed some real authority over his old "Duchy of France," the land immediately around Paris and stretching southward to Orléans on the Loire. This country has been commonly known as the "Royal Domain Lands." It was not, however, larger than the small American State of Massachusetts, and even within it, there were many petty barons who obeyed the King very reluctantly if they did so at all. Outside of this region the King had almost no effective power. The great Dukes of Normandy, Burgundy, and Brittany, and the equally lordly Counts of Flanders, Champagne, and Vermandois, could each put in the field as many armed retainers as the King, and they never hesitated to fight him when they harbored a grievance or an ambition. In the south of his nominal kingdom, the Duke of Aquitaine and the Count of Toulouse divided the rule over a folk who differed in language and local customs from their northern neighbors, and they usually did not trouble much about tendering the King even their outward and formal homage. The "South Country" (*Midi*) indeed differed so absolutely from northern France as to constitute almost a separate nationality. The Southerners spoke the melodious "Languedoc" dialect, as against the harsher "Languedoïl" used around Paris; their manners were more luxurious and showed more survivals of the old Gallo-Roman culture: and it was angrily claimed by the North French monks that their morals were far laxer than on the other side of the Loire.[1] In any case, the fusing of "France" and the "South Country" into a happily unified nation was one of the great tasks for the future, and would have remained a sore problem, even if it had not been rendered far harder by the general feudal anarchy.

Besides all these great nobles just named, there was a host of lesser counts, viscounts, and barons who ruled by the "grace of God" (that is, without heeding any suzerain), coined their own money, quarreled or made peace at their own pleasure, tyrannized over their subjects; in short, performed all the acts of petty sovereigns, with scant enough respect for "their lord the king" at Paris. Under these circumstances the real marvel is that the new dynasty of Capet ever built up an effective kingship at all; yet this was actually the case. Out of this feudal chaos was to rise the majestic monarchy of France.

A number of factors worked together to make the monarchy to wax and the barony to wane. Here are some of them.

While the various noblemen were continually resisting the King, these scattered princes could seldom forget their own bitter feuds enough to unite as a body against him. He had the support of *some* vassals in almost every war.

The Capetian kings were lucky in never lacking a direct heir down to 1328. The reigning king could always present a son eligible for election by the nobles, and for coronation as junior king in the older ruler's lifetime. For a long time, in theory indeed, the kingship was elective, with the great lords as the electors, but by about 1200 it was so clearly understood that only a Capetian was able to succeed a Capetian that the election became an empty form, and insensibly hereditary succession was established in its stead. There were no disputed successions and almost no wars *within* the royal family, to distract still further

---

[1] When King Robert married Constance of Arles, a Southern princess, about 1000, the North French monkish chroniclers recorded in dismay that the queen came with a most immoral rabble: "Their arms and dress were disordered; their hair cut short and even shaved in front [a Roman custom]; their beards clipped like mountebanks, and their high boots most discreditable to them."

the kingly power. Men became accustomed to the idea that a Capetian was the one possible ruler of all France.

Then again while several of these Capetian kings were mediocre men, none were entirely unworthy to rule, and several (and these in the most critical periods) were sovereigns of marked capacity. The personal equation was usually all on their side.

Another decisive factor was the ability of these kings to keep on friendly terms with the Church. The Popes, all through this period, were usually at strife or open war with the Emperors of Germany. All the more reason there was then for Rome to stand on good terms with the second most pretentious monarch in Christendom. The average feudal lord oppressed his neighboring bishop or abbot; the King would usually come to the latter's relief. The Church gladly repaid this protection by giving its own potent moral (and often its physical) support to the King against his vassals.

Also as time elapsed, and the non-noble lower classes, especially the dwellers in the towns, strove to win personal and local liberties, they often found a champion in the King against their baronial lords. The King reaped his reward in the subsidies these new subjects were glad to pay to him, and money has always meant power. Besides every detachment of subjects from the barons of course strengthened the monarchy.

Finally, be it noted, while the Capetian dynasty *lasted*, many feudal dynasties disappeared. Family feuds, local feuds, crusading warfare, and many similar calamities carried them off. The King would, of course, pounce upon the vacant fiefs and there would be few to gainsay him.

Thus it was that from a pitiful abyss the new French monarchy at last struggled upwards to greatness.

It was over a hundred years, however, before there were any substantial signs of a change for the better. The three Capetians who followed Hugh the Founder were among the most insignificant of their line. Robert (996–1031), Henry I (1031–60), and

Philip I (1060-1108) were all somewhat weak men, in addition to the ordinary handicap of facing a perilous situation. Philip indeed probably had somewhat smaller dominions than Hugh Capet. To make matters far worse in his day there had arisen a most formidable rival beside the King of Paris. Ever since their conversion and settlement the Dukes of Normandy had been little less than independent princes. Now in 1066, William "the Conqueror" had overthrown the Anglo-Saxon dynasts in England, and become the full-fledged king of a realm, which (thanks to his skillful and valorous policy) he held in a far tighter grip than his nominal suzerain held the bulk of France. It would have seemed a most ordinary turn of events if the Norman duke, now sovereign in his own right of England, had refused homage to Paris, and overthrown his one-time overlord by force of arms. This did not, however, take place. William I died in 1087. His sons quarreled over his possessions. Much of the best Norman fighting energy was drained away to the Holy Land on the First Crusade (1095-99) and perished there. France therefore had respite from absolute disruption, but the threat remained. So long as the Duke of Normandy held a great overseas dominion, whence he could draw gold and warriors, what chance of more than a precarious life had his "suzerain" the Capetian? The twelfth century was to prove critical indeed.

The Capetian monarchy was saved and exalted partly by the dissensions of its enemies, partly by the kind Providence which gave it *three* kings of very high ability. They were all among the prime builders of France. They were Louis the Fat, Philip Augustus, and last but nowise least St. Louis.

There was nothing sluggish about Louis VI "the Fat" (1108-37) but his body. Powerful war-horses groaned under the weight of this corpulent but vigorous king, as he hastened incessantly about his dominions exerting all his limited authority to make the king's law respected. The "Ile de France" (Royal dominions around Paris) had been infested beyond most mediæval regions with lawless petty nobles, who seized, plundered, and put to ransom travelers, pillaged the property of the Church, and made the whole land a ceaseless Gehenna. Louis found an admirable minister and assistant in the sage Abbot Suger, one of the first of those great royal administrators who were to do so much for the establishing of France. "It is the duty of kings," wrote Suger, "to repress by their power and the innate right of their office, the audacity of the nobles who rend the state by ceaseless wars, desolate the poor and destroy churches." These were high words for the twelfth century. Suger's master had often to let the great feudatories beyond his domain-lands work their will, but he at least became lord within his own limited house. One by one the robber castles were besieged and taken, and the worst oppressors taught a lasting lesson.

In his wars with his great vassals Louis, of course, had not the military strength for wide conquests, yet he at least struggled valiantly for his rights and not entirely in vain. The Normans were kept at arm's length, but in 1124, when Henry I of Normandy and England had made alliance with his son-in-law Henry V, Emperor of Germany, the Capetian King had to face a very serious danger. Henry the German led a great host into eastern France and even threatened Reims. Then it was there flashed the clear sign that Frenchmen were drawing together into a national consciousness, and could unite against a foreign peril. Louis VI boldly took the great "oriflamme," the flame-red silken banner of the realm, and called out all his vassals. For the most part they obeyed heartily and bravely. The great princebishops sent a host of men-at-arms. The Count of Champagne and the Duke of Burgundy led out all their retainers, and so did many lesser dynasts as well. Such an army was collected that Henry the German dared not abide the issue. He slunk home without risking a battle, and Louis reaped infinite credit. Everybody confessed that the King of France was no ordinary feudal overlord, but the consecrated chief of "the most noble and Christian nation of the French," its appointed champion against the alien. As a consequence of this prestige, Louis was able to meddle in the settlement of the troubled affairs of Auvergne (in the South Country) and in Flanders. In both cases he came away with credit, and demonstrated, as was then said, "that kings have long hands."

Another form of Louis's activities was even more menacing to the great nobles. Everywhere the towns of France were forming "free communes" and demanding charters of liberties from their overlords.[1] It was the beginning of a movement of the oppressed non-noble classes that was to bring much to the world. The King had little enough favor for such unsettling proposals *within* the royal dominions, but outside of them he craftily understood that they would undermine the power of his rivals, the great feudatories. Everywhere else, therefore, he used his influence to get charters from the seigneurs for the communes. It was not that he loved the communes, but the chance for a stroke at the great vassals was not to be resisted.

When Louis VI died (1137) the power of French monarchy was sensibly greater than at his accession (1108), although the danger from Normandy-England had by no means passed. The King had, however, arranged as he thought a most fortunate marriage for his son and heir Louis VII.[2] He had wedded him to Eleanor of Guienne, heiress to the great fief of Poitou and the still greater Duchy of Aquitaine — embracing the lion's share of the South Country. It should have made the royal dominions extend down to the Pyrenees, and rendered the king incomparably more powerful than any of his vassals. Unfortunately, however, Louis VII (1137–80), although not exactly a weakling, was by no means the equal of his energetic father. He was indeed so "pious, so clement, so kindly that on seeing him you might think he was not a king, but some good monk." Such a man was no match for the spirit of the times.

[1] See pp. 77–80.
[2] Louis VI had had an older son Philip, on whom he had rested great hopes, but in 1131, as the lad was riding out of Paris, a "diabolical pig" (one of the regular mediæval scavengers) ran between his horse's legs and threw the Prince, who died of the injury.

In 1149 after returning from the disastrous Second Crusade to Palestine, Louis VII quarreled with his high-spirited and not super-devout queen, and speedily divorced Eleanor, honestly returning to her the great dower of nigh all of the South Country. Eleanor was still marriageable and her vast fortune made her the "catch" for every lordly suitor. Almost to the ruin of France she presently married Henry of Anjou, who was not merely Count of Anjou and Duke of Normandy, but in 1154 became Henry II, King of England. This "Henry Plantagenet" was a prince of abounding energy and almost equal ability. In France his dominions extended now over an infinitely greater area than his nominal suzerain at Paris. He had all of England: he even commenced the conquest of Ireland. The sore quarrels in his own family, and the difficulty of controlling England, prevented him at first from a deliberate attack upon the Capetian, but from this time onward for nearly fifty years the "Angevin" (Anjou) peril hung over the French kingdom like a sword of Damocles, and Louis VII was not destined to live long enough to see it pass.

This twelfth century was, of course, an age when the French peoples if not the French kings were showing the effective power that was in them. The Crusades were at their height. The history of these vast military movements to rescue Palestine from the Moslem belongs strictly to the general annals of Europe, not to France. But France was their peculiar homeland, supplying probably more fighting men than all the other Christian nations combined, and endured corresponding sacrifices. It was at Clermont in Auvergne that in 1095 Pope Urban II had first preached his gospel of the sword, and had been answered by the mighty cry "God wills it!"; while of the chiefs who led the army that stormed Jerusalem in 1099, almost every one was either a Frenchman, a Norman, or at least came from the debatable lands of Flanders and Lorraine.[1] The Christian kingdom of Jerusalem

---

[1] Some of them, indeed, Normans who had emigrated to southern Italy and Sicily, founded dukedoms there, and thence passed on to the greater adventure in Syria and Palestine.

which lasted from 1099 to 1187 was almost a slavish imitation of feudal France transported to Oriental shores. In the abortive Second Crusade (1147–49) Louis VII had been one of the main participants, and in each of the five later Crusades which won so much futile glory, all but one (the Fifth, 1228–29) was to be largely under French leadership and with heavy French contingents. The sacrifices and agony of these expeditions were inevitably vast. Their failures were, of course, due to the pitiful ignorance of the conditions of Eastern warfare, but the resourcefulness and courage of the crusaders was superb: — a witness to the high intelligence, energy, and vast potentialities of the consolidating French people.

The reactions of the Crusades were not all of them simply religious and social. Not merely did the returned warriors bring back from Palestine a love for Eastern silks, sherbets, and other refinements, and learn how to improve the fortification of their castles: the political results were also marked. Many noble families were killed off. Many others became so impoverished by the sacrifices entailed by the expeditions they had to quit their fiefs. In any case the royal power was steadily the gainer.

The crisis of the French monarchy came in the days of the son of Louis VII, Philip II, who from his mighty deeds presently earned for himself the lofty title of Philip Augustus (1180–1223). More than any other one personage, *he* was the author of the greatness of France. When he ascended the throne the very existence of the monarchy was in question. When he departed, its victorious future seemed assured. He is therefore one of the cardinal figures in history.

Modern critics cannot, indeed, wax enthusiastic over this cold, cautious, firmly calculating man, who could, if need be, show himself the lion, but always by preference played the fox. He was not more unscrupulous and morally calloused and cruel than the run of his contemporaries, and there are few major crimes to be laid to his door. Chroniclers of his day give this not

unfriendly picture: "He was a well-knit, handsome man, bald (after an illness), of agreeable face and ruddy complexion, loving good cheer, wine and women, generous to his friends, niggardly to those he disliked, catholic [that is, pious] in his faith, far-seeing, and obstinate in his resolution." This king was fortunate in enjoying a very long reign, during which he saw his desire upon nearly all his enemies.

Henry II of England, Anjou, and Normandy had been prevented from throwing off his nominal dependence upon France by the strife within his own family and dominions.[1] There was intermittent fighting between him and Philip until 1189, when the news that the Saracens had retaken Jerusalem caused all the kings of Europe to dedicate themselves to the Crusade, and temporarily to drop their feuds. Henry II died almost immediately thereafter. He was a very able prince who had just missed founding a great empire. His son, Richard the Lion-Hearted (Richard I of England, of "Ivanhoe" fame), was a magnificent cavalier and field-captain, but without the political and diplomatic ability of his father. Late in 1189 Philip and Richard set off as brothers-in-arms for Palestine to recapture the Holy City. They departed as sworn friends, on the journey they quarreled, and their bickerings while in Syria went far to bring the unhappy Third Crusade to grief. In 1191 Philip washed his hands of the situation in disgust, and hastened back to France as soon as the strong city of Acre was taken. Richard more honorably stayed in Syria until 1192, when it was evident that Jerusalem was not to be recaptured. Then he made a truce with Saladin, the Moslem Sultan, and also started home. While, however, he was passing through Europe he was treacherously imprisoned by his enemy Duke Leopold of Austria, and held several years in German captivity — years which Philip used to full advantage to intrigue with all the disaffected elements in the Angevin lands and to undermine his rival's power.

[1] As Richard the Lion-Hearted stated pithily: "It is the usage in our family that sons should hate their father!"

In 1194 Richard was at liberty again, and such was his prowess as a general that Philip's schemes were effectively checked for five years, until the English King perished (1199) by a chance arrow while attacking a South French castle. This arrow was to determine much history. It is hard to tell the fate of France had this capable warrior enjoyed a normal lease of life. Richard's lawful heir to at least part of his dominions was very probably his nephew, Prince Arthur; but his younger brother John (King John of England, probably the greatest scoundrel who ever disgraced the English throne) put forth his hands upon all the territories. The great "Angevin" interest was divided. Philip, as the suzerain "bound to render justice," made haste to espouse the cause of young Arthur, whom he declared lawfully entitled to Anjou, Normandy, and Brittany.

John did not lack a certain military ability. He defeated Arthur, took him prisoner, and then completed the deed by murdering him. Philip had now a perfectly clear case under feudal usage. John had slaughtered the heir to three great fiefs and usurped them; he had "broken all the bonds of fealty." In the lack of proper heirs the fiefs lapsed back to the suzerain. John was so outrageous and so unpopular with the barons of France that Philip's other vassals for the most part supported the King gladly. John's vassals on their side often fought for him very slackly or not at all.

In the winter of 1203–04 John, like the coward that he was, took refuge in England. Philip then pressed the siege of the great Château-Gaillard, possibly the strongest castle of the time, which Richard had built at a vitally important spot to bar the passage from Paris down the Seine into Normandy. It was valiantly defended, but no outside relief arrived. One by one Philip's engineers forced its outworks, and in April, 1204, the great castle surrendered. In June of that year Rouen, the capital of Normandy, opened its gates, and nearly all the old duchy of Rollo the Northman was soon in Philip's hands. After that display of strength it took little more than a military promenade

THE KING ENTERS PARIS IN TRIUMPH

into the Loire territories in 1204 and 1205 to make Maine, Touraine, Anjou, and Poitou change fealty. By 1208 John retained little more in France than Saintonge and Gascony — a part of the old Aquitainian duchy in the South Country. The once great "Angevin Empire" had faded to a shadow.

John did not succumb, however, without a struggle. In 1214 Philip faced a genuine crisis. The Angevin interest had stirred up rebels and enemies in many parts of France, and above all had induced the Emperor Otto IV of Germany to invade France by way of Flanders. With Otto rode nearly all the dynasts of the Low Countries, those princelets of uncertain allegiance who wished neither France nor Germany to become too powerful. The danger was great. John himself was re-invading France along the line of the Loire, but Philip called out all his vassals, and was notably aided by the burgher militia of the new "free towns," anxious to prove their gratitude and value for their royal protector. At the bridge of Bouvines (between Lille and Tournai) French and German collided. It was a headlong mediæval battle, marked by little high generalship but by much valor. Philip was in the midst of the fray. The German footmen dragged him from his horse and almost took him prisoner till his knights thundered down to his aid. In the end the headlong charges of the North French chivalry cleared the field alike of the Germans and of their Flemish and English auxiliaries. Otto in turn barely escaped capture, and fled ignominiously, leaving six counts and twenty-five lesser barons captive in French hands as well as a swarm of ordinary knights and commoners.

Philip returned to Paris amid the rejoicings of the royal city. We are told how on the day of entry the *Te Deums* of the clergy mingled with the clang of the bells and the bray of the trumpets. The houses were hung with curtains and tapestries; the roads strewn with green branches and flowers, and citizens, churchmen, and university students all went forth to meet the King, singing canticles of praise. It was a truly national victory, for the militia of the communes no less than the feudal men-at-arms had borne their brave part in the battle.[1] The French people was finding itself and sensing its own unity and power. Bouvines therefore has to go down in history as one of the world's decisive battles.

After Bouvines, John quickly slunk back to England again, not risking a serious blow. The old heritage of the Norman dukes was definitely lost. Philip showed admirable ability in conciliating the factions in the conquered land, knowing how to take away the sting of conquest and yet to confirm his new power. His innovations for the management of the enlarged royal dominions, the introduction of *baillis* as high royal officers to supervise the lower *prévots* and to check up abuses, his skillful financial measures whereby he was able to fill his armies with soldiers[2] at steady wages, and not to depend merely on feudal levies, the marked favor he showed the new "free towns," which were giving scope and liberty to the lower classes — all these things, without entering into technical details, show him the great statesman as well as the successful warrior.

In 1223, when Philip Augustus died, he left a kingdom in which enormous blocks of territory from Picardy down almost to the heart of Aquitaine had been added to the direct royal domains. In 1180 these dominions had contained only thirty-eight provostships (*prévotes*), in 1223 there were ninety-four. The royal revenues had more than doubled. The feudal lords knew for a trembling certainty that they were henceforth only at best the privileged subjects of a mighty king. In other words, under Philip Augustus the great power of France was born.

During this reign also an important step was taken towards bringing the region of Toulouse, the eastern part of the South

---

[1] The battle probably was really won by the knights, not by the communal militia as over-zealous modern writers have contended, but it was much that "mere city-folk" should have proved of important military value to the King.

[2] Mercenaries, if regularly paid, could be employed in campaigning all the year long: feudal troops could be hardly held together, save in great emergencies, more than a couple of months unless chances of plunder were unusually good. Mercenaries also could be kept under far stiffer discipline than feudal levies.

THE LOUVRE OF PHILIP AUGUSTUS

This palace, which was at the same time a fortress, was much smaller than the present Louvre

Country, into dependence upon northern France. Philip had no direct part in the movement, though he did nothing to discourage it. In this soft and luxurious region the Catholic religion is said to have relaxed its hold and much of the population became infected with the "Albigensian" heresy; a hybrid type of half Christianity, half Oriental mysticism, which set at nought nearly all the orthodox dogmas. Milder efforts by preachers having failed, in 1207 the great Pope Innocent III caused a general "crusade" to be preached against the heretics. Many North French barons were delighted at a summons to pious warfare in a country near at hand and full of plunder. Between 1207 and 1218 lovely Provence, Toulouse, and other districts were ravaged from end to end; their towns sacked; their civilization stunted; and great numbers even of devout Catholics were slaughtered.[1] The power of the Counts of Toulouse, once nearly as independent as "kings," was almost completely broken.

At length the crusading fury burned itself out. The heretics disappeared, and the surviving Southerners turned in despair on the invaders and for the most part expelled them. But to secure any kind of protection, Count Amaury of Toulouse and other barons were forced to appeal to the King of France, and to pledge themselves to be his humble vassals. Under Philip's son Louis VIII, nearly the whole of this great fraction of the South Country was brought under royal control. The standards of the Capetian were thus to float proudly across the whole land from the gray Channel to the blue Mediterranean.

Louis VIII (1223-1226) apart from this achievement had too brief a reign to put any real impress upon his time. He left his throne to his twelve-year-old son Louis IX (1226-70), known to later annals as St. Louis, who was, next to Philip Augustus, to be the chief architect of the grandeur of royal France.

At the time of his nominal accession, the kingly power faced

[1] At Béziers some of the conquerors hesitated about ordering a general massacre, saying they could not always tell Catholic from heretic, whereupon the fanatical Abbot of Citeaux ordered, "*Kill all. God will know his own!*" — This command was obeyed.

what was always a grievous peril in any feudal monarchy — a regency. A weak rule would mean a perfect heyday for the great barons. But all the selfish dissidents missed their reckoning when it came to dealing with Blanche of Castile, the young King's remarkably capable and energetic mother. By the time her son was old enough to reign for himself the feudatories had been put effectively in their place, Henry III of England (John's son), who had dreamed of meddling in French affairs, had been beaten and chased home, and the royal grip upon Toulouse, established by Louis VIII, had been further strengthened. Between mother and son there seems always to have been perfect harmony and confidence. She continued to be the prop of his government for many years, remained as regent of France when he went to Palestine on crusade, and until she died (1252) it is hard to tell whether she or the king were the most powerful personage in the realm. The character of this puissant queen-mother seems sometimes hard and masculine, but no one can deny her great abilities and her use of them for the weal of France. In her we meet about the first of those remarkable women who were destined to play such a part in the annals of the French monarchy.

If we except the story of St. Louis's two crusades (whose details lie outside the scope of this history) there are few events in his reign that are dramatic and striking, but he made an enormous impression upon his age. From his friend and comrade-in-arms, the Sire de Joinville, we have a delightful memoir, giving a naïve, but loving and seemingly highly accurate, sketch of the personality and doings of this truly *good* man. We have him pictured to us as with a slender figure, large blue eyes, long blond hair, and "the manner of a young girl." But there was nothing timid in the manner in which he brought to justice malcontent barons who defied his law, or in which he charged to battle when his honest efforts had failed to maintain the peace. In him medieval piety shone at its best,[1] and proved that it was possible

[1] Louis seemed so flawless in character that his servants, seeking to find in him some trace of human frailty, were forced to fall back on statements such as "he was very difficult to manage when he was sick!"

ST. LOUIS'S CRUSADE TO PALESTINE

to be hyper-scrupulous in masses and fasts, to tend the sick, to give bread with one's own hands to beggars, to abound in building churches, hospitals, and every other like charity, and yet also to enforce law and order over a great realm, to chase away enemies, enact righteous laws, and make the wicked tremble at a king's just anger.

In 1248 Louis "took the Cross" for a crusade. The spirit of the first crusaders was waning. Men were no longer so anxious to save their souls by pilgrimage to Jerusalem as they had been a century earlier, but Louis conceived it his high duty to make another attempt to rescue the Holy City. The expedition was no more fortunate than its predecessors. The King landed in Egypt, where, after some brave fighting, he was taken prisoner by the paynims in 1250, and only released after paying a heavy ransom. By his heroic bearing in captivity, however, he won the admiration, not merely of all Christendom, but even of his Egyptian captors, who are alleged to have considered making him their sultan if he would only turn Moslem.

In 1254 he came back to France, and for the next fifteen years devoted himself to the happiness of his kingdom. He was undoubtedly the most powerful monarch of his age. Delightful are the pictures given us of how he used to love to award shrewd and speedy justice alike to high and low, sitting with his legal counselors under an oak in the royal forest at Vincennes. The Popes listened attentively to the respectful but very plain counsels he sometimes gave them about their miserable quarrels over secular issues. The great barons submitted their differences to him for arbitration, even when under feudal usage they were entitled to draw the sword. Turbulent factions or dynasts in England and Lorraine (not then part of France) requested him to judge between them. All this meant that the King of France was adding to his physical power that imponderable but often irresistible *moral* power which comes when worldly greatness, intellectual force, and spiritual worthiness are all united in the same person.

Louis was not a great innovator as a statesman, but without

striking any one violent blow at feudalism he steadily strengthened the royal authority. He used all his influence to prohibit or at least discourage the "noble right" of ordeal by battle, that is, the settling of the justice of a lawsuit by the blows between two champions instead of by honest evidence before a judge. The system of royal courts was developed, and the way made easy for appeals from the decisions of the seigneurial courts to those of the king. In time (with important cases at least) the "seigneurial justice" would become only a nominal preliminary before the "royal justice," and France would be further consolidated by being subject to a single set of tribunals. Another and even more direct stroke for national unity was this: Louis reformed the royal coinage and put it on an honest basis. Henceforth it circulated anywhere in the realm. The corruption and irregular standards of the wretched little private mints of the scores of barons made their coinage circulate only within each narrow seigneury. The natural result was that the king's good money presently drove out the feudal bad money — an incalculable factor for developing the economic life of France.

It is impossible to overestimate the gains in authority and prestige for the Capetian monarchy accruing from this forty-four-year reign of a genial, wise, valiant, energetic, and genuinely pious man. Louis IX met the perfect ideal of the thirteenth century for a royal layman. Even his misfortunes in Egypt seemed only sent from Heaven that his virtues might shine forth the clearer. His end added to the sanctity already associated about his name. In 1270 he went on a crusade again, although nearly all his worldly-wise intimates urged him against it. Europe was weary of crusades, and only the King's great personal influence induced a large army to embark. On the way to Palestine the host landed at Tunis in Africa to coerce its Moslem prince who was threatening Sicily. The camp was soon attacked by pestilence, the King sickened and died after a brief illness (1270). The expedition, of course, at once broke up, and returned to France with the casket of the beloved King.

The universal opinion of the age declared this ruler to be a "saint," and in 1297 (an unusually short time by Catholic usage) he was duly canonized at Rome, and placed in the Calendar. From that time onward French royalty could not merely boast in its line statesmen and warriors, but an accepted saint of the Church, worthy to rank with martyrs, holy bishops, and inspired doctors. The gain to the dynasty from such an honor, so long as the spirit of the Middle Ages persisted, was incalculable.

In 996 Hugh Capet had left a narrow domain land around Paris, and a fragile claim to the homage of various unruly feudatories, to his weak and distracted successors. In 1270, St. Louis, his lineal descendant, left a solid dominion, spreading from sea to sea, with great revenues and a formidable fighting power, to his son Philip III. France had reached a high estate in Europe, from which, notwithstanding many hours of sore trial, she was never really to fall.

CHAPTER V

LIFE IN THE FEUDAL AGES

THE mediæval chroniclers often make bare and uninspiring work of the barons and kings of feudal times. Conning their dry annals seldom stimulates our imaginations, unless we can reconstruct before our minds the world in which they lived. The life of the period of the earlier Capetians, when the royal power was weakest and feudal anarchy at its height, often seems further removed from us than the life of old Athens or Rome, despite the fact that Hugh Capet stands much nearer to us by chronology than does Pericles or Augustus. Anything like a perfect picture of feudal conditions is out of the question, even in a much longer book than this; and indeed matters were so confused in the Middle Ages that generalizations about how people lived, thought, and acted are more than ordinarily unsafe. Nevertheless certain things we may set down as typical and true; and even a very imperfect statement of the conditions under which the kings of France had to build up their monarchy will help us to realize the difficulty of their task and the slow and painful steps which the French people had to take before they could become a great modern nation.

In the Middle Ages there were really only three classes of people — feudal warriors, privileged priests, and servile peasants.[1] We will consider now the life of the first two of these classes — the only two classes then usually reckoned to be of real importance.

[1] Any artisans — carpenters, weavers, and the like — would ordinarily be numbered among the peasants, and probably would spend part of their time in agriculture. As for commerce, it had sunk to the importation of a few luxuries; for example, silks, spices for cooking, incense for the Church. These Oriental wares would be supplied through the rare visits to the castles by wandering peddlers.

EXTERIOR VIEW

Showing the bridge protected by a triple work; the donjon; at the left, the great hall; in the rear, living-quarters (these and the great hall are of the fifteenth century).

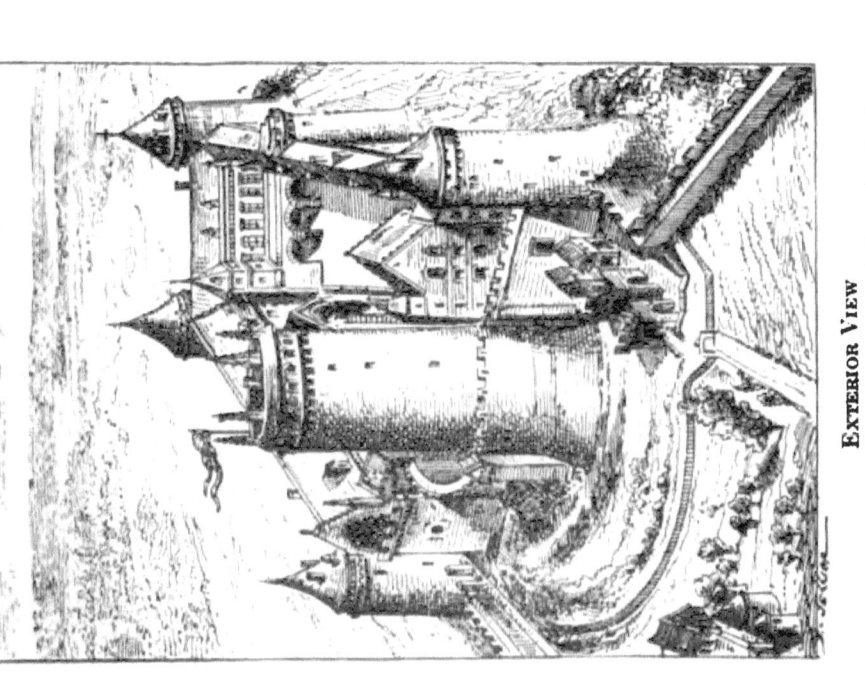

INTERIOR VIEW

At the right, the chapel and the donjon; in the rear, the structure defending the gate; at the left, living-quarters.

CASTLE OF COUCY (RESTORED): ERECTED A.D. 1225–1230

THE FEUDAL CASTLE 65

The regular unit of life in the Middle Ages was not the city or the open farmstead. It was the feudal castle — a more or less pretentious fortification, situated if possible upon a lofty hill, and often with a little village of the rude huts of the lord's peasants clustered close beside it. During the earlier feudal period these castles were of a very primitive nature. In most cases they would be simply a single huge wooden, and then later a stone, tower — round or square, with merely a rude palisade with a ditch for outworks. The height would baffle any scaling-ladder. There would be no opening in its blank masonry until a considerable distance from the ground. Then the narrow door would be entered only by a flimsy wooden bridge, easy to demolish, or by a frail ladder — drawn up every night. Inside this tower there would be a series of dark, cavernous rooms, one above another, communicating by means of ladders. The sole purpose of such a comfortless castle was defense: and that defense by mere height and mass,[1] not by any special skill in arranging the various parts.

Little by little this simple donjon became more complicated.[2] The original tower was kept, but only as the last citadel of a great complex of fortifications. There developed outer palisades, moats, flanking towers, gates defended by drawbridge and portcullis, a great courtyard surrounded by fairly habitable buildings, with the donjon still frowning down as the center of all. Great ingenuity was displayed in making a series of concentric lines of defense. To force the outer barriers meant simply that you had a far stronger inner bulwark before you. The best kind of mediæval castle needed only a very small garrison. From behind its walls even an inferior baron could defy a kingly army.

[1] There were many castles with donjons that rose over one hundred feet high and with walls fully twenty feet thick. At Coucy (in northeastern France), a relatively late and highly elaborate castle, there was a tower two hundred and ten feet high.

[2] Probably the mediæval castle-builders got many of their ideas of fortification through the Crusades — from the military art of the East Romans and Mohammedans. Castles kept getting more and more complicated down to about 1400, when the coming of gunpowder presently changed the whole system of building defenses.

In this castle (more or less extensive according to the power and ambitions of its owner) would live the feudal lord (seigneur), his family, and some scores or hundreds of personal retainers — men-at-arms, "varlets," and serving-women. For a normal mediæval nobleman there was only one legitimate calling — *warfare*, or the preparation for the same. In the earlier part of the feudal period a French lad of noble family would learn to read and write only by exception.[1] From his earliest manhood he would be taught the use of arms — to mount a "destrier," one of the ferocious war-horses; to leap and strike actively in ponderously heavy armor; to handle sword and lance with precision. Probably his father would send him to the court of his own feudal suzerain to be "nourished"; that is, taught all the things which pertained to a high-born warrior. Here as his lord's "squire" he would be given certain lessons in court ceremonial, in the courtesy due noblewomen, the waiting on banquets, fêtes; but his main education would still be military. When about twenty, his training would be complete. He would be a first-class warrior now; a match with his great horse and formidable armor for twenty less trained and poorly armed footmen. His lord at length would give him an elaborate feast, where the young noble would be given new spurs and girded with a new sword. Finally, the lord would give him the formal buffet on the head or shoulder — the accolade. "Be valiant!" he would enjoin. The young squire was henceforth a "knight"[2] (*miles*).

In due time this youth, if an eldest son, might hope to inherit his father's castle. A younger son must turn adventurer and try to win a vacant fief — or a rich heiress — by the grace of some prince in whose service he fought. The times which were spent

[1] This was surely true in the earlier Middle Ages; in the later Middle Ages, the nobles, of course, became increasingly literate, and presently we find high-born scholars and genuine patrons of learning.

[2] Knighthood was clearly at first only the public recognition that the young noble was now a full-fledged warrior. The idea of a religious ceremonial, "chivalric" vows and duties, an especial blessing by the Church, etc., all came in the later Middle Ages.

at the castle without actual warlike occupation could be whiled away by endless hunting, with dogs or hawks, with wild feasting (too often turning into bestial carousals), or with tournaments; that is, mock battles, in which the element of deadly risk was often great. The average feudal seigneur had few enough quiet avocations. He might make a winter's evening endurable by playing chess, or listening to a minstrel's tale of "the great deeds of Roland and Charlemagne"; but he was likely to find such diversions weary stuff.[1]

The women of the castle were of like temper with the men. The seigneur's dame had probably been married to him by her parents while a very young girl, with little heed paid to her own wishes.[2] At times he might treat her almost as brutally as he did his oafish serving-men; but she in turn would often be a hardened, masterful woman, well able to chastise her dozens of slovenly "weaving-women," and to command the castle garrison when her lord was off on the foray. The age was a strenuous one, and few weaklings would be able to survive the physical perils of childhood.

Theoretically the feudal system was a most humane arrangement between "lord" and "man" — of reciprocal loyalty and protection, service and reward. Actually it put a premium on contention, oath-breaking, aggression, and insurrection. Practically, every "noble" — that is, member of upper feudal fighting class — was a vassal[3] of some one, and had vassals under him. The vassal was bound to kneel before "his gracious lord," and take oath to be a faithful helper in return for the landed fief granted him. This was "doing homage." The main duties of a

---

[1] A list has been made of the possible amusements of a French mediæval seigneur; there are only fifteen: these included fencing, playing chess, eating and drinking, listening to songs, watching bear-fights, talking with ladies, holding his court, warming himself, having himself cupped and bled, and watching the snow fall!

[2] Hence so many of the romances that figure in mediæval lore are illicit — the woman, at least, has been already married in girlhood.

[3] "Vassals" were always noblemen: the term was never applied to peasants or townsmen.

trusty vassal were to give his lord good counsel,[1] to supply certain limited money aids, and especially to fight for him (along with his own followers) so many days each year, and, of course, never to do anything to injure the lord's interests. The latter in turn owed his vassal "justice and protection."

The value of this pact usually depended on the power and tact of the lord in enforcing it, and the necessities of the vassal. An ambitious, skillful prince could build up a great feudal dominion; under a weak heir, however, there would be a general "refusal of homage" — and the dependent fief quickly would crumble away from him. Many a baron nominally subordinate would "hold" his various fiefs of two or more suzerains at once — and often these might be at war: the result would be that the vassal would play off one against the other to his own great advantage. Often the "homage" became the merest formality, and the vassal was to all intents and purposes an independent prince.[2] Then, too, the question of the relation of his vassals to the overlord was always a delicate one. The overlord was always trying to get away the sub-vassals (of his dependents), so as to have them as his "immediate" (direct) liegemen, as being then more subservient and therefore more serviceable to himself. "The vassal of my vassal is not my vassal" ran the saying. Over these questions of "sub-infeudation" would come endless friction.

Feudal wars were incessant. Every baron was likely to nurse a grudge against his equal, — the lord of the next feudatory, — against his suzerain (or suzerains), and against his own vassals, for all kinds of reasons. The right of "private warfare" was cherished by even the lowest nobles. The Church, aided sometimes by the kings, tried to mitigate these local wars by the "Truce of God" (cessation of fighting between Wednesday night and Monday morning and on holy days) and by various other

---

[1] Especially in aiding the lord in pronouncing legal judgments, for the execution of which the lord and his advisers were naturally responsible.

[2] A case to the point is the story of Geoffrey of Anjou (eleventh century), who captured Thibaut of Blois, forced him to grant in fief his county of Tours, then "did homage" to his prisoner.

GENERAL WRETCHEDNESS OF FEUDAL LIFE 69

restrictions, but to settle one's troubles with sword and battle-axe was a "noble right"; it was really a concession, often, if the contending barons fought out their troubles in single combat (the so-called "judicial duel") before judges who arranged fair play, and did not call in their vassals, kinsmen, etc., and embroil the whole country-side in general warfare.

Quarrels over hunting and fishing rights, over boundaries of fiefs, over titles to fiefs, over the division of a fief between brothers, over the dowry claims of a widowed mother, over the right of the overlord to declare a fief vacant — these were a few of the pretenses for plunging a community into misery. Contrary to general belief, feudal wars saw few great battles.[1] The weaker bands would shut themselves up in their castles; the stronger party would try to coerce its foes by burning their open villages, ravaging their fields, driving off their cattle, persecuting their peasantry. What fighting there was usually came in single combats, raids, ambuscades, or in skirmishing on a small scale. The main sufferers were the wretched peasantry, the helpless prey of either party. At length one party would become exhausted. Peace would be made — and duly sworn to upon the box of holy saints' relics in some near-by church; but at any time the feud might be resumed if the side which was dissatisfied saw new hopes of victory. There was exceedingly little, therefore, that was morally ennobling in this warfare of the sometimes lauded days of "chivalry and romance."

The feudal anarchy was at its worst in the tenth century: from about 1000 onward matters steadily improved, yet even by 1200 law and order were woefully lacking in many parts of France, as elsewhere in Europe. It requires some stretch of imag-

[1] Of course, a good many real battles are recorded during the whole course of mediæval history. But they are decidedly few, considering the total amount of warfare which was going on. When they did occur, they were usually very unscientific; huge bodies of warriors rushed on one another; each man selected an opponent; the side which won the majority of the resulting duels would win the final day. There are almost no great strategists to be found among the mediæval captains.

ination to think of a time when war, not peace, was the order of the day, and when to "take one's weapons" was almost as usual as to don one's cloak. A journey of any length without arms for one's self, and if possible a strong escort, was (except for churchmen[1] and ragged peasants) practically unthinkable.

There were also many other drawbacks to life in the feudal ages, apart from this reign of armed violence. Outside of the Church practically all men were illiterate. Great barons and peasants alike were victims of crass superstitions. The Church did well to lay great emphasis on the warnings of hell-fire — it was only the animal fear of the eternal burning that kept many a sinful nobleman within the bounds of decency. Castles and hovels lacked the merest rudiments of modern sanitation and consequent healthfulness. On the floors of the great halls, where the lords and retainers feasted and drank deep, would lie a thick litter of rushes, changed only a few times each year. Into these rushes would be cast most of the scraps from the meal. What the numerous dogs did not devour would there remain until the distant day of sweeping. Probably as late as 1200, there was not a castle in Europe (even of a great king) where a modern visitor would not have been utterly horrified by very many matters to offend eyes, ears, and nostrils. Medical science was often mere quackery.[2] A great proportion of children were born dead: another great fraction died in infancy. In short, thanks to bad sanitation, lack of medical treatment, and ignorance of the laws

---

[1] Even monks and priests were subject to frequent attack and pillage by bandits and barons who defied the thunders of the Church. The average petty noble seems to have sat continually on edge, balancing the present advantages of plundering the rich churchman against the likelihood of the deed being avenged in the hereafter by an outraged heaven. Sometimes cupidity and sometimes piety would prevail.

[2] The best medical science of the Middle Ages was often derived from the Mohammedans, especially the Moors of Spain. Occasionally by the use of common sense and rough knowledge gained by experience, a mediæval doctor could accomplish real cures, but the average physician was often an unpunished murderer! We can notice the fearful mortality of young children even in the royal families, where the infants would receive the very best care then available.

of health, the proportion of persons who grew to old age (apart even from those cut off in war) was much less than to-day. Those were truly times of "the survival of the fittest."

The original feudal castle was merely a cheerless barracks, and fortunate it was that the folk of the Middle Ages spent as much of their time as possible in the open air. The later castles became more livable and in the end — in a crude way — luxurious, although never really comfortable in the gray days of winter. But to the man of modern ideas, the great drawback to mediæval life was its extreme mental limitations and monotony, — the lack of most intellectual pleasures, the extreme paucity of ideas, the narrowness of the human horizon,[1] the perpetual round of carousing, hawking, boar-hunting, tournaments, and downright warfare. It was amid this almost soul-deadening monotony that the great seigneur lived. Was there, indeed, any escape from such a melancholy stagnation, for men of weaker bodies and nobler intellects? The answer came — "in the Church."

From 900 to 1250, or later, the best intelligence of Europe was usually in the Church. It absorbed the energies which to-day are absorbed, not only by the clergy, but by the lawyers, physicians, teachers, and many of the more important forms of business. The Church had entered the feudal system. Possibly nearly one third of the lands of western Europe were held by churchmen— doing homage for them to overlords, and receiving the homage in turn of lay vassals. Many a dying baron, stricken in conscience after a turbulent life, had willed most of his estates to some bishopric or abbey "for the eternal profiting of his soul." Of course, the "one Catholic Church" was the only one allowed to exist by public law and public opinion. It was as inconceivable

[1] A great source of mental narrowness was, of course, the absence of easy communication: roads often were mere trails or tracks; dangerous fords in place of bridges; no decent inns; robbers everywhere. Practically all commerce had to be by pack-horses instead of carts. Under such circumstances ideas, no less than foreign commodities, can be exchanged only slowly.

to have two permissible religions on earth, as to have two suns in heaven; and by both secular and church law the stake and fagots awaited heretics as certainly as the gallows awaited murderers. No one dreamed of having things otherwise.

The churchmen fell roughly into two great classes — the "secular" clergy, who lived "in the world" and had the "cure of souls"; and the "regular" clergy; that is, monks subject to the monastic rule. The bishops had often great revenues from the estates of their "dioceses" (districts): they were usually feudal overlords of a considerable principality, and besides managing the churches of the region, were immersed in secular business. They were often the king's ministers, diplomats, and sometimes even leaders of his armies. Men of humble birth occasionally rose to be bishops, but as a rule they were noble-born — a neighboring bishopric proving a very convenient depository for the younger sons of a noble house when the eldest obtained the principality. The humbler parish priests were usually appointed by the rich layman (or his heirs) who had endowed the local church, and these priests were frequently peasant-born. Compared with the bishops they were inferior, indeed, but among their fellow peasants they were revered, not merely as the sacred intermediaries between God and man, but as the only individuals, often, in the parish who had the least education; that is, could read, write, and speak a little Latin.

Among the "regulars," the abbots of the monasteries often had positions of feudal influence almost equal to the great bishops. The monks were as a rule more learned than the parish priests, because they had less work to do among the laity and could devote their leisure to studies. At its worst, the monastic life was said to imply great idleness and gluttonous dinners: at its best, a monk was intensely busy with all kinds of peaceful arts and with continuous hard study. Neighboring abbeys differed often in character. One might be extremely lax; the next famous for its learning and pious austerities.

One thing all churchmen claimed in common: exemption from

trial in the ordinary lay courts. A priest must be tried by his bishop, a monk by his abbot. The Church was, in fact, "a state within a state."

Down to about 1200, almost all intellectual life seemed centered in the Church[1] — at first only in the monasteries, which maintained schools for the training of their novices or intended priests, and later in the schools attached to the great cathedrals. The learning preserved in these monasteries was almost entirely in Latin, and based either upon the Bible, the early Christian writers (the "Fathers"), or upon such old Roman authors as Cicero and Virgil. There was exceedingly little originality of scholarship, almost no personal investigation of the phenomena of nature, and a great willingness to say, for example, "thus says St. Jerome," and to consider all discussion of the case closed by merely citing a time-honored authority. This, of course, often led to many absurd notions, when either the ancients themselves were wrong, or when (very often) their real meaning was misunderstood. Nevertheless, it was of great merit that the monks kept *any* intellectual life at all in the Middle Ages, considering the general storm and stress. Also, it was of no less service that the gains for civilization by the ancients were in the main preserved until the next age could build a nobler civilization upon them. The mediæval monk, despite his slavish bowing to the dicta of "Master Aristotle,"[2] his endless parchments upon the obscure mysteries of theology, his hopelessly unscientific "chronicles" which record so imperfectly the annals of his own time, should nevertheless be the hero of an age when to fix one's ambition on anything save feudal glory must have been infinitely hard.[3]

---

[1] This was so much the case that it was often assumed that if a man could read he was a "clerk"; that is, in churchly orders.

[2] Aristotle wrote in Greek; but some of his works had been translated into Arabic, and then, by a curious roundabout process, into Latin. Other of his writings were available in a sixth-century translation by Boëthius. Aristotle was the great authority of the Middle Ages in all matters of secular learning.

[3] Any complete discussion of Mediæval France would have to take into the

By about 1200, we find the hitherto despised "vernacular" of the laity — North French, Provençal, etc. — beginning to express itself in literature, but for a long time the stately Latin of the mediæval churchmen held its own as the language of all learned men. It had been hardly displaced by the age of the Protestant Reformation.[1]

In its own especial way this mediæval society was intensely religious. It showed its zeal in a series of great architectural monuments which remain as the most glorious witnesses to the best in the Middle Ages. The great mediæval churches cover, indeed, Germany, Italy, northern Spain, and England, but especially in France did they find their most elaborate and noblest development.

Sometimes great barons built them, sometimes bishops or abbeys, but often whole communities united in one great offering to God — devoting their wealth and energy for a century more or less to building a stately cathedral.[2] At first these were in the Romanesque (rounded arch) style. After about 1150, they began to rise in the more elegant Gothic (with pointed arches) which seems to have originated in the "Île de France" near

account the University of Paris, which became consolidated late in the twelfth century; but which had existed as a less unorganized center of learning for a considerable period earlier. For a long time no other European university had such distinction: the decisions of its theological doctors had to be weighed seriously even when they collided with the dicta of the Popes, while in all matters of secular learning the opinions of its faculty were almost the last word of authority. The existence of such a renowned body in their capital added much to the prestige of the Capetian kings.

[1] Among learned men, thanks especially to the influence of the Church, this mediæval Latin came much nearer giving the world a "universal language" than anything we have to-day.

[2] A cathedral is, of course, the especial seat of a bishop (his *sedes* = seat; hence the word "see"). Often the ordinary parish churches or the abbey churches were built with a magnificence equal to a cathedral. We can imagine many starving villages of peasants' huts, squalid and utterly mean, clustered around a parish church which would be the cynosure of any modern city. Usually the mediæval cathedrals were undertaken on such a magnificent scale that a whole generation could build only a small part of them. It has been well said, "No Gothic church has ever been finished!"

Paris.¹ The climax came in such French cathedrals as Notre Dame of Paris, and, even better still, Amiens, Chartres, and Reims — with many others such as Tours on a hardly inferior scale. These "symphonies of stone" — with their soaring towers, lofty vaulted roofs, elaborate stone carvings, multitudes of sculptured saints, vast windows of inimitable stained glass — are witness to the truly devout and artistic life that could develop in the Middle Ages, as well as proof of wholly admirable technique, and tell us how despite the feudal anarchy the forces of civilization and righteousness were steadily winning the victory.²

The knights and the priests with their swords or their pens made nearly all the history of the earlier Middle Ages; yet barely one man in forty belonged to these two favored classes taken together. It is time to say a little of the less favored thirty-nine.

In 1000, the bulk of the peasantry in France were serfs — bound to the soil, subject to the extremes of forced labor and personal taxation, able to marry only with the consent of the seigneur, and able to transmit their little farm and personal belongings to their children only by the payment of a heavy tax, paid again to the seigneur. They could be actually bought and sold, but only along with the land to which they were unalterably attached.³ If they ran away, they could be chased down as "masterless men" and reclaimed like runaway slaves. There were, however, also an increasing number of free peasants.

---

[1] More technically, we can say that diagonal ribs are used in Gothic churches to hold up the masonry vaulting, so that the weight of the roof is all on the capitals, none on the walls (which can be very thin, and have elaborate windows). A few genuinely Gothic churches have rounded arches.

[2] It is an interesting fact that often in the mediæval churches the inner side of sculptures, etc., is elegantly finished, although set so as not to be exposed to any spectators. "But God can behold if our work is imperfect!" a mediæval craftsman would have said.

[3] In being thus bound to the soil, and having the real use if not actual ownership of a little farm, the mediæval serfs differed from absolute slaves. There were a few genuine slaves in the Middle Ages, but not enough to make them a real factor.

These men could marry and change their abode at will, and transmit their property. But their social status was scarcely better than that of the serfs. They were without effective protection against the lords, who could tax and maltreat both "serfs" and "freemen" with almost impartial brutality and arbitrariness.

Nobles and churchmen alike taught that it was the duty of these "villeins"[1] to submit cheerfully to their lot, to support the upper classes with their labors, to thank Heaven if they were treated with a modicum of justice, and to endure patiently if the feudal lord flogged and otherwise abused them (as too frequently) a little worse than his dogs and cattle.[2] Truth to tell, the villeins were probably a brutish lot. Their days were consumed in grinding field labor with very clumsy spades and mattocks; their homes were mere hovels of wood, sun-dried brick and thatch; their clothing a few coarse rags; their food always scanty. Of their intelligence, manners, cleanliness, nothing need be said. In the average peasant's hut, the dirty, half-naked children would struggle on the earthen floor along with the little pigs and the poultry. "How could God and the saints love such creatures?" — Betwixt peasant and noble there was surely a great gulf fixed!

In the Middle Ages the towns were at first few and insignificant, and nearly all peasants lived in miserable huts on the feudal estates. Agricultural methods were extremely primitive; a drought or a wet year meant famine and misery for a wide district. During times of great shortage there are grim tales told of feasts on human flesh, and of the multiplication of wolves, human and quadruped. Even the rights which the feudal law secured to the peasant were seldom enforcible if his seigneur were an unscrupulous man: — for how could the serf ever hale

[1] That is, dwellers in a villa or farm, whence later came the idea of a "villain" as a clownish, rascally countryman.

[2] Well down to 1789 to cane one's peasantry seems to have been a standing privilege of the average French gentleman.

his mail-clad lord to justice? Sickening stories of extreme tyranny and cruelty abound. Nevertheless, little by little, the peasantry found their lot improve, for various reasons:

(*a*) On the ample Church lands, the churchmen as a rule treated their peasants with greater humanity than did the average seigneur.[1]

(*b*) The Church declared the freeing of serfs a most meritorious act for a nobleman. Frequently a conscience-stricken baron would try to square accounts with Heaven by freeing all or a part of his peasants.

(*c*) Especially in crusading times the lords had great need of ready money for their wars. Wretched as the serfs were, individuals or villages had often saved up a little private stock. They could now "buy their freedom" by one lump payment.

So the serfs were always tending to become "free peasants." They were still despised villeins and "non-noble," but they were not quite so defenseless. They were next able to make an agreement with their lords so that the taxes they paid on their lands, and the amount of forced labor requirable of them, should be limited to a certain fixed amount. Besides, the kings were growing in power. They would give a certain protection to the peasants, as a makeweight to the nobles. Nevertheless, the country villeins continued to be as a rule oafish, ignorant, and outrageously oppressed all through the Middle Ages. The non-nobles of Europe first found their opportunity and their power in the growth of the towns.

The Roman Empire had been covered with stately cities. Many of these had perished outright; others were, in the last Carolingian era, merely starving villages inside the ruins of the old walls. But in the decades following the year 1000 came a revival of civic life. Sometimes a reviving commerce reawoke a nigh-dead community; sometimes an unwontedly intelligent seigneur fostered its growth; sometimes the presence of a pros-

[1] Especially the peasants dependent upon an abbey could count on being fed by the monks in times of famine.

perous monastery was the decisive factor. By 1100, there are signs of city life over western Europe. By 1200, cities are numerous and relatively important.[1]

At first these cities were mere collections of a few nobles and a mass of peasants who preferred trading to farming. Ordinary feudal law (or lack of law) obtained in a community. The peasants were subject to about the same burdens as if they had worked in the fields. But in these towns the non-nobles could join together as never in the open country. They soon learned their numbers and their strength. Merchants and master artisans were becoming wealthy. They, too, were no longer utterly defenseless against the seigneur. The towns soon built walls which could defy an ordinary feudal army. Inside the gates the mounted knights — so formidable in the open field — were almost helpless in the narrow streets when stones and boiling water rained on them from the houses above. During the twelfth and thirteenth centuries the cities of France were winning charters from their king or lords.

Occasionally these charters were freely granted by magnanimous and intelligent princes. Often they were purchased — through an extraordinary payment by the townsfolk. Sometimes, also, the king or great suzerain would grant them — perhaps in the teeth of the local feudal ruler — to set up a rival power beside that of the dangerous baron. Or often city folk rose *en masse:* the gates would be closed; the great alarm-bell rung; the residence of the local prince or prince-bishop would be stormed, and the charter would be granted before the threat of gleaming weapons. The ordinary result in any case is the same, a carefully drafted and sealed document creating a "free town"; that is, with specific rights of local self-government, and all taxes and other obligations due to the lord defined and limited. Hereafter the inhabitants of such a town are no longer helpless peas-

---

[1] The small size of these "cities" must be clearly realized. In the Middle Ages 1000 inhabitants would make a very passable town; 10,000 a "great city," indeed.

ants. They are called (in France) *bourgeoisie*, — "free-burghers," — with their own especial rights. They elect their own magistrates, levy their local militia, raise their own taxes; and if fortune favors, the bond uniting them to their old feudal lord becomes very frail indeed. The cities then become veritable little "city-states" — almost on the old Greek model.

This new order of burghers, which intruded itself between the two favored upper classes and the peasants, was unwelcome, indeed, to the former. "Commune — a name new and execrable!" cries a priestly chronicler. But the nobles and churchmen were fain to make the best they could of these intruders; for wealth, intelligence, enterprise, and new ideas made haste to find their way to the free towns.

The government of a mediæval city differed with time and country. In any case the mediæval city was never a democracy. Sometimes various petty nobles actually settled in the town, fraternized with the non-nobles, and made a civic aristocracy. More often, the great merchants, the heads of the trading and craft guilds, etc., formed a body of city "patricians," which dominated the city council, and usually supplied the "mayors," sheriffs, or however the head magistrates were variously called. Yet while it was an aristocracy, such a government was usually intelligent and public-spirited. A "mayor" could hardly dare to imitate a feudal prince in his contempt for the wishes and rights of the lower classes. The government of a "free city," in short, would often be founded on efficiency and practical justice, though not on human equality.

As presented to the eye, a typical mediæval city would be a remarkable sight. Its extent would be small, both because of the limited population, and the need of making the circuit of the walls to be defended as short as possible; but within these walls the huge, many-storied houses would be wedged closely together. The narrow streets would be dirty and ill-paved — often beset by pigs in lieu of scavengers; but everywhere there would be bustling human life with every citizen elbowing close to everybody else. Out of the foul streets here and there would rise parish churches of marvelous architecture, and in the center of the town extended the great square — the market-place — where the open-air markets would be held; close by it, dwarfing the lesser churches, the tall gray cathedral, — the pride of the community; and close by, also, the City Hall (*Hôtel de Ville*), an elegant secular edifice, where the council met, where the great public feasts could take place, and above which often rose the mighty belfry, whence clanged the great alarm-bell to call the citizens together in mass meeting, or to don armor and man the walls. The magnificent houses, walls, churches, and civic buildings of many French towns to-day, testify to the glories of most of the greater mediæval cities toward the end of the Middle Ages.

Such, then, were some of the physical, political, and social conditions under which the great nation known as France advanced to unity and strength. Everywhere things ugly and iniquitous struggled with things virtuous and lovely. The contrasts of life were probably far more pronounced in every respect than with us to-day. But whatever else be said, there was power, energy, and indomitable courage in those nation-builders of the feudal centuries. The school of the Middle Ages was often a very rough one, but it was an efficient school, and the peoples which survived it were trained for mighty deeds alike of the body and of the spirit. To-day, it will doubtless be asserted, Europe and France have nearly completed the process of casting away the relics of the Middle Ages — relics to which France at least clung, all too closely, down to 1789. But it is not good for any country to be ashamed of its past, and the France of the twentieth century has no reason to be ashamed that it was the heir of the France of Philip Augustus and St. Louis.

CHAPTER VI
THE DAWN OF THE MODERN ERA: 1270-1483
THE HUNDRED YEARS' WAR

St. Louis left a truly magnificent kingdom. There was no longer any great dread of the old-line feudal nobility. It still existed, with much wealth, pomp and circumstance, splendid castles, "seigneurial rights," and high claims to social privilege and legal favor; but all knew it was merely an aristocracy, a "bulwark of the throne," demanding the king's favor, indeed, often with peremptory words but not really demanding the lion's share of his sovereign power. Nevertheless, for the next two centuries the royal authority, and with it the happiness of the nation, did not go forward as might be expected. There were three prime reasons for this time of disappointment and even reaction.

In the first place under any real monarchy much always depends on the person of the monarch. The Capetian line had provided several very able princes; now the quality of the royal stock was to degenerate. Several of the kings of this period were very unfit rulers indeed. France paid for their inefficiency. Again, although the old *feudal* aristocracy was waning, a new *royal* aristocracy was coming to the front. It was composed of younger scions and kinsmen of the royal house. In theory these princes believed in the unity of France and the greatness of the dynasty. In practice they often quarreled outrageously for the high places at court, the royal governorships, the control (if the king were a weakling) of the monarch's person; and they often sought "appanages"; that is, parts of the royal dominion, which they could govern for themselves as semi-independent viceroys. Some of the worst foes of French monarchy were thus to be in its own household.

Finally against France was to come a great foreign peril. The

Norman Kings of England, losing their old duchy, but becoming identified with their new island peoples, were to build up a formidable military power, and to direct systematic attacks upon the Continent, which attacks almost ended in nothing less than the conquest of France.

From 1314 (the death of Philip IV, the grandson of St. Louis) to 1483 (the death of Louis XI) was to be a time of grievous testing for the entire French nation. At least once the entire realm seemed lost. Several times it was in grievous danger of being permanently dismembered and crippled. In the end, the genius of the people enabled them to shake off the foreign peril and to thrust the recalcitrant royal princes into their proper place. The dawn of "modern times" saw France again rich, progressive, and powerful.

It is difficult to characterize this long and troubled period without becoming swamped amid a mass of names and details. Some of the main incidents were these:

Philip III, "the Bold," son of St. Louis, had a somewhat brief and undistinguished reign (1270-85), but his son Philip IV, "the Fair," ruled longer and also wrought mightier deeds (1285-1314). No man can praise the character of this grandson of the Saint, but Philip IV falls into the catalogue of those grasping, unscrupulous men, who in a wholly uncommendable way really advance the world's progress. A large part of his reign centered around his famous quarrel with Pope Boniface VIII, himself one of the most self-seeking and imperious pontiffs who ever ruled the Church from Rome.

The immediate issue was whether the King had the right, which he asserted, to tax the wealthy French clergy. Boniface denied this right, and Philip of course was not anxious to have the wealth of at least one fifth of the lands of France escape permanently from his treasurers. Actually behind this contention lay the greater issue whether in secular matters the Pope could override the authority of kings, and constitute himself a kind of super-monarch, merely deputing the temporal government of the world to such princes as would serve faithfully as his crowned viceregents. It was substantially over this issue that there had been bloody wars between the Papacy and the Emperors of Germany, and the Papacy on the whole had seemed the victor. But the Capetian kings had now a much firmer grasp upon their realm than ever the Saxon or Hohenstaufen Emperors had had upon Germany, and Frenchmen were entirely unwilling to have an Italian prince (as Boniface certainly was) intermingle in their own distinctly secular affairs. When after preliminary negotiations and compromises, the Pope came to open threats of putting Philip under the ban of the Church, the King countered by a dramatic stroke.

In 1302 he convoked the States General of France at Paris. Philip was an utter despot in his aims and methods, but in facing so great a power as the Papacy he understood the need of securing the loyal support of all elements of his people. It had been fairly common, long ere this, for the kings to consult about public affairs with Councils of their nobles and their higher clergy. Now, for the first time, the representatives of the "city dwellers" (*bourgeois*) were invited to be present and to give their support and wisdom to their liege lord. Needless to say, the men from the "Third Estate" were immensely flattered at this association with the secular and clerical nobility. They readily voted their approval of all the royal policy and joined with the upper orders in advising the King to take an uncompromising attitude toward the Pope. From this time onward we have occasional meetings of this States General — the representatives of the three great orders of French society — to aid the king in national issues, although thanks to a multitude of reasons this extraordinary body was never able to develop into a regular legislature with periodic meetings like the English Parliament.[1]

[1] The chief reasons why this seemingly promising attempt at representative government came to nothing were, first, because the "three orders" met separately, had very diverse interests, and thus, without unanimity, almost nothing

France thus stood stoutly behind Philip, and all the threats and anathemas of Rome could not put his throne in danger. The King even sent armed agents into Italy and actually arrested Boniface as a pretender to the Papacy (1303); [1] and although the Pope was soon rescued from prison by his friends, the shock and humiliation of the affair were so great that he soon died utterly discredited. His successors (timid and pliable men) made haste to be reconciled with a monarch who could read them so terrible a lesson. In 1309 they actually withdrew their residence from Rome to Avignon in southern France, there to remain till 1376. During this long "Babylonish Captivity," the Papacy was to be under the very shadow of the formidable "Eldest Son of the Church" who reigned at Paris, and the whole Papal policy was often directed in the secular interests of France: — a matter of terrible ecclesiastical scandal, but something which of course increased the influence of the French kingship in every part of Christendom.[2]

could be done; and secondly, because the States General never obtained undoubted control of the treasury, and could not coerce the king by refusing to vote taxes. See Appendix.

[1] This was the famous "Assault of Anagni," a small city near Rome, where the Pope was sojourning.

[2] An infamous episode in the reign of Philip IV was the persecution and downfall of the Knight Templars. This powerful military order of monks, sworn to show their religion by fighting the Infidel instead of by the usual austerities of the convent, had waxed extremely powerful and correspondingly wealthy. It owned great properties in France, as well as in other European countries, and in 1306 its "grand master" is said to have come back to France from the Levant with 150,000 gold florins and ten horse-loads of silver. The Templars were becoming the object of grave suspicion on account of their secret conventicles, and stories were circulated as to immoral practices at such meetings. The arrogance and covetousness of the order gave point and currency to these sinister reports.

Such a wealthy, semi-secret, suspected organization made an excellent victim for a covetous and unscrupulous King like Philip IV. In 1307 he suddenly arrested De Molay, the grand master, and sixty of the leading brethren. A little later nearly all the other Templars in France were accused. Broken by threats and torture, De Molay and his companions confessed to "denying Christ and spitting on the cross," though they still would not admit the charges of gross immorality.

Pope Clement V was wholly at Philip's mercy. After vain protests, he ordered

THE SALIC LAW

Philip IV was survived by three sons. None of them, however, in his turn left sons to succeed him. When, after a colorless reign of two years, Louis X (1314-16) died leaving only a daughter, his next brother came promptly forward with the claim that women could not inherit the crown of France. A weak, female rule was not popular with responsible men; it opened the possibilities of all kinds of confusion. The crown lawyers and the States General therefore confirmed, or rather invented, the so-called "Salic Law" (alleged to be derived from the Salian Franks) that no woman could be a reigning queen over France.[1] Philip V (1316-22) accordingly reigned in his brother's stead, but after another short, uneventful government he also died without a son, and in his place came the third brother, Charles IV (1322-28). No better fortune attended him. Like the rest he died in his prime without male heirs. Pious folk wagged their heads, and said that a curse was resting on the Capetian line for the insult offered Pope Boniface VIII. In any case Charles was the last ruler of the direct Capetian line. The crown passed to his cousin, Philip of Valois, the son of a younger brother of Philip IV. With this change in the dynasty evil days were to come to France.

Philip VI "of Valois" (1328-50) was not an entirely incapable prince, but he was inconsistent, reckless, and anything but an ideal ruler for guiding the nation in a time of dangerous attack

the Templars suppressed throughout all Christendom. As for Philip, he proceeded to have his wretched prisoners tried for heresy, blasphemy, and various vile crimes, and between 1310 and 1314 the greater part of them died at the stake. De Molay perished (1314) summoning both the tyrannous King and the pliant Pope to appear promptly with him at the judgment seat of God — a summons that, as men later recalled, was soon followed by the deaths of both potentates.

The consensus of opinion is that the Templars were largely innocent of the charges brought against them. Their confessions were extracted by coercion or torture. Philip wished for their vast property, and stuck at no measure which could enable him to confiscate it.

[1] This law seems the more curious as in few kingdoms have women exerted more real influence in political life than in France.

from abroad. He was not tactful in dealing with his great nobles, and, in particular, he soon quarreled with Robert of Artois, a prince of the blood, who presently fled to the court of Edward III of England and stirred up mischief. The King also became embroiled in Flemish affairs. The freedom-loving Flemish cities had resisted their local prince, and Philip took sides with his vassal, the Count of Flanders, against them. The wealthy and powerful burghers, "the most industrious, the richest and the freest people in Europe," promptly began negotiating with Edward III, who was impelled to help them because Flanders was the great market for the English raw-wool exports.

Edward was the less disinclined to dip in French affairs because he had colorable claim to the crown of Philip himself. If there had been no Salic Law, Edward would possibly have reigned in Paris as well as in London, thanks to the rights of his mother Isabella, daughter of Philip IV. The English King was a thoroughly capable monarch, a skillful captain, and he possessed (as Europe was soon to know) a military weapon in his "long-bow archers" that was to make him a great power in Europe.

Fighting began in a desultory way in 1337, at first in an attempt of the English to detach Flanders from French control. Nothing decisive eventuated. Then in 1341 the strife deepened, when two claimants struggled for the ducal crown of Brittany.[1] Philip upheld the claims of one faction; the other naturally turned to Edward, who, to give color to his intervention in France, made more or less bold pretensions to the French crown itself. However, the Breton war, although not decisive, in the main favored the French party. It was not until 1346 that Edward found his hands sufficiently free to cross the Channel in considerable force. In July of that year he landed at Cape la Hogue, with 32,000 men: a decidedly large army for mediæval times.

[1] Brittany, surrounded by the ocean on three sides, was the last of the great feudal states to pass under the French crown. Its dependence upon France remained very nominal indeed, until its annexation in 1491.

Up to this point, the contest had considerably favored Philip. The English had failed to master either Flanders or Brittany. But now Edward trusted no longer to local risings to help him, but to the strength of his good right arm. He quickly captured Caen, swept across Normandy almost to the gates of Paris, then turned north — burning and pillaging the open country but seldom stopping to besiege the cities. If Philip had trusted to Fabian tactics the English must have presently retreated from the devastated land with little really accomplished. But it was intolerable for a king of France to see his country devastated like the fields of a petty baron. He called out the entire levy of the realm. The French nobles responded with alacrity. A great force of Italian cross-bowmen were hired to offset the English archers. At Crécy, near Abbeville in Picardy, on the 26th of August, 1346, the French at last brought their foes to bay and forced a great battle.

Then all the world was to learn that a new factor had come in warfare. Hitherto upon any kind of a fair field, the feudal knights on their great war-horses and clothed in ponderous armor, had been able almost always to ride down even the best and bravest footmen. Edward, however, used his English archers with consummate skill. These long-bowmen with their great yew bows and "cloth-yard" arrows could shoot many scores of paces with remarkable speed and accuracy, and with force enough to penetrate all but the very best armor. The long-bow was in fact more powerful than the later musket, until generations after the coming of gunpowder. All day long, with mad and disastrously brave valor, the French knights strove to charge home through the deadly volleys of the bowmen. In the evening the remnants of the assailants drifted in rout from the field. Never had Frenchmen met so terrible a defeat. The King of Bohemia (Philip's ally) lay slain, and with him eleven princes, eighty knight-bannerets, twelve hundred knights, and, it is alleged, thirty thousand of the rank and file. France was stunned for the moment by the loss.

Edward made hard-headed use of his victory. He laid siege to Calais, the chief door into France from across the English Channel, and starved the town out (1347) despite a very brave defense and vain efforts of Philip to send in succor. Henceforth the English had a most convenient sally-port from which to invade France, whenever they listed. Calais was to remain in English hands until 1558.

Philip of Valois died in 1350. He had been saved from further defeats and losses more by the advent of the Black Death, a terrible plague which swept over Europe in 1348, destroying French and English impartially, and for the nonce suspending all wars along with almost all peaceful forms of life, than by any forbearance on the part of Edward. In his stead reigned his son John, a brave, impetuous, but entirely light-headed and extravagant prince, who soon emptied the treasury by his luxuries and his careless generosity to his courtiers, and then almost ruined the economic life of the land by his equally reckless debasement of the coinage in a vain attempt to make money out of nothing. Such a king was no leader to confront a second great English attack.

In 1356 Edward, the Prince of Wales, often called the "Black Prince" to distinguish him from his father, commenced another invasion. This time the English started in from Bordeaux and Guienne (a fragment of which they had always retained out of the wreck of the old possessions of Henry of Anjou) and worked northward, headed possibly for Calais. It was an exceedingly risky venture, even if the Black Prince were at least as able a general as his father. His force barely exceeded eight thousand men, and he was in danger of being swallowed up in a hostile land. King John again called out all his liegemen and again the French chivalry loyally responded. With over fifty thousand men, he hemmed in the English upon a hill near Poitiers. The odds seemed so uneven that if the King had only held his lines in a tight blockade the invaders must have been starved into surrender. But no such tame victory would content John and his adventurous counselors. The shame of Crécy must be effaced in a fair battle, therefore battle there was; but it did not efface Crécy. The French horsemen with indescribable folly charged up a narrow lane whereof the hedges on either side were lined with English archers who shot down their foes at ease. When the attacking host reeled back in confusion, the Black Prince counter-attacked. The King's divisions failed to coöperate: they were cut up piecemeal. In the end John, after showing much personal valor, was taken prisoner along with his youngest son, thirteen counts, an archbishop, seventy barons, and some thousands of lesser warriors. It was really a far greater disaster than at Crécy. France was not merely defeated but deprived of her head.

The next few years were little better than anarchy. The King was prisoner in London. The nominal regent was the Crown Prince, the "Dauphin,"[1] Charles, as yet inexperienced, weak, and cowardly. Charles the Bad, King of the little country of Navarre,[2] and a great French noble to boot, contested the government in an unscrupulous manner, and added to the terrors of foreign invasion all the miseries of civil war. The Dauphin convened the States General, but no real help came from this gathering of the estates of the realm. A radical party led by Étienne Marcel, provost of the merchants of Paris, seized the opportunity to try to cut down the royal authority, and to set up a kind of government by the representatives of the Third Estate. Moderns will sympathize with this bold move towards democracy; but in truth it was no time for rash political experiments. The radical party soon indulged in deeds of bloody violence. Marcel was presently murdered while trying to surrender Paris to Charles the Bad. A desperate revolt of the demoralized and starving peasants (the *Jacquerie*) was quenched

[1] So called from Dauphiny over which he was supposed to rule, just as the English heir was "Prince of Wales." The last feudal Prince of Dauphiny resigned his power to the king in 1349.
[2] Navarre lay in the Pyrenees wedged in between France and Spain.

in blood, and something like peace returned to the land when John was set free following the treaty of Brétigny (1360).

It was not a pleasant treaty for France. Edward did not, indeed, press home his very dubious claim for the French crown, but otherwise his demands were galling. John had to pay a ransom of three million gold crowns (an enormous sum for that age) and cede an absolute sovereignty not merely Calais, but practically the whole of old Aquitaine. The French monarchy thus lost fully half of the South Country, and the Black Prince set up a viceregal court for his father at Bordeaux. The best that could be said was that at last there was peace, and a chance for rehabilitation. No real improvement could be expected under John, however, but that headlong, pleasure-loving King died in 1364.

The Dauphin now took the crown as King Charles V (1364–80). His experience and record as crown prince had assuredly been unlucky, but he had learned by adversity. There was nothing heroic about him, but also nothing rash. His physical weakness gave him the aspect of a recluse and student. He was destined to go into history as "Charles the Sage," one of the cleverest monarchs of the whole French line.

The English menace was waning. After all, Edward III disposed of a realm as yet relatively poor and unable to send a succession of new armies year by year to the Continent — the only proceeding that could really endanger France. The Black Prince was presently induced to march from Bordeaux into Spain to reinstate a very evil king of Castile, Pedro the Cruel, whose subjects had justly banished him. The Black Prince was victorious (1367). Pedro was temporarily put back upon his throne, but he proved an ungrateful protégé. The English leader had exhausted the strength of his army, and had weakened the fealty of his new Aquitainian dominions by the heavy taxes he forced upon them. The Southern malcontents soon appealed to Paris, and Charles gave them a ready ear. He had quietly reorganized his army, filled up his treasury, and was ready to throw over the Treaty of Brétigny. In 1370 the war was renewed.

Charles was fortunate in finding a very able captain — Bertrand du Guesclin, a valiant Breton knight, who never shunned battle when it promised advantage, but who understood clearly the folly of trying to ride down the English archers by serried lines of horsemen. The Black Prince marched again through the land, but everywhere he met cities with barred gates and with no chance for open fighting. These guerrilla tactics presently wore down the small English armies. "Never was there a king of France who fought less," spoke Edward III angrily, "and yet never one that gave me so much trouble." The Black Prince sickened and returned to England to die (1376). The leaders left in his place were no match for du Guesclin. Troubles at home prevented the coming of English reinforcements. By 1380 the islanders held only the coast towns of Calais, Cherbourg, and Brest in the North, and Bordeaux and Bayonne in the South. The first great English attack on France was over.

Charles the Sage died at the age of only forty-three. His passing was a national calamity. His eldest son Charles VI (1380–1422) was only twelve years old, and never developed any great clearness of intellect. In 1392 he became insane, although possessed of recurring lucid intervals which made it impossible actually to depose him and to appoint a regent. His nominal reign was one long misery for his people. First his covetous and incapable uncles quarreled over the possession of his person and of the reins of government: then their place was taken by factions of younger nobles, with the immoral and unprincipled queen-consort Isabella of Bavaria as the guiding spirit in many of their intrigues. Presently the contending parties passed from plottings to assassination. In 1407 the powerful Duke of Orleans was stabbed at the direct instigation of the Duke of Burgundy, his rival. This made the quarrel unhealable. The "Burgundian" party, notwithstanding this crime, lost possession of the kings' person, which fell to the rival "Armagnac" [1] faction of the

---

[1] So named from a Count of Armagnac, who became a leader in the Anti-Burgundian party.

nobility that soon became the stronger because the young Dauphin had joined them. John the Fearless, Duke of Burgundy, was able, however, to embroil almost all the kingdom in civil war, when suddenly a new terror descended — the English under Henry V (Shakespeare's winsome "Prince Hal") renewed their invasions.

It is difficult to withhold personal admiration for Henry V, but the fact cannot be disguised that he was reviving a worthless claim to the throne of France, and that his coming produced nothing but misery for that already distracted kingdom. He landed at Harfleur in Normandy (1415), took that town, and then began a difficult march across the country to Calais.

His army numbered barely fifteen thousand effective men. If the French Armagnac, princes who claimed to represent the royal government, had known how to handle their forces, they ought to have cut him off, as surely as John might have cut off the Black Prince at Poitiers. But these turbulent leaders had learned nothing from the past sixty years. The mounted knight, with lance couched at full charge, was still their only idea of warfare. With fifty thousand men, under the nominal leadership of the Dauphin, the French attacked Henry at Agincourt near Calais. It was the story of the old battles over again. The wet, slippery ground made quick movements impossible. The closely packed formation of the men-at-arms merely improved the targets for the English archers, when the French strove recklessly to advance. The battle ended almost with a massacre when the longbows had finished their work, and the English charged out upon their demoralized enemies. The Dauphin fled leaving ten thousand men slain on the field, and very many great noblemen captive with Henry. The whole royal power of France was shaken.

Henry used his victory well. He let Armagnac and Burgundian rend one another in the interior, while in 1418 and 1419 he gathered in Caen and Rouen and other strongholds in Normandy. In 1419 the Armagnacs retaliated for the murder of the Duke of

A BATTLE IN THE FIFTEENTH CENTURY

ATTACK AND DEFENSE OF A CITY
IN THE FIFTEENTH CENTURY

Orleans by assassinating, under circumstances of great treachery, John the Fearless, Duke of Burgundy. The Dauphin was mixed in the plot,[1] and the deed threw Philip of Burgundy, John's son and heir, into the very arms of the English.

Burgundy was already a great principality; many of its domains lay outside of France in "the Empire." Philip was more formidable than many kings of his day, and to him had joined the unnatural Queen Isabella, who hated her own son the Dauphin so much that she plotted to dethrone him in favor of Henry. Burgundy and Isabella negotiated in the name of the helpless Charles VI the shameful Treaty of Troyes (1420) whereby the Dauphin was to be disinherited, Henry was to marry Catherine the daughter of King Charles, and on the death of Charles was to become king *both* of France and of England. The Dauphin was still holding out south of the Loire; nevertheless the grip of the English on all of North France seemed tightening. Paris was in their hands and a great block of the old Capetian lands to boot, when in 1422 Henry V died, followed in a few weeks by the crazed old Charles VI. The latter had had one of the most calamitous reigns in all French annals.

Henry V left by Catherine a ten-months son, the unfortunate Henry VI of England. This child's regents were in actual possession of practically all France north of the Loire, also of the country around Bordeaux. He was recognized as "king" by the Duke of Burgundy and by the Parlement of Paris, the supreme legal body of France. South of the Loire, most districts now acknowledged the Dauphin as Charles VII (1422–61). He was "a young man of nineteen, of engaging manners, but weak in body, pale in countenance, and deficient in courage." He was charged with being engrossed in ignoble pleasures. The taint of

---

[1] The Dauphin was still a boy, but he let depraved courtiers induce him to invite the Duke of Burgundy to an interview at the bridge of Montereau. There, while the latter knelt at the Prince's feet, he was foully massacred by Tanneguy-Duchatel, one of the chiefs of the Armagnac faction.

the murder of John of Burgundy clung foully to him. No one could deny that he seemed to lack energy, and was all too content while the aggressive English regent — the Duke of Bedford — seemed plucking away his kingdom.

Most of the French governors and nobles of the South Country adhered to Charles. The prejudice against an English king was violent. The Duke of Bedford's armies were small if very efficient, and it was clear enough that Henry was acknowledged as king in the North only because of constant acts of coercion. Nevertheless the case of France seemed almost desperate. Charles's government was so weak that he was usually known as the "Dauphin" not the "King," or was sarcastically called "the King of Bourges," his residence city, the one place he held in fairly sure possession. His captains and noblemen were constantly at odds. His treasury was empty and the taxes were nigh uncollectable. The South Country was regularly harried and terrorized by "free companies" of roving mercenary soldiers, who, when they were not fighting for the pay of some prince, were wandering hither and yon, eating up the land and plundering impartially on every side. Alike in North France and the South commerce and orderly economic and cultural life appeared to be perishing.

Under those circumstances, it seemed to Bedford as if one bold, fierce stroke would win the undisputed crown for his nephew Henry. In October, 1428, the English laid siege to Orléans, one of the chief cities still held by Charles, and the greatest obstacle to the penetration of the invaders southward from the Loire. By May, 1429, the position of Orléans was very serious. The defense had been brave; but efforts at succor had failed, and provisions were running low. The fall of Orléans would probably have seen the English marching victoriously down into Aquitaine.

Already for years there had been a keen sense of national humiliation passing through all thoughtful Frenchmen. The English had been often tactless and brutal in their dealings with the conquered. The terrible miseries of the land, economic prostration, famine, pestilence, massacre, were all traceable to one cause — the invader. Yet the case seemed so hopeless, the Dauphin's government so inert, that, even while men ground their teeth and gripped their sword hilts, they said there was no help possible "save from God." Then came what many have called a miracle, what all must call a heaven-sent leader.

It is very hard to exclude the personal story when dealing with Jeanne Darc;[1] but this is a sketch of French history, not a study of even its most important and interesting characters. In bald, matter-of-fact language, what happened was this:

1. Jeanne Darc was born a peasant girl in 1409 in the village of Domremy, on the borders of Champagne. The region was one of the few eastern districts still held by Charles. As she grew up as a pious village maid she began to have elaborate visions of a France redeemed from the yoke of the English, and the Virgin kept telling her, "Jeanne, go and deliver the King of France, and restore him to his kingdom." Psychologists may determine of what these visions, her "voices," consisted. There is no doubt she honestly believed that she had them.

2. In 1429, when Orléans was at its last gasp, she appeared at the court of the Dauphin at the castle of Chinon, near Tours. She convinced even the skeptical court and the prince that hers was a divine commission and that she should be entrusted with an army to rescue Orléans. The force placed under her command she handled with considerable military skill, conducted it through the English lines into the city, and then directed a successful sortie. The French fought boldly, confident in being under the orders of a saint. The English archers broke in terror, being pitted (so they swore) against a diabolical "sorceress." "All things prospered," wrote Bedford angrily to England, "until a disciple and limb of the Fiende called the *Pucelle* [maid] used

---

[1] It seems wholly unscientific to say Jeanne (or Joan) " of Arc." There was no village named " Arc " near her birthplace, and her people were humble peasants with no claim to the nobleman's " de." " Darc" was simply an ordinary surname.

false enchantment and sorcery." Orléans was completely relieved.

3. Jeanne now successfully conducted Charles across a country partly held by the enemy to Reims. Here he was crowned King of France in the great cathedral, and was "Dauphin" no longer. At the coronation ceremony Jeanne stood proudly by the altar holding the royal standard.

4. Jeanne had now fulfilled her original mission. She is said to have stated "she would be glad to be sent back to her father and mother, that she might tend their sheep and oxen as she was accustomed." But the English still held Paris and a great block of northern France, and she felt bound to attack them. Her warfare was now less successful. At the court, jealous captains and selfish counselors began to intrigue against her. The support of the King grew cold. Was it dignified for a King of France to owe his throne and power to a peasant maiden?

5. In 1430 Jeanne was taken prisoner by the Burgundians when she led a sortie from Compiègne. Duke Philip deliberately sold his captive to the English who were greedy for vengeance. The disloyal and subservient Bishop of Beauvais undertook to serve them by acting as her judge and trying her in the Church courts on the charge of "witchcraft." If Charles could be proved to have owed his recent success to an emissary of the Devil, it of course would be a great blow to his prestige! Every art, coercion, and some of the milder forms of torture were used to trap Jeanne into a confession of guilt. At last (although resisting her questioners with great adroitness) she went through the forms of a recantation. It was easy then by a little trickery[1] to allege that she had lapsed back to her former "damnable practices." On May 30, 1431, she was burned alive in the great square at Rouen as an incorrigible sorceress. Her bearing at the stake,

[1] Jeanne had worn male clothing. In prison she had been promised pardon, if among other things she should resume female attire. One night the woman's clothes were taken away, and the old male garments substituted. Having nothing else to wear, Jeanne put them on. She was at once declared a "relapsed" heretic.

however, was heroic and devout, her executioners trembled, and brutal English archers were filled with terror. "We are lost," cried one of King Henry's secretaries, as he turned away; "we have burned a saint!"

The guilt of her destruction was shared by many: by the venal Burgundians, by the infamous bishop, by the terrified and pitiless English, and last but not least by Charles VII himself, who callously let the woman who had probably rescued his crown be done to death, and yet never stirred, although he could readily have saved her by the threat of retaliation upon several great English noblemen he held as prisoners.

Even at the moment, not many took the charge of "sorcery" against Jeanne very seriously. The English gained nothing by her murder. In 1456 the Pope solemnly annulled the decision against her and declared her blameless. In 1908 she was enrolled at Rome among the "Blessed," as an immediate preliminary to canonization by the Church.

The English were still in the land for some time after the martyrdom of Jeanne, but her work was accomplished. The French patriotism had been roused, the invaders thrust upon the defensive, and finally a new spirit seemed to possess King Charles. He fell under the influence of a mistress, Agnes Sorel, who (however irregular their connection) seems to have been a contributing cause to his improvement. He discovered wise counselors and skillful captains. The Duke Philip of Burgundy was wearying of the English alliance, and began to quarrel with his old associates. In 1435 the Duke of Bedford, a great friend of Burgundy, died. The English thus lost their best leader and Duke Philip openly went over to the French. Charles made solemn avowals of sorrow at the murder of the Duke's father, and as a more material consideration, ceded considerable territory. The results of this shift in allegiance came quickly. In 1436 Paris opened its gates to the King, and the English garrison filed gloomily forth, departing under a capitulation.

After that the war lagged. The French won back Normandy

and the other occupied countries bit by bit. There were intermittent truces. England was now becoming involved in home difficulties, thanks to the feeble reign of Henry VI. She no longer had archers and men-at-arms available to pour across the Channel. In 1453 came the last important battle. It was in the South Country near Bordeaux. There at Castillon Charles's troops defeated a last English army sent over under the old Earl of Talbot. The English were roundly beaten. Bordeaux was besieged and surrendered (1453). For the first time, therefore, since the days of Louis VII the English kings held not a single fortress in the South Country. Nothing now was left of all the conquests of Edward III, the Black Prince, and Henry V, but Calais and two adjacent villages in the extreme North.

The "Hundred Years' War" was over.[1] It left France terribly scourged and desolated. Misgovernment, outrageous taxation, the devastations of hostile armies, the demoralization of trade and commerce, the exactions of the hosts of mercenaries employed by all the combatants had almost ruined many once flourishing districts. Probably France was a less populous, civilized, progressive land in 1453 than in 1328, the year of the first Valois King. But in any case, the nation had been welded together, as were then few mediæval kingdoms, by this awful visitation of constant war. The necessary common effort to expel the alien naturally redounded to the advantage of the royal power. One direct and important consequence was that it became recognized that for the defense of the realm, the King might continue to levy taxes (beyond the recognized "feudal dues") without the consent of the States General. The other, of equal consequence, was that royalty became possessed of a permanent standing army entirely apart from any feudal levies. These new forces, "lances"[2] of cavalry, "free archers," etc., could be used

[1] Of course it really lasted longer, 1337 to 1453, but there were long periods of truces and of nominal "peace."

[2] A "lance" consisted of six men: a first-class man-at-arms, his page, three archers, and a soldier armed with a dagger — all mounted. Charles VII had 1500 lances — 9000 cavalry; also 16,000 "free archers," — royal footmen.

by the King without any essential outside control, noble or democratic. An irresponsible use of the public purse and an obedient standing army have rightly been counted as corner-stones of autocracy.

Charles VII, after so feeble a beginning to his reign, died in a blaze of glory. His son Louis XI (1461-83) had lived on very bad terms with his father, and was actually in exile at Duke Philip of Burgundy's court when Charles died. It was generally expected the new King would prove merely the adjunct of his formidable vassal, but within two months after Philip had aided in crowning Louis at Reims, the twain quarreled. As a matter of fact the greater part of Louis's reign was to be taken up in a struggle with Burgundy, the swelling greatness whereof had become a standing menace to the safety of France.

Louis XI has made an interesting place for himself in French annals. "A bad man but a good king" is a phrase that describes his policy and deeds not inexactly. Majestic in his person he certainly was not. "Ungainly with rickety legs, eyes keen and piercing, but with a long hooked nose which lent grotesqueness to a face marked with cunning rather than dignity," such was his aspect. We are told also that he delighted in wearing mean gray clothes, that he would travel on a mule with only five or six servants, and that he invariably wore an old felt hat, ornamented with the leaden saint's figure, whereon he superstitiously set much store. He was wont to wander about *incognito*, and to select as his associates men of the middle or even the lowest stations of life, who were delighted to find themselves on familiar terms with "their lord the King." He distrusted (not unjustly) the loyalty of many of the higher nobility; by contrast therefore many of his councillors and even ministers of state were menials or little better. To be the King's barber meant probably to have more influence than to be a prince of the blood. This King, too, was superstitious, pouring out money on gifts to the shrines of influential saints, worshiping holy relics of dubious authenticity, and surrounding himself with astrologers and quack doctors. He was careless of human life and suffering. His dungeons were usually full, his hangman close at his hand and always busy. His most solemn promise was likely to prove unreliable. And yet — and herein lies the antithesis to all the above statements — his deeds in the end greatly redounded to the weal of France. Most of his victims deserved few tears; and as has been well written of him, "Louis was one of the few men destined to do really great things, and yet not himself be great."

Louis did indeed many things, but the most important of his deeds was this — he blasted the attempt of the House of Burgundy to found a "Middle Kingdom" between Germany and France, hemming in France and tearing away from her many essential provinces. In 1467 Duke Philip, "the Good," died. His son and heir was Charles the Bold. Charles's "ducal" crown was worth far more than the "royal" crowns of Scotland, Portugal, or Denmark as those kingdoms then went. Probably he seemed richer and more powerful than the King of England, now that the latter was driven back to his island. Thanks to inheritance, conquest, marriage treaties and the like, the Burgundian dukes, besides their old French duchy, held a great scattering of territories from the North Sea to the Alps. They were Counts of Holland and of Flanders, controlling the lion's share of the Belgium and Holland of to-day, and drew enormous revenues from all the teeming industrious Flemish cities. They had a considerable sprinkling of territories going into modern Alsace. The Holy Roman (German) Empire was now becoming very weak and its Emperor, Frederick III, was no stronger than the Empire. Charles confidently expected to be able to bribe or browbeat him into giving him a royal crown. Then he could write as an equal to his one-time suzerain and soon-to-be "brother" at Paris.

There were still obstacles in the way of Burgundian greatness. Charles's territories were large, but very scattered and heterogeneous. The weavers of Ghent and the peasants near the Swiss cantons had little in common. Charles's title to some of his dominions also was not beyond fair dispute. But the new Duke was a man of much ability as well as ambition. His resources were vast, he was brother-in-law to Edward IV, the new King of England, and his energy was too great rather than too little. Charles the Bold has indeed gone into many histories as Charles "the Rash." His project on the whole seemed very feasible. He would take advantage of all the disaffection of many great French nobles against their niggardly, uncourtly king; he would egg on the English to renew their invasions to recover their lost provinces; then he would strike home hard for himself. The blow at the future of France might have been almost as deadly in the end as that which Jeanne Darc averted. It was averted now by a very different character: by Louis XI, one of the most skillful human foxes who ever knew when to run and when to bite.

Charles was of course greatly assisted by the fact that Louis had bitter foes in his own household. Especially did his own brother, the Duke of Berri, systematically conspire with the common enemy of France in order to wring money and governorships out of the King. Louis fought back with all the subtle weapons at his command. He is alleged never to have met his enemies face to face in fair battle. No man was ever the incarnation of the word "policy" more than this son of Charles VII. A contemporary likened him to a spider who quietly spun his web, then calmly waited for the unlucky gnats. There was much force in the simile.

In 1465 Louis had to confront a general uprising of the French nobility headed by the Duke of Berri and boldly championed by the Burgundians. The insurgents hypocritically called themselves "The League of the Public Weal," and made cynical professions of anxiety for the oppressed bourgeoisie and peasants (who were indeed being very sorely taxed), but there had actually never been a movement more selfish. Louis's armies seemed overmatched. He unhesitatingly made peace with his rebellious subjects, giving concessions right and left to their leaders; especially Berri was given the great government of Normandy, and to Burgundy was awarded various towns, especially Boulogne and Péronne.[1] Louis had only done this to make his foes quiet down, that he might divide them and ruin them piecemeal.

It took him some years to do this. There were more combinations and re-combinations against him. Presently the Duke of Berri was induced to exchange Normandy for Guienne, a pleas-

[1] THE PÉRONNE INCIDENT

A famous and humiliating incident in the career of Louis XI was when his intriguing nature over-tripped itself at Péronne in 1468.

Wishing to conclude his bargain with Charles the Bold, the King visited the Duke in person, coming with only a very small escort, and trusting to his powers of cajolery and persuasion to induce the haughty Burgundian to give in to the royal claims. Charles issued a safe-conduct to the King, and received his guest with apparent friendliness, although surrounding him with over-many "guards of honor."

Very soon, however, was verified the saying of the contemporary historian, Commines, "Great is the folly of a prince who places himself in the power of another!" While Louis talked smoothly at Péronne, the news suddenly came that his own agents, sent by him some time earlier and not headed off, had stirred up the citizens of Liège to revolt against their prince-bishop, Charles's ally, and that the bishop had been brutally slain in an uprising. The Duke's fury knew no bounds. For three days he held Louis practically as a prisoner, almost threatening his life. Presently he cooled enough to agree to release the King provided he would consent to a treaty very disadvantageous to France, and then, as a crowning humiliation, ride with his own troops along with Charles's to punish the Liège rebels. Louis, in fear for his skin, abjectly assented to all this, and swore "on the true cross which St. Charlemagne wore" to keep his word.

The King therefore appeared with a contingent among the Burgundians at the siege of Liège. The wretched citizens vainly displayed the royal standard upon their walls and shouted "Vive la France!" They were soon overcome, their town was brutally sacked, and many of the men whom Louis had egged on to rebel, were executed almost before his very eyes — with never a plea from him in their behalf.

According to the stories of the day, the King (on returning home) had to issue a proclamation to punish the uttering of "songs, rondeaux, and ballads reflecting on his conduct," and to send out his officers to seize "all caged pies, jays, and owls," lest they had been taught to cry in derision "Péronne!" — And yet this King was permitted to do a far greater work for France than many relatively worthy and honorable sovereigns.

The "Péronne incident," of course, forms the basis for Scott's excellent romance *Quentin Durward*.

ant principality, but one that put him at a greater distance from his ally in Burgundy. Charles the Bold was alternately fought with and cozened. In a lucky moment for Louis, his brother Berri died (1472),[1] and Charles could now be treated more roundly. War was renewed (1472), and the Burgundian with a great army forced his way down from the North towards Paris. The Duke penetrated as far as Beauvais. He had sworn to teach Louis a lesson by putting all his subjects and lands to the fire or sword; and the country along the Somme was ravaged almost as pitilessly as in a greater war in more recent times. At Nesle the Burgundians slaughtered a multitude of men, women, and children who had taken refuge in the village church. Such "frightfulness" usually brings its own punishment. When Charles appeared before Beauvais the inhabitants nerved themselves up to a desperate defense. A stalwart young woman, Jeanne Hachette, distinguished herself by leading on the fighting men. The Burgundians lost fifteen hundred men in their assaults and then had to decamp discomfited. The result was a truce, which was really equivalent to a great defeat for Charles. The King was coercing or buying off his French allies one by one, and the Burgundian would have to face his nominal suzerain without their help.

Charles had still great hopes from the English alliance. In 1475 Edward IV crossed to Calais with a fine army, but Louis promptly sought an interview with the invader, convinced him there was little to gain by playing the selfish game of Burgundy, and sweetened his arguments by seventy-five thousand crowns cash in hand, and the promise of a pension of fifty thousand more each year. Edward rather ingloriously went home. Charles found himself most decidedly left in the lurch.

He had still brave prospects and a great power, but he believed he could gain more by attacking the weak principalities near

[1] So lucky, indeed, that Louis's enemies charged him with making use of poison. This is not proved, though this king was anything but squeamish. There is not the least doubt, however, as to his joy over the death of Berri.

Germany than by another attack on Louis. In 1475 he seized the Duchy of Lorraine, and then in an evil hour he decided to subdue the free Swiss cantons. For many years now the Swiss mountaineers had defied the military power of Austria, but Charles had learned no lessons from the old stories of Mortgarten and Sempach, and other Swiss victories. Louis sat back quietly, allowed Charles to march his pretentious armies into difficult mountain country where his formidable cavalry and artillery [1] were useless against the rush of the Swiss pike and halberd men, and shrewdly waited the results. The King had calculated very correctly. Charles was disgracefully routed at Granson, and fled for his life (1476). With furious energy he assembled another army and invaded Switzerland again. This time the highlanders caught him at Morat, on the verge of a lake, and slew eight thousand to ten thousand Burgundians besides those who were drowned.

The exiled Duke of Lorraine now came on the scene to reclaim his heritage, and seized his old capital of Nancy. Charles had strength enough to collect still another army to retake it, but now Louis sent active help to his rival and urged on the Swiss to take the offensive. In January, 1477, Charles the Bold fought his last battle under the walls of Nancy. His army was scattered or slain, and the prince who had almost founded a new independent kingdom in Europe was among the fallen. Louis did not conceal his joy.

Charles the Bold left only a daughter, Mary, eight years old. Louis promptly seized the greater part of her father's possessions in eastern and northern France. He did not have the power or hardihood to make a stroke for the great domains in the Low Countries which were eventually to pass under the influence of Hapsburg Austria. In 1482, by a treaty with Mary's guardians, France acquired Picardy, Artois, the Duchy of Burgundy — all with many dependent lands. Louis had also gained territory

[1] Field artillery by this time was developed enough to be of some use in open warfare, but only under very favorable conditions.

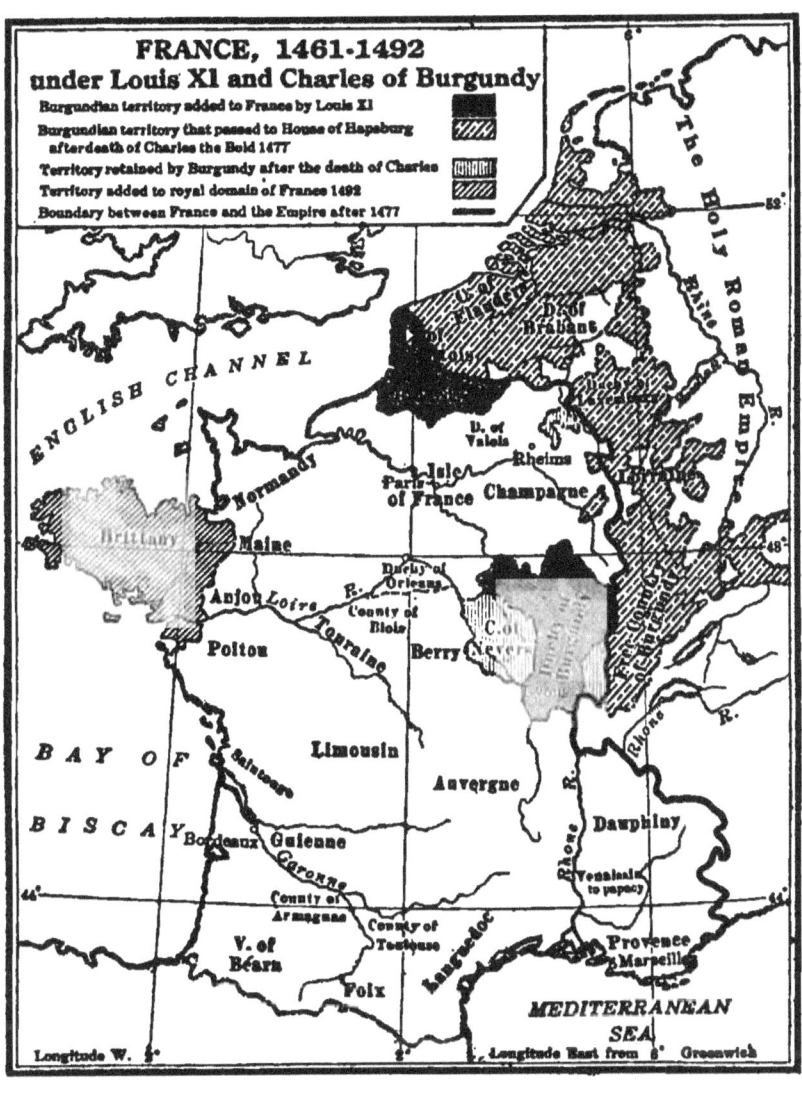

toward Spain, and absorbed many of the provinces held as governments by the great nobles. Since the expulsion of the English no French king had added such territories to the realm as did he.

Louis did not spend all of his reign either in intrigue or in battle. Unable to trust the loyalty of the nobles, he not merely filled many of his great offices with members of the bourgeoisie ("city-folk") or even low-born peasants, but he did not a little to elevate the whole lot of the lower classes, to better their legal condition, and to extend the rights of self-government in their towns. We find him improving highways, summoning to his court expert merchants to advise on the means of promoting French commerce and industries, creating new fairs and public markets, and encouraging Italian craftsmen to settle in France to manufacture glass. His interests ranged as widely as from the promotion of mining to considering schemes for the scientific codification of the royal laws; and last but not least we find him founding new universities and schools of law and medicine, and giving his patronage to the young invention of printing.

Louis XI thus deserves exceedingly high praise for having been able to fend off the Burgundian danger, and actually to turn it to the enlargement and strengthening of France, for, reverting to Philip IV's usage, introducing the non-noble classes into a share in the government offices, and for once more putting the great lords in their proper place. He "contributed more than any one else to establish the French monarchy, and is in certain respects the representative of the new spirit in politics." Nevertheless, when we return to the personality of this sordid King, a sense of his repulsiveness returns also. He won necessary battles with despicable weapons. He not merely kept high-born conspirators and rebels in needful custody; he held them for years in noisome "cages" and dungeons with all the refinements of mediæval cruelty. To this day the crypts and dark cells of his grim castle of Loches are a potent reminder of how cruel were the mercies of this wicked King; and if he was pitiless to the great lords who defied his power, he was equally pitiless to such of the wretched bourgeoisie as resisted his grinding taxation. On one occasion when these revolted, we hear of the leading insurgents being hanged on trees all along the roadsides, or being flung into a river, sewed in sacks, whereon was written, "Let the King's justice pass!"

His superstition continued to the end. In 1482 the Flemish envoys came to him to get his oath to the treaty of peace with Mary of Burgundy. The King lay dying of paralysis: he caused the Gospel to be brought, upon which he was to swear to the pact. "If I swear with my left hand," spoke he, "I pray you excuse it, my right is a little weak." But then, fearful a treaty sworn with the *left* hand might seem invalid, by a painful effort he touched the Holy Book with his right elbow! — He duly exhausted every possible appeal to the saints and to saints' relics to prolong his life, but the end came in August, 1483.

It is well written that "there was nothing noble about Louis XI but his aims, and nothing great but the results he attained," yet, however different he might have been, he could not have done more, for *what he achieved was the making of France.*

In 1483, at the end of the Middle Ages, France was the most populous, the richest, most consolidated country in Europe, and probably the best governed. Thanks to the marvelous recuperative power of the French people, so often displayed, the ravages of the Hundred Years' War had been completely eliminated. A great future seemed about to open before the nation.

CHAPTER VII

THE TURBULENT SIXTEENTH CENTURY: 1483-1610

Louis XI died in 1483. The Turks had taken Constantinople in 1453. At almost exactly that same time Gutenberg at Mainz had produced the first printed book. Columbus was to discover America in 1492. Luther was to nail up his famous theses and to commence the Protestant Reformation in 1517. Manifestly, therefore, Europe, and with Europe of course France, was on the eve of that great transition in men's activities and ideas which we call the beginning of "Modern Times."

In this first "modern" movement, France was not to be precisely a leader. The reasons for this were several. She had recovered from the Hundred Years' War amply in the sense that the burned hamlets and cities had been rebuilt, but the progress of French culture had been stunted. French architects, poets, sculptors, troubadours, philosophers, and churchmen were no longer giving the example to the artistic and intellectual life of Europe as they had done in the thirteenth century.

Another and very serious reason was that another great monarchy had arisen on the Continent. At first it did not openly threaten to destroy France, as had the English peril, but for a long time it certainly overshadowed France, humiliated her, and mingled most ruinously in her affairs. This power was Spain, for a long time a congeries of weak, turbulent small kingdoms, now at last united in a powerful military monarchy under the famous Ferdinand and Isabella; and then (following 1516) under the power of the Austrian Hapsburg dynasty, which had come into the old Burgundian heritage of the Low Countries along with the Austrian lands in Germany; and likewise for much of the time into possession of the crown of the "Holy Roman Empire" itself. From the days of Hugh Capet, France had never had such a dangerous foreign rival to her east and south. All this, of course, meant that her destinies were clouded until the Hapsburg-Spanish menace waned.

In addition to this must be restated the obvious fact that under a real monarchy, the prosperity of the country depends to a perilous extent upon the character of the monarch. Charles VII, in his later days, and Louis XI had been highly efficient kings, and their country had reaped the reward, but from 1483 to 1589 it is not too much to say that not one of the monarchs of France deserves more than very stinted praise, and the majority can only be condemned as weaklings or tyrants. The kingdom was to pay the full penalty for the worthlessness of every king; this fact constituting, of course, one of the standard miseries of autocracy.

The years between 1483 and 1610 constitute a very well-defined chapter in French history. At the beginning of this epoch France had lived down the dangers of the Hundred Years' War, but was hardly strong enough as yet to adventure herself in schemes to dominate Europe; at the end of this time the Spanish menace was fading, and if only France could have great kings or great ministers she was certainly well able to play the part of the first power in Western civilization. Within the long period there are three well-defined divisions: (1) from 1483 to 1559, the time of so-called "Italian Wars," when the French kings vainly and foolishly strove to annex at least a large portion of Italy; (2) from 1559 to 1589, while all France was racked by religious wars between Protestant and Catholic; (3) from 1589 to 1610, when a great king, Henry IV (the famous "Henry of Navarre"), terminated the religious wars, repelled Spanish intervention, healed the domestic griefs, and put his kingdom again on the road to prosperity.

Barring this last sovereign, all the monarchs of France during this time are mediocrities or worse. There is often no need of dwelling on their particular "reigns" because they usually were the creatures of forces more powerful than themselves. It is much clearer to dwell upon the different issues of this age without overmuch reference to the royal actors.

Louis XI left a full treasury, an obedient kingdom, and a powerful army. It was too much to ask that his successors should remain peacefully at home, busy themselves with internal improvements, and not proceed forthwith to fish in the very troubled international waters of their day. The condition of Italy at the end of the fifteenth century was a constant invitation to an invader.

The Italian people were now enjoying the apogee of their wonderful Renaissance — that revival of the Græco-Roman art, letters, and learning, which had begun not long after 1300. Florence, Milan, Rome, Venice, Perugia, Siena, and dozens of smaller cities were the centers of a progress in painting, architecture, and sculpture as well as in all varieties of literature and erudition with which France had little to compare. The southern peninsula, too, was very wealthy. Italian craftsmen were the most skilled technically in the world. Their cities were full of refinements and luxuries unknown north of the Alps. Along with all this magnificence, however, went a lack of political unity that was lamentable. Milan had its own independent prince, or better, "despot." Venice was an aristocratic republic. Florence was a nominal republic controlled by the great Medici family. The Popes dominated central Italy as extremely "secular" princes. The south was held by the King of Naples. There were a number of smaller and weaker states. These petty governments were constantly at war, and were perfectly willing to invite the foreigner to help them crush their unfriendly neighbors. Italy was thus liable to prompt conquest by any great outside power. The only real question was whether it would be by France or Spain.

It is difficult not to express moral detestation for these "Italian Wars." They were entirely without serious provocation, and they were conducted almost exclusively for the "glory" of the various contending monarchs: but the ethics of 1500 were not those of twentieth-century America.

Charles VIII (1483–98), the light-headed and impolitic son of Louis XI, invaded Italy with a splendidly equipped army in 1495. He had been invited in by a usurper over the Duchy of Milan, and he had also vague claims to inherit the crown of Naples. During the first advance of his magnificent army, Charles easily conquered Naples, but he soon found that the North Italian powers were arming against him. His retreat and return to France were even more precipitate than his advance. The native princes and Ferdinand, the canny King of Spain, who soon intervened, drove out the last French garrisons beyond the Alps. Charles died of an accident in 1498.[1] Nothing seemed left of his startling campaign save a memory, but the indirect results were considerable. The effects of the Italian Renaissance were now brought home to Charles's subjects. The French had been brought in direct contact with a civilization far more advanced and artificial than their own. Italian architects, artists, cooks, tailors, mountebanks, Greek and Latin professors — all alike streamed north of the Alps, in far greater numbers than before, to receive a warm welcome at the King's court, at the great noblemen's châteaux, at the University of Paris, and almost everywhere else. The culture of France was profoundly modernized.[2]

Louis XII (1498–1515), the next king,[3] was a much worthier person, but not much wiser in his foreign policy. Considered merely as a ruler at home he was one of the best monarchs France ever enjoyed. Taxes were lightened, honest measures taken to increase the prosperity of the lower classes, and the

[1] While passing down a dark gallery, in the château of Amboise, he struck his head on the top of a low doorway, with such violence that he soon died.

[2] In 1491 Charles VIII married the Duchess of Brittany and thus brought that great semi-independent principality into a "personal union" with France. Complete incorporation only came some years later.

[3] He was not the son of Charles VIII, who died without direct heirs, but the grandson of a brother of Charles VI. With Charles VIII the original Valois line ran out.

expenses of the court were largely confined to the income of the King's private estates. There was a general cutting-down of needless pensions and of other extravagances. "I would rather," proclaimed the King, "see the courtiers laughing at my avarice than the people weeping at my extravagance"; and in 1513 he declared in an ordinance, "On no account will we lay further burdens upon our poor people, knowing the hardships of their life and the heavy burdens, whether in the shape of *tailles* [direct taxes] or otherwise, which they have hitherto borne and still bear, to our great regret and grief." There is also excellent testimony that this benevolent home policy had its proper reward. "For one rich and prosperous merchant [it was written] that you could find in the days of Louis XI at Paris, Rouen, Lyons, or any other of the great cities of the realm, you may find in this reign more than fifty." Indeed, the national prosperity was so great that the royal income nearly doubled, even when the taxes were abated. The general wealth of France thus made Louis XII the envy of other kings.

Unfortunately he threw away all this just glory by his fatuous Italian policy. His whole reign was one succession of treacherous intrigues, alliances, counter-alliances, wars, truces, and renewed wars to gain possessions in Italy, especially the Duchy of Milan. He fought with the Pope, with Ferdinand of Spain, with Maximilian the Emperor, with Venice, and finally with Henry VIII of England, who had made alliance with Spain. More by bad luck and by the incapacity of his generals than because of the feebleness of his armies, Louis XII failed all along the line. For a time he held Milan, then was ousted from it, and finally, to fend off an English attack, he had to promise Henry VIII the city of Tournai and one hundred thousand crowns to boot (1514). When he died France had no more footing in Italy than it possessed after the unlucky Charles VIII. Louis's undertakings had devoured vast sums of money, and cost the lives of tens of thousands of Frenchmen, while his foes, especially Spain, seemed stronger than ever.

The next monarch was a distant cousin of Louis, Francis I (1515–47). His foreign policy was on the whole no better, and his internal policy was much worse. Francis was a showy, pretentious man who, by his patronage of artists, architects, and poets trained in the Italian school, did much to advance French culture. He was also ready to dip into the treasury for ambitious building schemes, and he encouraged his rich nobles to do likewise. This was therefore the epoch for the erection of many elegant châteaux — stately residences and palaces, not mere comfortless, frowning castles as in the now departed "Middle Ages." The region around Tours is to this day dotted with the magnificent buildings which recall a stately and luxurious age. Chambord, Chénonceaux, and Blois are merely random examples of the famous châteaux which were either erected or remodeled in the days of this splendor-loving king. For wise heed for the weal of his subjects, however, it was useless to look toward Francis. He was immoral, extravagant, and selfish in his person, and the riches of France, so far as they were not squandered on a court full of glittering parasites, were spent still more uselessly on a series of wars for power in Italy; wars which in the end brought little more than defeat and desolation.

Early in Francis's reign the Hapsburg-Austrian House saw its heart's desire when the venerable crown of the German Empire, and the more valuable personal lordship over the Austrian lands, the Low Countries, and the entire Kingdom of Spain, all passed to the single prince who is known in history as Charles V (of Germany).[1] This ruler was a far steadier and more adroit man than Francis; he also wielded much greater resources if they had been concentrated. Practically the whole of Francis's reign was taken up with a great duel with Charles, directly for the domination of Italy, less immediately to settle the question whether Austrian or French royalty was to seize the leadership

---

[1] His power was of course soon to be increased further when by the conquests in America of Cortez and Pizarro, his captains, he became possessed of the vast riches of Mexico and Peru.

of Europe. There followed a weary succession of invasions of Italy by Francis or his generals, leagues and treaties with the Pope or against the Pope, as the secular interest of the Holy See was now pro-French and now pro-Spanish, occasional victories for Francis, but on the whole far more of defeats.

There were in all four set wars between Francis and Charles. In the first war, Francis invaded Italy, but was defeated and taken prisoner at the battle of Pavia (1525). "All is lost save honor," he wrote back to his mother, the Queen Regent. The King purchased his freedom by a very disadvantageous treaty of peace, which he made haste to repudiate as soon as he was at liberty. The later three wars were less disastrous. Whenever Charles tried to throw his Spanish and German armies across the French frontiers, they were roundly repulsed. Henry VIII of England sometimes appeared as Charles's ally, but he was on the point of breaking with the Catholic Church (which Charles stoutly championed) and did not prove a very steady foe to France. Charles was handicapped also by the constant hostility of the then formidable Turks, and by the extreme disaffection of the new party of "Protestant" princes of Germany who bitterly resisted his efforts to restore the old Church. When Francis I died (1547) the great debate between Valois-Capetian and Hapsburg was not ended, but the map greatly favored the latter. Spanish viceroys were ruling firmly in both Naples and Milan, while there was hardly a French garrison left beyond the Alps.

Under Henry II (1547-59), the son of Francis, although the King was no whit better personally than his father, the struggle with the Hapsburgs took a turn for the better. Taking advantage of the civil wars in Germany between the Emperor and the Protestant princes, the French seized theree great frontier cities of Toul, Metz, and Verdun (1552). Charles made a desperate effort to recover them, and besieged Metz with sixty thousand men. The Duke of Guise, Henry's governor, however, made a gallant and skillful defense. Forty thousand cannon-shot (an unprecedented number for the old-style artillery) were fired into the town in the course of a two months' investment; but still the city held out, and Charles, having lost two thirds of his army, was fain to raise the siege. "I see plainly," he cried bitterly, "Fortune is a woman. She favors a young king more than an old emperor!"

In 1556, Charles V abdicated in favor of his son Philip II of Spain. Philip had married Mary the Catholic, daughter of Henry VIII, and thus brought England again into collision with France. In 1558, by a very sudden attack the Duke of Guise caught the small English garrison in Calais quite off its guard, and easily took this gateway to France. Peace was made in 1559. The Spaniards had won a considerable battle near St. Quentin, but Philip was anxious to have his hands free to crush Protestantism wherever it lifted its head. He therefore made easy terms with Henry, who retained alike Verdun, Toul, and Metz, likewise Calais — notwithstanding the humiliated rage of the English.

Henry II hardly survived the treaty. At a court tournament he was accidentally wounded by the broken lance of his guard captain, the Scottish knight, Montgomery. The great religious wars were about to rack and harry all France, but there is not the least evidence that Henry II had any abilities to cope with the situation.

The Reformation movement in France is harder to analyze than that of Germany, England, or elsewhere. It began assuredly as a sincere protest against the usages and dogmas of the Catholic Church, but before it gathered full strength a political element intruded, perhaps more markedly than in any other country that was touched by those great convulsions which began with the posting of Martin Luther's "Ninety-five theses" at Wittenberg, Saxony, in 1517.

At that time the French Church was being subjected to the same general criticism of worldliness, degeneracy, and false doctrine which Catholicism had to face almost everywhere outside

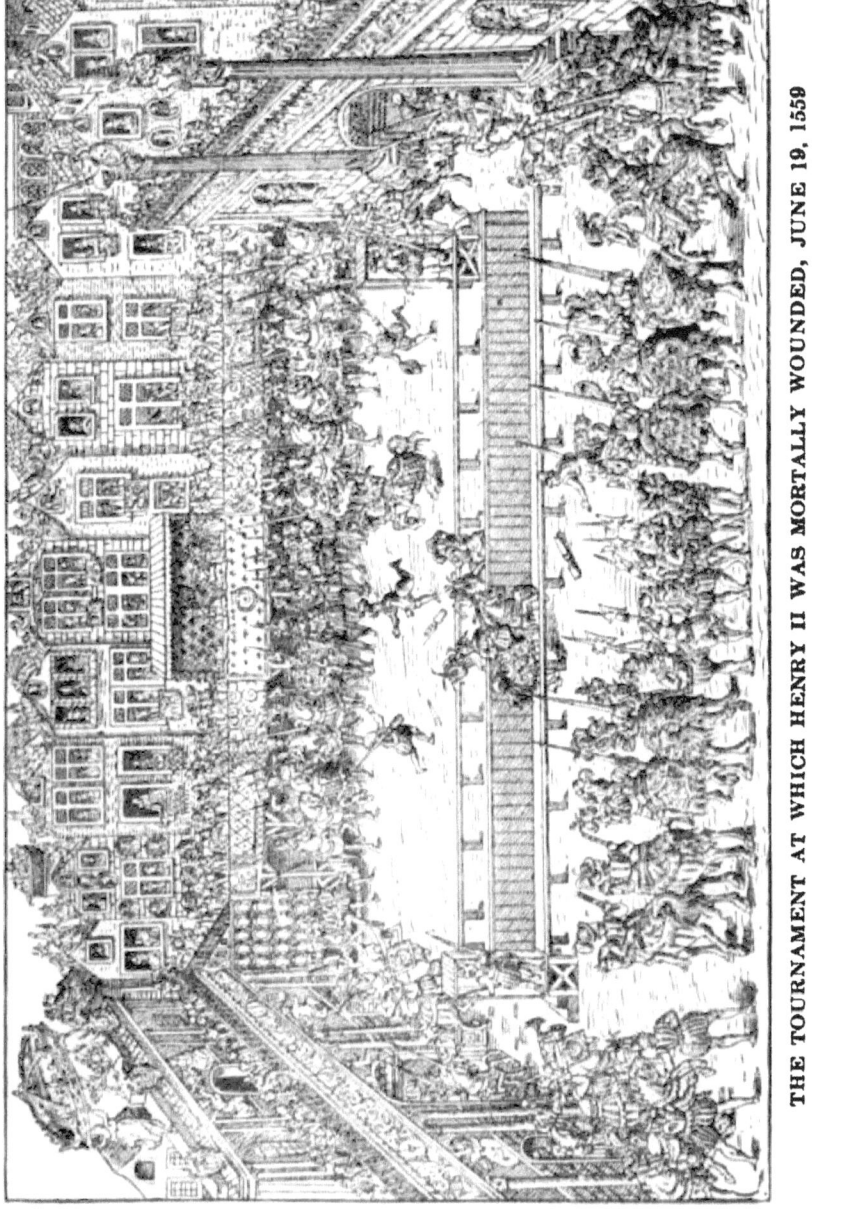

THE TOURNAMENT AT WHICH HENRY II WAS MORTALLY WOUNDED, JUNE 19, 1559

of its strongholds in Italy and Spain; and with probably about the same degree of justice or injustice. As early as 1520 there was a group of radical theologians at Meaux, a small city on the Marne, near Paris, which translated the New Testament and taught unsettling doctrines. The strong arm of the Government heresy-hunters soon made malcontents to scatter. But the greatest of French Reformers did his work elsewhere: Jean Calvin, born in 1509 in Noyon, the quiet little Picard city which was to see so much bloody history in 1917–18. He spent most of his life as the pastor, public prophet, and uncrowned ruler of the Swiss city-republic of Geneva, on the confines of France, but not under the King's control. His was assuredly one of the mightiest intellects that ever came out of France. To-day his "Institutes of the Christian Religion" may seem cold, nay, repellent enough, as a theological document, but in its generation this famous book, clever in its appeal and irresistible in its logic, was to send armies to battle, to make men die cheerfully on the scaffold, and to array kingdom against kingdom. Between 1541 and 1565, Calvin lived in Geneva, sending thence a perfect host of eloquent disciples, trained in the most robust and aggressive type of Protestantism, and able (thanks to their French connection) to obtain much more acceptance in France than the followers of Luther's strictly German type of propaganda.

Under such stimulus Protestantism grew rapidly during the reigns of Francis I and Henry II. Both kings, especially the latter, furbished up the old heresy laws, and did not spare with the rack, fagots and stake. There were a considerable number of executions for religious belief, and a prominent member of the High Court (Parlement of Paris), Anne Dubourg, who ventured to plead the cause of the persecuted to Henry II, was himself put to death. Nevertheless, the number of dissidents multiplied far beyond the ordinary means of repression. Great numbers of the lesser nobility joined the "Reformed Religion," and they were presently reinforced by some of the greatest princes of the blood — especially the powerful Prince of Condé, by Coligny the High

Admiral of France,[1] and other magnates on the very footsteps of the throne. By 1560 matters were quite ready to come to a climax.

From the outset the French Protestants, however, labored under a heavy handicap. All sides admit that both in Germany and in England the desire of the local princes or king to get control of the church offices and particularly of the church wealth was a very moving factor in inducing many rulers to listen favorably to the Protestant theologians. In France this was never the case. In 1516, Francis I had signed at Bologna with Pope Leo X a famous *concordat* (treaty with the Papacy) whereby in return for an assurance to the Pope of a considerable share of the income of the French clergy, the appointment and general control of that clergy, including large financial claims on the same, were remitted to the King. The King thus disposed of both the great offices and much of the wealth of the French Church like so much secular patronage — of course a matter of incalculable advantage to the royal power. This *concordat* reflected little credit on Pope Leo, who thus sacrificed much of the spiritual freedom of the French Church for a mess of financial pottage sent directly to Rome; but the King on his part now had such a firm grasp upon the Church that there was nothing in the temporal way for him to gain by risking his soul and embracing a new religion!

The "Wars of Religion" began in France in 1562 and cannot be said to have ended until 1598. They form a period troubled, confused, and one which brought misery to many parts of the nation; on the other hand, there were always considerable districts which remained in comparative peace. The Protestant party speedily gained the name of "Huguenots," alleged to have been a corruption of the German term *Eidgenossen* ("Confederates"). Its main strength was in the South Country, but the new religion had also scattered strongholds in the North. Particularly the

---

[1] The French "Admiral" served at that time almost exclusively as a land general.

THE WARS OF RELIGION

Huguenots gained and kept La Rochelle, an important seaport town on the Bay of Biscay. This harbor sometimes enabled them to get reinforcements from the Protestants in England and Holland. They also (when they had money) were able to hire mercenaries in the Lutheran parts of Germany. Their great strength, however, was in their dashing cavalry supplied by the swarms of petty nobles who had embraced the new religion. Their standing weakness was the fact that, besides being continually at odds with the King, court, and of course the whole formidable organization of the Church, especially with the admirably directed Jesuit order, the Huguenots were not able as a whole to make a deep impression on the peasantry and bourgeoisie of France. In some few districts the lower population accepted the new religion, but only a few. The city of Paris also remained fanatically loyal to Catholicism. A Protestant service, even in times of legal toleration, could not be held openly within its walls.

Under these circumstances it was plain the chances of Protestant victory were at best dubious. After 1560 the new religion made few new converts. The question was whether it could win reasonable toleration alongside of the Catholic majority. Whether if it had continued as a strictly religious movement it could thus have secured a legal place is uncertain: the fact is, however, that the Huguenot nobles soon began mixing with their religious zeal a distinct animus against the royal authority. Sympathy with their religious cause or admiration for the high character of some of their leaders should not prevent moderns from realizing that the Huguenots often represented a movement for strictly political disintegration which menaced the strength and happiness of France. It was all too frequently another part of the long duel between central authority and expiring feudalism. If the Huguenots could have won over the King and the lower population well and good; if not, they certainly added a political to a religious schism in the nation.

Between 1559 and 1589 the Kings of France were successively three sons of Henry II. Each of these rulers died without leaving a son himself. All three were selfish men of luxurious and debauched habits, without the least pretense to statesmanship or even to ordinary political intelligence. The true ruler of France was more frequently their mother, the Italian Princess, Catherine de' Medici, a woman of no morals, but of considerable low shrewdness, who now lied, now conceded, now was clement, now was cruel or perfidious, all to keep the royal power intact in a time of infinite peril to the same.[1] The reign of Francis II extended only from 1559 to 1560; that of Charles IX, his brother, from 1560 to 1574; that of Henry III, a third brother and probably the worst of the trio, from 1574 to 1589. During this time there were no less than *eight* civil wars, all nominally between the King and the Protestants, but often under conditions that made the royal family almost as dissatisfied with victory as with defeat.

The facts were that, thanks to the weakness of the kings, two great princely houses were putting forth their hands toward the

---

[1] Henry IV (who had no reason to love her) spoke thus of Catherine, after he had come to power following her sons: "What could a poor woman have done, with her husband dead and five small children on her hands and two families, who were scheming to seize the throne, our own and the Guises? I am astonished that she did not do worse!"

These three kings, sons of Catherine, are the most shadowy of all the rulers of France since the revival of the monarchy in the twelfth century. It is impossible to think of them as solid personalities. They are only important historically because various things were done by others for or against their "royal" authority.

Francis II was only sixteen when he became king. His wife was the brilliant and beautiful Mary Stuart, the famous Mary, Queen of Scots, just now at the beginning of a troublous and ultimately tragic career. Had he lived (he was from the first sickly) his energetic wife might have made his reign noteworthy, but he died after barely a year upon the throne.

Charles IX was only thirteen when he succeeded his brother. He was "tall, graceful, dignified, sensitive, and intelligent"; he was, however, entirely unsteady in his likes and prejudices, and very subject to evil counsel. Despite the massacre of St. Bartholomew's, he was, however, probably the best of these three last Valois kings.

Henry III was of mature years when he received the crown, but he was beyond a doubt the *worst* of these three royal brothers. "Scandalous and effeminate in his life, his palace was the home of bloodshed and intrigue, of love and murder, of the worst passions in fullest license." Such a king was, of course, defied by the Protestants and bullied by the great Catholic nobles.

LOUIS XI

CATHERINE DE' MEDICI

HENRY IV

MAXIMILIEN, DUKE OF SULLY

SPASMODIC AND CONFUSED WARFARE

throne. On the Protestant side was the powerful House of Bourbon and Condé. Antoine of Bourbon married Queen Jeanne of the little Kingdom of Navarre. He was thus something more than an ordinary "Prince of the Blood"; but the most important item was that his son, "Henry of Navarre," would by right of inheritance be heir to the throne of France if the reigning Valois dynasty ran out — as there was every chance it might do. Young Henry was being brought up a Protestant, to the infinite horror and anxiety, of course, of many pious Catholics. On the other side were the formidable Dukes of Guise. They had not the same direct expectations of the crown, but as time went on their ambitions very clearly pointed toward the supreme office. They were ultra-Catholic. The weak Valois kings (who really were often more interested in preventing ruinous civil wars than in suppressing heresy) were seldom orthodox enough for them. The Guises put themselves at the head of the extreme Church party, backed, of course, by the indefatigable Jesuits, and presently, as the movement spread, by the money and influence of the King of Spain. The Guises in fact deliberately traded on their orthodoxy. Their relations with their royal "masters," in whose alleged behalf they fought and won many battles, were often the worst. They aimed to put the kings in complete leading-strings, and even the feeble Valois were acute enough to realize this fact. Finally, in the later period of these wars, the Guises organized the ultra-Catholics into a Holy League, under the patronage of Philip II of Spain, for the avowed purpose of annihilating the Protestants, and for the hardly concealed purpose of setting a Guise on the throne of Hugh Capet.

The details of these wars are confused and very uninteresting. The fighting was now here, now there, in almost any part of France where the Huguenots chanced to have some strongholds. There were vain attempts by moderate men to promote toleration and conciliation. The Chancellor L'Hôpital, one of the few real statesmen of his time, in 1560 made a noble appeal at the States General at Blois for tolerance. "Let us attack heresy," he urged, "with the arms of charity, prayer, persuasion, and the words of God that apply to such a contest. Kindness will do more than severity. . . . Let us drop the wicked names of [our] factions. Let us content ourselves with the title of Christians."

Such high-souled words were lost on the contending passions of the day. The wars ran their course, broken by ill-kept truces. The Huguenots lost most of the pitched battles, but, until 1572, they had in Admiral de Coligny a leader of admirable firmness in adversity and skill in averting the worst consequences of a defeat. Repeatedly the Queen-Mother Catherine granted them a "peace" which permitted large elements of toleration, mainly because the final defeat of the Huguenots would have left the royal power at the complete mercy of the Guises.

In 1572 came one of the most melancholy incidents in French history, and one that has left an abiding stain upon the names of Valois and Guise. In that year not merely was there again a temporary "peace," but the Royalists and the Huguenots were showing marked signs of reconciliation, at least in political matters. Coligny was in Paris and seemed to have won great influence over the unsteady King, Charles IX. Many Protestant noblemen had flocked to the capital in the train of their leader. Great schemes were on foot for the healing of home quarrels by a general attack on the national foe, King Philip of Spain. But at the last moment the Queen-Mother Catherine seems to have recoiled. She dreaded a decisive struggle with Spain. She dreaded still more having Coligny take the place of Guise as the dominator of the royal counsels. By a curious reaction she swung temporarily back to the party of Guise, convinced the young King that he must escape from Protestant tutelage, and joined in the most sanguinary advice. The Huguenots, it was urged, must be removed by a general massacre. Charles IX, weakling that he was, hesitated at the proposed crime.[1] At last he gave way, saying

[1] To this day the precise motives and lines of reasoning which induced Catherine to urge this revolutionary change in the royal policy remain considerably obscure.

QUARRELS WITH THE ULTRA-CATHOLICS 121

angrily: "If you must kill them, kill them *all*, that no one may be left to reproach me."

On the night of August 23-24, 1572 (the ill-fated St. Bartholomew's Night), a general massacre took place of the Protestants in Paris. Coligny was stabbed in his bed. The city was full of fanatics who were delighted to execute the commands of Guise. "Comrades," announced the Duke joyously, "continue your work, the King orders it!" The slaughter continued systematically for three days in Paris. At least two thousand Huguenots were slain there in cold blood; then the massacre extended to the provinces, where, by the lowest estimate eight thousand Protestants also perished.[1]

The Huguenots were, of course, staggered by the blow, but they were not exterminated. On the contrary, they soon made such desperate resistance that they again gained temporary edicts of toleration. But no lasting settlement was possible while the question of the royal succession was open, and while the Guises and the Holy League were demanding the physical extermination of every heretic. In 1584 died the last Valois prince who might be expected to follow upon the throne, and by every law of France the heir was Henry of Navarre, a Huguenot. The Holy League and its adherents, who absolutely controlled Paris, were frantic. The Guises brought extreme pressure upon the feeble Henry III (probably the worst and weakest as well as last of his line) to make him submit to their disloyal policy, and they even schemed at last to dethrone him outright on the ground that he could not be relied upon to resist the claims of "Navarre." Henry III, however, after many humiliations, turned like a beast at bay. At Blois in 1588 he caused the Duke of Guise and his brother the Cardinal Louis to be brutally assassinated. He then made alliance with the nominal rebel, Navarre, and marched to besiege Paris.

The fanatics of the League soon struck back in true sixteenth-century fashion, and avenged their champions. A young friar,

[1] Other fairly careful estimates carry the numbers to three thousand and thirty thousand in Paris and the provinces respectively.

Jacques Clément, made his way into the King's presence, pretending he had "secret matters of great importance to communicate," and drove a dagger into Henry III's abdomen. All was over with the last of the degenerate Valois. Catherine de' Medici, the old Queen-Mother, the center of much intrigue and much evil, had died a little earlier. The House of Bourbon now was to grasp the crown of France.

Henry IV (1589-1610), or "Henry of Navarre," as he was familiarly called long after his accession even, is one of the most sympathetic as well as most honored figures in all the long list of French royalty. His had been a most turbulent youth. His position as Prince of the Blood had made him the chief of the Huguenots' party, and his years had been spent in almost incessant warfare. The petty Kingdom of Navarre had given him little more than a royal title and a standing above ordinary uncrowned princes. His mother had been a devout Protestant, and had had him educated in the religion of Calvin, but surely there was little enough real devotion on his part to the abstract principles of that iron theologian. Henry IV has been characterized as "affable to the point of familiarity, quick-witted, a true Gascon [Southlander], good-hearted, indulgent, yet skilled in reading the characters of those around him," and, when the need came, severe and unyielding. In battle he was personally brave to rashness. He was not a great strategist, but assuredly he was an admirable field captain. He knew how to draw competent advisers around him, to command their affectionate loyalty, and to profit by their counsels. As for his private morals, they were anything but "Calvinistic." The story of his irregular love-affairs is more interesting than edifying; and he had several bastard children by his principal mistress, the famous Gabrielle d'Estrées. Such peccadilloes did not count seriously against a king in the sixteenth century. The Parisians were horrified, not at his morals, but only at his theology!

The day after Henry III died, Henry IV proclaimed that he would not attempt to use his power to undermine Catholicism in favor of Protestantism; but no such simple announcement satisfied the frantic nobles and Jesuits of the League. They made haste to proclaim a superannuated old ecclesiastic Cardinal Bourbon as "Charles X." The Cardinal was childless and obviously would soon die; by that time the Leaguers, headed now by another member of the Guise family, the Duke of Mayenne, hoped to upset the line of succession altogether. Philip II of Spain gave them steady support with men and money, although not entirely because he was everywhere the avowed champion of Catholicism. Philip had himself arguable claims of inheritance to the French crown, if the Bourbon line could be eliminated, and he was biding his time to press them. In fact, had the hated "Navarre" once been ruined or slain, Mayenne's candidacy and the hopes of Philip might have clashed in open battle. Thus the extreme Catholic party was divided in ultimate aims, yet their power was great enough to make the position of Henry IV almost desperate.

At first he held only about one sixth of France, a city here and a district there. Not all the remainder sided with the League. A good many provinces and powerful nobles remained studiously neutral, trying to keep the ravages of war at arm's length and waiting to see how the issues would presently lie. Of course, Henry could reckon on the Huguenots, but they were probably less than ten per cent of the nation. He also received certain succor from Elizabeth, the Protestant Queen of England, but his best hope was in his own sound legal title to the throne (which fact presently brought many moderate Catholics over to his side) and in his good right arm which had never failed him. At the beginning his forces were heavily outnumbered by those of Mayenne, who for three weeks long attacked him at Arques in Normandy, striving to break his fortified lines, but the Leaguers were roundly repulsed. Henry delighted in the mere joy of manly battle. "Go hang yourself, brave Crillon," he wrote to an absent general; "we fought at Arques, and you were not there!" Mayenne had to shrink back into Picardy discomfited.

At last the genial, hard-hitting "King of Navarre," the heir of desperate fortunes, was the very powerful King of France. He needed all his power for his task. Since 1580 alone it was estimated that 800,000 persons had perished by war or its accompaniments, nine cities had been razed, 250 villages burned, and 128,000 houses destroyed. Commerce and industry were of course prostrated, as well as, in many regions, all agriculture. Between the civil wars and the sheer inefficiency of the last three Valois monarchs the royal finances were naturally in terrible disorder. The public debt amounted to the then astonishing sum of about $60,000,000. This was merely *one* symptom of the general upheaval.

Thirty-eight years of warfare, usually of a devastating guerrilla nature, had destroyed the ordinary processes of administering justice in many districts. Not merely were certain great nobles, the Montmorencys, Guises, Birons, and D'Épernons, treating their governorships like hereditary kingdoms; the petty nobles, each in his château, were ruling like feudal lords before the days of Philip Augustus, and playing the part of irresponsible princelets. Downright brigandage had multiplied. Roads were unsafe. Merchant caravans were often plundered. In the towns industries were prostrated. All this called for wise handling, and in many instances for stern and unswerving justice. It was not until 1605 that the turbulent nobles were taught to obey the King's law and not their own. In that year Henry made a progress through the South Country dealing out Roman justice and abruptly "shortening" (with the axe!) various great trouble-makers. In Limousin alone, it was pithily written, "some ten or twelve heads flew." The unruly Duke of Bouillon was chased over the border into exile in Germany. All this was much-needed work and quite to the King's hand.

Much earlier, however, he had accomplished a capital act of healing. For the sake of peace and Paris, he had "taken the plunge" (as he himself put it) from Calvinism to Catholicism, but he did not forget his old Huguenot supporters, who were now very distrustful. In 1598 he proclaimed the "irrevocable" Edict of Nantes, giving the Huguenots more ample toleration than was then permitted to religious dissenters in any other country of Europe, and putting France far ahead of its bigoted age. The Huguenots were given liberty of worship within their own castles, in all towns where they had already established the practice, and in at least one city or town in each *bailliage* (district). They were given access to the universities and other seats of learning, and to public offices. Every three years they were permitted to hold general synods to present complaints to the Government. They were likewise given a share of the judges of the high courts (*parlements*) of Paris, Toulouse, Grenoble, and Bordeaux, for all cases where Protestants were concerned. Finally they were given the right to hold several towns with their own garrisons, as "guarantees" for their liberties, and especially to hold their beloved La Rochelle. The edict was, of course, too tolerant to please extremists. The ultra-Catholic party railed violently against it, and cast innuendoes at the sincerity of the "conversion" of the King, but Henry forced its general acceptance as a part of the law of the land. It remained a fundamental statute of France until 1685, when, in an evil hour, the great King's grandson was to repeal it to the capital detriment of his realm.

It was the glory of Henry IV and of his chief Minister and personal friend, the Duke of Sully, that, after having been constantly in harness since almost their early youth, they now, unlike so many victorious captains, were able to conduct genuine and far-reaching pacific reforms. In truth, so great have always been the recuperative powers of France, such were the personal energy, thrift, and intelligence of the run of the French people, that given ordinary conditions of mere *peace*, they were reasonably sure to revive and prosper. But Henry IV and Sully went far beyond this minimum. Their reforms and innovations were not spectacular, and it is far easier to summarize the result of a great battle than to describe clearly but briefly a whole series of somewhat minor administrative and economic measures, each inconsiderable in itself, but in the aggregate producing national happiness. The best thing that Sully probably did, in fact, was to introduce common honesty and efficient business methods into the royal administration. A hard-working, strictly upright man himself, who shrank from no detail, he gradually cleared up all the mass of "graft" (to use a significant American expression), extravagance, and downright peculation which had begun in the court and spread its foul tentacles out to almost every petty treasury officer.

It was estimated that the "leakage" in the collection of taxes was such that when the people paid out 200,000,000 livres [1] per year, the State barely received 50,000,000. All this iniquity Sully attacked, punished, and abolished. He did not abolish various institutions derived from the Middle Ages — for example, the peasants' *taille* (direct tax) — which were inherently bad, and easily opened themselves to abuses; but at least for the time he abolished most of the abuses. His economies were rigid. After twelve years as "Superintendent of the Finances" he could see the public debt reduced by one third, the needful expenses of the State honestly discharged, and in the cellars of the Bastile, the King's castle in Paris, lay a reserve of 40,000,000 livres against the day of need.

Such drastic economies and the cutting off of fine perquisites or spoils of course awakened violent outcry in powerful quarters, but Henry IV stood by his Minister. King and lieutenant alike seem to have had a real desire to benefit the lower classes, not merely because a rich peasantry would add to the royal income, but because of a genuine benevolence toward their people. Frenchmen loved to repeat the wish of the King "that soon there might

---

[1] The French livre ("pound") at that time seems to have been worth about 88 cents in silver. Of course its purchasing power was then much higher, say $1. The value of the livre gradually sank to about 19.5 cents at the time of the Revolution, when it was renamed the "franc."

The above estimate for "leakage" in taxation may be exaggerated, but the waste undoubtedly was outrageous.

be a fowl in the pot of every peasant on Sunday"; and Sully with more practical energy, used the royal precept and treasure not to maintain an extravagant court, but to build roads, to make canals, and especially to introduce better methods of agriculture, asserting that fertile fields and pastures of fat cattle were "the real mines and treasures of Peru" for France.

The one point wherein he betrayed the prejudice of an aristocrat and a soldier was when he opposed efforts to promote more extensive manufacturing in the country, declaring that the handicrafts "did not produce men fit for soldier work." But here the Minister collided with the King. Henry seconded all that Sully did to promote agriculture,[1] but he was fain to advance French industries also. Thanks to Henry silk-culture was introduced into the kingdom — the beginning of that silk industry which was to bring such wealth and credit to France. Other industries favored and introduced by the King were those of fine textiles, of gold thread so much in demand for the country's wardrobes, of high-warp tapestries, of gilt-leather, of glass and of mirrors — articles hitherto almost monopolized by the workshops of Italy.

The King also found time to improve and beautify Paris. The capital still had great quantities of squalid houses and filthy streets with here and there an elegant palace or church. Thanks largely to Henry IV the royal city now began to develop into the best-built, most refined, and presently the most magnificent capital in Europe, and he made considerable additions to the already huge palace of the Louvre.

All these things seemed to indicate that Henry IV had ceased to remember the plumed knight of Ivry, but such was in no wise the case. Through Sully's economies the King was able to assemble a formidable army without overtaxing his subjects. In 1595 there had been only four regular regiments in the French army.

[1] Henry IV showed his interest in agriculture by causing a very sensible book by a Languedoc gentleman, Olivier de Serres, on *The Management of Farms*, to be read to him ever day after his dinner. Thanks to the royal example the book had wide circulation and decidedly benefited French agricultural methods.

In 1610 there were eleven. The artillery was greatly improved and increased, and the royal arsenals well stocked and multiplied. Large bodies of foreign mercenaries were hired.[1] Henry confidently looked forward to the time when he could, with all the resources of a wealthy and loyal kingdom behind him, strike another blow at the old national enemy — the Hapsburg dynasts in Austria and Spain. In 1610 that time seemed to have come. The Protestants and Catholics in Germany were already involved in those bitter disputes which were soon to lead to the Thirty Years' War (1618-48). Henry prepared actively to intervene on the anti-Hapsburg (Protestant) side.

The issue was a decidedly secular one over the succession to the lands of the Duke of Cleves and Julich, but the mere fact that the King was mobilizing a great army to strike on the side of the Lutheran heretics was enough to alarm many extreme Catholics. They had never accepted his conversion for more than its face value and the favors he had shown to the Jesuits had been more than offset by the execrated Edict of Nantes. Now malignant spirits began to work upon a convenient tool for their purposes. In 1610 it was said that the King was gloomy and impressed with dire forebodings, although he was seemingly at the height of his power and prosperity. On May 14 he drove in his coach to visit his old friend Sully, who was ill. In five days Henry was to join his great army on the march to Germany. The postillions had neglected to clear the way in a narrow street. The lumbering royal car stopped an instant, when a man scrambled up by one of the hind wheels, reached into the coach, and stabbed the King twice. Henry was driven at full speed to the Louvre, but he died before any aid could be rendered. The murderer, one Francis Ravaillac, was a weak-brained fanatic, who declared "the King was going to make war on the Pope, and therefore to kill him was a good

---

[1] The French nobility regarded it as degrading to serve on foot, and tradition and policy were against arming the common peasantry too freely; consequently to get sufficient infantry recourse was often had to foreigners, mostly Swiss and Germans.

deed!" It is needless to say the wretch was executed with every refinement of post-mediæval tortures.

Henry IV was by all odds one of the worthiest kings in the whole French line, probably the worthiest since St. Louis. Looked at as a private individual one cannot, of course, commend his social morality: following the death in 1599 of his favorite mistress Gabrielle d'Estrées, "his court showed little more respect for monogamy than that of the Sultan of Turkey." He cared little enough for his lawful consort, the stupid Marie de Medici of Tuscany. But the seventeenth century judged lightly the vices of a monarch, and considered as a ruler and builder of France, Henry IV must be ranked very high, indeed. The results of his wise policy were to show themselves in the days of his grandson Louis XIV.

CHAPTER VIII
THE GREAT CARDINAL AND HIS SUCCESSOR

WHEN the news that the dagger of Ravaillac had ended the life of Henry IV was brought to the Duke of Sully, the latter cried out in distress, "France is about to fall into foreign hands!" He was not wrong. The new King, Louis XIII (1610-43), whose nominal reign began the instant his father died, was only a helpless minor. The government passed to his mother Queen Marie de Médicis, an Italian lady, "heavy and lethargic," of very mediocre ability and quite willing to let herself be controlled by unworthy favorites. Sully quitted office in disgrace, and for seven years the true ruler of France was an Italian, Concini, "who had been made a marshal without ever having been under fire." Needless to say his domination, foreign birth, and arrogance made him utterly unpopular among the high-spirited French noblemen, and in 1617 he was assassinated in a bold and successful plot; being shot down at the very gates of the Louvre, by high-born conspirators who alleged that he was "resisting the orders" the young King had given them for his arrest. Louis XIII was now old enough to assert himself, although not to rule intelligently. He replaced the favorite of his mother with his own favorite, the clever, supple, and unprincipled De Luynes, who was practically Prime Minister until he died in 1621.

Under such a government, one faction of selfish nobles contending against another, and the interests of the nation being recklessly sacrificed, it is needless to say there was lamentable decadence from the brave policies of Henry IV. That redoubtable monarch had seen a foe in every Hapsburg, and had counted Austria the dearest rival of France; but Marie de Médicis and her custodians deliberately played up to the Hapsburgs, and

N.B. Nominally independent principality of Lorraine was peacefully annexed under Louis XV: 1766

caused the young King to marry the Princess Anne of Austria. A government that could not sustain the interests of France abroad was not likely to be strong at home. The great nobles began to follow their lawless whims in the good old feudal manner. The Protestants and Catholics resumed quarreling over political issues. In 1614 the weak administration tried to calm public sentiment by convening the already antiquated and discredited States General, that inefficient parliamentary body wherein the Nobility, Clergy, and "Third Estate" met in three separate bodies to petition the King, ventilate their grievances, contend, and then to disband. The meeting of 1614 was even more contentious than usual. Practically no effective measures for bettering the realm were suggested to the Government, and the worthlessness of the States General as a helper to the King was so advertised, that the body was never reconvened until the eve of the great Revolution in 1789.[1]

Then, just as the feeble government seemed cracking, as France seemed about to lapse, if not into feudal anarchy, at least into a long period of weakness and misrule, a firm hand took the helm of state. Louis XIII was a man of very ordinary abilities, but he was a far more fortunate monarch than many a more capable king; he had found a truly great Prime Minister and he had the firmness and common sense to keep him in office. We thus come to one of the genuine builders of the splendor of France — Richelieu.

Armand Jean du Plessis, Duc de Richelieu, was born near Chinon in 1585. Like that of many another famous man, his family was "poor but noble." His first education was for the army, but young Richelieu soon found that for him at least the quill pen was a far better weapon than the sword. He entered the Church, and family influence was sufficient to get him the bishopric of

[1] Of course there were very powerful influences in 1614 which prevented any democratic tendencies in the States General from becoming formidable and efficient; nevertheless the very nature of the body made it almost worthless as an instrument for the liberalizing and regeneration of France.

Luçon, "the most wretched and disagreeable bishopric in France," as he afterwards testily stated. The young prelate was doubtless a sincere Catholic, but no one claimed that he ever looked on the Church as anything but a means to worldly advancement. He seems to have spent as little time in the ruling of his clergy as possible, and devoted his main energies to pushing his fortunes at court where his immense practical and social talents soon carried him far.

In 1614, Richelieu was a member of the States General, and became disgusted at the selfishness and political inefficiency of its members. In 1616 for a short time he was a minister of state, but so long as Concini or De Luynes lorded it, there was no real scope for his talents in the government. Richelieu steadily grew, however, as a power at the court. In 1622 he received the red hat of a cardinal, and in 1624, Louis XIII had the intelligence to realize that in this Churchman was a "First Minister" who could order his land for him. For the next eighteen years it may be fairly said that Louis XIII reigned, but that Richelieu governed. The monarch only shone by the light reflected from his mighty vicegerent.

Richelieu had a very genuine devotion to the weal of France, but he saw that weal coming from her glory in war, not from her quiet economic prosperity. He was determined to eliminate all opposition to the royal power at home, and to advance the boundaries of the kingdom by fair means or foul. He did not shrink from harsh and utterly unscientific methods of taxation. He had only scorn for the relics of "popular liberties" surviving from mediæval times. The experience of the States General of 1614 had convinced him that the best government was an intelligent autocracy. He was drastic and unscrupulous in his methods, but it may at least be said he never descended to wanton cruelty, and some of the opponents he crushed assuredly deserved their fate. Early in his career it had been written of him, "His is an intellect to which God has set no limits," and his deeds went far to justify the saying.

Richelieu's performances may be summed up in three sentences: He robbed the Protestants of political importance. He reduced the nobility to genuine dependence on the Crown. He created a formidable army and launched it in victorious war against Austria. In simpler words, he consolidated the royal power at home and he made it terrible abroad.

Richelieu's quarrel with the Protestants was political and not religious. He did not attempt to tamper with their consciences or their right to hold religious gatherings; but ever since the Edict of Nantes it had become plain enough that the privilege therein granted them of garrisoning sundry fortified towns and of holding meetings for political purposes, were so many opportunities for unruly noblemen wherewith to undermine the royal authority and to breed civil wars. Twice Richelieu, in the King's name, drew the sword against the Protestant nobles. The second time the war was on a really large and bloody scale. La Rochelle, the Huguenot stronghold by the sea, made a desperate defense (1627-28) and resisted Richelieu's blockade until the children died of famine in the streets. The Protestants hoped for succor from their fellow religionists of England, but the incapable Charles I could not find admirals valiant enough to force their vessels through Richelieu's dikes across the harbor. When the English ships retired, La Rochelle surrendered, having held out until the survivors were "so wasted they resembled in looks the dead." Thus ended the Huguenots as a political party. They had failed, but they had gone down with honor. Richelieu (wiser than Louis XIV afterwards) left them their religious privileges, and for fifty years thereafter French Protestant lived with Catholic in a peace and harmony seldom seen elsewhere in any part of Europe save in Holland, because (in the Cardinal's own sagacious words) "we must trust to Providence, and bring no force to bear against [the Reformed doctrines] except the force of a good life and a good example."

This was Richelieu's first hard task: but the curbing of the high nobility was even more essential and much more difficult.

The haughty malcontents were able to carry on intrigues against the hated minister in all the closets of the palace. At any moment Louis XIII might succumb to some backstairs influence, yield to the Cardinal's enemies, and fling him out of office. But it was absolutely required that the aristocratic dissidents should be taught their place if France was to be great France, and the Prime Minister did not flinch from the ordeal.

"The four corners of the King's cabinet," he declared, "are harder for me to conquer than all the battles fought in Europe." The Cardinal had not merely to fight against subtle intrigues and ordinary conspiracies, but against wholesale lawlessness on the part of the majority of the entire nobility. The practice of dueling among the French aristocracy had risen to a national evil. A competent writer affirmed that more gentlemen had perished in these private combats than in the entire "Wars of Religion." Duels took place on the most trifling possible provocation: because two "men of honor" would not step aside on the street, because one chanced to look at another coldly or arrogantly, because he would not look at all, because the two had touched one another in passing, etc. Each adversary had his witnesses; the "witnesses," who in no wise shared the original provocation, did not content themselves merely with seeing fair play, they fought personally, possibly without in the least knowing what the dispute was supposedly about. The quarrel of a nobleman thus sometimes involved all his near friends. The combats were frequently waged in deadly earnest, and not one, but five or six persons might perish in the swordplay. There were royal ordinances against all this, but the French aristocracy were as accustomed to laugh at such enactments of the King as at very many other laws. These seventeenth-century duels were therefore becoming really more destructive to life than the old mediæval tourneys and ordeals by battle!

Of course under all this blood-letting rested the ancient feudal notion that it was discreditable for a true nobleman to let his quarrels be determined by any means save his good right arm. Richelieu set himself stubbornly against this wholesale dueling, probably quite as much because it implied defiance of royal authority as because it was morally outrageous. In 1626 the Cardinal applied the anti-dueling edicts with a severity which soon alarmed the malcontents. A certain gentleman, the Count of Boutéville, a scion of the great House of Montmorency, had been exiled to Brussels for having had part in twenty-two duels. After pardon had been refused him by the Government, he had the boldness to beard the lion, by deliberately coming back to Paris and fighting a combat at high noon in the Place Royale (1627). The hand of the Cardinal was instantly upon him. Boutéville and his second, the Count de Chapelle, were promptly arrested, tried, and condemned to die. The protest from the high nobility against this "cruelty" was tremendous. Every kind of influence, social and political, open and backstairs, was invoked to induce Louis XIII to pardon the offenders. But the King, though probably not without sympathy for the "high sense of honor" of the victims, dared not discredit his great minister by an act of pardon. The offenders died, and as Richelieu observed, "Nothing serves better to keep the laws in full vigor than the punishment of persons whose great rank is equal to their crime." Dueling was not indeed completely swept away by acts like these. It long continued to curse the French nobility, but its worst features disappeared, and in any case a vigorous lesson had been taught the lawless.

About this same time Richelieu struck another and far more effective blow at the bold spirits who might feel tempted to defy the King. There were still many venerable castles over France, strong enough to defy anything but a regular siege with heavy artillery. Their mere existence was a suggestion to their noble owners of schemes for insurrection. The Cardinal ordered the wholesale dismantlement or downright destruction of these castles. To the French middle classes and peasantry, long the victims of feudal insolence or even of wholesale oppression, this was the most popular edict imaginable. Thousands of willing hands aided the royal officers to throw down battlements or to demolish entire donjons. As a consequence, a great number of once magnificent castles sank into ivy-clad ruins: the remainder would be made over into elegant, but undefendable open châteaux. Antiquarians of a later day might regret this destruction of the stately relics of feudalism, but the peace of the land was infinitely the gainer. Hereafter if there were to be soldiers or strongholds, they were to be ever increasingly at the sole service of the King.

So long as Richelieu was dealing only with the seigneurs of petty or average rank, his position was secure enough. It was different when his policies collided with the King's own kinsfolk. In truth, the Cardinal was so masterful a ruler that no dignitary could be very comfortable in his presence, and even the King himself dreaded and somewhat disliked him, at the very time when he told himself that his redoubtable "servant" was indispensable. In 1626 several very formidable personages combined against Richelieu. Gaston of Orléans, the brother of the King himself, and heir to the throne, was nominally the center of the conspiracy, but he was a decidedly stupid man and the brains of the undertaking were really with Marshal d'Ornano, whom Richelieu had earlier favored and promoted. Nearly all the other French princes seem to have known something of the plot. Their object seems to have been to depose the Cardinal by force, since the King refused to dismiss him, and to substitute some more pliable and obsequious minister. These high-born gentlemen speedily learned, however, the dangers of plotting against one who admirably combined the fox and the lion. Richelieu got wind of their schemes: let them drift along, then suddenly began arresting the leaders right and left. Ornano was clapped into the fortress of Vincennes and in a few months died in custody. The Count of Chalais, another leading spirit, had to die on the scaffold. The cowardly royal princes were let off easily, mostly with a term of exile, and Gaston of Orléans, after a fit of helpless rage, went through the forms of reconciliation with the King and his Minister. The Cardinal had wisely refrained from touching the blood royal, and for a time his credit was higher than ever. The King granted him a bodyguard of a hundred men, as if he too were a royal personage, while the great offices of "Constable" and "Admiral of France" (posts that had hitherto given two great nobles a considerable control respectively over the army and the navy) were suppressed, thus bringing the armed forces more completely under the monarch's authority.

So Richelieu met and flung back the first personal danger which confronted him. But he had now won for himself the standing enmity of the two queens. The Queen-Mother, Marie de Médicis, "had turned against her 'ungrateful' minister with a hatred intensified, it is said, by unrequited passion." Anne of Austria, Louis's consort, had been on very bad terms with her mother-in-law; her dislike of Richelieu, however, had presently led to a reconciliation with the older princess. In September, 1630, Louis lay very ill at Lyons, and the Queens, working upon him, won his tentative promise to dismiss the Cardinal. The King declared, however, nothing could be done until peace should be made with Spain. When tidings of the truce of Regensburg reached the court, Marie hastened to recall the promise. If she had been more tactful and less violent, probably she would have had her way. On November 10, 1630, when the court had returned to the Luxembourg Palace in Paris and the King had recovered, the Queen-Mother created a scene before her son, denouncing Richelieu and his favorite niece, Madame de Combalet, "in language that would have disgraced a fishwife," and driving the Cardinal, who did not venture to defend himself, from the room. It was one of those moments when, as is possible in monarch-ridden countries, a violent domestic quarrel can make or mar the fortunes of empires. Richelieu, and, it is not unfair to say, the immediate hopes of France were lost if

Louis wavered. The King, however, though loath to quarrel, and listening to his mother in silence, was still more loath to dismiss a minister whose chief fault obviously consisted in being more devoted to the Sovereign's interests than to those of the Queen Dowager. After Marie had left him, Louis did nothing, and certain of Richelieu's friends confirmed him in his resolution not to jeopardize the weal of France by succumbing to female tantrums.

Meantime the Queen Dowager had swept out of her son's cabinet conveying the impression of triumph. The courtiers crowded around her with time-serving congratulations. The rumor spread that the Cardinal was packing his valuables for flight. This was hardly true, but Richelieu was in genuine fear lest the King had deserted him, as indeed had almost all others; but while he desponded, and while all the toadying Parisian world waited for the name of the new "First Minister," there came the messenger of the King announcing that his master had no intention of displacing his great vicegerent. "Continue to serve me," said Louis, "as you have done; and I will sustain you against all who have sworn to destroy you." This "Day of Dupes" (November 11, 1630) was therefore to become famous in French annals. Many pompous magnates who had shown their joy at the Queen-Mother's alleged triumph were promptly stripped of their dignities. Marie de Médicis vainly attempted a reconciliation with the Cardinal, but her humiliation was too great — in 1631 she fled to Brussels and never again entered France, dying in gilded exile.

If the Queen-Mother could not displace Richelieu, no lesser worthy surely could turn the trick, although there were other conspiracies. In 1632, indeed, Henry, Duke of Montmorency, undertook an open revolt in Languedoc — a blunder which promptly cost him his head. In 1642 a young favorite of the King, Cinq-Mars, a vain and futile courtier, dabbled also in treason, and perished in turn upon the scaffold. On the whole, however, from 1630 onward Richelieu was the uncontested

THE STRUGGLE WITH THE HAPSBURGS 141

master of France. He could devote himself to greater things than nipping closet intrigues and boudoir conspiracies.

Richelieu was by no means a skillful civil administrator. Taxation meant to him simply the means of raising huge armies, without respect to the miseries of the taxpayer. The *taille* (the main tax on the peasantry) was doubled to meet the cost of the wars with Spain. The distress of the rural population was often extreme. In 1634, in the South Country, and in 1639 in Normandy, there were serious insurrections of the peasants, and the name of the Cardinal became execrated by all the lower classes even as by the great nobles.

But the Cardinal surpassed as a master diplomat and organizer of wars and coalitions. Probably no statesman, in the days when diplomacy was said to consist of "lying for one's country," ever handled the sinister weapons of intrigue, private correspondence, and underhanded bargain more adroitly than he. Besides his accredited ambassadors and open agents, he made incomparable use of confidential representatives and downright spies. A certain Father Joseph, a supple and sanctimonious ecclesiastic, was his special private deputy at various important conferences, and probably had a large part in the making of much significant history.

The aim of Richelieu's foreign policy was very simple: to humble the House of Hapsburg and to make France recognized as the first power in Europe. The Hapsburgs were a divided dynasty: one branch was reigning in Austria, another in Spain, but the family alliance was fairly well maintained. Spain was still theoretically a great monarchy, with vast dominions and a redoubtable army, but already there were plenty of signs of that dry-rot within her fabric which was to bring her low without any one crushing disaster. In 1618 the Emperor of Austria (or more officially the "Emperor of the Holy Roman Empire") had become engaged in a life-and-death war, at first largely over religious issues, with the German Protestant States. By the time Richelieu grasped power, however, in 1624, it was evident enough that the question was partly this — Could Austria, with the aid of Spain, subjugate and consolidate under her centralizing sway all the lesser princes of Germany, especially those of the North? The Protestants were being steadily defeated, thanks to Spanish gold and Spanish pikemen. For several years it seemed likely they would go under. In that case a huge Hapsburg dominion would hem in France from the East, with a territory running clear down from the Baltic to the Adriatic. Against such a disaster to France, Richelieu struggled with all his might.

For years, however, this very belligerent and secular-minded Cardinal could hardly draw the sword along the Rhine. He was too busy at home crushing rebellious Huguenots and malcontent noblemen. But the same warrior-prelate who pressed the siege of La Rochelle against the French heretics was busy pulling wires and sending money in behalf of the German heretics who were the foes of his hated Austria. The inconsistency of this policy troubled Richelieu not a whit, even if his enemies denounced him as "The Pope of the Huguenots, and the Patriarch of atheists." Finally, in 1631, Richelieu made a direct treaty with Gustavus Adolphus, the Lutheran King of Sweden, paying that great captain a heavy subsidy if he would invade Germany and humble Austria. Gustavus, of course (as Central European history duly records), fulfilled his entire share of the bargain. He broke the power of the Hapsburgs over the North German Protestants by his famous victory at Breitenfeld (1631), and although he fell himself in battle in 1632, there was no longer any serious danger of the extermination of German Protestantism. Richelieu, however, was interested, not in the safety of Teutonic heresy, but in the prestige of French monarchy. His hands were now becoming untied at home. He could therefore devote his main energies to organizing France for foreign war.

Hitherto, despite the vast resources and martial population sustaining them, French campaigns had been conducted most

VICTORIES OVER AUSTRIA

unscientifically. The standing army had been very small. There were plenty of country gentlemen to make a dashing militia-cavalry, provided the term of service was short and the discipline lax. A good many of the infantry regiments had been made up of mercenaries — German, Swiss, Scotch, Irish, etc., who found the King a steady paymaster. The generals had often been royal courtiers and favorites, but by no means always men of military ability or even of decent training. All in all, the French armies up to 1630 could not be compared in organized effectiveness with the best of those of Spain.

Richelieu deserves the honor of being the first real builder of the modern French war-machine, later so terrible to every adversary. He made grievous mistakes. He too often mistook mere numbers of men for disciplined armies. He sometimes selected very incompetent generals; but he profited by his own blunders; repaired defeat and disaster with dauntless energy; and before his death he began to reap his reward.

The history of the foreign wars of Richelieu is largely a history of the later phases of the miserable Thirty Years' War in Germany (1618-48); a war which began as a struggle over religion, and which, after 1632, continued almost exclusively over the sordid question whether Austria on one side or France allied with Sweden on the other should reap the greatest material advantage at the expense of the helpless, devastated lesser states of Germany. In 1635, France actively intervened in the war, beginning active hostilities against Spain and Austria. Richelieu had gathered very large armies, but they were still only partially trained, and in 1636 the Spaniards were thrusting down from the Belgian provinces and were even threatening Paris, only halting at Corbine-on-the-Somme. By courageous efforts Richelieu turned this stroke aside, and soon the tide flowed steadily in his favor. In 1638 the German leader Bernard of Saxe-Weimar, fighting, however, in the French pay and interest, took the greater part of Alsace (excluding Strassburg), and on his death in 1639 this coveted territory was turned directly over to France. By this time Richelieu's armies were everywhere on the offensive, and before the great Cardinal died in 1642, they were striking at the Hapsburgs and their allies across the Pyrenees, in Italy, in Flanders, and across the Rhine. The older Spanish Monarchy was being pushed at every point upon the defensive.

A year after Richelieu departed, the forces which he had organized under the generals he had commissioned won a smashing and decisive pitched battle at Rocroi in Champagne (1643), when the stout squares of Spanish pikemen crumbled and collapsed under the charges of the French cavalry, and 7000 Spaniards fell and 6000 were taken prisoners. "The victory of Rocroi marked the end of the military preponderance of Spain, and the beginning of the military preponderance of France." It was won by the superior intelligence of the French leaders and soldiers as stimulated and organized by Richelieu, though the Cardinal never heard with mortal ears the tale of his greatest triumph.

However, Richelieu died a happy and fortunate man, even if he did not live till the day of Rocroi. Everywhere the power of his royal master had been consolidated; and victories were being already reported from every frontier. In 1621, Louis XIII had possessed an army of 12,000 men. In 1638, it had risen to 150,000. In 1642, it was still greater. Above all, Richelieu had fostered the training of two young generals — the masters of war, who were to enable France almost to dominate the world — generals known to history as Condé and Turenne. The House of Hapsburg was already very hard-pressed in Germany. In six years it would have to sign the humiliating Peace of Westphalia; and already French standards were floating over the Alsatian fortresses beside the Rhine.

Richelieu died late in 1642. His life had been one of incessant intrigues and wars. Probably if a more peaceful existence had been granted him, he would have proved a lavish patron of art and letters. As it was he dabbled in literature himself, left some interesting and significant memoirs, gave legitimate patronage to the poet Corneille, and in 1635 found time amid his martial cares to found the famous French "Academy," which was to have so important an influence upon the life of the nation.

It was fortunate, of course, for the Cardinal, that his royal "master" was not a man of sufficient sensitiveness and energy to feel his dignity hurt by the princely state affected by this overpowering "First Minister." Richelieu built for himself the great "Palais Cardinal" at Paris, later the well-known "Palais Royal." He was never modest in appropriating his share of the royal revenues. In 1617 as a "poor bishop" his income had been 25,000 livres. In his later years it was 3,000,000. His table cost him 1000 crowns per day, and he delighted in sumptuous fêtes. His nephews and nieces ranked almost as "Children of the Blood," and great nobles were compelled to lacquey this omnipotent ruler of the King.

Richelieu is described to us as having looked his stately part, despite a sickly frame and a drawn face. Before his stern, august presence all France quailed, including Louis himself. Cunning, unscrupulous, and sinuous in all his ways, and adamantine to every foe, the Cardinal was nevertheless capable of acts of high courage and even of generosity. His interpretation of the "public weal" was pitifully narrow, and excluded a thousand acts which governments now count needful to make the governed happy; but at least he was never swerved from what he considered his duty to France and her King, by reason of threats, danger, or desire to win popularity and applause. More than any other great Frenchman he can be likened to another famous Prime Minister of a later day — Otto von Bismarck. Their moralities and ambitions were very much the same; but with this extenuation for Richelieu — he lived in the fetid atmosphere of the courts of the seventeenth century. Bismarck lived in the later nineteenth — an ample time for the standards of the world to change.

Louis XIII died seven months after his great minister (May 14, 1643). He had been, to say the least, a very inconspicuous king, but he deserves a place in history for one crowning virtue — in the face of infinite opposition he had kept Richelieu for eighteen years in power.

Those eighteen years were to prove decisive in the history of France. Under the successors of Louis XIII and of Richelieu, France was in a position to advance from strength to strength.

That the next decade, following the death of Richelieu, was not one in which the full power of France was brought to bear upon Europe, is largely due to the fact that the great Cardinal's nominal master left only a boy of five years to be his heir. Once more the kingdom had to undergo the sorrows and weakening of a regency. Anne of Austria, mother of Louis XIV (whose official reign was to extend for the extraordinary term of seventy-three years, from 1643 to 1715), was no woman to play the part of Blanche of Castile, the regent for an earlier Louis. She was perhaps a shade more capable than her mother-in-law, the unlamented Marie de Médicis, but in any case she was absolutely under the influence of the new First Minister, Cardinal Mazarin, around whose policies and destinies the next eighteen years were largely to revolve.

Mazarin was a smooth, shrewd, supple, and extraordinarily calculating Italian ecclesiastic, who had come to France in 1634 and had become an invaluable lieutenant to Richelieu. That magnate had promoted him, secured him the Cardinal's hat, and doubtless would have been pleased could he have known he was to be his successor. Mazarin was certainly a lesser man than Richelieu, less original, daring, or willing to use courageous methods; but he was nevertheless a statesman of genuine ability who faced great difficulties and skillfully overcame them, albeit not always by heroic methods. The fact that he was an Italian naturally made the native aristocracy hate him; the other fact, that the King was a minor and that the

CONSECRATION OF LOUIS XIV AT REIMS

grasp of the Regent and her Minister on the government was none too strong, of course made these same lords also feel that the time had come to throw off some of the humiliating restraints cast upon them by Richelieu. When that master of men at length vanished, for the last time France was racked by an aristocratic reaction.

The days were long departed when the great feudal vassals had dreamed of dismembering the kingdom. What the noble counts, marquises, dukes, and "Princes of the Blood" now really wanted was to be allowed to have their full share of the royal offices, patronage, and treasury receipts. The idle, frivolous life of a seventeenth-century court put a premium on boudoir plottings and parlor conspiracies, merely as a means of escaping ennui.[1] No higher motives than these stated led certain lace-collared monseigneurs and mesdames into hatching schemes against "the Italian"; but it must be said there were other more legitimate causes of discontent with the Government. Richelieu had been an abominable financial manager. Mazarin was little better. The superintendent of the treasury was an Italian, Emeri, who shared his patron's unpopularity. Taxes were being collected with merciless rigor. Public offices were being sold to eke out the exchequer. Money was being borrowed at twenty-five per cent, yet the Thirty Years' War was still dragging to its expensive as well as its painful close, and Mazarin was charged, not unjustly, with feathering his own private nest at the cost of the State.

Such conditions enabled the high-born conspirators to obtain considerable popular sympathy, especially in the city of Paris, when they talked much of drawing the sword to rescue the young King from "his evil ministers." In addition to that, the high

[1] The irresponsible spirit of the Fronde leaders is well summed up in this description of the Duchesse de Longueville, the most prominent of the noble ladies who fanned the revolt: "She was impelled by vanity and ennui in to rebellion to her king, treason to her country, and infidelity to her husband, until at length a penitential retirement to Port Royal rescued her from the intoxicating grandeurs, cares, and pleasures of the world." (Stephen.)

judicial court of France, the Parlement of Paris, was quite willing to assert its power. The members of this court were all of them noblemen, holding office as a matter of hereditary right, and they had long claimed the privilege of a practical veto upon the royal decrees by refusing to "register" them — that is, enroll them as legally binding.[1] They had also under their eye the example of the much more powerful legislative "Parliament" of England, which was just then gaining the mastery over Charles I in the Puritan Revolution.

These three elements, therefore — discontented nobles, dissatisfied taxpayers, and a self-assertive judiciary — came together in a series of insurrections which made young Louis XIV sit very uneasily upon his throne. In 1648 began the wars known as the "Fronde" (1648–53), the detailed history whereof is not important, although it forms the basis for numerous racy and romantic court memoirs. For some time the two great royal generals, Condé and Turenne, were the mainsprings of the action. Both had their grievances against Mazarin, both were for a while in revolt against the Government, although not always simultaneously, and both (though more particularly Condé) struck hands with the Spanish enemy against their own King. The battles in these wars were sometimes bloody, but seldom were very decisive. The Parlement, and presently the Parisian city-folk, came to realize that the lofty aristocrats, who professed such zeal for the woes of the lower classes and for the respect due the laws, were themselves fighting mainly for pensions, patronage, and high commands. When the tempest was at its height, Mazarin had sagaciously withdrawn from court, but the moment the royal armies gained the advantage he was back (1653) and more powerful than ever. In that year Paris surrendered to Turenne, who was now again firmly on the King's

---

[1] The King could indeed overcome this veto by holding a solemn session (a "bed of justice"), at which he declared the proposed law binding without the consent of the Parlement. This method, however, was cumbersome and highly unpopular.

DEFEAT OF SPAIN

side. The Parlement and the citizens made their peace with the young King, and Condé fled into exile among the Spaniards. The old aristocracy, which had been a thorn in the side of every king since the crowning of Hugh Capet, had fought its last battle.

Peace did not come instantly with the collapse of the Fronde commotions. Spain had not shared in the pact of 1648, when the Treaty of Westphalia, with the German Powers, had awarded the bulk of Alsace to France. The proud Castilians had been very loath to confess that their dream of world domination was forever ended, and that north of the Pyrenees had risen a power mightier than they. When Condé fled his native land, he was welcomed at Brussels by its courtly governors, and they gladly gave the famous general the command of their armies. But Condé probably misliked the part of a rebel. In any case his new Spanish troops were not equal to his old French regiments. He won few successes over his one-time comrade and now opponent Turenne. In 1657, since the war dragged, Mazarin put his pride as a Catholic into his pocket, and made alliance with Cromwell, the redoubtable Puritan "Protector" of England. The latter sent over to the Continent a division of his stoutest, psalm-singing "Ironsides." In 1658, Frenchmen and English fought shoulder to shoulder against the Spaniard in the once famous Battle of the Dunes, on the sands near Dunkirk. The Spaniards were routed. Their power was near its end; and the proud Philip IV submitted to the terms dictated by the two nations which Philip II, his ancestor, had hoped to conquer. Dunkirk was ceded to England.[1] France received parts of Artois, Roussillon (in the Pyrenees), and also various districts in Lorraine, whose unlucky Duke had sided with Spain. It was also agreed that Louis XIV should marry the Infanta Maria Theresa. The Princess was to bring a dowry of 300,000 gold crowns, in consideration of which she was to waive all claims to her father's throne.[2]

[1] It was sold by the venal Charles II to France in 1662.
[2] The non-payment of this dowry was to have very serious consequences. (See p. 189.)

This Peace of the Pyrenees (1659) definitely settled the question whether Spain or France was the first power in Europe. The only issue remaining was whether France would push her ambitions further. Mazarin's foreign administration thus wound up in a blaze of glory. The young King was seemingly his obedient pupil, content to imitate his father and let a capable minister steer the ship of state for him. The last powers of resistance had been squeezed out of the great nobles. Henceforth they were to be merely gilded, obsequious ornaments of a splendid court, or at most the faithful commanders of the royal armies.

In Richelieu's time (or possibly earlier) there had, however, developed a new type of royal administrator in districts roughly corresponding to the various provinces. These new administrators, *intendants*, were men of humble origin who owed everything to the King, and expected everything from him; and although they did not formally replace the old royal governors, who were still great nobles, they speedily stripped them of most of their functions. The *intendants* by 1660 were becoming indispensable agents of monarchy, and were enabling the royal ministers to centralize the government at Paris, so that never since the fall of the Roman Empire was any pretentious monarch to have a more complete grasp upon the persons and property of his subjects than did Louis XIV.

In 1661, Mazarin died. He had completed the work of Richelieu, and he left his master the most splendid and powerful monarch in the world. If he had let the public debt accumulate, and otherwise proved himself a worse civil administrator than he was diplomat and court intriguer, he had at least looked well to his private fortune. He bequeathed an estate valued at 100,000,000 livres, had married his numerous nieces to great Italian or French noblemen or princes, had made his nephew a duke, and his brother (once a poor Italian monk) a cardinal. To crown his success, he had found in the young King a docile ward and admirer, and he had tried diligently to implant in him all those devious methods of statecraft which the age accounted the highest worldly wisdom.

Louis XIV was twenty-two years old when this minister and mentor left him. Hitherto the young King had seemed content to lead a life of courtly pleasure. It was expected he would immediately name a new First Minister and resume his royal vanities, but when after Mazarin's death the lower ministers came to him asking to whom they should report for orders they received an astonishing answer. "*To me!*" replied the young King.

Louis XIV had determined not merely to reign, but also to govern.

CHAPTER IX
LOUIS XIV, THE SUN KING — HIS WORK IN FRANCE

WE come now to the most important reign in French annals save possibly that of Philip Augustus. Louis XIV was a very imperfect ruler, but no one can deny that in a limited but genuine sense of the word he was "great" — that is, he exercised a profound influence over the lives, actions, and imaginations not merely of all Frenchmen, but of all Europeans. For at least four decades in his reign it seemed possible that France might become not merely the most powerful, but the overwhelmingly dominant power of Europe, ambitious to make Paris another Imperial Rome. To understand the circumstances which enabled this king to occupy the very center of the world's thoughts it is needful to study his personality, the principles of his government, the achievements of his ministers, the discipline of his armies, the ceremonial of his court. Only then can we see how he was able to make France the cynosure of Europe.

On the day after the death of Mazarin, Louis XIV, as narrated in the last chapter, assembled his Secretaries of State. "Hitherto," he announced, "I have let others transact my business. For the future I will be my own First Minister. I will be glad of your advice when I request it. I request you to seal nothing without my orders and to sign nothing without my consent." The Monarch thus indicated his will to be *really king*. He was then twenty-two years old. He died at the age of seventy-seven. In this period of fifty-five years (1661 to 1715) the wish which he had manifested on the first day of his actual government never left him for an instant. He never had a First Minister. He was constantly the King.

Louis XIV was of moderate height, but he imposed himself on all beholders, thanks to an air of nobility and of majesty

LOUIS XIV

CARDINAL RICHELIEU

JEAN-BAPTISTE COLBERT

Mme. DE POMPADOUR

without arrogance, which expressed itself in his least gestures, and which, as said his contemporary, the Duke of Saint-Simon, "in his dressing-gown even as at the fêtes," at the billiard table even as at the head of his troops, caused him to appear "the master of the world." He had only moderate intellectual acuteness; but he had much good sense, and he seldom decided a matter until he had been well informed by those supposed to know. He was naturally inclined to the right. "He loved truth, equity, order, and reason." He had also much moral courage and a firmness of character which appeared especially in his disastrous later years, when he saw his armies beaten, his country invaded, and nearly all his family carried away by death.

This King had few personal ideas. He had *one*, however, that from his youth had become embedded in his intellect and which dominated his whole life. From infancy he had been told that he was a "visible divinity," a "Vice-God." The first copy-book set for him to learn writing read, "Homage is due to kings. They do that which they please." He was penetrated with this dogma — that he was a being set apart, holding his crown by the divine will, King by the grace of God, His lieutenant upon the earth. To God, but to God alone, he must some day render account for his deeds.[1]

Practically all the French world then admitted the validity of this idea. One of his subjects, La Bruyère, wrote bluntly: "He who considers that the face of the monarch causes the felicity of the courtier, whose life is occupied with the desire of seeing him and being seen by him, may understand how the sight of God suffices for the glory and the bliss of the saints." For Louis XIV such views had two very important consequences.

[1] Louis XIV wrote in his own historical memoirs, or "Instructions for his Son": "The worst calamity which can befall any one of our rank is to be reduced to that subjection in which the monarch is obliged to receive the law from his people. . . . It is the essential vice of the English monarchy [contrasted with the French] that the King can make no extraordinary levies of men or money without the consent of Parliament, nor convene Parliament without impairing his own authority."

In the first place, as lieutenant of God he had to be the absolute master — free to dispose of the goods, liberties, and even the lives of his subjects, who owed him implicit obedience, "without discernment." In the second place, he had the obligation upon his conscience to discharge, to use his own expression, "his profession as king." He ought to "do everything for the weal of the State" and only to employ his power "to labor more efficaciously for the prosperity of his subjects."

Louis XIV did not always provide this prosperity, but at least he was a faithful worker. "It is only by labor that one may reign," he wrote for his son; "and it is ingratitude and defiance toward God and injustice and tyranny toward man to wish for the one thing without the other." As a consequence a certain proportion of every morning and afternoon was devoted by the King to public business, either working alone or with his Secretaries of State. Every day and hour was arranged according to a rigid schedule, so that, as Saint-Simon writes, "with an almanack and a watch, though you were three hundred leagues away, you could tell exactly what the King was doing."

The idea that he was the lieutenant of God had filled Louis XIV with indescribable pride. He rejoiced in the name the "Sun King." He almost allowed his obsequious courtiers to "adore" him after the manner of a saint or a demi-god. His dependents, if traversing his empty chamber, when they came before the royal bed or the chest in which was kept the royal napkins, made a profound reverence as they might before the high-altar in a church. They organized "the cult of the royal majesty," and each of the King's ordinary acts of daily life, arising, dining, taking a walk, hunting, having supper, going to bed, became a public ceremony with minutely regulated details — all known as the "royal etiquette." [1]

[1] Students of antiquity will take cynical interest in noticing how intelligent Frenchmen of the seventeenth century were thus allowing their conduct to revert to the elaborate ceremonial which made the Egyptian Pharaohs the first slaves of their own "divinity."

The "Sun King" rose at eight. The courtiers were introduced into the bedchamber by groups, known as *entrées*. For the *lever* there were six *entrées*, and after the last of these some hundred persons at length found themselves in the royal presence. The most favored were those admitted at the moment when His Majesty arose from bed and assumed the royal dressing-gown. The least fortunate were those who entered only when he wiped his hands with a napkin moistened in alcohol and finished putting on his garments. The "etiquette" indicated what persons should present each separate garment: for example, the "day-shirt" wrapped in an envelope of white silk had to be presented by a son of the King, a Prince of the Blood, or, failing them, by the Grand Chamberlain. The right glove had to be presented by the First Valet of the Chamber; the left glove by the First Valet of the Wardrobe. The Master of the Wardrobe passed the lieutenant of God his breeches and assisted him to button fast the same.

Having thus been clothed, the King entered his cabinet, gave his orders for the day, and then went to mass. Quitting the chapel he held council with his ministers until one o'clock. At that time he dined, alone, in his chamber. The "etiquette" then was no less minute than for the *lever*. Each plate was borne in by a gentleman, preceded by an usher and by a *maître d'hôtel* and escorted by three life-guardsmen, musket on shoulder. Five gentlemen stood regularly behind the King. If he wished to drink, it required three gentlemen to provide him with a glass of water or wine. This was the "etiquette" for ordinary days. On gala days, and days of the *grand couvert*, usually Sundays, the King, although still alone at table, had around him some thirty persons, about half of them armed guardsmen. On those days the public was permitted to come in and contemplate the *grand monarque* eating.

After dinner the King would go outdoors; either for a walk or more often for a trot on horseback, and frequently for a hunt. A regular multitude would follow him. On return he changed his dress with all the morning ceremonial; then shut himself again in his cabinet to read the reports of the State Secretaries or to write his own letters. Thus he would work one or two hours. At ten o'clock he supped with his family, again with great ceremony. After supper came a game of cards; then finally came the solemn *coucher* — going to bed, a process as public and complicated as the *lever*.

The French court had become elaborate and brilliant in the days of Francis I. During the "Wars of Religion" it had been entirely disorganized. Under Henry IV it had become extremely simple and even severely military. Now, under his far from simple grandson, it received an astonishing extension. It consisted of the military household, some ten thousand men in magnificent uniforms, a guard corps worthy of the most formidable monarch in Christendom; and of a civil household, containing at least four thousand. The service of the "Kitchen of the King" (*la bouche du roi*) — that is, the group of individuals employed for the royal table and the royal table alone, — contained 498 persons. But besides the King's household there were those of the Queen, Dauphin, Dauphiness, and those of their children. A daughter of the Dauphin, when aged *two* years, had for herself a "household" (*maison*) of 22 persons, including three governesses and eight waiting maids.

The chiefs of these "services" were drawn from the highest nobility. The "Grand Master of France," chief of the service of the royal table, was none other than the first Prince of the Blood, the Prince of Condé himself, who might also be the selfsame terrible general whose victories smote fear into all Europe. Usually these functions were actually discharged in person, and were not handed over to deputies. It was a coveted honor to pass the King his shirt or to hand him a dish. There were plenty of inferior noblemen who merely waited around in the royal presence, hoping that after the evening game of cards the King might make them happy above their fellows by asking them to carry a candle to light him to bed.

THE GREAT STATE OFFICIALS

The King thus had the once arrogant and self-sufficient nobility of France completely tamed. He wished to see the *noblesse* always dancing attendance upon him in the huge royal residence at Paris, or, after he built it, at the still vaster Versailles. Daily he passed in review his courtiers as he went along his galleries, or the alleys of his great parks. Whoever did not come to court could hope nothing from the royal favor. "He is a man I have not seen," the King would say, when asked a boon for some one absent. "*I do not know him*" — which was the most terrible possible criticism.

All the nobility of France, therefore, which could find the means drifted to the royal court. The country châteaux were deserted by all save the poverty-stricken, the disgraced, or the scandalously unambitious. The nobility, to live in state, built their own elegant "hôtels" around the royal residence, and consequently, when Louis XIV moved to Versailles, they aided to create a regular city.

Although the nobility thus became really *his* nobility, Louis XIV only gave to it very meager opportunities for a career. A nobleman could serve in the King's army or navy; he could enter the "civil household" to pass a napkin or to uncover a dish; he could hang around the palace as an obsequious courtier without definite functions. But the King almost never employed the nobles in the ordinary civil government and administration. "It is not in my interest," he once wrote, "to choose men of the highest eminence. It is important that the public should know, by the rank of those who serve me, that I will never share my authority consciously with them."

The regular agents of the Central Government were the Chancellor, the Controller-General of the Finances, four "Secretaries of State," various "Ministers of State," and also "Councillors of State." These functionaries for the most part had existed in earlier reigns. The Chancellor, the Controller-General, and the Secretaries formed what would be called to-day in France the "Council of the Ministers." The Chancellor was the head of the administration of justice; he was likewise president of all the royal councils in the absence of the King. The Controller, of course, had charge of the treasury and all its problems. The four Secretaries were those of the "Royal Household," of "Foreign Affairs," of "War," and of the "Marine," but each of them, in addition to these designated functions, was entrusted (following a rather old usage) with the charge of the general civil administration of an assigned portion of the country. Theoretically these secretaries were mere recording agents for the pleasure of the King, to whom they were bound to report everything, and then to execute his commands "without rejoinder." In fact, of course, they had large powers and much personal leeway.

Under these high officials were four great councils made up of "ministers" (who were really only high councilors), and ordinary "councilors." The King himself, if he wished, presided over these councils. They were the "High Council" for many major affairs, but especially for war and diplomacy; another of "Finance"; another of "Dispatches" (that is, from local officials, to handle interior administration); and finally that of "Parties" which conducted all important legal business in which the Government was interested.

This was a decidedly simple machinery for governing a great autocratic state, where all kinds of public business was being concentrated ever more firmly at the King's court. Obviously everything depended on the abilities of the Sovereign, the Chancellor, the Controller, and the four State Secretaries. Their grasp upon the realm was maintained by the all-important *intendants*. There were still, indeed, provincial "governors," each set over an old province, — for example, Toulouse, Normandy, — and appointed from the highest *noblesse*. But the once viceregal governor had had his powers so sadly curtailed that his was now little more than a pretentious honor. Usually in any case his royal lord kept him in residence at court far from his "government." The actual working administrator was the non-noble *intendant*, set over a *généralité* (a district often considerably smaller than an average province).[1] Unless the King's ministers stopped him there seemed little an active *intendant* might not do. If he wished he could sit as presiding judge in the courts. He supervised and controlled the local finances, the administration of the cities, and all the public works. He levied and led the militia of the district if there were disturbances and handled any military situation which did not demand a regular royal general and elaborate warfare. In short, as was then said of him, "The *intendant* is the King present in the province." Thus he remained until the Revolution of 1789.

For the first and by far the most prosperous portion of the reign of Louis XIV, the most important Royal Minister was Jean Baptiste Colbert. Sumultaneously he was Controller-General, Secretary of the Marine, and Secretary of the Royal Household. He was the most powerful of all the King's subjects, and without him his master could hardly have risen to the wealth and power which made him overshadow Europe.

Colbert (1619–83) was the son of a dry-goods dealer ("draper") of Reims. In his youth he went to Paris, and became the manager of the private estate of Mazarin. That clutching ecclestiastic was quick to recognize the financial talent which conserved and increased his property. At his death he formally commended Colbert to Louis in his will as being "very faithful." At this time the future Controller was forty-two years old.

When Mazarin died the finances had been in the hands of a certain Fouquet, a man of great abilities and ambitions, who seemed so intrenched in his position that he could enrich himself with impunity and use his vast wealth as a basis for schemes

---

[1] For practical purposes "provinces" and *généralités* may be considered the same from this time down to the abolition of both in 1789; there were, however, important differences often in their precise boundaries, and their names were by no means always identical.

to win permanent political power. One of Louis's first acts of personal authority was to depose this overweening minister, strip him of his dubiously acquired wealth, and condemn him to perpetual imprisonment (1661). In his place was set Colbert, a man whom the King discovered would never abuse his authority.

Colbert had a genuine mania for work. He was heard to declare that "he could not live six years if condemned to idleness." At half-past five in the morning he would enter his cabinet, and if he saw there his desk loaded with dispatches he would rub his hands as a gourmand before a feast. His regular working hours were sixteen per day. To disturb him at his labor was an unpardonable offense, and his icy habits gained him the epithet "The North." The tale runs that once a lady fell on her knees before him while soliciting a favor. Colbert promptly fell also on his own knees facing her, saying, "I beseech you to let me alone!"

The activities of Colbert can best be understood by stating that for twenty-two years he united in his person official positions that are to-day shared in France by no less than nine cabinet ministers. He has been styled the "work ox" of Louis XIV. He toiled, however, not merely out of personal inclination, but because of genuine patriotism. His devotion to his King and to France was unlimited, and he labored for them because he wished them to be the first king and the first kingdom in the world. To them he dedicated all his unbounded talents.

Colbert's leading idea was very simply *to make France rich*. For this end he used every possible means to attract money to the kingdom, and also to reduce the wealth of rival states;[1] and very specifically he strove to reorganize the public finances, to develop industry, and to promote commerce.

In handling the finances he first of all dealt rigorously with all

---

[1] Those, of course, were the days of the crude economic theory that to make a country prosper and grow wealthy, it was necessary to impoverish its neighbors.

COLBERT BUILDS UP FRENCH INDUSTRY

who, under Mazarin's lax régime, had plundered the treasury. Some hundreds of wealthy magnates were prosecuted and compelled to disgorge the equivalent of over $85,000,000. At the same time the general disorders of the finances were abated. The exchequer management was always the weakest point in the French royal régime down to the great crash in 1789, but things went better under Colbert than ever before or after. He enforced a rare thing then in Government financial circles — a strict accounting for every sou; and also a genuine attempt to keep expenditures inside of receipts. He had, indeed, something like a very elementary budget. From 1661 to 1672 it may be said that France was kept away from the threat of a deficit. Then, following 1672, the incessant wars and the endless expenses of building the royal château at Versailles brought back the evil days. Colbert lived to see the public finances sinking again into deplorable disorder.

His real achievement was in developing the manufactures of France in a way which made her a great industrial power — a position from which she has never permanently declined. He took up the lines of development dropped too long since the days of Henry IV. Thus he put the energies of the Government behind the older industries which already existed — cloths, tapestries, and silks; and then went on to introduce and promote industries hitherto almost unknown in France, such as glass, porcelain, laces, and iron-work. It is from his day that dates, for example, the steady output of admirable silks from Lyons, porcelain from Sèvres, lace from Chantilly, etc. — articles or objects of elegance which made the name of France honorably famous wherever there were persons of taste. Colbert secured this progress partly by means of large money prizes to successful artisans, partly by granting privileges to foreign craftsmen who would settle in France, but especially by advancing funds for the purchase of raw material and for the erection of factories of a size remarkable for that age. In place of the "family work-room" where a master-craftsman and a few apprentices labored on a very small scale, there were developed really large manufacturing plants such as are familiar to the present age. Thus certain of Colbert's industrial foundations employed hundreds of workers each, and at least one — a cloth-works at Abbéville, in Picardy — employed sixty-five hundred "hands" — a number not unworthy to be ranked with the largest type of factories of the present day. Colbert was, therefore, not remotely, one of the fathers of the modern factory system.

The great Minister's ambitions, however, went beyond merely making France economically independent. He intended to have foreign lands economically dependent upon France. For that end he desired that French products should be the most reliable, durable, and elegant of their kind in the world. Accordingly all the processes of manufacture were carefully prescribed by law. There were no less than thirty-two sets of regulations and one hundred and fifty edicts issued on the subject. For example, the length and width of pieces of cloth were carefully regulated and the number of threads in the warp and woof. Every craftsman had to put his distinguishing mark upon his products. These were carefully inspected, and in case of defective workmanship the offending articles were seized, exposed publicly upon a post with the name of their manufacturer, and then deliberately torn to pieces and burned. If the offense was repeated, the manufacturer himself was exposed upon the post for two hours along with his dishonest wares. Colbert defended these severities by saying pithily, "I have always found manufacturers *very obstinate* in sticking to their errors!"

Colbert achieved his end by these measures. French-made articles speedily gained a reputation of being the very best in the entire market. "Such is the vogue of these products that orders flow in for them from every quarter," wrote a Venetian ambassador. It is thus to Colbert that French industry owed its reputation for the high quality of its articles — a reputation which has remained one of its best assets even to this day.

GREAT COMMERCIAL COMPANIES 163

To promote the sale of these products Colbert made a corresponding effort to promote French commerce in general. His attempts to improve the conditions of *interior* trade were, indeed, not entirely fortunate, but he certainly gave the foreign trade of France a marked impetus.

Within the kingdom each French province was almost an independent state economically. It had its own customs, barriers, and special weights and measures. A merchant of Auvergne paid a tax for the privilege of introducing his goods into Languedoc, those of Champagne to enter Burgundy. This, of course, was one of the evil remnants of feudalism. The roads were also few and very bad.

Colbert could not sweep away many evil conditions which were to defy reform until 1789; but he greatly improved and multiplied the roads, and particularly he developed the river and canal system already exploited by Henry IV. From his day onward the inland waterway system became a decisive fact in the economic life of the country and even a passing substitute for railroads. In foreign commerce the great Minister could accomplish more. This had the greater importance in his eyes, for it enabled France to extend her power among the nations. To grasp at the valuable "spice" trade with the Orient, which had brought such wealth first to Venice and later to Holland, he created several elaborate "Companies for Ocean Commerce" whereof the most important was naturally the "East India Company" — a formidable rival to similar English and Dutch corporations. As an inevitable part of this undertaking he devoted himself to fostering an efficient French merchant marine. The existing taxes levied on foreign ships (especially Dutch) that entered French harbors were carefully maintained, and simultaneously a system of bonuses for the building and maintenance of merchantmen was introduced. As a consequence French cargo-carriers began to compete with the Dutch and the English on all the oceans of the world.

Behind a great merchant fleet, however, Colbert realized

there must be a great war navy. Richelieu had undertaken to make his king formidable upon the seas, but Mazarin had less advisedly allowed the royal navy to dwindle. In 1660, Louis XIV was master of only 18 very inferior men-of-war. In 1683, when Colbert died, the King had 276 vessels of greatly improved types — galleys, useful indeed only on the Mediterranean, ships-of-the-line carrying up to 120 guns, and frigates for scouting and cruising. Instead of using the outrageous "press gang" in the port towns, a barbarous method which kidnaped French seamen at haphazard intervals into a regular slavery, Colbert substituted a regular method of naval recruiting among the seafaring population. Qualified persons were obliged to serve one year in four in the royal navy between the ages of twenty to sixty. In recompense they were assured a pension in their old age. The King thus disposed of 60,000 reliable seamen. Thanks to Colbert's efforts Louis XIV, during the first twenty-five years of his reign, was almost as powerful on the ocean as he was upon land.

Colbert thus put his quickening hand on French finance, industry, commerce, merchant marine, and navy. In him we see the solid, constructive qualities of the great bourgeois class given a real opportunity to show what they could accomplish for the nation. Far more than any other minister he was the builder of the glories of his King. Yet before he died he saw much of his work in ruins. The King's head had been turned by pride, victories, and "glory." The treasury was again showing a deficit. Louis was no longer trusting a minister who forever preached peace, economy, and the promotion of very prosaic and workaday industrial projects. Colbert died in 1683 with France already embarked on a series of disastrous wars which were to blast her prosperity.

The aggressive military policy of Louis XIV brought about a complete transformation of the military system of France; earlier, in fact, than in the other great states, and this in large measure accounts for the success of French arms up to 1700. Richelieu had, indeed, paved the way by his energetic innovations, but the war machine of the Bourbon Monarchy did not see perfection until the next generation. The fundamental alteration was, of course, the substitution of a regular standing army for armies improvised from war to war. The leader in all the innovations was Louvois.

Without the genius of Colbert, France could not have been rich enough to sustain the grandiose projects of Louis XIV; without the genius of Louvois, it would have been impossible, in a military sense, to have attempted them.

Louvois was the son of one of Mazarin's Secretaries of State. In 1666 he succeeded his father in the great position of Chancellor. He was much younger than Colbert, but had a large share of that great man's unemotional character, zeal for hard work, and love of order. Unlike Colbert he never risked his royal master's favor by contending against the extravagances of the court, and especially against the waste of public money in building Versailles. On the contrary, he was a systematic flatterer and presently he gained much greater influence over Louis than was possessed by the Finance Minister. We find him brutal, violent, and harsh, and to him are attributed the idea of the *dragonnades* of the Protestants, and of the devastation of the Palatinate — two of the foulest blots on the history of the Sun King. No one can deny, however, Louvois's ability as a secretary of war. Hitherto it had been usual, even in a great monarchy like France, to disband the bulk of the armies the moment peace was declared. When a new war began, its first stages were consumed, not in fighting, but in painfully mustering troops, hunting out competent officers, and improvising a new organization, etc. In case of a sudden attack by a better prepared foe, the situation was soon desperate. Also since Gustavus Adolphus the Swede had demonstrated in his German campaigns that the art of war could be put on practically a scientific basis, the time required to train competent officers and men had been greatly increased. The inevitable consequences were: (1) the preparations for war had to be made in times of peace, and (2) the royal army had to become a strictly permanent force.

Louis XIV had already in 1661 a body of regular troops which other kings duly envied: especially the Household Troops (*maison du roi*), an excellent guard-corps; and twelve standing regiments of infantry. Around this basis Louvois built a great military organization. In 1670 there were some sixty infantry regiments; about 1690, ninety-eight; and, when the War of the Spanish Succession broke out (1701) Louis had the then almost incredible number of two hundred, although some of these, indeed, were certainly created for the emergency. But even in peace times the "Grand Monarch" issued his daily orders to 47,000 cavalry and 127,000 foot; all properly barracked and armed, and supplied on a well-matured system. No other king in Europe had anything equal to this peace establishment.

Unlike other armies of the day this French army had also a uniform dress, discipline, and system of tactics, in great contrast to the previous age when every regiment had been a distinct law unto itself. It was, for example, a great gain when all the ordinary field guns in the army could use the same cannon balls interchangeably. The troops were recruited by private enlistment, for conscription in our sense of the term was unknown, though the plausible recruiting sergeants made a practice of visiting famine-stricken or otherwise unhappy districts and inducing the despairing peasants to enlist by lying tales of the luxury, fine quarters, and lax discipline of the King's service, when actually on reaching the barracks the recruit found that "one bed for three men, some bad bread, and five sous per day for sustenance" was the real life before him.

Discipline in seventeenth-century armies had been often so slack as to compromise decisive battles. Louvois's forces were held down by martinets. Floggings were the lot of disobedient privates; but the War Minister insisted upon equal obedience

NEW WEAPONS

from officers also. No longer could irresponsible young noblemen lead a gay life around the camps. Breach of orders brought them quickly to the guard-room. Vainly the high-born lords protested that Louvois was insisting on their "learning to obey before they could command" — which was precisely what he had intended.

The changes introduced in arms and tactics were not radical, but it is worth noticing that with this age armor practically disappears from the soldiery, except in certain élite corps of cavalry, where it remained more for splendor than for defense, and with the armor went also the pike, practically the last surviving form of the venerable spear of antiquity. Hitherto it had been absolutely needful to keep a certain number of pikemen in every regiment to avoid its being ridden down by a bold charge of cavalry against its files of slow-firing musketeers. But well before 1700 there appeared the now familiar bayonet, which transformed every musket into a pike in an emergency, and made special pikemen unnecessary. The first bayonets had, indeed, the great drawback that when fixed they covered the muzzle of the musket so that it could not be fired, but about 1701 means were found to attach them so the firearm could still remain in full play. This invention, therefore, not merely retired the old spear to practical oblivion, but went far to give the infantryman a great advantage in resisting the charges of cavalry. He could shoot down the onrushing horsemen, even while maintaining a hedge of steel points against the charge.

This army would, of course, have been worthless had there not been ability and often even genius in the higher command. In Condé and Turenne, Louis XIV inherited from Mazarin's régime probably the two best generals in Europe. Condé, indeed, was more a dashing tactician than a great strategist; Turenne was certainly the best soldier seen in Europe between the days of Gustavus Adolphus and Frederick the Great, and possibly was the peer of either. In 1660, Louis had made this modest, well-poised man "Marshal General of the Camps and Armies of France." He possibly lacked Napoleonic inspiration, but he could execute with magnificent audacity the schemes which he had previously worked out with scientific precision.[1] His movements were of lightning rapidity compared to the average general of the day, whose maneuvers would be so slow that whole campaigning seasons would be wasted while working up to a single siege or unimportant battle. "Our father" his devoted men nevertheless called him on account of his long calculations to avoid needless sacrifices. When Turenne died in 1675, Louis XIV had no captain really equal to taking his place. He had still two more than ordinarily competent generals, however, the Duke of Vendôme and Marshal Villars. But in the King's later days he seems to have run through his first-class leaders, and he was unable to find successors to any but their high titles. French generalship experienced a great decline after 1700, and king and kingdom alike suffered.

Turenne also surpassed most of his contemporary generals in his willingness to force and to accept battles. Considering the amount of campaigning in the period, this time, like the height of the feudal era, saw comparatively few great pitched engagements. The ideal campaign was one in which an invader outmaneuvered the defending army and forced it to watch helplessly while one fortress after another was besieged and taken. It was almost reckoned as something wrong in a general that he should get caught in a situation which made a regular battle unavoidable. He might win the battle and yet fall slightly short of playing the best military game. Louis XIV in his wars took peculiar delight in sieges. Repeatedly he would let his generals arrange for the investment of a Flemish or German city, and then appear in person at camp to watch at safe range the advance of the trenches, and finally to receive the sword of the commandant on surrender.

The "Grand Monarch" took just pride in "his" sieges, for

[1] It is not unfair to say that in his scientific military methods Turenne was the intellectual father of Von Moltke (the elder) and of Foch.

VAUBAN, THE GREAT ENGINEER

the art of attacking and defending towns had been brought to an even higher perfection by his Commissioner-General of Fortifications, Vauban, than had ordinary strategy and tactics by Turenne. Vauban in fact was possibly a greater military asset to Louis than even his more famous contemporary. Considering the short-range artillery of the day, his schemes of attack by parallels, "ricochet" fire, "batteries of approach," etc., seem marvels of ingenuity. When once a town was taken, Vauban would devote all his superb genius to remodeling its defenses so as to render them impregnable. It was boasted that "no city which Vauban fairly attacked was ever saved: no city he had once fortified was ever taken." In a word, to this officer, whom Louvois and Louis discovered as a simple captain and honored as a Marshal of France, is due the system of siege warfare and fortification which lasted clear up to the present age, when changes were forced by the coming of long-range artillery and extra high explosives.[1]

Thanks to the genius, therefore, of Colbert, of Louvois, of Turenne, of Vauban, and last but not least of Lionne, a remarkably adroit and effective Secretary for Foreign Affairs, Louis XIV not merely possessed a great realm, but one in which the full economic and military resources lay completely under the King's hand, and with highly capable public servants and generals ready to do their master's bidding. Considering the education, ideas, and ambitions of Louis, there is therefore no difficulty in seeing how he was able soon to spread his name to every corner of Europe.

[1] Vauban was more than merely an engineer and soldier. He was a man of high general intelligence and wide humanity. Before he died in 1707 he had fallen somewhat into disgrace because he had dared to make very keen criticisms upon some of the worst abuses of his master's reign; to plead the cause of the down-trodden peasantry and to make pertinent but unwelcome suggestions for reforms.

CHAPTER X
LOUIS XIV DOMINATOR OF EUROPE

THE nature of the monarchy and power of Louis XIV have been set forth in the preceding chapter. It remains to be told what use this king made of an opportunity hitherto unparalleled in French annals. It was not merely that Louis's own power was great. The old rivals of his dynasty were falling away. Spain was sinking into hopeless lethargy caused by disastrous wars, an utterly unenlightened government, and the intellectual numbness inflicted by the Inquisition. The Thirty Years' War had left Germany rent into some hundreds of weak, poverty-stricken principalities, with their nominal leader, Austria, shaken and discredited. Italy was, of course, as divided and as helpless as ever. In England the mighty Cromwell was dead, and in his place was coming the profligate Charles II, a prince so absolutely without royal self-respect that he was presently willing to become his cousin Louis's actual pensioner. Holland seemed strong upon the seas, but the Dutch Republic, as events were to show, lacked the population and physical resources to make successful head by land against the first monarch of his age. The remoter Powers, such as Sweden and Poland, hardly counted, although the matchless French diplomatic service often arrayed them upon its master's side. As for Turkey, still a pretentious empire of belligerent infidels, her Padishah was very willing to strike hands with "The Very Christian King" so long as the object was alike a war against Austria, their common enemy. The whole situation in Europe was thus most favorable to grandiose schemes on the part of France.

Louis, nevertheless, did not engage in warfare for quite a few years after he assumed the personal government. This was the happy time when Colbert was allowed to give his reforming genius full scope, and when the treasury figures steadily reflected the growing prosperity of the kingdom. Louis gave speedy evidence, however, that he intended to claim the leadership among all monarchs. In 1661 the Spanish Ambassador in England, in an evil moment, ventured to claim precedence at a court function over his French colleague. A curious armed brawl took place in London between the Spaniards and French there resident, as to the rights of their respective envoys to precedence in Charles II's court processions, with the English watching the fray with grinning neutrality. The Spanish party won and killed the horses to the French Envoy's coach, while the Spanish Envoy's coach drove away triumphantly after the coach of King Charles. The news of this insult had no sooner flown to Paris than Louis thundered for revenge and made ready for war. Conscious of its weakness, the Spanish court made abject apologies, disgraced its over-zealous London Envoy, and formally ordered its ministers in all the courts of Europe never to claim precedence over the representatives of France. Such a diplomatic triumph over what had been hitherto the proudest monarchy in the world was a proclamation to the four winds of the prestige of the "Sun King."

In 1662 Pope Alexander VII was also to feel the breath of his anger. The then Pope had been on bad personal terms with Mazarin. When, in an affray, the Papal Corsican Guard fired into the palace of the French Ambassador to the Vatican, and killed several of the suite, no serious punishment was inflicted on the rioters. Louis was a sincere Catholic, but he never hesitated to bully the Holy Father in any matter of secular interest. Now he hastily ordered an army of 24,000 men to enter the Papal States,[1] while the University of Paris learnedly condemned the doctrine of Papal authority over kings. Alexander

[1] Louis took pains to show that this was a strictly "Catholic" army, dealing with purely temporal matters. The soldiers were ordered to pay special attention to fast days, and the commissary was to serve nothing but fish and cheese on Fridays in lieu of meat.

vainly looked for help to Austria and Spain, and a few days before the French army penetrated to Rome he had to present profound apologies and indemnity, and to send his own nephew Cardinal Chigi to Paris as special envoy to convey the profound regrets of His Holiness. Louis could, therefore, boast of having humbled the Pope, no less than the heir of the terrible Philip II. A great awe of the King of France and of those whom he protected fell on all the potentates and peoples of Europe.

In 1662 Louis also added a fair city to his dominions. Dunkirk, on the edge of Flanders, had been wrested from the Spaniards by Cromwell; but Charles II now needed money and had no pride in keeping a second Calais for England. He promptly sold this important place to France for 5,000,000 livres. Louis thus at a relatively trifling expense obtained a city which might have been a perfect thorn in the side of his realm if held by a more aggressive English Government.

In this manner, down to 1668, the King continued to increase the prestige of his monarchy without any serious fighting. Colbert was winning bloodless economic victories every day. The old nobility had ceased intriguing and conspiring — it was becoming content with its position as gorgeous butterflies in the splendid court. The industrial and commercial genius of the French middle and lower classes was receiving unhindered encouragement. The Huguenot minority was living at peace with the Catholic majority. If the King was an autocrat, in these years autocracy was showing its fairest and most efficient side. Never for a very long period, earlier or later, was France to seem more prosperous, tranquil, and happy than in this golden epoch of 1661 to 1668.

Not unnaturally this orderly government and wide material prosperity were accompanied by a literary and intellectual movement worthy of a truly "great" age. Corneille, the founder of modern French tragedy, did not die till 1684, although perhaps his greatest works had been produced before Louis XIV began his direct reign; but to the Sun King's own brilliant day belonged Racine (1639-99) whose tragedies deserve almost equal fame with Corneille's, and above all Molière (1622-73), that prince of comedians, the Gallican Aristophanes, whose characters have become immortal literary types, and whose genius would possibly be reckoned equal to that of Shakespeare if only he could have added the tragic to his comic muse. These are only three names out of very many contemporaries enrolled among the Olympians, such as La Fontaine, whose fables became a classic; Bossuet, the eloquent court preacher whose sermons and discourses expressed all that was best in Catholic Christianity; Fénelon, that other literary ecclesiastic of hardly lesser renown; Pascal, the mathematician and philosopher; and, to select a quite different type of genius, Madame de Sévigné, whose "Letters" give us an inimitable picture of the life and intellectual horizon of the court and noblesse of the age.

The literary life was not unnaturally accompanied by a development of the fine arts, architecture, painting, sculpture, especially such as was calculated to minister to the magnificence of costly palaces and noble "hôtels." The art was formal, heavy, over-elaborate: but none might deny its elegance or the genius that often breathed through the florid façades, or the ingeniously wrought battle-pieces and galleries of portraits. Had he determined to pose as a purely pacific king, Louis could have justly argued that the rapid development of his people in every kind of peaceful endeavor and conquest would speedily give to France the cultural mastery of the world without the need of firing one cannon shot. Considering, however, the nature of his education, his own inherent bents and talents, and the temptation set for him by the distracted state of Europe, such renunciation of martial schemes lay in the land of the impossible. Louis XIV was to make his attempt to become military master of Europe.

Four times since the end of the Middle Ages has a great military power made a distinct and formidable bid for something that may be fairly called "world-empire," and until that soaring project has been firmly thwarted, there has been no peace for the world. The first attempt thus to imitate ancient Rome was made by Philip II of Spain, and was defeated by the combined valor and skill of Elizabeth of England, William of Orange, and Henry IV of France. The second attempt was made by Louis XIV in the name of Bourbon France. The third attempt was by Napoleon, also (albeit under very different auspices) in the name of France. The fourth was to be made by Germany in 1914 when the hosts of William of Hohenzollern marched forth to "world-power or downfall."

Louis XIV did not, of course, consciously announce, perhaps even to himself, an intention of conquering the entire world. He simply started his monarchy along lines of least resistance which, since one conquest invariably leads to another, would have brought about such a colossal expansion of France that the planet could hardly have contained another power which might be treated as a free equal. The King's more obvious and avowed ambition was to execute a formula attributed to Richelieu: "Extend France to every place where once was Gaul." Such a project, of course, implied immediately very considerable territorial expansion; the conquest of all the Low Countries, at least as far as the Rhine, and perhaps beyond it; the annexation of all the small German States west of the Rhine; and finally the absorption of those relics of the "debatable lands" east of France, such as Lorraine and the "Free County of Burgundy." This last was a part of the old dominions of Charles the Bold, not permanently annexed by France when that potentate came to grief, and which had been long held in a very uncertain grasp by Spain.

By 1668 Louis had thoroughly imposed himself upon the imaginations of all Europe. "Each morning the princes of the [German] Empire, the grandees of Spain, the merchants of Holland, and the cardinals of Rome asked eagerly for the latest news of the King of France. The dangers to be feared from his

NATURE OF LOUIS'S WARS

ambition, and the magnificence which characterized his life were discussed in every council chamber, in every coffee-house, in every barber-shop in Europe." In 1668, Louis, hitherto (his position considered) a remarkably pacific prince, began a series of four wars which at first added immeasurably to his "glory," but ended by leaving that glory tarnished and the prosperity of his kingdom absolutely destroyed. These wars ran until 1714, one year before the King's death. Between them there were conditions of truce and of uneasy quiet rather than of genuine peace. They were nearly always waged against the same set of inveterate antagonists, and upon nearly the same fields for campaigning. All civilized Europe participated in them or preserved at best a very uneasy neutrality. These contests, therefore, constitute a long and important period in general world-history.

These wars, however, are extremely uninteresting. Down to the last and decisive struggle they are marked (as has been already indicated) by few great pitched battles, by very few in fact which decided the fate of a campaign. In almost every case they consist of advances by one side or the other against the enemy's fortresses, the siege of the same, and the efforts of the defending side to raise the investment. In the earlier wars the French are nearly always on the offensive. They are the besiegers; their foes are happy if by delaying tactics they can prevent too many fortresses from being taken. In the later struggles the fates begin to turn, and finally we see France defending her national boundaries with the courage of despair. This monotony and lack of exciting incidents in Louis's wars make it needless to do more than state in a few words their main events and decisions, and to explain a little of the diplomatic setting which led to each renewal of the protracted struggle. In this attempt to secure dominion over Europe there was not a Salamis nor a Waterloo nor a Marne.

In 1667 Louis laid claim to a considerable part of the Spanish Low Countries (Belgium) on the strength of certain terms (defensible only by very special pleading) in the Flemish law. The King alleged that his wife, a Spanish princess, was entitled to inherit these lands rather than her half-brother, the feeble-minded Charles II of Spain. Turenne easily overran a great fraction of Flanders and Hainault. It was clear enough that left to herself Spain could only take the decision from her great northern neighbor. However, this threat to the territories that had been a barrier betwixt themselves and France smote fear into the then rich and influential Hollanders. The Dutch made hasty alliance with England and Sweden to halt the French advance by their united threats and pressure. Such was the power of Louis that he might have rushed ahead, defying the whole alliance, but prudent counsels for once prevailed, and he signed the Peace of Aix-la-Chapelle (1668), whereby Spain was let off by the cession of certain Flemish towns, especially Lille and Tournay. The great King was merely biding his time.

When next Louis struck it was not directly at Spain. The territories of that vast ramshackle empire would be his far more promptly when once he had disposed of certain less pretentious but more solid opponents who had vexed him sorely. France and Holland had long been friends and allies, but Louis hated the Dutch, not merely because they had checked his schemes for the conquest of Belgium, but because they were Republicans, whose system of government ran counter to his whole idea of lawful authority; because they were Protestants; and finally because in commercial relations they had proved themselves very shrewd dealers with France. He took first of all the precaution to make close friendship with Charles II of England, that base monarch who welcomed a foreign pension to render himself free from dependency upon the money grants of his Parliament. In 1670, this heir of Edward III and Henry V deliberately sold himself by the formal though secret Treaty of Dover to the heir of Philip of Valois. English foreign policy was to be subservient to that of France and in return the "Merry Monarch" was to receive £200,000 per year while the projected

SECOND WAR: ATTACK ON HOLLAND 177

war lasted and 6000 French troops to repress any insurrection in England when Charles declared himself a Catholic — as he solemnly agreed now to do. "Charles told the French Minister that he wished to treat with Louis 'as one gentleman with another,' and on this basis of easy courtesy he proceeded to sell himself and his people." Louis was now confident of the help and not the hindrance of English sea power and he could deal roundly with Holland, having already secured (as he thought) the neutrality of the various German States by wholesale money gifts to their several princes. Louis had no genuine grievances against Holland, but, as he wrote in 1674, "the origin of present war may be charged to the ingratitude and the unsupportable vanity of the Dutch!" As he also more candidly wrote of himself at another time, "When a man can do what he wishes, it is hard for him to wish only what is right." He therefore attacked the Dutch in 1672 with all his incomparable forces.

Holland then possessed what was possibly the first navy in Europe, but her land defenses had fallen sadly into decay, and her chief statesmen, the brothers De Witt, up to almost the last were fatuously unconvinced of the evil designs of the King. Turenne easily conducted his sovereign and 100,000 men across the Rhine, took the few Dutch fortresses that attempted resistance, and seemed on the point of seizing Amsterdam. The terrified Hollanders in vain offered large concessions for peace. Carried away by a belief in his omnipotence, Louis demanded such terms as would have stripped the Dutch of a large fraction of their lands and left the remainder in abject vassalage to France. He forgot he was dealing with the descendants of men who had proved too much for Philip II of Spain. A great popular revolution at Amsterdam swept the Francophile De Witts from power. The young Prince William of Orange, a direct descendant of the famous William the Silent, was proclaimed Stadholder (captain-general). The Dutch armies rallied with the courage of despair, and while Louis waited in his camp for the trembling delegation to come to announce submission to his terms, he was informed that the defiant Republicans had cut the dikes, letting the sea flow in as an impenetrable rampart before Amsterdam. There was nothing for it but for the Sun King to retrace his march rather ingloriously, and settle down to a long, grueling war with the various powers that were now hastening to the aid of the Dutch.

The conquest of Holland would have been a direct preliminary to the conquest of Belgium from Spain and to unlimited aggressions in Germany. Now that the first rush of attack was past, Austria, Spain, and various German princes, especially the powerful Elector of Prussia-Brandenburg, intervened actively in the war. Seemingly France was fighting nearly all Europe, save only England, which, despite Charles II's promises, proved only a very halting ally. But so great were Louis's resources, so excellent the war-machine which Louvois had built for him, that he not merely held his own, but made steady gains at the expense of his enemies — mainly at the cost of Spain. The coalition against him had, indeed, no general who seemed a fair match for Turenne, or even for Luxembourg, after Turenne was killed in 1675. William of Orange, for all this, proved himself a resourceful and indefatigable leader. It was, indeed, spitefully alleged by the French that "no other 'great captain' had lost so many battles, or been forced to raise so many sieges as he"; but though William was often defeated, he was never disastrously defeated; he never lost courage when the situation was dark, and what is more, he never let his associates and followers lose courage for themselves. His distrust and detestation of Louis were extreme. He consecrated all his matchless talents as a diplomatist to building up against France one great coalition after another; and in the end this cold, unsympathetic, iron-tempered man was to go far in pulling down the whole power of his mighty rival.

In 1678, however, both sides had wearied of the war. France had made great gains, but had not "knocked out' the hostile coalition. The coalition had been utterly unable to disable

THE HUGUENOTS UNDER LOUIS XIV 179

France. The Treaty of Nimwegen (near The Hague) restored to Holland her territories intact; Spain, however, had been forced to cede still another slice of Flanders including Valenciennes and Cambrai, also the whole of Franche-Comté, and various small concessions were made by Austria along the Rhine. Louis had not ruined Holland as he had designed in 1672, but his acquisitions from this war had been large enough to send the court poets and historians into ecstasies. He had fought almost all Europe and come away the gainer. There were already signs, however, that his wars were undermining grievously the general prosperity of France.

Between 1678 and 1688, the formal beginning of the next great war, Louis was to see his position seriously compromised. Colbert died in 1683. The finances of France were already in disorder. The great minister had preached economies, and had been nearly repudiated and disgraced by his master as a consequence. After his death, however, Louis had good reason to regret him. Never again was the King to see the civil administration entrusted to ministers of more than very mediocre capacity. The fine company of able civil servants which Mazarin had bequeathed to the Government was running out.

It is doubtful if Colbert could have dissuaded the King from what a liberal Catholic (Duruy) has called "the greatest mistake in his reign" — the revocation of the Edict of Nantes. Since 1630 the Protestants had ceased to be the slightest menace to the peace of the State. They had been loyally quiet during all the turbulent years of the Fronde. Very many of the great noble houses which had once supported the Huguenot cause, the Condés, Colignys, and the like, had drifted back to Catholicism now that early reforming fervor had cooled, and court favor had been clearly for the friends of the old religion. But the bourgeois and peasant elements of the Protestants had stood fast — thrifty trades-people and artisans for the most part, respected for their industry, sobriety, and honesty. Colbert had found them very useful in his schemes and employed them frequently in his new factories or commercial ventures. Duquesne, one of the greatest seamen of France, and Van Robais, the chief manufacturer of Abbéville, had been Protestants.

These harmless, self-respecting, and highly valuable people were now decidedly less than ten per cent of the whole population. Worldly-wise Catholics decidedly favored letting them alone. "This little flock feeds on poisonous herbs," said Mazarin the Cardinal, "but it does not wander from the fold." When Louis XIV took over the government he distinctly declared that while he would show the Protestants no favor, he would respect the rights the laws secured to them. He was himself a bigoted Catholic who had little room for liberal theological opinions, but it was not until after 1678, when peace existed and the King felt his hands free, that serious moves were attempted against the Huguenots. Louis was probably sincere in his detestation of heresy, but he had at least two extra-religious motives. In the first place, he was on chronically bad terms with the Papacy over questions of secular interest, and was anxious to prove to the world that he was still "The Eldest Son of the Church" even if he wrangled with the Pope over the right of his embassy at Rome to give asylum to outlawed cut-throats, or over the question of the election of a pro-French candidate as Prince-Bishop of Cologne. Secondly, it probably irked him sore that in a realm where he claimed plenary authority, and considered his own autocratic decrees as the law for all his subjects, a considerable body of Frenchmen should declare that in one very important matter their ways were not the ways of the King.

At Louis's elbow were many powerful elements which urged him to play the persecutor. Great courtiers, ladies of irregular morals but unblemished orthodoxy, and eloquent and eager bishops and leaders of the Church, brought constant pressure upon Louis to undertake the conversion of his dissenting subjects. The first step was to cut off all privileges from the Protestants not carefully secured to them by the existing law; they were excluded from the teaching and medical professions and from all public offices. The next step was to send preachers into Huguenot communities to attempt by eloquence, cajoleries, and threats to sow the good seed. The next, and far more sinister, was to enact that at the age of seven a child could select its own religion. If a boy or girl could be tricked into making some statement indicating that he or she wished to be a Catholic, the child could be taken from its unbelieving parents and placed in some kind of non-heretical custody, although the parents had still to pay a pension for its upkeep. The next stage — beginning especially in 1681 — was the deliberate process of "dragooning"; billeting soldiers in the houses of peaceful Protestants who did not encourage "instruction," and allowing or even inciting barrack topers to insult the women and to carouse all night like beasts. "They entered an orderly and religious household, and existence there became like life in a brothel or dramshop."

Under these circumstances tens of thousand of Protestants professed themselves convinced of the tenets of Catholicism. The Archbishop of Aix "confessed that the fear of the dragoons persuaded many more than either his money or his eloquence," but although it was admitted that many "conversions" were rotten or debatable, it was also boasted that at least the children would be brought up in the true faith. The court was delighted at exaggerated tidings of the numbers of the converts. "Every bulletin," writes Madame de Maintenon, "tells the King of thousands of conversions"; while Te Deums were sung, guns fired, and the palace grounds illuminated at each victory of true religion.

In 1685 Louis was honestly convinced that practically all the French Protestants were converted, and that the Edict of Nantes could be repealed, as having become needless for the present, and merely a blot upon the statutes of "The Very Christian King." The Royal Council voted unanimously for revocation. On the 18th of October, 1685, the King signed the revocation of the Edict of Nantes, and ordered all Protestant forms of worship forthwith to cease and all Protestant chapels and "temples" to be immediately destroyed.

The Catholic population of France received the mandate with unconcealed joy. The aged Chancellor Le Tellier exclaimed, "Lord, now lettest thou thy servant depart in peace!" as he put the great seal on the document abolishing heresy. Bossuet, the enlightened and humane court preacher, was delighted. "The work is worthy of your reign and of yourself," he told the King: "heresy is no more. May the King of Heaven preserve the King of earth," while Madame de Sévigné, a mild and estimable noblewoman, wrote ecstatically in a letter, "Nothing could be finer: no king ever did, or ever will do, anything so memorable."

Hardly were the rejoicings over before it became clear that a great mischief had been wrought to France. Thousands of Protestants had turned under coercion, but thousands more had kept their faith. There seemed no alternative to the most brutal type of persecution.

Under the terms of the new law all the Huguenot pastors were to be banished from France, but none of their laity were to be permitted to quit the realm under extraordinarily heavy penalties. Protestants who refused promptly to conform were subject to more brutal dragooning than ever. "His Majesty decrees," wrote Louvois, who highly approved of the persecution, "that every means shall be used to make it clear that no rest or mercy is to be expected by those who persist in a religion which displeases the King." The prisons and galleys were soon full of Protestants convicted of various offenses against the new edict, or of trying to save themselves by sham conversions and then of lapsing from the Catholic faith. But despite threats, brutal soldiery, bonds, and gibbet the consequences of the persecution were almost instantly disastrous for Louis. By tens of thousands the Protestants smuggled themselves across the frontiers. They filled England, Holland, and Lutheran Germany with their outcries. Themselves among the best artisans and merchants of France, they transferred their commercial abilities and industries to her most bitter national rivals. In all, over two hundred thousand Huguenots seem to have emigrated, giving thus of the very life of France to England, Holland, and Brandenburg, and also to the English and Dutch colonies, notably to South Carolina and to the Cape of Good Hope.

The persecution had thus been one of the most suicidal acts by any French king. Not merely had Louis's enemies been strengthened economically, but the revocation, coming just at the moment when the great war costs of the Government were already undermining the wealth of France, produced an economic crisis by ruining a great fraction of the thriftiest citizens. Some years later, Vauban, who was a careful student of public problems as well as a great military engineer, formally charged that the emigrants carried an enormous amount of wealth out of the country; that many arts and manufactures were utterly destroyed; that French commerce was prostrated; that eight to nine thousand of the King's best sailors had gone over to the enemy, and with them some twelve thousand soldiers and over five hundred admirable officers. Certain it is that in the next war one of William of Orange's ablest generals, Schomberg, was a Huguenot exile, and several of his doughtiest regiments were made up of these outcast Frenchmen, who had forsaken native land, though only at the call of conscience.

Even the persecution within France did not succeed. The Huguenots lost over half of their numbers, but in the South Country a sturdy remnant held out and maintained their worship "in the desert," in the open air among the hills, with scouts watching to give warning of a raid by the soldiery. In 1703 in the Cévennes district there was the serious armed insurrection of the Camisards.[1] A royal army had to be sent against the rebels at a time when all the regular troops were sorely needed else-

[1] So called from the habit of the insurgents putting their shirts on over their clothes, to identify one another in a night attack.

where. Even then the Government had to make terms with the malcontents and offer pardon to those who submitted. After that all men realized that the Huguenots of France could not be exterminated. They continued despised, maltreated, under heavy legal handicaps and without formal toleration for their religion until shortly before 1789, but their mere existence was a proclamation that here was a task too hard for "Louis the Great." Then with the Revolution came full religious toleration and the Church of the Huguenots remains a potent factor in French life unto this day.[1]

While Louis was thus committing a blunder which tarnished his splendor and cost France dear, he was also drifting into lines of extravagance which added grievously to the economic burdens of the kingdom. What he did not spend on wars and upon a super-magnificent court he spent on colossal building projects. The King disliked Paris. It had memories of the disloyal Fronde of his boyhood. Its palaces also reminded men of earlier princes before his own blaze of glory. The Tuileries were, indeed, enlarged, and more structures piled upon the already colossal Louvre, but the King was deliberately resolved to build a residence city. Unconsciously he was perhaps determined to imitate other mighty despots, as the rulers of old Egypt and Assyria, or Alexander the Macedonian who scattered his new "Alexandrias" over a conquered world. As early as 1664 Louis authorized the architect Mansard to undertake a royal settlement at Versailles, then an insignificant hunting château of Louis XIII, some ten miles southwest of Paris.[2] Here the Sun King created an enormous palace and all the lesser buildings, parks, recreation grounds, and other necessary impedimenta for the most pretentious court in Europe. Thirty thousand soldiers were needed to work upon the aqueducts and other channels

[1] Many Protestants were lost to France when Alsace was seized by Germany in 1871. These, of course, reverted to reinforce French Protestantism in 1918.

[2] The royal residence was not ready for occupancy until 1682, and not actually completed until 1695.

THE CHÂTEAU OF VERSAILLES BEFORE THE END OF THE SEVENTEENTH CENTURY

in France, although she never was openly put forward as the royal consort, and exercised her great influence very discreetly behind the scenes. Thanks to her tactful efforts there is little doubt that Louis became less luxurious and immoral, and that an atmosphere of religion, if not of genuine decency, overspread the court in the last two decades of the reign. There were other reasons, however, for this quieting change. France had been plunged into two very unhappy wars.

After the peace of Nimwegen, Louis had gone to no pains to conciliate his rivals. In 1681, in a time of international quiet, he had seized the "free-city" of Strasbourg, to the no great anguish of the inhabitants, it is true, but to the enraging of its nominal overlord, the Emperor of Austria. In 1688 he quarreled so bitterly with Pope Innocent XI over various issues, but especially over the Pope's right to "invest" the Prince-Bishop of Cologne, that the Holy Father was willing to wish fair fortune to William of Orange, the champion of Protestantism, when that potentate went from Holland to England, overthrew the Catholic James II (Louis's ally and co-worker for tyranny), and became William III of England. In this year another great war blazed up. Louis's ambitions seemed to know no bounds. He had enraged every Protestant Power by his treatment of the Huguenots. He had almost equally offended the Catholic States by his bullying treatment of Innocent XI. Austria, with most of the lesser German States, Holland, Spain, England (now under William), and Savoy (Northwestern Italy), all joined in a mighty coalition against the common danger.

This war, waged against Louis by the "League of Augsburg," was even less interesting than the one that preceded it. England was now definitely against France. Her navy, plus that of Holland, gave the coalition the control of the seas, but Louis tried to strike back at his rivals by giving his unwilling guest, the exiled James II, an armament and an army, with which to reduce Ireland as a preliminary to recovering England.

James landed in Ireland and seized the greater part of that oft-afflicted island, but in 1690 all his hopes were blasted by a crushing defeat at the hands of William in the battle of the Boyne. Soon James was back in France, thrusting himself again upon the hospitality of Louis.

On the Continent the war was bloody and indecisive. Most of the fighting was in luckless Belgium, for all the centuries the battle-ground of Frenchman and German. Louis's general, Luxembourg, as a rule proved more than a match for William who led the armies of the coalition, and in 1693 the French King himself joined his own host and confronted his great rival close to Louvain. William had barely fifty thousand men and the French nearly one hundred thousand. It was in their power to force a decisive battle. Luxembourg is said to have gone down on his knees while begging the King to strike a great blow, but Louis declared himself contented with the results of the campaign and returned to Versailles. Various reasons could be given for his decision, but the real fact seems to have been that the Grand Monarch feared, despite the apparent odds in his favor, that something might slip and his splendor be compromised by a defeat. He seems never to have played the general again, but a similar opportunity for a great victory was never given to his various lieutenants.

Peace came in 1697. Louis had had the advantage in perhaps a majority of the sieges and battles on the Continent, although he had been defeated in Ireland and on the sea.[1] French military prestige had not been shaken, although it was now evident that the King could not carry off so many successes as in the days of Turenne. But two factors disposed Louis strongly to peace. His ministers could not conceal from him that France was now suffering terribly from taxation and commercial prostration and must not fight on indefinitely. Also every day increased the likelihood of the wretched Charles II of Spain dying without

[1] Particularly the French lost a decisive naval battle off Cape La Hogue (on the Breton coast) in 1692.

direct heirs. It was very needful for Louis to clear up all his former disputes in order that he might be free to protect what he considered the interests of his dynasty, in case the huge, lumbering Spanish Empire were suddenly dissolved. The war was therefore wound up by the Treaty of Ryswick. Louis XIV was very conciliatory. He recognized William III as King of England, thus leaving the exiled James II in the cold. He restored nearly all the Belgian and German cities he had seized since 1678, although retaining Strasbourg. He made various concessions to Holland. It was, in short, by no means the kind of a treaty the Great Monarch might have been expected to make, but the facts were that he was intensely interested in the fate of the Spanish Empire, and expected to win for his family at least several rich provinces if not the throne of Philip II itself.

Peace thus came in 1697. France sorely needed a long rest, with an economical government by a Sully or a Colbert. She was to have fitful quiet for four years, and then twelve years of a new grueling, exhausting, and utterly disastrous war.

Few matters are less easy to explain briefly and clearly than how Louis XIV had a discussable claim for his sons to the throne of that selfsame Spanish kingdom with which he had spent so much of his reign in hostilities. It is one of the miseries of monarchy, that under the principles of hereditary succession empires can be handed about or split up and parceled out, like an estate of farms or dwellings among a number of distant and quarreling heirs. In all the bloody debate which was to rack Europe the obvious question, "Which ruler was capable of doing the most good to the Spanish people?" seems never to have been discussed. The Spaniards themselves appear to have been so despot-ridden that at first they hardly expressed a wish in the matter; their only national desire apparently was to have the great dominions of Charles V and Philip II kept intact and undivided. What manner of man might be their personal master hardly troubled the most intelligent grandee.

RIVAL HEIRS TO THE SPANISH THRONE 189

Out of the great snarl of diplomacy preceding this execrable "War of the Spanish Succession," the following bare facts emerge:

1. Charles II of Spain, a prince feeble alike in body and intellect, was without children, and his nearest direct heirs were the sons of Castilian princesses, especially Louis XIV and the Emperor Leopold of Austria, each of whom in their turn had married a Spanish infanta. Each of these ambitious rival potentates had thus a good chance of doubling his realm, if only the other Powers would stand aloof.

2. For either France or Austria to get such a vast increase of power as would be implied by taking over all the Spanish dominions was sure to be resisted to the death by all the rest of Europe. Schemes were therefore entertained for a parceling-out of Charles's dominions; for example, another less formidable claimant, a Prince of Bavaria, was to have Spain, but the Milanese province in Italy was to go to Austria, and Naples and Sicily to the Dauphin, the son of Louis XIV, etc. This was (according to the notions of the day) a fair division of the inheritance. Unfortunately in 1699 the Bavarian Prince died, and all the ambassadors at the rival courts had to resume their long interviews and hurried correspondence.

3. Louis still hesitated to claim all of Spain's dominions for his sons (pressing for their mother's alleged rights).[1] He had the good sense to realize that France could ill afford a great war to the death, and he therefore negotiated with his old rival William III of England. It was agreed that Spain itself was to go to an Austrian archduke, but that other territories, somewhat larger than previously agreed upon, especially including Lorraine, were to be assigned to the Dauphin of France.

4. Charles was terribly angered, fool and weakling that he was, to hear that his dominions were being thus portioned out while he was still living. His Spanish pride demanded that his vast

---

[1] The non-payment of her dowry was alleged to have cancelled her renunciation of rights to the throne. See p. 149.

territories should still be kept intact. Acting as if the empire that embraced Spain, Belgium, much of Italy, the Philippine Islands, and most of South America, could be treated like a private country-seat, he determined to make a will. There was a great contest and infinite intriguing between the Austrian and French Ambassadors at Madrid. The French Envoy was far more clever. He won over the dying king's confessor and other powerful ecclesiastics, who worked on their superstitious master. In 1700, Charles II made a will giving his entire dominions to Philip, Duke of Anjou, Louis's second grandson.[1] In less than a month this utterly incompetent king was dead, leaving a heritage of disasters for all Europe.

5. Louis was faced with an overwhelming temptation. He had feared that if Charles made a will, it would be in favor of Austria, hence his willingness to compromise. Lo! the whole Spanish Empire was proffered to his own grandson. The King called a solemn privy council at Versailles. Should the treaty just made with the other Powers be kept? There were various considerations, of course, suggested to palliate the charge of bad faith against France. On November 16, 1700, a great levee was held at Versailles. The courtiers gathered eagerly when the great doors of the King's chambers were thrown open, and the now aged monarch emerged leaning on Philip, his second grandson: "Gentlemen," spoke Louis, "behold the King of Spain!"

Philip was promptly received by his new Spanish subjects who were glad to have the young monarch's mighty grandsire guarantee to him the integrity of his dominions. There was, of course, one cry of rage from Austria, from Holland, and presently from England. It was firmly believed, erroneously as it turned out, that Spain was about to become hopelessly subject to France, thanks now to the kinship of the neighboring monarchs. A great war was from the outset inevitable.

[1] The Spanish Empire was not given to the Dauphin, or to the elder grandson, because the Spaniards did not wish the same man to be king both of France and of Spain. It was generally believed, however, that Spain would become completely subservient to French influences.

WAR OF THE SPANISH SUCCESSION 191

Louis may have consulted his own greatness when he thus treated a solemn treaty as a "scrap of paper." He certainly ignored with studied deliberation the happiness of France. The French nation had not the slightest interest as to who might reign at Madrid, provided Spain continued a weak, unaggressive power — as under *any* ruler she was very sure to do. For the glory of Louis's family and the interest of one of his grandsons, Frenchmen were called upon to engage in an utterly exhausting general war. The Spaniards were now, indeed, their nominal allies, but were allies who demanded much and who gave little. The main burden fell on France alone.

In 1701 began the war of the "Grand Alliance" (England, Holland, Austria, the German States, and Portugal) against France and Spain. The Elector of Bavaria was on Louis's side, his only important ally, indeed, except his own grandson. William III, the King's old and implacable foe, died in 1702, but Queen Anne, his sister-in-law, continued the war for England. And now it was that the numbing effects of the Grand Monarch's despotism began to be painfully evident. The finances, already in a slough of despond, were abandoned to very incompetent ministers. The army absolutely lacked first-class generals. Turenne had left no real successor. On the other hand, the enemies of France for the first time found two really great leaders, the Duke of Marlborough, a man of despicable personality, but possibly the ablest Briton who ever commanded an army,[1] and Prince Eugène, the highly capable chieftain of the hosts of Austria. Marlborough and Eugène, unlike many "allied" generals, usually worked together in confidence and harmony. Before their united attack France was destined to go down to humiliation.

The annals of this long War of the Spanish Succession (1701–13) are needless to trace. There was fighting in Italy and much

[1] Of course Cromwell was an infinitely greater as well as better statesman than Marlborough, but it may be doubted if he was quite equal to the wily Duke considered merely as a military leader. In any case Marlborough was in command of much larger masses of troops in battle.

fighting in Spain, but once more the main collisions were in Germany and Belgium. In 1704 Marlborough and Eugène, having skillfully united their forces, gave battle to the French and Bavarians under Marshal Tallard and the Bavarian Elector at Blenheim in South Germany near Augsburg. The French fought bravely, but Marlborough's cavalry broke their line, and presently all was lost. Tallard himself was taken prisoner, and all Germany east of the Rhine was lost to Louis. There had not been such an utter disaster to France since the battle of Pavia.[1]

Campaigning was still very deliberate, even when it was not unmercifully slow. The next decisive stroke came in 1706. Marlborough here forced a pitched battle on Marshal Villeroi at Ramillies, near Namur, in Belgium. The French were not merely beaten, but routed. They were then cleared out of nearly all of Belgium, and only great exertions saved French soil itself from invasion. The humiliation of Louis was extreme. So far from winning the war, he was now hopelessly on the defensive.

The King, however, held his ground manfully even when every day brought new tidings of ill. He had no word of reproach for brave if unsuccessful generals. "Monsieur le maréchal," said he to the elderly Villeroi, when the latter appeared at court after Ramillies, "at our age one is no longer fortunate!" In 1708 the French lost another great battle at Oudenarde; the kingdom itself was invaded. Louis doffed his pride, and for the sake of his people, of whose miseries he was at length becoming conscious, he asked for peace. Had his foes been reasonable the war would have ended speedily, but although Louis was willing to leave Philip in Spain to fight for himself, he refused to send a French army to drive him from a throne where the Spaniards were anxious to keep him. "Since I *must* make war," declared Louis, "I would rather fight my enemies than my children."

For the first time in his reign Louis condescended to make a

[1] See p. 118.

THE TREATY OF UTRECHT

public appeal to rally to save sovereign and native land from humiliation and invasion. The appeal was not in vain. Volunteers streamed into the army. In 1709, at Malplaquet, although the allies won a technical victory, the battle was practically a draw. There was no longer danger of a general collapse of the French armies; and in the meantime events were working somewhat in Louis's favor. It was becoming very evident that the Spaniards would never endure the Austrian Archduke whom the allies were trying to thrust upon them. In England also Queen Anne was falling out with the Whig (pro-war) faction which had been Marlborough's mainstay, and was going over to his pacifistic Tory enemies. Englishmen also realized that if Philip remained in Spain, he was not likely to be subservient to France, and they were not anxious to continue fighting merely to aggrandize Austria.

Negotiations began in 1711, but the main treaty was not signed at Utrecht until 1713, and that with Austria at Rastadt until 1714. Considering his great defeats Louis did not lose as much as might have been expected. He retained Strasbourg, which earlier in the war he had seemed likely to lose, although he had to cede Newfoundland and Acadia (Nova Scotia) in America to England, and to grant the English also a favorable commercial treaty. What the war really effected was the breakup of the European dominions of Spain. Belgium, Milan, and Naples all passed for the moment to Austria, and Sicily to the Prince of Savoy; while Gibraltar, seized in this war by the English, was duly retained by them. So ended a struggle that by a little good faith and tactful policy on the part of Louis could have been readily avoided. The finances of France were in utter confusion. In 1683 her indirect taxes had brought in 118,000,000 livres: in 1714 they had fallen to 46,000,000. All this told a story of commercial and industrial prostration, and of widespread hardship and famine for the lower classes. The glory of the Grand Monarch had been sadly dimmed by these long sufferings inflicted upon his people.

Louis XIV, it must be said, bore his disasters more nobly than he had his prosperity. He met ill-fortune with dignity and without complaining. His last years were personally very sad. All the great administrators who had contributed to the splendors of his early reign were dead. His grandeur had left him without true friends. In 1711 the Dauphin died; then one member after another of the royal family was stricken as if by some relentless curse upon the dynasty. In 1715 the King found himself nearing his end with his nearest heir his great-grandson, the Duke of Anjou, a child of only five years. The unavoidable regency would have to go to the King's nephew, the Duke of Orléans, a man for whom Louis had profound personal dislike.

On September 1, 1715, the Sun King, no longer dazzling Europe as of old, departed forever. In his last moments he seems to have realized many of his errors, and his dying words were not without grandeur. "Why weep?" he said to his domestics in tears; "do you think me immortal?" And then he commanded that his little great-grandson, the boy about to become Louis XV, should be brought to the bedside. "You are soon to be King of a great realm," spoke the dying monarch. "What I commend most earnestly to you is never to forget the obligations you owe to God. Remember that to Him you owe all that you are. Try to keep peace with your neighbors. I have been too fond of war: do not imitate me in that, or in my too great expenditure."

Louis XIV died at the age of seventy-seven, having reigned seventy-two years. There were in France many white-haired men who had never known any other king. His passing seemed to be the withdrawal of one of the hitherto immutable things in the Universe. "*God alone is great,* my brothers," Massillon, the famous court preacher, had need to say at the beginning of his funeral oration. Louis had raised his realm at one time to a pinnacle of glory, but all he had in the end added to France, in return for the treasure and blood poured out in his behalf, were a part of Flanders, Franche-Comté, Strasbourg, and a few lesser cities. His death marked the close of a distinct epoch in European history.

"In spite of his faults," wrote Guizot a century and a half later, "and his numerous and culpable errors, Louis XIV had lived and died like a king. The slow and grievous agony of olden France was about to begin."

CHAPTER XI
THE WANE OF THE OLD MONARCHY

Louis XIV had enjoyed an unprecedentedly long reign. His successor, Louis XV, was to enjoy one almost equally long. He occupied the throne of France from 1715 to 1774. These two kings between them covered a decidedly wide span in the world's history. When the earlier of them was proclaimed, the first Puritan settlements were just fairly taking root in New England. When the second of them reached his dishonored end, the British colonies in North America were almost in the very act of organizing that armed resistance which was to lead straight to the battle-smoke of Lexington, Concord, and Bunker Hill. It is the transition from the age of Charles I and of Cromwell to that of Franklin, George Washington, and the Declaration of Independence. Much water surely had run through the nation's mills!

During all the long reign of Louis XV there were to be no important changes in the system of government for France. Wars there were to be, but they were to change the European boundaries of the kingdom very little, though they were to cost her most of her colonies and bring her grief and not glory. The epoch was not to be one of any great outward strokes of public policy, but of a gradual intellectual and social change, which, radiating from France, was to affect the philosophy and cultural life of all Europe, and then, passing at the ripe moment from the realm of theory to that of action, was to produce the greatest political explosion the world has so far known — the French Revolution, a revolution which affected by no means only France, but all civilized Europe.

The domestic annals of the reign of Louis XV are seldom significant. The old monarchy seems to stand as before; there is a semi-divine king with the solemn *levers* and cult of royalty, and Versailles with all its pomp and circumstance; but the master, Louis XIV, who, with all his faults, knew how to put on genuine majesty, is no longer there. The splendors become tawdry; the ceremonial hollow; and men come to recognize ever more clearly that instead of worshiping a god they are only bowing before an idol. At length the pretense wears thin. The Old Régime is then approaching ruin.

Probably the march of events would then, in any case, have ultimately destroyed the prestige and authority of the "Lieutenant of God" such as Louis XIV felt himself to be. But the process was assuredly intensified and hastened by the wretched personality of the new King. The Grand Monarch, despite his sins, knew how to look and to play his part. His great-grandson did everything possible to destroy the "divinity which doth hedge a king," not merely by the evils of his private life, but by his utter lack of dignity, his unabashed frivolity, and his gross and notorious neglect of public business. No man was ever a more dangerous if unconscious foe to autocracy than this very absolute Louis XV.

The new King was only five years old, when amid an awful hush the French courtiers were told that "Louis the Great" had passed away. A regency was of course indispensable, and the first Prince of the Blood was Philip of Orléans. The late King had left a will carefully designed to hamper this magnate whom Louis XIV had disliked, but Philip promptly swept the document aside, aided in his purpose by the Parlement of Paris, glad to assert its authority now that its great master was gone forever. The last years of the late reign had been spent in an atmosphere of piety and even of a kind of asceticism, as Louis XIV outgrew his youthful dissipations. Instantly now the restraining hand was relaxed. All France breathed easier. The Regent hardly pretended to be a pious Catholic. He is said to have celebrated Good Friday with an eleborate feast and revel. Everywhere there was a letting-down of old barriers and prohibitions. The oppressed Protestants lifted their heads a little. There were some attempts to reform the finances. A number of royal prisoners were let out of their dungeons. It was, in short, a general period of mental, moral, and political relaxation. France was learning to live her life without the oppressive supervision of her long-time autocrat.[1]

Philip of Orléans was a debauchee, but he was no fool. He was on bad terms with his kinsman, the King of Spain, and therefore he leaned to friendship with England. France needed rest from wars, and down to 1733 she was, for all practical purposes, given conditions of prosperous peace. The Regent had as his main confidant and Prime Minister Cardinal Dubois, a man of low birth and equally low character, who had nothing sacred about him but his red robe,[2] but who was, like his patron,

---

[1] A famous episode in the Regency was the attempt at a financial revolution by John Law. The latter was a clever Scotchman, half-charlatan, half-financier, who gained the favor of the Regent by his financial proposals, and by various successful private banking ventures in 1717. In 1718 he was allowed to open a "Royal Bank," with practically the entire credit of the State behind it. Supplementing the bank was a marvelous "Mississippi Company" for exploiting the newly acquired colony of Louisiana. The shares in this company (which accomplished little that was practical with its vast capital) were soon manipulated to enormous values. Speculation convulsed the French financial world. At the same time the Government was paying off its obligations with notes of the bank, which were issued recklessly, and without the slightest sound system behind them.

In 1719 all classes of Frenchmen seemed plunged into stock-jobbing. A tailor was reported to have made 70,000,000 livres; thus beating out the Duc de Bourbon who, with his mother, had to be content with 60,000,000. The Regent speculated himself, along with the meanest upstarts.

By the end of 1719 the Bank had issued over three billion livres of notes, more than four times the entire specie in France. Prudent persons began to withdraw their deposits, or to sell their shares and turn them into solid wealth — lands, gold, jewels, etc. Law vainly struggled by desperate expedients to head off the inevitable crash, but he fled the kingdom in 1720 an impoverished man. The speculators who hung on too long were of course ruined also. The net result of the whole adventure (besides many broken fortunes) was the addition of some $2,500,000 to the annual interest on the public debt. The Regent was naturally left a sadder and wiser ruler, after this lesson in "high finance."

[2] Saint-Simon, who hated him, tartly says, "All vice, perfidy, avarice, debauchery, ambition, and the basest flattery, struggled in him for the mastery."

clever and not without insight into what France required. It was therefore not at all as calamitous an epoch for the country as the personal character of its rulers might have indicated. In 1723 Louis XV was declared of legal age, although only thirteen. Orléans and Dubois expected to retain their essential power, for a boy of thirteen cannot actually govern, but both of these very equivocal men died in that same year.

After a brief interval the young King entrusted the management of affairs to another adroit churchman, the Cardinal Fleury; a personage of considerably superior quality to Dubois, and one who rejoiced in a singular piece of good fortune. He was one of the *very* few individuals for whom Louis XV maintained a real affection. So long as he lived, Fleury retained office, and he consistently favored peace and kept out of wild-goose foreign adventures. Diplomatic events were too strong for him at times. Twice he had to see France drift into serious hostilities,[1] but at least the faults of the aggressor were not his. According to his light, and so far as his master let him have the power, he tried to reorganize the state finances and to do away with abuses which seemed to have become inveterate. In 1738 there was an event rare in the annals of the Old Régime. The royal finances balanced. It was the first time since 1672, in the days of Colbert, that a year had closed without a deficit. There was not to be another such year in France till the days of Napoleon Bonaparte. In 1743 the aged Fleury died. Henceforth in name at least Louis XV governed for himself.

France was still passionately attached to its monarchy, which seemed to sum up the glory of the country. Frenchmen taunted Englishmen with having murdered their king, Charles I — no such stain rested on the annals of "the Great Nation!" Louis XV was, for the first part of his reign, the recipient of an amount of popularity and affection which nothing in his character could warrant. "Louis the Well-Beloved" his subjects styled him. When, in 1744, he lay sick at Metz, all Paris seemed

[1] The War of the Polish Succession, 1733-35; the War of the Austrian Succession, 1740-48.

rushing to the churches to say prayers for his recovery. In the chapel of Notre Dame alone six thousand masses were required by the people in his behalf. Toward the end of his reign this popularity ceased completely, but there was never an end to the flattery and lip-service before the King's face.

Louis XV was, indeed, utterly unfortunate in his childhood and in his education. He was first left an orphan, then he became a monarch at five. His tutors taught him to bow and to dance gracefully, and to carry his part at court functions; otherwise they left him profoundly ignorant of everything that pertained to his great-grandfather's "profession of king." The young boy was filled with extreme notions of his own irresponsibility and importance. "Sire, all these people are yours!" said his tutor, the supple old Marshal de Villeroy, when from a balcony the King saw thousands of Parisians gathered to catch sight of him. The King was personally handsome: he was (when he chose to amuse himself by thinking) not without a fair amount of intelligence; but there is universal testimony to his selfishness, sensuality, and brutality. Said Choiseul (who served him later in the reign as a high minister), "He was a man without love, without spirit, liking the evil as children like to torment dumb animals, and having the faults of the vilest and most sordid." It is probable that he realized that all was not well in the Government, and that the whole State was drifting toward calamity. Deliberately he remained inactive — reforms would require unpleasant exertions, and as he remarked with iniquitous cynicism, "The machine [of government] will last through my time!" Louis XIV had, at least, always devoted weary hours to all the minutiæ of state policy. His successor's ministers counted themselves lucky if their master could spare them half an hour per day for serious business. Hunting — of which he was very fond — chatter with his favorites, drinking coffee in the apartments of his daughters, reading the reports of the secret police, and going through private correspondence which had been intercepted by his agents, consumed most of his time — when he was not indulging in pleasures ultra-sensual. Possessing all the world, this king could really enjoy nothing. "From youth to age the King was bored. He wearied of his throne, his court, and of himself: he was indifferent to all things and unconcerned as to the weal or the woe of his people, or of any living person."

All through the reign of this unworthiest of monarchs the royal prerogative seemed absolutely untouched. The fortunate ecclesiastics who were invited to preach before royalty in the chapel in Versailles exhausted their ingenuity in what was technically known as "the complement." Said one preacher in 1742, "The Lord has rendered Your Majesty the support of kingdoms and empires, the subject of universal admiration, the beloved of his people, the delight of the court, the terror of his enemies; yet all this will but raise your great soul above what is perishable and lead you to embrace virtue and to aspire to universal beatitude." Louis's own theories of his power would have rejoiced his great-grandfather. He wrote in 1766, ten years before the American Declaration of Independence: "In my person alone is the sovereign authority. Legislative power belongs to me alone. Public order emanates from me. I am its supreme guardian."

Louis was entirely wrong in his assertions of autocratic independence. The most powerful personage in France was by no means always himself, but was very often the woman he chose to take as his chief mistress. The King's life was vile; his concubines numerous enough for a Solomon; but there was usually *one* female whom he chose to honor above all others and to allow to interfere freely in the public destinies of France. From 1745 to 1764 this woman was Jeanne Poisson, a clever, merry, artistic bourgeoise, whom Louis XV made famous under the title of the Marquise de Pompadour. She lived at Versailles, and everybody recognized her high position and honored her accordingly. She made and unmade ministers, gave or withdrew the command of armies. Great state treaties were discussed in her boudoir. It was thanks to her, very largely, that France threw over her old alliance with Prussia, made league with her ancient foe Austria, and embarked on the utterly disastrous Seven Years' War. She was not without refined tastes, and gave to Voltaire and other prominent men of letters a modest amount of patronage. No ordinary woman, indeed, could have maintained the ascendancy which she did over a creature like Louis XV down to the very time of her death; but it was useless to look to such an uncrowned queen for any wise policy for France. Her whole aim was to use the State to reward her favorites, to pay off her grudges, to gratify her whims, and to confirm her hold on the King. Obsequiousness to her interests was a surer passport to high office than great abilities and years of faithful public service. The treasury to her and her minions was not a trust, but an opportunity. Such was the woman to whom Providence consigned the destinies of France in years when the national enemies were to be led by Frederick the Great of Prussia and the elder Pitt (Chatham) of England. Not wrongly did the French people declare her to be the author of their public woes and execrate her name before she died.

After she departed, Louis presently (1769) consoled himself with another "first" mistress, a woman of much coarser grain, the notorious Countess du Barry. She was little better than a handsome prostitute, selfish and brazen, on whom the now senile old King squandered his wealth and affection. One of the first acts of the next reign was to dismiss this woman from court, but her evil memory was not to be forgotten. In 1793, when the Revolution was running its course and the guillotine was very busy, the Jacobins arrested her, revived old scandals, and sent her to the scaffold. They slew more innocent victims.

With such a king and such female dictators the only ministers who could keep office for long were those who made it their first object to serve the royal pleasures, their second, possibly, to benefit the State. Not all of the fifteen of Louis's ministers were hopelessly mediocre men. The King could make intelligent choices when he tried, and the Pompadour also understood the practical advantages of having things go well rather than go ill; but no minister could count on any consistent support in a given policy, much less on anything but opposition if he undertook any radical reform; and as a matter of fact France became involved in two serious wars, the first expensive and indecisive, the second expensive and absolutely calamitous, which between them made anything like a firm home policy impossible. As for "economies" the very word was hateful to Louis XV. Were not the revenues a synonym for the privy purse of an absolute monarch? "When you speak to His Majesty about economy and retrenching court expenses," ruefully wrote d'Argenson, "he turns his back on the ministers who talk to him!" The expenses of the royal court ate up a calamitously large percentage of the entire national revenues. The Pompadour seems to have enjoyed alone the personal spending of about $1,000,000 per year. The King was very fond of fireworks displays. On these nearly $1,000,000 was literally "burned up" in 1751. Even in times of peace there lacked funds to pay the army, while the salaries of the officers were in chronic arrears. Always the treasury receipts were being "anticipated"; always, after Fleury, there was a deficit; always borrowing was resorted to as an ordinary source of public income. The King was told all these things and cynically ignored them: "The only way to pay these debts is to declare bankruptcy," he coolly remarked — and continued to send in his sight drafts on the treasury.

The external history of France in this long, bad reign is largely summed up in two wars. Neither of these wars was quite so wantonly provoked as that of the Spanish Succession; but both could have been avoided by firm, peace-loving diplomacy.

In 1740 the Emperor of Austria, Charles VI, died without a son. Could a daughter, Maria Theresa, inherit all that huge conglomerate of peoples even then ruled by the German Hapsburgs? Instantly every other covetous Power began scheming to dismember her dominions. France supported the claims of Frederick II of Prussia to the great province of Silesia. Prussia then seemed a very young and feeble kingdom, quite useful to France as an agent for humiliating and tearing to pieces her old Austrian rival. Louis XV plunged into this war wholly unprovoked by Maria Theresa, and against the advice of his shrewd old minister Fleury. The war soon took on a wide scope. Maria Theresa resisted stoutly. England came to her aid, attacked France by sea and sent armies to the Continent. Louis had indeed the good fortune to find in Marshal Saxe a really competent general. In 1745 he won a famous and hard-fought battle at Fontenoy in Belgium over the allied Dutch and English. It was a combat conducted with chivalrous bravery on both sides,[1] and the result reflected great credit upon the victors, but Louis XV lacked the energy to follow up such a success. Frederick having gained Silesia was anxious to drop the war, and almost everywhere else Maria Theresa, the Austrian Empress-Queen, was holding her own. In 1748 peace was signed at Aix-la-Chapelle. Each side gave up all its more important conquests, save only Silesia which was kept by Prussia. The French had overrun much of Belgium, but Louis made no serious attempts to use these conquests to get better terms for France. In the meantime the English navy had nearly ruined the commerce of her great rival and driven her fleet from the seas. This war therefore brought nothing to Louis XV and his subjects except some glorious but useless victories, economic prostration, and a debt increased by the equivalent of nearly $600,000,000. The next war was to bring things even worse.

In 1750, despite governmental torpor and blundering, France

[1] It was in this battle that when the French had advanced to within fifty feet of the British line, Lord Hay stepped in front of his regiment, pulled off his hat to the French officers (who promptly returned his salute), and said courteously, "Tell your men to fire." "No," replied the Comte d'Auteroche, with equal politeness, "we never fire first." Such sometimes were the usages of war rather long before the days of Hindenburg and Ludendorff!

seemed on the point of possessing a great colonial empire. The story of her attempt to use Canada as the center for a great adventure to make all North America subject to Versailles rather than to London, is a tale reasonably familiar to every American who has studied the history of his own country. It is by no means so well understood how close the French were to becoming the lords of India at the very moment their voyageurs and traders were building blockhouses along the Great Lakes and the Mississippi. There can be no higher tribute to the inherent genius and capacity of the French people than this fact, that at a time when their Government seemed addicted to almost hopeless blundering, this same Government's subjects, not because of it, but *in spite of* it, seemed on the point of making their King the lord alike of North America and of the Golden East. This attempt, however, was now about to fail, and the failure was not entirely chargeable to the gross ineptitude of Louis XV, the Pompadour, and their selected minister.

It may be fairly granted that as a people the French have taken less readily to maritime hazards than have their English contemporaries, and that their talents have been less naval than military. Also, it may be granted, the French peasantry was held more firmly by home ties than the English, emigrated less readily, and were less open to the lure of foreign adventure. These facts, however, do not go to the root of the matter. The truth was that in the seventeenth century Louis XIV was throwing dice for the military supremacy of Europe. To humiliate and to cut short Austria, Spain, and Holland by land fighting demanded all his best energies, and in the end the task proved too great even for him. The efforts of Colbert had created for the Grand Monarch a navy able to compete on fairly equal terms with that of either England or Holland. The French ships were excellently designed, the sailors brave, the admirals skillful. When, however, the King's policy drove Holland and England into alliance, his sea power was simply overmatched. A great naval defeat at La Hogue (1692) had left the French hopelessly at a disadvantage upon the seas. They could not hope to regain the maritime leadership, unless their Government saw fit to resign nearly all its Continental ambitions and to devote the main energies of the nation to building and sustaining a navy and a great merchant marine. This neither Louis XIV nor Louis XV was ever able or willing to do.

French naval power, therefore, continued as merely second-rate. Holland was sinking in decline, but the English fleet was becoming ever more formidable. The French colonies as a consequence remained a risky experiment. However they might prosper, the link that bound them to the home country might be severed and each colony left isolated, and doomed to be reduced separately the moment the English asserted their mastery of the seas. Nevertheless, despite this second-class navy, the attempt to found a great colonial empire came very close to success.

In 1750 France held, besides Canada, Louisiana, and her great claims on the rest of North America, the rich "sugar" colony of Hayti (western San Domingo), Martinique and Guadeloupe in the West Indies, some trading posts on the Gold Coast of Africa, other posts in Madagascar, the prosperous islands of Mauritius and Reunion in the Indian Ocean, and a whole string of valuable trading posts on the coasts of India itself — these last so many potential starting-points for the actual conquest of India. Devoted Jesuit missionary, hardy trapper or trader, indomitable Norman or Breton seaman, clever and insinuating Bordeaux merchant — all these had coöperated first with Richelieu, then with Colbert, then with less prominent ministers to make the white flag of the Bourbon monarchy float over northern woods and tropic seas. It was a great heritage, and in the eighteenth century it was growing rapidly. The French traders, missionaries, and administrators were on the whole more flexible and adroit in conciliating the various types of natives they dealt with and ruled, than were their English rivals. The English colonial and commercial enterprise was, however, growing by leaps and bounds even faster than the French. Collision, humanly speaking, was inevitable. Had Louis XV and his ministers been statesmen, they would have recognized that there were only two things France might do: either (1) to keep out of every kind of land hostilities near home, and to concentrate the national wealth and energies upon creating a naval power fit to compete with the English: or (2) frankly to resign all schemes for colonial dominions, give up the seas to the English, and expect greatness for France solely as a land power. They did neither. They neglected the fleet, they mishandled their army, and they very naturally met with a great disaster.

The period between 1748 and 1756 was one of the most prosperous, economically, which France had ever known. All the port towns reported increased exports and imports. The sugar and coffee of the French Antilles were driving out the similar products of the English colonies. In the Turkish Levant, French commerce was likewise flourishing. It was, however, only a lull before a calamitous hurricane. Already in India an enormous opportunity was being frittered away. In 1740 the English and French alike had possessed a number of small "factories" or trading stations, mostly along the east coast of Hindustan. The English headquarters had been at Madras and Calcutta, the French at Pondicherry.[1] So long as the power of the Mogul Emperors had been formidable, both sets of European visitors had been content to pose as mere traders. But the Mogul Empire was now breaking up. The various nawabs (viceroys) and rajahs (petty princes) had been eager to put themselves under the protection of whichever foreign invader could give them the amplest guarantees against their rivals. Native troops (sepoys) were quite willing to fight under European orders, provided the Western leaders could have a small body of their own countrymen to stiffen their armies.

[1] Pondicherry was on the east coast of Hindustan, ninety miles southwest of Madras. The French still hold it.

In India the Governor of Pondicherry had been Dupleix, a man of remarkable adroitness and energy, very skillful in winning the allegiance of the natives. He never ceased dreaming dreams and seeing visions of a great Indian Empire governed by France. In 1746 the French had actually taken Madras from the English, but it had been handed back by the treaty of peace in 1748. Had Louis XV realized that in Dupleix he had a servant who might win for him the splendid crown of the Indies, and sustained him heartily, French and not English might at this day be the official language for three hundred million Hindus. But no such support was accorded the Governor. He made various blunders which impaired his power over the natives. In 1754 he was most foolishly recalled at the very moment when the English were finding in young Robert Clive the very conqueror and proconsul that Dupleix might have been had he been well seconded by his King. The natives were not slow to discover which of the European intruders seemed the more aggressive and successful power. In 1757 Clive was to win the Battle of Plassey, which immediately gave his country control of the great province of Bengal; and which ultimately determined the fate of mighty India. A new French governor had been sent out, the brave, incompetent Lally; who came too late to prevent Clive from getting complete ascendancy over the natives. France and England were now again at open war. Lally was defeated in a pitched battle at Wandewash (1760), Pondicherry was taken, and the whole chance for an Indian Empire escaped from the French forever. It was one of those chains of blunders and disasters which make world history.

Simultaneously another like chain of disasters was destroying "New France" in North America. The friction between the two mighty colonizing powers in the Great Lakes region and at the head waters of the Ohio had already become acute before formal war was declared. The French, thrusting out from Canada, had nominally preëmpted vast regions in the Northwest and the Mississippi Valley, hemming in the British seaboard colonies by their line of forts and trading posts. But the inherent weakness of the French colonial system was already evident. There had been a vast deal of tactless interference and unintelligent regulation of Canadian affairs from Versailles; and above all French peasants had been as a rule very loath to quit their ancestral farms in sunny Touraine or Champagne to settle in a cold and utterly primitive country a thousand leagues away. At this very moment when Canada was trying to extend its boundaries so as to cramp its British neighbors, it barely reckoned 90,000 inhabitants to its rivals' 1,200,000 or more.[1] Left to itself, therefore, Canada was bound to be cut off and destroyed, except as it was constantly sustained by men and supplies from France.

All this implied sea power and an intelligent policy at Versailles, things not to be expected in the days of Louis XV. The Government did, indeed, at the outset send to Canada an extremely able general, the Marquis of Montcalm, a leader of the best French type, also a small body of reliable regular troops to eke out the Indian allies and the Canadian militia; but from 1756 onward "New France" was practically left to shift for itself. No effective help was sent across the Atlantic, and superior British sea power was to throttle the French navy so effectively that a warship with the Bourbon colors was hardly able to show itself upon the great waters. In 1759 the battle of the Plains of Abraham, when Montcalm was slain gallantly fighting before Quebec, was to register a situation absolutely certain to have come to pass unless Louis XV made a great naval effort to relieve Canada — an effort under the circumstances simply impossible.

Formal war between England and France had been resumed in 1756. This was the once famous Seven Years' War, when by a reversal in alliance, Austria and Russia joined with the old foe

[1] Of course, too, the more enterprising and progressive character of most of the English settlers in America, compared with the extremely conservative Canadian *habitants*, was an additional handicap upon the French colony.

of the Hapsburgs, the Bourbon Monarchy itself, in an attack on the upstart power of Frederick of Prussia — a prince who had thus to fight three great Powers at once with only England for a powerful ally. Not the slightest good reason really existed for this reversal of all diplomatic traditions by Louis XV. He was under no obligations to Maria Theresa of Austria to recover for her the Silesian province which Frederick had seized earlier. Every sign pointed to a desperate struggle with England that would consume the full resources of France, but Kaunitz, the clever Austrian Ambassador to Versailles, had worked successfully on the Pompadour to incline her favorably to his mistress, Maria Theresa, and Frederick had earned the bitter wrath of the royal favorite by his pungent criticisms of her frivolities.[1]

In this war, although occasionally the French armies were sufficiently well led to live up to their old traditions, the national record was one of general incompetence and disaster. The Pompadour often took upon herself to name her favorites as generals. They were pitifully unequal to dealing with Frederick the Great, who ranks among the very first captains of modern times, barring only Napoleon Bonaparte. The French armies were wretchedly organized, munitioned, fed, and led into battle. If Frederick had possessed a greater kingdom, and if his Austrian and Russian enemies had been as incompetent as their ally, he would have been overwhelmingly victorious. As it was, with little more than financial and naval assistance from England, he fought the three greatest empires in Europe and held his own. In 1757 the French were not merely beaten but disgraced at Rossbach in Saxony, where the amazingly incapable Soubise, the nominee of the Pompadour, with 50,000 men was utterly routed by Frederick with 20,000. The French lost 7000

---

[1] Frederick's over-ready tongue won him potent enemies. He is alleged to have remarked that "*three old cats were governing Europe.*" The "old cats" were Maria Theresa of Austria, Elizabeth, Czarina of Russia, and the Pompadour, the left-handed ruler of France. This *bon mot* did not ingratiate him with these powerful felines!

prisoners and 63 cannon. It was as great a disaster as Blenheim and far less honorable.

In the maritime struggle with England the French were at first aided by the mediocrity of King George II's Minister, but in 1757 the power passed to the elder Pitt, one of the mightiest war ministers ever known to history. Against the genius of his leadership the appointees of the Court of Versailles had pitifully slight chance. In 1759 Quebec was lost; the battle of Quiberon Bay destroyed the remnant of French naval power; and, if Pitt had continued in office, it is likely he would have enforced conditions utterly ruinous upon France. As it was, in 1761 he was forced out of the Ministry by the new King, George III, but his work was largely done. In 1763, completely at the end of his power to save his colonies or to accomplish the scheme for destroying Frederick of Prussia, Louis XV assented to the Peace of Paris. It was one of the most humiliating documents ever signed by an heir to Philip Augustus. France ceded Canada to England and part of her holdings on the African coast; she received back, indeed, her small factories in India, but under conditions which condemned her to look on helplessly while her rivals rapidly extended their power over the Hindu natives. The war both by land and by sea had exhibited the entire incompetence, not merely of Louis XV, but of the whole system for which he stood, and the pride of the French nation had been wounded to the quick by the unprecedented defeats and losses. When Wolfe won the battle before Quebec he had not merely decided that North America was to speak not French but English; he struck a deadly blow at the prestige and very existence of the Old Régime in France.

But as Louis XV had wickedly remarked, the old order "lasted through his time." After the treaty of peace there was a reasonable recovery of commercial prosperity, while a really patriotic, though not great, Minister, Choiseul, devoted himself not ineffectively to rebuilding the fleet, and succeeded so well that in the next war the French navy was to be able practically to hold its own upon the seas. He also was successful in 1768 in purchasing the island of Corsica from the decrepit Republic of Genoa. The consequence of this was that in 1769 a certain infant there born, who was christened Napoleon by his parents, came into the world as a French citizen.[1] Various reforms were to be attempted in the judiciary [2] and other half-hearted efforts were made to bring about better things. The Government continued, however, in its evil courses. The Pompadour was dead, but Du Barry, her successor, was even viler. Choiseul refused to cringe to her, and she united with his other foes to work on the King to dismiss him. In 1770 he was deposed as minister and banished to his estates. From this time until the end of the reign France was ruled by unprincipled and supple courtiers, whose one object was to keep office by pleasing the senile King.

Louis XV continued in his debaucheries to the end. When threatened with illness he would vehemently profess his penitence ("because his sole religion consisted of a fear of hell") only to resume his old usages when health returned. Suddenly in May, 1774, he was smitten with smallpox, and Du Barry's power vanished abruptly on the 10th of that month when with "a mighty noise absolutely like thunder" a crowd of courtiers rushed down the great staircase at Versailles to announce to his grandson that Louis XV had gone to his long account.[3] The new rulers, Louis XVI and his wife, Marie Antoinette, fell on their knees at the tidings: "God help and protect us," they prayed aloud, "we are too young to reign!"

They had need of the prayer. No great nation was ever more

---

[1] Imagination breaks down when speculating on the destinies of Europe, if Choiseul's negotiations had broken down and the "Man from Corsica" had grown up as a humble Genoese subject.

[2] See p. 220.

[3] To the shame of the French Church this King received many eulogies. The Bishop of Arras declared: "I will not talk of the great achievements of this mighty king, his glory, his successes, his victories. A prince so dear to human hearts must have been according to God's heart." The Bishop of Alais more honorably spoke of the evil example which Louis XV had set before his people.

sorely in need of drastic reforms than was France in 1774; and for now over a generation there had been internal forces at work which might have warned any clear-sighted man that if her rulers could not give her reform they would themselves become the first victims of revolution.

CHAPTER XII
FRANCÉ THE HOMELAND OF NEW IDEAS

THE War of the Spanish Succession had blasted the dream of making France the physical dominator of Europe. The Seven Years' War had almost destroyed her claim to be the first single Power in Europe, and yet, by a most curious paradox, never was French influence, throughout the civilized world, more potent than during this evil, degenerate reign of Louis XV. There had scarcely been a like instance since the distant day when Athens, overpowered in arms by Philip and Alexander and their unpolished Macedonians, saw her language, her letters, her art, and her philosophy imposing themselves upon an intellectually conquered world.

In the eighteenth century French was the invariable language of the diplomatist and the statesman. Frederick the Great spent much of his public energies in fighting the King of France; he spent much of his private energies in writing decidedly mediocre French verses. The world had its fashions for wigs, silk breeches, and ladies' gowns dictated from Paris. French dancing-masters ruled every ballroom. French novels lay on every great lady's table. French was chattered in preference to Russian by the great boyars and princesses of Czarina Catherine's showy and wicked court at St. Petersburg. The habits and ceremonies of Versailles were likewise slavishly copied by all the pretentious little "Highnesses, Graces, and Serenities" who ruled over and afflicted the hundred petty states of Germany. Things were about the same in the insignificant courts of Italy. Every young English nobleman would try to spend a year in Paris and Versailles to learn the language and to acquire the indefinable polish of what were admittedly the "politest" people in the world.

This leadership of France was not merely confined to the realm of the dancing-master and the costume-maker, nor to the purveyors of *risqués* novels or vivacious comedies. A great intellectual contribution was being made to Civilization. A series of writers upon the most serious themes was coming forward, which was to dictate the thought of the nations. These writers were not to excel merely as literary artists. There was no Sophocles, no Cicero, no Shakespeare among them. Outside of France comparatively few save historical students read their works to-day; but in their generation they were to have an incalculable effect, first on all theories of physical science, moral philosophy, political science and government, and then upon the application of those theories to very practical life. "Liberty, equality, and fraternity," the great doctrine of the Revolution, was the direct product of ideas advanced by writers who in the days of Louis XV, frequented the fashionable salons, or were perhaps flung for a disagreeable interval into the Bastile.

It is also not quite correct to say that under this sinful monarch there was no change in the political life of France. On the contrary, there arose something which might be described in modern language as a regular "opposition party." This party came to center around the oft-discussed Parlement of Paris. After the unlucky wars of the Fronde the high law court of the capital had perforce been obliged to adhere pretty closely to merely legal business, and to refrain from political meddling. Louis XIV had been only sixteen when, probably at Mazarin's suggestion, he had appeared before that pretentious tribunal, "booted and spurred and with whip in hand, to tell the members roughly that he demanded an unquestioning obedience."[1] Under the weaker rule of the Regent Orléans and of Louis XV this corps of hereditary "noble" judges grasped eagerly for its old authority. Especially did it claim the right of refusing at

[1] Modern criticism has attacked the tradition that Louis XIV actually carried his riding-whip when he stalked before the Parlement. There is no doubt, however, that he read its members the severest kind of a lesson.

will to "register" (that is, enroll, promulgate, and put into effect) the royal edicts. This amounted to a veto upon the King's power of legislation, and the only method of overcoming the same was by means of a formal session called a "bed of justice," at which the King was present in person, where the monarch on his own direct authority commanded that the edicts should be registered.[1]

The Parlement of Paris was far from containing men of unselfish and progressive ideas. Its members were quite ready to defend all kinds of old abuses so long as those abuses were profitable to themselves and to their class. Quite as many worthy edicts were refused registration as iniquitous ones; but when all was said, here was *one* body that was not absolutely at the mercy of King and favorites; that could interpose a very modest constitutional opposition to royal autocracy; and that could be a focus for something like real political life. The Parlement, therefore, often commanded an attention and a popularity which it did not always deserve.

The latent friction between royalty and the Parlement expressed itself most characteristically in a struggle nominally centering about religion. As early as 1638, when Richelieu was lording it in France, a certain Catholic bishop, Jansenius, had died in Flanders. This prelate had written a theological work of wide acceptance in which he ventilated certain opinions about "grace" and "predestination." In the age of Louis XIV many distinguished Frenchmen had held these views, but they had awakened the angry criticism of the powerful Order of Jesuits. The matter had seemed to end when the Jansenist opinions were condemned as heretical and squinting toward Protestantism, first by Louis XIV, and then in 1712 more officially by the Pope. But the Jesuits, by their arrogance and intrusion into worldly affairs, as well as by their influence at court, had rendered themselves extraordinarily unpopular with the French legal classes and with the upper bourgeoisie. It was claimed, not

[1] See also p. 148, note.

without plausibility, that the Pope had only condemned the Jansenist doctrines because of extreme pressure from the Jesuits, and consequently a friendliness toward this very mild form of religious dissent became one of the methods of registering disapproval of the whole decadent political régime.

The adherents of Jansenism enjoyed all the advertising which comes from a spasmodic and very unpopular persecution. In 1732 it was claimed that miracles were being wrought at the tomb of a certain prominent Jansenist at the cemetery of Saint-Médard in Paris. The Archbishop of the city gravely attributed the alleged wonders to the Devil and induced the Government to stop the scandal by closing the cemetery. A satirical epigram was soon spread all over France —

"By order of the King : it is forbidden to God
To work miracles, in this place!"

The official clergy were ordered by their bishops to refuse the last sacraments, unless the dying man had accepted the Bull "Unigenitus" condemning Jansenism. Thence naturally arose scandals, contentions, bitterness, and finally lawsuits. The Parlement claimed that the much-disputed bull had never become legally part of the laws of France. Finally, in 1752, it ordered the Archbishop of Paris's excommunication of dissenters to be burned by the public hangman, seized his "temporalities," and issued an order, which American lawyers would call a "mandamus," commanding priests to administer the communion to the sick, even if suspected of Jansenism.

All theological issues had now been utterly lost in a grievously secular political broil. The King stood unequivocally committed to defend the Archbishop and the Bull "Unigenitus." How the case would have been handled by Louis XIV admits not an instant of doubt. But Louis XV had inherited only the Grand Monarch's formal prerogatives, not his masterful energy. He indeed ordered the Parlement to refrain from interfering with the clergy; then in 1753, when its members proved recalcitrant and proceeded to resign office by way of protest, he commanded them to be exiled by *lettres de cachet*, and talked of abolishing their court altogether and substituting a more subservient tribunal. But on the side of the Paris Parlement were all the lesser provincial Parlements and the entire legal body of France. The King recoiled before the evident popular support for the dissidents. The Parlement was reinstated after consenting to register a decree ordering silence on all religious matters, and in 1756 the Vatican tactfully intervened with conciliatory counsels. While, therefore, in theory, the decisions against the Jansenists still stood, the whole affair had wrought harm alike to the King, the clergy, and their Jesuit backers.

In this same year (1756) the Parlement protested again — this time on a very vital political matter, the right of the King to impose new taxes to meet the expenses of the war. It required a very solemn "bed of justice" to make the obstinate lawyers give way. Their motives were actually selfish. They feared lest they were in danger themselves of being exposed to taxation, but their attitude took on the color of patriotism. "We demand our rights," they declared in their protest, "only because they are the rights of the people." This was an utterance calculated to call the very ghost of Louis XIV in horror out of its grave.

A little later the Parlement was also destined to win an unequivocal victory. Its old enemies the Jesuits were losing alike their popularity, their piety, and worst of all their astuteness. They still felt secure in the friendship of the King, but at the critical moment the all-powerful Pompadour turned against them, and allowed them to go down in ruin.[1] The Jesuits had engaged extensively in trade in the West Indies. This decidedly secular occupation involved them in a bankruptcy proceeding which turned into a serious lawsuit that was brought before the Parlement of Paris (1760). The Parlement rejoiced in its

---

[1] The Jesuits had no cause to feel ashamed of the enmity of this woman. They had endeavored, with a zeal for good morals they did not always display, to get the King to dismiss his chief concubine.

QUARREL OF KING AND PARLEMENT

chance to investigate the whole nature and organization of the Jesuit Order, and under the cover of a judicial decision gave the opinion that the Jesuits as a body should be suppressed in France, as dangerous to the good of the realm, that their schools should be closed and their great property confiscated to the Crown (1764).[1] Pope Clement XIII vainly interceded in their behalf; so did the Queen, so did the Dauphin. All these dignitaries weighed far less with the King (with whom the final decision lay) than did the influence and enmity of the Pompadour. Besides, Louis XV was genuinely afraid of the Parlement, and did not wish to quarrel with it on what was to him no vital matter. In November, 1764 the once powerful Jesuit Order — the persecutor of heresy and of advanced opinions everywhere — was itself suppressed in France, and in 1774, largely at French instigation, it was to be temporarily suppressed by Pope Clement XIV throughout the entire Church.

The contest between royalty and Parlement, however, had only reached a truce. In 1770 there was again a bitter contest over the attempt of the King to interfere in an important trial then going on before the High Court. The Parlement loftily declared that "the exercise of absolute power, against the spirit and letter of the constitutional laws of France, revealed a design to change the form of government." Louis XV was a weakling, but some of his ministers were men of a certain bravery. When, early in 1771, most of the high judges resigned and closed their law court as a means of coercing the King, the latter struck back.

On the night of January 19, 1771, the royal musketeers routed all the Parlementarians out of their warm beds, commanding them to sign "yes" or "no" to the question, "Will you reënter the service of the King?" The tale is, that it was Du Barry who had worked Louis up to the striking point, by pointing to a portrait of Charles I of England and saying,

[1] The Jesuits had already been attacked in Portugal and expelled from that kingdom by the reforming Minister, Pombal (1759). The Jesuits were detested by many other branches of the Catholic clergy.

"*Your* Parlement will also strike off your head!" Most of the high judges refused to sign "yes"; and all the malcontents were at once sent into various places of exile. The provincial Parlements sustained the senior body. "You are King," warned the Parlement of Dijon, "by virtue of the law, and without the laws you have no right to reign." There was even talk of "the States General." But Louis XV had for once plucked up courage. The entire system of parlements, greater and lesser, was declared abolished, and in their place were set up various "Superior Councils" which would transact legal business quietly without meddling in politics. By the end of 1771 fully seven hundred French magistrates were in exile, and a great blow seemed struck at the main source of opposition.

This change lasted only till Louis XV was dead and Du Barry was in helpless banishment from court. The new judiciary had been absolutely unpopular and its members were very mediocre men. Public opinion clamored for a return of the Parlements, and Louis XVI, the inexperienced new King, was anxious to have as few enemies as possible. The old high judges were all summoned back and their old tribunals reëstablished. They were ordered to abstain from "fatuous opposition to the decrees of the Crown," but the future was to show that their temporary suppression had taught them no meekness. They had really been champions of privilege, not of liberty, but their quarrels with the monarchy had been so many deadly blows to the existence of the Old Régime.

The Parlement of Paris had been able to defy the "absolute" authority of the King because of a profound intellectual change which had penetrated the minds of nearly all the intelligent elements in Europe and especially in France. This change is best summed up by stating that educated men came in the eighteenth century to accept (in name at least) the guidance of "*reason*, that is to say the affirmation of truth, evident or demonstrated. Reason could not fail to be revolutionary, because it denied tradition and built on a *tabula rasa*. It seemed at first to be entirely disinterested, lofty and serene, but very soon it stooped to regard life, manners, and politics. Finding these *unreasonable*, it began to wage war against unreason, and became the philosophy of the eighteenth century." [1]

From 1517 down to say 1700, the efforts of human thought had been mainly directed to the attack or defense of the Catholic Church during the Protestant Reformation and all the struggles that came after it. By 1700 most of the Western world had settled down as either permanently Protestant or permanently Catholic. Neither by blows nor arguments could either side eliminate the other, and the zest of contest was therefore lost. Men were drifting away from the questions of admission to heaven or hell, and (even as in the Italian Renaissance) were reverting to the problems of this present world. The interest in natural science was intense, old mediæval notions were sloughed off, and the foundations were to be laid for nearly all the great achievements of the nineteenth and twentieth centuries; but the practical inventions and discoveries were to be often by Anglo-Saxons and not by Frenchmen. James Watt the Briton was to invent the steam engine. Benjamin Franklin the American was to demonstrate the connection of electricity and the lightning. Nevertheless, the French achievements are not to be slighted. Lavoisier (1743-94) was to lay many of the foundations of modern chemistry; and Buffon (1707-88), a man of enormous and curious learning, was to make notable contributions to the understanding of natural history, and was even to drive one of the wedges which led to the doctrine of evolution.

What the French writers of the eighteenth century excelled in was handling the literature of politics. For the first time in many centuries the relations of man to his government, the nature of that government, its claims to obedience and to mere existence, its various kinds of faults, and the expedients whereby

[1] Lavisse.

it might be made better, were to be subjected to a violent, penetrating, and extremely skillful scrutiny, and the results of that scrutiny were told in such a striking literary form that they received instant attention.[1] These writers "passed in review all the ideas hitherto accepted, criticized them, and in place of those which they judged vicious or false proposed new ones, which would serve as the basis for a general reorganization" of mankind.

It is needless to say that the instant the government and social organization of France was surveyed critically in the eighteenth century, the only question for a bold man of clear vision could be, "Which evil shall I *first* attack?" In government there was the absurdity of "divine right"; in society, the existence of outrageous "inequality"; in religion, a régime of abominable "intolerance." Everywhere also in minor matters there were relics of feudal barbarism, excessive and wrongful regulations and restrictions upon economic liberty — shackles, in short, on mind and on body repulsive to every intelligent, freedom-loving man. The precise evils of the Old Régime will be discussed a little later.[2] It is enough here to say its armor was utterly penetrable.

These critics had the incalculable advantage that they wrote in the most lucid, animated language in Europe. The great authors of Louis XIV had been anything but champions of liberty, but they had at least evolved from the French tongue a magnificent literary vehicle, in which it was easy — even when dealing with very sober themes — to be brilliant and almost impossible to be dull. Furthermore, French seemed then in a fair way to becoming a universal language for all Christendom. A book by Voltaire needed neither translator nor lexicon before it could be read by almost every cultivated Englishman, German, Italian, or Russian. This literature, therefore, though

[1] Of course there had been other very important writers on political science in other lands — for example, Machiavelli, Locke, etc. — but they had addressed only limited contemporary audiences and were by no means part of a great general literary movement among their countrymen.

[2] See pp. 243-67.

primarily for Frenchmen, was to win its way quickly through all the world.

It is far easier to summarize the causes and results of a war than of a great intellectual movement. Between 1730 and 1789 the literary activity of France was to be intense and Paris became "the brain of Europe"; nevertheless, the spirit of the age may be summed up in four words — Montesquieu, Voltaire, Rousseau, and the Encyclopædists. In them were to lie almost all of the Revolutionary law and the prophets.

Montesquieu (1689-1755) was a South Country nobleman, who became a "President" of the Parlement of Bordeaux. There was nothing of the revolutionist about this thoroughly worthy and responsible high magistrate. He was the least radical of the men we shall mention, but not the least to be responsible for pregnant ideas. In 1721 he wrote a brilliant satire, the "Persian Letters," which, under the guise of letters sent home by two Orientals traveling in France, forms a clever and really scathing criticism of the foibles and vices of the day. Subsequently he visited England, became acquainted with English leaders and institutions, and in 1748, after twenty years of meditation and composition, published his great work, "The Spirit of Laws," possibly the most important book on political science since Aristotle wrote his "Politics." Montesquieu was not a rabid iconoclast. He undertook to seek out the foundations for various types of laws and political institutions; he analyzes the different kinds of governments, so far as known in his day, and states their weaknesses and excellencies. He is bitter in his arraignment of "despotism," and although the most obvious type of despotism was found in the East — for example, in Turkey — he hardly conceals his opinion that France was a despotism also. He makes still less concealment of his admiration for the already well-developed constitutional liberties of England, which he pretty plainly commends to the French for a national example. Very calmly and deliberately also he attacked other evils of the day, such as religious intolerance (Protestants were still occasionally being executed in France) and slavery. The book produced a great effect "in a society which is sometimes described as wholly frivolous. In eighteen months there were twenty-two editions."

But Montesquieu was the mere forerunner before a more famous and loud-voiced prophet of the new liberalism. Not many persons to-day can realize the influence and prestige enjoyed in the second half of his life by François Voltaire.[1] Certainly no other writer in modern times received half of the honors showered upon this "prince of philosophers" by contemporaries. Kings were presently to be his correspondents and patrons, and to tremble at his sarcasms. The Pope in the Vatican was to dread him like a second Mohammed. He was, it is fair to say, the most terrible personal foe the Catholic Church ever encountered, barring only that very different champion, Martin Luther, and on the political side he was the most formidable enemy the Old Régime ever encountered, barring none. To-day only a sprinkling of Americans and probably not very many Frenchmen read even a twentieth of his voluminous writings, yet in his day a new book or pamphlet by Voltaire would be on every parlor table in Europe. He was, in short, a man of his age, and with the passing of his age his influence declined correspondingly, for he was, when all is said, a propagandist, not a literary artist; and the worst evils he attacked are to-day as a rule buried in the limbo of history.

Voltaire (1694–1778), be it noted, came of a good bourgeois family and was duly sent to school at a Jesuit seminary, to be given the preliminary education for the bar. He became disgusted alike with the life of a lawyer and with his sanctimonious professors. By 1717 he had fallen into evil courses, quarreled with his family, and got himself clapped into the Bastile for a violent lampoon on the Regent. He was not imprisoned long, but for some years he led a struggling existence, writing plays

[1] "Voltaire" was a name he assumed in 1718 when he began his literary career. His father's name was Arouet.

VOLTAIRE'S CRITICISM OF THE CHURCH

which had only slight success. Then finally he had a personal quarrel with a member of the powerful Rohan family; was flung once more into the Bastile, and when again released was banished to England (1726). This banishment was to cost the champions of the Old Régime sorely. Voltaire made the acquaintance of many English rationalists and advanced thinkers, and became steeped in the more destructive parts of Locke's philosophy.[1] When he came back to France in 1729, he had been equipped with a full battery of radical ideas about politics, philosophy, and religion, which his own versatile genius soon expanded, then used with terrific effect.

Voltaire had from the outset displayed a willingness to criticize Church and State, and to attack religious persecution as iniquitous and irrational. Now he became far more confessedly the champion of "reason" and "philosophy" as the true guides for intelligent men, as against "superstition," which it was clear enough was very concretely the Catholic Church. Christianity to Voltaire meant simply Catholicism,[2] and that too the grievously worldly and unspiritual Catholicism of the French Church.[3] How easy to hold up to ridicule a bishop who was clamoring for a new dragooning of the Huguenots, when the

---

[1] Any complete study of French political thought in the eighteenth century would have to take into account the influence of the theories and political philosophy of several famous English writers and thinkers. Locke (1632-1704), by his economic writings and his discussions of the basis and justification, etc., of governments, had an influence on French "liberals" which can hardly be overestimated. Another Englishman of far less steadiness and integrity than Locke, but who probably did much to modify French thought, was that brilliant non-moral free-lance — deist, philosopher, and political theorist — Viscount Bolingbroke (1678-1751).

The French students of these writers, more logical than Englishmen, and less fettered by the conservatism which is inherent in every Briton, took up the theories of their preceptors, expanded them, and gave them a new, brilliant, and ultimately startling dress, before which the grave and modest Locke at least would have recoiled in dismay.

[2] He never seems to have made a genuine attempt to study the better types of Protestantism, and it must be admitted that the Protestantism of his day had many weak joints in its armor.

[3] See pp. 256-259.

holy man himself enjoyed all the palaces, valets, and love-intrigues of a luxurious marquis! The Church was the cornerstone of all the traditionalism, mediævalism, intolerance, and political absolutism as it then existed in France. It defended the abuses of the monarchy, because the monarchy provided it with dungeons, fetters, and gallows to repress heresy, and also with revenues for its luxurious prelates. Therefore Voltaire turned loose his full batteries of ridicule, sarcasm, and direct criticism upon the Church. He was himself, he professed, not an atheist, but a "deist." To-day he would probably be found connected with some vague form of Unitarianism. Late in his life he was to fall out with the extremists who after attacking the Church were to attack the need of a deity also.

By almost every possible literary means Voltaire smote upon the old order, ecclesiastical and political. He had a long life and he was an astonishingly prolific writer. Satires, novels, epic poems, dramas all came from his pen, in unending succession. He wrote a "Treatise on Metaphysics," an historical sketch on "The Age of Louis XIV," *risqué* comediettas and also pompous tragedies. Soon after his death in 1778 there appeared a final edition of his works. It required *seventy* volumes. Voltaire was not a literary artist of the very first order, but he was a past-master of an extremely pungent style. His paragraphs cracked like a whip over the backs of hypocritical ecclesiastics and obscurantist defenders of old abuses. In their day many of his books and pamphlets were a delight to read. Even those who cringed and cried out at his attacks on themselves, were enchanted with his genius the moment he turned to attack some rival. Had he been living to-day he would doubtless have won fame as the editor of an incomparably audacious, widely read, hated, and popular newspaper.

This man's personal history cannot quite be ignored. His private-life gave no lessons in morality. After his return from exile in England, he lived in relations of notorious intimacy with a clever, licentious, married lady of quality, Madame du

Châtelet. For a short time, about 1745, he made his peace with the court and was made royal historiographer at the instigation of none other than the Pompadour herself; but within a little over a year he outwore his welcome and was glad to quit Versailles. Madame du Châtelet died in 1749 ending a very sordid romance.[1] In 1751 Voltaire visited Berlin at the pressing invitation of the other most distinguished European of the eighteenth century, Frederick the Great. The King of Prussia boasted that he was a philosopher and guided his state by the rules of enlightened reason. Why should he not patronize this second Plato? But the King was too masterful, and Voltaire, as a guest, did not prove well-mannered, discreet, or submissive. In 1753 the great Frenchman quitted Potsdam in high dudgeon, after having lost all his favor by publishing a satire upon Frederick himself. In 1758 he settled on a handsome estate near Geneva and there spent his old age, his pen busy up to the end, delighting in innumerable controversies, often in behalf of the oppressed Huguenots. Finally in 1778 he revisited Paris after an absence of twenty-eight years. The court gave him little welcome, but by the Academy, by distinguished foreigners, and by all men of science and letters he was hailed as the chief champion of "enlightenment" in the world. At the performance of his play "Irene," he sat in his box crowned with laurel amid the plaudits of a great audience; but the excitement of the celebrations were too great. On May 30 he suddenly sickened and died. The tale is that the priests thrust themselves to his bedside, but that he petulantly motioned them away, and the Church was denied the final capitulation of one of its most inveterate enemies.

From such a versatile writer it is impossible to expect any

---

[1] The morality of a certain type of society in this age can be judged by the story told after the death of this lady. After her departure Voltaire and her husband "opened a locket the dead woman had worn most sacredly. The two strangely suited mourners looked at the portrait the locket contained — and silently closed the case. It [the picture] was of neither of them, but of *a third man*."

well-defined programme or philosophy. Voltaire's boast and aim was to dethrone "superstition" and to substitute "reason." He worked in the eighteenth century, when modern science was in its childhood, and when many solutions for natural problems, which as answers had seemed delightfully sound and plausible, had not yet been exploded. It was his constant puncturing of shams, his pitiless and ceaseless attacks on old abuses which stood merely because they were venerable, his ardent championing (sometimes at considerable personal risk) of individuals obscure and oppressed, that made his main impression on the life of the age. Full as he was of dreams for the future, he believed the world was about to reform itself without serious struggles and without bloodshed. He expected kings to learn to govern in the spirit of philosophy, and that these "enlightened despots" would render popular rights unnecessary. He was no believer in democracy. "We have never pretended to enlighten shoemakers and servants," he wrote. "What the populace wants is guidance and not instruction." Although he had quarreled with Frederick the Great, he recognized in that extraordinary Prussian all the benefits which a thoroughly efficient king could confer upon his people. Voltaire's ideal was simply of another Frederick with whom he could live in personal harmony! But the lesson which Voltaire impressed upon his age was not that of submission to a superior type of kings — it was to question or actually to deny every kind of existing authority.

The part of constructive philosopher for the new day fell to a very different genius. Jean-Jacques Rousseau (1712–78) was the son of a Geneva watchmaker. He was therefore born in a small Swiss Protestant city that was not subject to France, but his whole influence lay in the greater country, and he there spent much of his life. In him again we meet an individual of deplorably vagabond and non-moral tendencies, whose life was a flat contradiction to very many of his famous dogmas and

VOLTAIRE

JEAN-JACQUES ROUSSEAU

MIRABEAU

LOUIS XVI

preachments. By his own statement he had, during his life in Paris, five children by a certain mistress, all of whom were promptly consigned to the foundling hospital. Later he became famous as an author, received the patronage of the great, visited England, and although his later years were turbid, he died in a state of comparative reputability in 1778. In the final decade of his life he was certainly abnormal, and very likely was not quite sane; indeed, there is a tinge of abnormality running through *all* his writings, a fact which no doubt tended, within certain limits, to add to their effectiveness.

Rousseau's writings almost defy classification. They can hardly be called novels, though some are cast in a very thin narrative form. They are not poems, not even high-falutin prose poems. They are hardly formal essays. He is extremely, from a modern standpoint he is absurdly, sentimental, but this quality was received with far more sympathy and enthusiasm in the eighteenth than in the twentieth century. Above all, he is "a describer — a describer of the passions of the human heart and of the beauties of nature"; and able, it should be added, to apply this interest in the passions to the problems of economics, laws, and political science. In other words, with Rousseau political philosophy became intensely human — and consequently easy to understand by persons who would have been left numb by any formal treaties.

Rousseau's most famous work was the "Social Contract," in which his doctrine for the State was stated in extremely remarkable language. More than any contemporary he not merely denounces the abuses of the age, but argues that man has gone through a long process of degeneracy, thanks to the iniquitous developments of civil law, church authority, and social custom. Rousseau had read many travelers' tales, and he solemnly held up the unclothed islanders of Tahiti (about the most remote region he could think of) as unspoiled, virtuous, and happy beings, to whose innocence it would be no disaster for us to revert. "Man is born free," he declared in a most striking sentence, "and everywhere he is in chains."[1] He goes on to examine the basis for all kinds of authority, and describes society as growing "out of an ideal primitive condition of individual independence, by means of a 'social contract' whereby all individuals consented to abandon their individual liberty, not into the hands of any King or Governor, but of the community." The corollary of this doctrine was very plain. Monarchs had usurped the authority which had once belonged to the sovereign people. But no length of time could make this usurpation valid. The right of the community to determine its own destinies was inalienable and inviolable, and "all the rulers of the earth were mere delegates of the people, who, when they are displeased with the government, have the right to alter or abolish it."

It requires little insight to see where such a theory left the power of Louis XV. The "Social Contract" naturally did not make pleasant reading for the royal censors. It was wisely published in Amsterdam in 1762,[2] and its appearance was one of the reasons why Rousseau was obliged to depart very suddenly from France to Switzerland that same year. But it was beyond the power of King, censors, or Parlement of Paris, as things then went in the realm, to prevent the book's wide circulation. Government displeasure added to the reader's zest and drove home the argument. Rousseau did not stop at criticizing monarchy. He not merely attacked the Catholic Church (Voltaire was doing that): he proposed a kind of denatured "Civil Religion" with all dogmas about the supernatural omitted, and accent laid on the mere existence of the deity and the bare

[1] In his *Émile* or *Education*, Rousseau expands his "back to nature" views much more clearly. "All our wisdom consists in servile prejudices. All our customs are but suggestion, anxiety, and constraint. Civilized man is born, lives, dies in a state of slavery." "*The Caribbeans are more fortunate than we by half.* Observe Nature, and follow the path she traces for you."

[2] French authors of that day regularly published in Holland such books as were likely to be prohibited in France, then duly smuggled the edition home. A great fraction of all the best French works thus came from Amsterdam or Leiden.

moralities. He denounced all forms of religious intolerance as great sins against the State, because the moment the priests began to make the civil magistrates do their bidding to punish heretics, "the sovereign is no more a sovereign even in temporal matters. From that time the priests are the true masters, the kings are only their officers."

Rousseau also expressed a marked distrust for what we should call "representative" political institutions. The best type of government for him was that in which all citizens participated very directly. He was thus the advocate of extreme democracy. He knew very little of the history of his own times. His examples were frequently drawn from old Athens and Rome as he imagined them from a reading of Plutarch, and as was later to be confessed of himself by one who accepted Rousseau's doctrine and followed it to the bitter end (Vergniaud), "he had dreamed they were in Rome, and he woke to find they were in France!" All this is simply saying that the acid tests of time and experience have made sore havoc with Rousseau's dogmas and theories. But their influence and effect in a feebly critical age were electric. The "Social Contract" and its associated and hardly less famous books, were passed out by the lending libraries, not by the day, but by the hour. To half-educated young lawyers like Robespierre, to generous young girls like the one who became Madame Roland,[1] they seemed a new gospel, an infallible interpretation of life, and a clear message of how to remedy its many evils. "They did not merely gain an intellectual adherence from many, but they inspired a fanaticism equal and closely akin to religious passion. The 'Social Contract' became the 'Bible of the Revolution.'"[2]

These three writers were the moving personalities, but the spirit of the new age expressed itself also in a great literary

[1] Madame Roland was so caught by the admiration for classical "liberty" then prevalent, that she declares "she had often wept to think that she was not born a Spartan girl."
[2] Grant.

work, the "Encyclopædia." There had been earlier compendiums of human knowledge, and in fact the work in question was directly inspired by "Chambers's Encyclopædia" in England. But the eighteen formidable tomes of the set which appeared in France between 1751 and 1772 were much more than a catch-all for what then passed as sound information. The moving spirit and editor was Diderot (1713–84), a profoundly iconoclastic philosopher, who could far exceed the skepticism of Voltaire, and he was assisted by a kindred spirit, the famous mathematician D'Alembert (1717–83).

Their famous "Encyclopædia" sought not only to give information, but also to guide opinion. The prospectus announced it as "a general tableau of the efforts of the human mind in all its variations and through all the ages." It was manifestly opposed to the Church and it committed the unpardonable crime of treating religious dogma historically. As it progressed, as the opposition to it and the vain attempts to suppress it increased, it developed into a regular "war-machine" attacking both the Church and the still more despotic Government in general, as well as the whole Christian religion. All this made the history of its publication very troubled. Repeatedly its issues were suspended, its editors harassed, the sheets and plates solemnly seized at the printers and carted to the Bastile, only to be released after anxious delays. But the best intelligence of France was supplying the subject-matter for the "forbidden" book. The non-controversial articles (of course an extremely large part of the work) were authoritative and admirably written. Voltaire encouraged the undertaking and was a considerable contributor. Kings and emperors were on the list of subscribers despite the censor's oft-repeated (and oft-remitted) bans. It was impossible in the end to suppress a work edited by such a man as Diderot whose fame was such that when he was in personal difficulties Catherine the Great, Czarina of Russia, helped to pay his debts; and when many of his colleagues and collaborators were of hardly less influence and prestige in Europe.

THE NEW IDEAS PENETRATE DOWNWARD

The "Encyclopædia" popularized and made widely available the new science and the new philosophy. It supplied a perfect arsenal of well-assorted facts for every critic of the old institutions. The articles were alike clear and clever, and possessed readable qualities rare indeed in works of reference. The viewpoint of the new "philosophy" cropped out everywhere. At each turn of the pages there were arguments for freedom of person, freedom of thought, freedom of the press, as well as commercial and industrial freedom, coupled with a constant war on all religious institutions as forming an obstacle to liberty.

Space fails, to discuss the other intellectual leaders of the day, especially the "Economists" who added their pungent criticisms to the existing economic order. Quesnay, court physician to Louis XV, was supple enough to retain his important post, while constantly preaching a doctrine of non-interference by the authorities in ordinary human affairs, which would have seemed utter heresy to Colbert. "Not too much government: not too much regulation!" were his constant maxims.

And so these ardent "philosophers" wrote their books, spun their theories, or conversed in the salons of duchesses. As was said of the hospitality of one of them, Holbach, at his house "ten or twenty guests gathered to enjoy good fare, excellent wine, superior coffee, and the best talk in Europe. Religion, philosophy, and government, literature and science were discussed in their turn; there was no theory too bold to be advanced or to find supporters."

Only slowly, very slowly, was all this fine talk by the "enlightened" to penetrate outside of the circle of bag-wigs and silver buckles into the lesser nobility and lower bourgeoisie and then into that great vulgar mass of the unenlightened in whom these elegant gentlemen who started the movement took such great theoretical interest. Yet there is ground for saying that there was a great, if almost silent, penetration of a large fraction of the French people, at least of the population of Paris, between say about 1750, when Voltaire first displayed his ascendancy, and 1789, when the full results of the new gospel were to become astonishingly manifest. In the meantime these good philosophers went happily on their way, believing that merely by expounding correct theories society would painlessly reconstitute itself. As a distinguished historian, Lavisse, wrote of this age: "When, owing to the faults of its kings, the country detached itself from royalty, it raised itself all at once to *the idea of humanity*. French writers in the eighteenth century rediscovered this idea, which had been lost since the time of Plato, Seneca, and Marcus Aurelius, or, at least, had been replaced in the Middle Ages by the ecclesiastical idea of Christianity, and later on by the political idea of [a united] Europe."

It remains to see the events which preceded the hour when the new theories were to be translated into action.

Louis XVI (1774-92) was the grandson of Louis XV. If he had walked in the evil ways of his predecessors few might have blamed him, but thanks to a wise and pious mother he was a far more excellent man. Even as he himself protested, it was a misfortune that he came to the throne so young. He had been trained in paths of personal rectitude, but he had received no serious education in his "profession of king." Few rulers ever had better intentions, and few had greater difficulties in giving effect to honest desires. When he was proclaimed at the age of twenty, he is described as "a large boy, heavy, powerful, with a great appetite, very fond of physical exercises, of hunting, or of working as a lock- or black-smith." Such a personage would never make an effective "Sun King" or a "First Gentleman of Europe."

The real question was, of course, would he make a tolerable ruler? He was honest and high-minded, but he soon showed that he was without acute intelligence. He distrusted himself greatly, and was constantly weighed down by the fact that "every one of his actions influenced the fate of 25,000,000 human beings."

This consciousness did not, however, spur him on to resolute action. It made him awkward, self-conscious, and very willing to lean on others, and those others were not usually the wisest men in France, but the King's own family and familiars who had the right of access to him. He was often painfully unstable. His own brother declared that the King's mind was like two oiled billiard balls, impossible to keep in the same place together. To Louis's own great hurt he was especially in the hands of his wife, the famous and unfortunate Marie Antoinette.

The Queen was the daughter of the puissant Maria Theresa of Austria, a sage lady who wrote the younger Princess many letters of excellent advice which she seldom followed. Marie Antoinette was one year younger than her husband. At first it had not been a very happy marriage — a vivacious, pleasure-loving young Queen, and a King awkward, shy, and ponderous. Gradually, however, the two grew together the marriage was a really happy one; but the increasing influence of his wife was to bring no good to Louis.

Marie Antoinette had the saving qualities of being really a pure woman with good intentions and physical courage. If she hardly knew how to live, she in the end knew how to die. But she was destined to be the evil genius of the Old Monarchy in France.[1] Thanks to her, more than to any other single culprit, the last chance of peaceful evolution was to be thrown away. She was ignorant, frivolous, impatient of all restraint. She let herself be involved in compromising positions, and she enjoyed compromising friends among the nobility. Her high-born confidants gained an evil fame for their rapacity, their defense of all kinds of abuses, and for their efforts to check any reform which threatened their own precious profits and pleasures. This Queen, who loved to whirl in masked balls at the

[1] Modern critics, comparing her with the unfortunate Czarina Alexandra ("Alix") of Russia, and her malign influence in that country, 1914–17, will soften their judgments upon Marie Antoinette. For all that, her influence was disastrous to France.

Opera, could never view the political situation from other than a personal standpoint. She could be a gracious hostess at an extravagant court fête at Versailles, but could never discover wherein the public treasury really differed from the King's private purse. There is no real evidence that she looked on the widespread miseries of the French lower classes as calling for more than so much patronizing charity, or discovered that the crown of France was not given her husband for one form or another of kingly enjoyment. It was therefore a national calamity when this beautiful, versatile, strong-minded woman gained a mastery over the weaker mind of Louis XVI.

Her malific influence was directly supplemented by the King's two brothers, the Count of Provence and the Count of Artois. Both of these princes had views substantially as shortsighted as their sister-in-law's. They consistently opposed all reforms, and intrigued against every minister who threatened to show himself a reformer.

The reign of Louis XVI between 1774 and 1789, when the Old Régime ceased to control the destinies of France, revolved mainly about two things; they were very different theoretically in their nature, but both of them aided to topple down the Monarchy. These were the desperate struggle to put through certain reforms and to avert national bankruptcy, and secondly there was the war with England in behalf of America.

Louis XVI began his government admirably, by taking for his Finance Minister Turgot, one of the ablest and most enlightened statesmen in the kingdom, a man who had collaborated in preparing the "Encyclopædia," and who, as *intendant* of the great district of Limoges, had shown himself a first-class practical administrator and reformer. Turgot made a truly noble attempt to put a stop to the almost eternal deficit, to cut off the grosser forms of extravagance in the royal household, which ate up so much of the revenues, and most important of all, to uplift the economic prosperity of France by abolishing the absurd and famine-producing restrictions upon the free trade in grain throughout the kingdom, also to work to the same good end by destroying the hopelessly outworn trade corporations which had been strangling French commerce and industry.[1] Finally he abolished the royal *corvées* upon the peasants; that is to say, the obligation to render a certain amount of unpaid labor upon the roads and other public works. In place of this forced labor for the peasantry alone was to be substituted a "territorial tax" to be spent for the same objects, but to be paid by *all* the proprietors of the district benefited — noble or non-noble.

These were not fundamental or revolutionary reforms, but they might have been the opening wedge for greater things. Turgot was not a democrat. What he did, he strove to accomplish only by means of the royal authority, or, as the age loves to call it, by "enlightened despotism"; but instantly all the beneficiaries of privilege, all the petty recipients of pickings and stealings, all the great magnets who battened upon the old abuses, were at him in wrath. The Parlement of Paris (just reëstablished over Turgot's protest) hastened to protest against his edicts, and finally the King, who had put him in power, and who had tried honestly for a while to sustain him, deserted Turgot when Marie Antoinette added her criticisms. "Only Monsieur Turgot and I really love the people," remarked Louis plaintively — but he let him depart May 12, 1776, not heeding the prophetic words his Minister had written him a little earlier, "Do not forget, Sire, that it was weakness which brought the head of Charles I to the block."

With the dismissal of Turgot went the last real chance — though men knew it not — that the Old Monarchy could reform the country and itself without a cataclysm. From 1776 to 1789 all that the royal ministers could do was to try to stave off the inevitable.

Turgot's successor was, however, in a narrower way, a really capable man — Necker. Being a Protestant and a citizen of

[1] See p. 263.

Geneva, he was only given the title of "Director" of the King's finances, but he was in truth a most formidable minister. Necker was a financier pure and simple. His aim was not to reform rotten social institutions, but to administer in a business-like manner the King's resources such as they then were. Wealthy men trusted him and loaned the Government money on favorable terms; but constant loans are an unsatisfactory method of filling the treasury, and to make things worse, in 1778, France went to war with England to secure American independence. The cause was a good one, but modern wars are never inexpensive. The embarrassments of Necker were increased by the heavy demands for war funds. He had perforce to render himself unpopular at the court by constantly preaching "economy" to King, Queen, and satellites, even if less harshly than had Turgot. Finally in 1781 he published a formal official statement of the condition of the finances. For the first time it seemed possible to tell *just* where the public moneys went. The court favorites and pensioners were scandalized to have all the details of their great incomes from the treasury blazoned over France. Their rage against Necker was indescribable. In May, 1781, the King sent him the way of Turgot. The Old Régime had set its face, not merely against reforms, but even against a decent business administration.

After an unimportant interval, in 1783 there came a new Finance Minister, Calonne, who pleased the royal circle much better. Calonne was a supple courtier. He knew his post depended on the good graces of a rapacious cabal. He had an avowed philosophy which carried him a considerable distance. The only way to get money was to borrow it, "but a man who needs to borrow, must appear to be rich, and to appear rich one must dazzle by one's extravagance!" For the three years following life at Versailles had never seemed so gay, the court so luxurious, money so easy. It was as if Calonne was giving the royal and noble ladies and gentlemen their last brave fling before exile or the scaffold. Pensions, palaces, extravagant fêtes, every kind of lavish expenditure — Calonne found money for everybody and everything. Peace had been made with England, but Calonne did not curtail expenses. In three years he borrowed the equivalent of $280,000,000 — more than Necker had borrowed to sustain the whole war for America. For a little while he succeeded in his policy: rich bourgeois bankers loaned him great sums. Then suddenly in August, 1786, the fact dawned on the court that the treasury was empty, that another loan was impossible, and that something desperate had to be done.

What followed is the mere succession of one stop-gap after another: a meeting of "Notables" (selected noblemen) to counsel with the King on the evil state of the nation; the dismissal of Calonne (1787); the assumption of the finance ministry by a worldly churchman, the Archbishop of Brienne; a fierce quarrel between the new minister and the Parlement over some proposed edicts, followed (1788) by an audacious decree of the Parlement declaring that "France is a monarchy governed by the King according to the laws," and asserting that only the States General could change the fundamental laws of France. Matters were obviously drawing to a climax.

Bankruptcy was not the only force, however, which was hurrying the Monarchy along to the precipice. The story of how France intervened in our behalf in the War for Independence is of course known to all Americans. The motives of Louis XVI and his ministers who took up arms against England in 1778 were not entirely those of sympathy for the struggling democrats beyond seas, whatever might have been the enthusiasms of the young Marquis de Lafayette. Vergennes, the Foreign Minister, was a cautious and crafty old statesman who would not send more than money, munitions, and other indirect aid to America, until the surrender of Bourgoyne made it fairly evident that the colonists stood more than an even chance of victory. Then the opportunity to inflict a great humiliation on the old British foe, and to avenge the loss of Canada and India was not to be resisted. But it is not to be denied that France would never have entered upon an expensive and distant war, where the chances of direct gain were scanty, if the best intelligence of the nation had not been swept into sympathy with the ideals of the homespun colonials three thousand miles away. When Jefferson, inspired by the philosophy of Locke,[1] wrote that "all men were created free and equal," he struck an answering chord in the hearts of the great intellectual class that had saluted Voltaire as a sage, and studied the books of Rousseau as those of a prophet.

In this war the French fought far better than they had twenty years earlier. There was little land fighting save in America where Rochambeau with a sturdy corps of French veterans rendered invaluable service in strengthening Washington's army, and delighted their allies both by their valor and their good discipline. It was on the sea that the French showed they had not lost the grim lessons of the Seven Years' War. Their navy had been largely rehabilitated. The English were put to the unwonted experience of having to fight several drawn naval battles; and, finally, in 1781 the crowning mercy for Americans at Yorktown would have been impossible save for the presence of the great blockading fleet of Comte de Grasse, which hemmed in Cornwallis by sea while Washington throttled him by land. De Grasse was indeed the next year to lose a considerable naval battle in the West Indies, but the whole course of the war showed clearly enough that it had not been national ineptitude, but sheer governmental inefficiency which in the past had kept the French navy from fighting the English squadrons on equal terms.

The war had ended in 1783. The English had not been beaten badly enough to warrant demanding severe terms, except, of course, the release of America, but France recovered several of her minor colonies which had been seized earlier and the whole

---

[1] Whose influence on the movement for enlightenment and "reason" in France was very demonstrable.

CALL FOR THE STATES GENERAL

struggle ought to have added to the prestige of Louis XVI. That this did not happen was partly due to the new strain upon the treasury, but still more to the inevitable reaction from contact with America. Thousands of young Frenchmen were to return home to tell of an unspoiled land, without privileged classes, artificial customs, or high taxes; and where seemingly all the more practical parts of Rousseau's theories were being put into execution most happily. In Paris itself, Dr. Benjamin Franklin, that canny Bostonian, who was American Envoy to France between 1776 and 1785, exerted an incalculable influence, not merely in behalf of his country, but of democratic ideals in general. Lofty monseigneurs and bejeweled countesses went into delight over this seemingly guileless Yankee, with "his bland face, his unpowdered hair, his gray clothes, and his general patriarchal simplicity which seemed like the incarnation of the 'natural man.'"[1] And the envoy had received all the homage with never a smile upon his crafty old lips, doubtless glad of anything which might serve his country. He was innocently and probably unconsciously undermining the power of the very King from whom he was soliciting men, money, and ships.

Peace with England had been made in 1783. Five years later Brienne had been defied by Parlement when he tried to get it to register new laws, to give the King more money. After that events marched rapidly. In the provinces local parlements and estates (representatives of the three "orders") were calling for a "States General" — the representatives of the *whole* French nation — as the only authority entitled to cure the grievously diseased body politic. There had not been a States General since 1614, but its memory was not lost. It seemed the one thing possible and needful. The treasury was empty. New taxes might have meant a revolt. On August 8, 1788, Brienne an-

[1] Jefferson later wrote of him, "more respect and veneration attached to the character of Dr. Franklin in France than to that of any other person in the same country, foreign or native."

nounced that the King would convene the States General of France on the 1st of May, 1789. In the meantime, to tide over the finances, the King soon dismissed the incompetent Brienne himself and restored Necker, at the magic of whose name trustful capitalists consented to arrange a new loan.

The fall, winter, and spring of 1788–89 were spent in intense political bustle and anticipation.[1] A great nation, pathetically ignorant of free political life, was trying to hold a general election of popular representatives, to conduct an orderly discussion of public affairs, to make up a programme of reasonable reforms, and to set its face toward a changed future.

All Europe was watching France. She was confessedly the intellectual and cultural leader of the Continent, yet the kings and emperors beyond her borders were not greatly disturbed at happenings around Paris. Surely, they comforted themselves, their "brother" Louis XVI was in a perilous way with his subjects, and would be in no condition to attack his neighbors. That the ideas just penetrating the French masses would also penetrate and agitate the masses of Germany, Italy, and Russia entered no man's head. Governmental Europe heaved a sigh of relief when it saw the nation of Louis XIV seemingly engrossed with wholly domestic problems. Where was the prophet to tell them that eight years after 1789 a young man, born beneath the French flag in Corsica, would be dictating the Peace of Campo-Formio to the trembling Princes of the House of Hapsburg, and that the world would be on the eve of another, and a most skillful and almost successful attempt, to found a new Roman Empire?

[1] The Government stimulated a flood of pamphlets by openly requesting information as to the methods of holding the States General, its historical powers, etc.

CHAPTER XIII
OLD FRANCE ON THE EVE OF THE REVOLUTION

THE French Revolution can be understood only by a careful examination of the political, economic, and social conditions from which it sprang. It did not appear, first to convulse France, and then to confound the entire world, because France was more miserably afflicted by public ills than other quieter nations. On the contrary, it was precisely because the French were probably, all things considered, the most progressive, enlightened, and in general fortunate people of Continental Europe, that they were the first who dared to throw aside the great barriers which mediævalism still erected in the way of human development. If we examine the condition of average sections of Germany, Austria, Italy, or Spain as compared with France, those conditions would have seemed decidedly worse; old abuses and hoary tyrannies much more obnoxious; the governed still more severely exploited by the governing classes; the traces of popular liberty even less in evidence. But while Italians, Spaniards, Germans, etc., were as a people too helpless and ignorant to do more than mutter in despair, hopeful at best of a "good king" and a slight mitigation of the worst abuses, in France a great fraction of the people were becoming keenly alive to two great facts: (1) that very many things in the body politic were absolutely wrong; (2) that, as men of energy and intelligence, it was alike their right and their duty to take the remedy into their own hands. These specific evils and this consciousness of both the need and the power to remedy the evils: to which, it should be added, the whole philosophic temper of the age, which predisposed men to an optimistic faith in "reason" and in the perfectibility of human nature by merely changing its environment, led as a consequence to drastic but wholly untested schemes for reform. The result was to produce the French Revolution, the most far-reaching political and social explosion in all European history.

In 1789 France presented the utterly anomalous picture of a great kingdom, of nearly 25,000,000 inhabitants, leading the world in most of the civilized refinements and luxuries of life, and numbering a high proportion of high-spirited, educated, and well-intentioned men, but which nevertheless was cursed with political and economic institutions which had been growing threadbare ever since Louis XI. In its heyday Capetian royalty had been an enormous asset to France. It had been the kings who had rescued the land from feudal chaos. In the olden days the King and the lower classes had more or less made common cause against their common enemy and oppressor — the barons. Only by the loyalty and the unfeigned consent of the lower classes had French royalty been able to rise to power. Often had the King fought against his dukes, counts, and seigneurs, but very seldom against the burghers of his "good towns" or the peasants of his villages. But when the victory had been won, the monarchy had promptly kicked aside its humble helpers. Louis XIV had no more intention of asking the Third Estate to aid in his government than he had of sharing his throne with a Condé or a Bouillon.

The Monarchy in 1661 had seemed to be absolute and owing no duty to any Frenchman, save the general duty of governing with responsibility "only to God" the people with which Heaven had entrusted it. The monarchical theories of Louis XVI we have already seen.[1] We have seen, too, the circumstances, especially the disastrous and disgraceful wars, which undermined the prestige of the Monarchy both with the world at large, and with its own subjects. Nevertheless, in 1789, in legal theory, Louis XVI possessed a power not a whit less absolute than his several-times grandfather Louis XIV. That earlier monarch had

[1] See pp. 236-37.

said, "All the State rests in me: the will of the entire people is shut up within myself." In 1787 Louis XVI had said, "This thing is legal — because I wish it!" and again, "I am answerable only to God for the use of the supreme power." The "States General," that feeble attempt at a legislature which had developed in the later Middle Ages, had not been convoked since 1614; and very few men, until shortly before 1789, claimed that this half-forgotten body had possessed much more than consultative powers. The King could make war, make peace, spend the public revenues as he would, and also make new laws, all by his own arbitrary fiat. In theory, and partially in practice, too, he held authority over the very lives and thoughts of his subjects. No book, no paper, could appear without the consent of his censor. The King could confiscate a man's entire property without obligation to give payment.

Worse still, he could take away his liberty without any process of law. In the days of Louis XVI, even as in the days of Richelieu or of Louis XIV, the usage remained of issuing the famous *lettre de cachet* (literally "sealed letter") which was simply a royal order to seize and lock up the special individual named in the document in some designated fortress — the Bastile at Paris, Pierre-Ancise at Lyons, Pignerol in the Alps, etc. No crime had to be mentioned; no period set for the imprisonment. It was all "at the King's pleasure." Louis XIV had thus kept the unhappy Duke of Lauzun in close custody for ten years. Other victims had probably languished longer. Under Louis XV these notorious documents seem sometimes to have been solicited by noble families for locking up and bringing to repentance unruly sons who were on the point of contracting imprudent marriages. Under Louis XVI, probably, they were not often issued save for dealing with very unworthy persons who deserve scant sympathy; but issued they still were, over a thousand of them between 1774 and 1788. The mere fact that the King could use them proves the "first gentleman of Europe" to have been essentially a despot, only a little more varnished and self-restrained than the Sultan at Constantinople.[1] There was, however, this important difference. Turkey was described as a "despotism tempered by assassination." France was now surely a "despotism tempered by inefficiency." The royal power was wearing thin in places. The King's commands were being only imperfectly executed. The amount of inertia the monarch had first to overcome in order to execute any unwelcome change was inconceivably great. Whatever the *theory* of his authority, long before 1789 the King of France had to take into very serious account two forces — the wishes of the court around him, his family and noble intimates; and also the trend of public opinion in France. For the ruin of the Monarchy these two forces seldom failed to collide. This "absolute" King in the end was to be destroyed largely because of the *practical* weakness of his power.

Versailles was still the center of the court and of its royal master. Here were some eighteen thousand persons directly in the service of the reigning family, or at least eating of the King's bounty. About half were in the "military household," a guard corps which had perhaps been a little reduced since the days of Louis XIV; the remainder were in the "civil household" which had grown rather than diminished. Besides the King's host of attendants there were the households of the Queen (at least five hundred souls), those of his children, his brothers, sisters, sisters-in-law, aunts, and cousins — each with an establishment worthy of a second-class sovereign.

The court was extremely luxurious and with an utterly disorderly type of luxury. There were nineteen hundred horses in the royal stables and two hundred carriages. To maintain the King's stables required annually the modern sum of $4,000,000. The service of the royal table (after certain very unpopular economies had been ordered!) cost some $1,400,000 per annum.

---

[1] Of course the French claimed that their King could not sit as judge of his own cause, order a man to be executed without forms of trial, or do other things familiar in the Orient. The fact remained that there was no legal way of checking the King if he chose to do these things.

The waste and downright embezzlement was incalculable. Every one of the highly salaried and seldom employed servants had his or her special line of well-defined perquisites. Thus the group of "first waiting-women" between them added fully $30,000 per year to their incomes by disposing of the partly burned candles used in lighting the palace. Queen Marie Antoinette required (according to the royal account-books) four new pairs of shoes each week — but probably no such number ever touched the royal feet. It was notorious also that everything sold to the King was charged at a far higher price than when sold to humbler mortals. Thanks to utter lack of management, "graft," and downright pilfering, in 1789 the total cost of the royal household, civil and military, it is alleged, mounted to the equivalent of nearly $17,000,000.

Yet the cost to the King did not really stop here. His Majesty was expected constantly to make "royal gifts" on a scale corresponding with his greatness; also to award pensions to favorite courtiers, and to friends of the Queen; for example, to families of noble harpies like the Polignacs who had particularly the Queen's ear.[1] Between 1774 and 1789 the able finance minister Necker calculated that the King had thus given away to his family or courtiers what amounted to $114,000,000. Already under Louis XV it had been said, "The court is the tomb of the nation." This was still more true under his well-meaning successor.

The Government of which this court was the axis was still the same in form as under Louis XIV. Great ministers and royal councils were at Versailles, and France at large was divided into thirty-six *généralités* each under its omnipotent *intendant*, who, taken from the bourgeois class, found himself a petty king in all governmental matters so long as his lord and master deigned to keep him in office.

One royal minister, however, was standing out beyond all the

[1] This particular notorious family seems to have fastened on to pensions equal to nearly $400,000 per year, modern reckoning.

others. The Controller-General of the Finances was coming more and more to be the chief servant of the Monarchy. His salary was over $112,000 per annum. He was gaining power, because the one test of successful administration in France was coming to be the ability to satisfy the insatiable demands of the treasury. Without money the "Very Christian King" was helpless.

In the *généralités* the provincial regions were subdivided into smaller districts usually known as "elections," and each was ruled by the intendant's appointee and direct agent, the "sub-delegate." The power of these petty officials was very great. They could override every other kind of local authority, but in turn had to refer almost every variety of question to their intendant and he often to Versailles. If a bridge was to be repaired, the roof of a public building retiled, a prison made secure or habitable, the papers usually had to go a weary way to the King's court and come back again. Delays were interminable and all governmental agencies seemed strangled with red tape. France thus was a highly centralized monarchy, but there was none of the prompt efficiency which can characterize the less iniquitous forms of despotism.

France was also, if a centralized monarchy, anything but a *unified* monarchy. Within the kingdom were all the economic barriers and variations which one would expect to-day when passing across a dozen separate nations. Thus the weights and measures differed radically going from district to district. In Paris a "perch" implied the equivalent to thirty-four square meters, but it was fifty-one meters in some provinces; and it was forty-two meters in still others. France was divided into at least seven customs districts, each with its own barriers and special tariff, as if between unfriendly kingdoms. There were also seven different groups of territories (each with its own sets of rates) for the obnoxious and notorious salt tax. In a minor fraction of the provinces, *pays d'États* (literally "Countries with Estates"), there were local bodies which partially

VARIATIONS IN LEGAL SYSTEMS

represented the people and which had something to say about the levying of taxes. In the rest of the provinces, *pays d'Élection* all this lay directly with the agents of the King.

There was also no *legal* unity in France. Practically all the southern half of the realm was subject to the so-called "Written law," to a system based very directly upon the old Roman codes. In the northern half there was the "Customary law," "a confused jumble of 295 different codes" derived from old feudal usage, and traceable in theory back to Frankish times.[1] Going across France, therefore, as Voltaire well said, "one changed the laws as one changed post-horses." This line of legal differences cut across France in a most arbitrary manner, and especially the great province of Auvergne was split in twain by the distinction, one city, Aurillac, being under the civil law of the South and the next, Clermont, under the customary law, though both towns would be subject to the jurisdiction of the Parlement of Paris as their high court.

These divergences had originally arisen because the Capetians, in making their conquests, had wisely refrained from treading on local customs while their own power was just consolidating. But long after the reasons for any such tenderness had vanished, inertia on the part of the Government and the influence of magnates interested in the old systems, had kept the latter in vogue. Despite their harmfulness, many districts were proud of the barriers that cut them off from their neighbors, and even up to 1789 they strove to maintain their provincial insularity. As Mirabeau was to say in a striking phrase, France was, up to the Revolution, "an unconstituted aggregation of disunited peoples."

If the laws were complicated, the administration of the same also left much to be desired. There were still plenty of remains of the old seigneurial justice of the Middle Ages. In most villages,

[1] This very complex and imperfect legal system was well adapted to breed a host of clever, hair-splitting lawyers who were to come to the very front of public affairs in 1789 and onward.

petty crimes and complaints went before a judge named by the old feudal lord of the manor. His jurisdiction, however, was subject to appeal to the king's courts in all important cases. The only practical effect, therefore, of the feudal courts was to delay the final decision, and to make extra pickings for the insignificant seigneurial judge. Once a case, however, was in the royal courts, it was caught in a perfect network of tribunals. The ordinary superior judges were known as "presidents," about one hundred in number. It was complained there were not enough of them to attend to the legal business of the realm, and consequently every kind of litigation was grievously delayed. Above the presidents were the parlements. The most dignified and honored of these parlements was the famous one of Paris, but really it was the supreme court for only about one third of France. There were twelve other parlements each acting for some province or group thereof or subdivision of the realm. They were less esteemed than the Paris tribunal, but not subject to it. If there was any higher jurisdiction, it could come only directly from the councils of the King.

All the high judicial magistrates held office on a basis incredible if not diabolical to modern ears. They gained their posts either by inheritance — for example, a son inheriting his father's position as judge — or by downright purchase, one incumbent selling his position to an aspirant. This rule of venality of positions applied as a matter of fact to a multitude of high governmental posts.[1] There were some required precautions to prevent notoriously unfit men from securing places which it would ruin the King to have them administer; nevertheless the fact remained that under the "absolute kingship" the monarch could not prevent a great judicial office from changing owners like a country house. Another set of grotesque customs made it incumbent on litigants to present a regular gift to their judges: the

---

[1] The sale of public offices was a regular expedient in difficult times to fill up the treasury. After they had once been awarded, their disposition lay largely with the purchaser.

CRUEL PENALTIES AND TORTURE 251

only thing expected was that these "spices" should be fixed in an equal amount for each side.

The methods of these courts were, as might have been expected, often abominable. The criminal law was terribly severe. The hangman punished many "crimes" which to-day would be settled by a small fine. The penalties for poaching on hunting rights approximated those for arson and murder. As was complained in 1789, "the life of a rabbit was balanced off against that of a man." Torture was a regular feature of a criminal trial. In 1780, by a great reform the "preparatory" torture, before condemnation, was given up; but until 1789 the "preliminary question" — that is, use of the rack after condemnation and before execution — was carefully retained to extort from the wretch some facts about his accomplices. The sight of the gallows, with corpses hanging in chains and with the carrion crows busy around them, was terribly familiar in every region in France. Condemnation to the galleys (a living death in life) was only a pretense at mercy.[1] Really serious crimes would be punished by breaking on the wheel, drawing and quartering, and every other refinement of cruelty which had lived on from the truly "dark" ages.

The Achilles heel of all this strange and evil polity, or rather demi-chaos, was the financial system. It must never be forgotten that the *immediate* reason why the Absolute Monarchy broke down was because the Lieutenant of God could not pay his own most necessary debts. Had the King of France remained decently solvent his old government might have survived some years longer.

In 1789 the financial situation was briefly this: The annual expenses came to about $265,000,000; the receipts to $238,000,-

---

[1] Once chained to the oar as a galley slave, prisoners were often kept for years after their legal sentences had expired. A case was brought up in 1679 of a man sentenced for five years in 1660, and not yet released through sheer administrative inertia.

000, and the interest on the public debt came to $105,000,000 (well on to half the total receipts!) Under Louis XVI alone the public debt had increased by $570,000,000 (2,850,000,000 francs present French money). This deplorable situation was not due alone to the blunders of Louis XVI and of his ministers. It was traceable back to the policy of every French king since Francis I, save only Henry IV and Louis XIV during the golden days of Colbert. The whole spirit of the royal policy, however, had been summed up by the Count of Artois (brother of Louis XVI and himself the later unhappy Charles X): "The expenses of the King ought not to be governed by his receipts, but his receipts by his expenses!"

A deficit was the standing situation in the treasury department. The only way to meet this deficit was by such doubtful expedients as the creation and sale of new offices or privileges, or by the regular contraction of a greater debt. The situation as to taxes was so bad that almost any proposal to augment them would have shaken the nation. The "Absolute Monarch" could not arbitrarily increase a poll-tax lest the consequences destroy his throne. Therefore the drift to bankruptcy continued.

The existing taxes were numerous and most of them of long standing. The chief direct tax was the famous *taille*. It was traceable back to at least the Hundred Years War with England. In the South Country it was usually levied on lands and houses; in the rest of France it was personal, levied on the presumed fortune of the tax-payer, whatever its origin. In any case it was wholly arbitrary and was imposed without any rational basis for the assessment. The sight of a few hen feathers at a wretched peasant's door, implying that he was acquiring more than a starving living, was in itself enough sometimes to increase the poor wight's *taille*. Such acts, of course, put a deliberate discount on the habits of thrift.

The *taille* was the *roturier's* (non-noble's) tax. It fell only on peasants, craftsmen, and bourgeois. The lands and incomes of

OTHER DIRECT TAXES

the noblesse and the Church (the two wealthiest classes) were proudly exempt. The noblemen paid the King by their "blood" when they served in battle; the ecclesiastics paid by their prayers. They were not to be subject to this grievous impost which was in itself a sign of inferiority.

There were, however, two other taxes which the nobles and the clergy were supposed to pay along with the peasants — despite much groaning. These were the "capitation tax," and the "Twenty" (*vingtieme*). The first tax was a proportional levy of so much per head, according to the twenty-three classes into which all the King's subjects were assigned. The first class was headed by the Dauphin, who was taxed in theory about $1000. The poor folk of the twenty-third class paid nothing. The "Twenty" was supposed to be a general income tax of twenty per cent. Such was the letter of the law. In usage, however, the privileged classes received almost wholesale exemption. With the upper bourgeois the chances of exemption would vary. The clergy "redeemed" their taxes by a "free gift" to the King, much less than their lawful share. As for the nobility, their quotas were always estimated with calculated leniency. The "Princes of the Blood," who should have paid about $1,200,000 as their total "twentieths," actually paid only about $90,000. In the region around Paris, when a marquis was levied for $200 in place of his just $1250, a bourgeois was held for $380 in place of his just $85.

These taxes were levied so harshly upon those they struck, and the exemptions of wealth and privilege were so wholesale, that it is reckoned that fifty per cent of the entire earnings of the non-noble classes were swept in by the *taille*, the capitation tax, and the "Twenty" alone — and yet that was by no means all for which the tax-gatherer stretched out his hands!

Besides the direct taxes there went the elaborate indirect

---

[1] Such estimates are of course highly general. Many non-nobles, by fair means or foul, were more fortunate. But their share in the tax-burden was always excessive.

taxes. What made these worse was the fact that they were regularly "farmed out" — that is, the privilege of collecting them was sold to "farmers," speculators, who paid a lump sum to the King, then levied as much as they could stretch the law to allow them in order to get a fat profit. This was a sinister revival of the "publicans" who disgraced ancient Rome, and who were justly execrated in New Testament Palestine.

The *gabelle*, the salt monopoly, was open perhaps to the most grievous abuses. Every subject above the age of seven was legally obliged to purchase at least seven pounds of salt annually. Not to purchase this was almost as serious a crime as perjury or house-breaking. This salt had to be used exclusively in cooking or on the table. To use such a supply for salting provisions implied a fine equal to at least $150. The agents of the public salt-dealers frequently would search dwellings from attic to cellar to make sure that no unauthorized stores were therein secreted. They could easily tell the government salt — it was of such very inferior quality! Naturally there was a great trade in contraband salt. The risks were great, but the legal price of the article was so high that it paid to take chances. In 1787 a high official (Calonne) asserted that 30,000 persons were arrested per year for breaking the salt laws and 500 were condemned to the galleys or gallows for contraband salt running. Of course a small army of detectives and revenue officers had constant employ, enforcing this *gabelle* alone. All this did nothing to increase the respect of the lower classes for the laws against genuine crimes.

The *aides* were petty taxes almost as intolerable as the *gabelle*. They struck various articles, but especially wine — in France a staple of consumption such as Americans can hardly understand. Wine was subject to a small tax when it was manufactured; another when it was sold to its first handler; and then again, while in transit, at every possible halting-place on the road (thirty-five to forty separate places in going from Languedoc to Paris); again when it entered a city; again when it passed to the retailer. A cask of wine worth 150 francs ($30) in Montpellier in the South had paid out 122 francs in these small taxes before it was drunk in Paris. Most vexatious of all was the check kept upon the consumer. Every family, whatever its size, was entitled to four puncheons of wine per year, without extra tax. If they needed more, however, it had to pay a surtax; this on the principle that the extra wine might be sold *sub rosa* and the Government cheated.

The *aides* and the *gabelle* alike were most unequal over France. In some regions the salt tax was so small as to constitute no serious grievance. In others, it was almost the chief public burden. As for the aides, we find certain parishes on opposite sides of a river; on one bank the inhabitants were subject to a heavy *aide* on their wine, on the other they were wholly exempt.

The evils of this taxation system were so patent that no one attempted to defend them. Even the privileged classes recognized that these fiscal iniquities were the source of a large proportion of the violent unrest which was afflicting the country and threatening the whole social order. No finance minister dared propose heavier taxes until a better system could be devised, and yet the system could not be changed without touching the whole edifice of social and financial privilege upon which the French upper classes doted. The absurd situation was therefore presented of an "absolute monarch," with a realm well able to pay much larger taxes than actually existed (provided they were evenly adjusted), but not daring to add a fraction to the imposts already laid upon his people, and therefore himself drifting into bankruptcy. The statement would be comical had not the results been tragic. Behind the shadow of the deficit was rising the guillotine.

The abuses in taxation were inextricably tied up with the abuses in personal privilege. The kings had stripped the nobility of their political authority, but they had done anything but establish a dead level of subjects all under one common master. Inequality was the principle of French society, and all the nation was legally and avowedly divided into three great orders — the Clergy, the Noblesse, and the Third Estate. The first two orders were styled "The Privileged." Their precious rights varied from that of preferred admission to the royal court to mere exemption from the *taille* which smote all the lower classes. So far as numbers went, the privileged orders were in a glaringly small minority. The whole population was then about 25,000,-000. The two noble orders each reckoned about 130,000 to 140,000 members; say 275,000 "nobles" in all. To these, in fairness, should be added about 300,000 bourgeois who held official positions and enjoyed exemptions and prestige far above most of their contemporaries. In all not over 600,000 Frenchmen were thus singled out by law and custom for a position highly enviable as compared with 24,000,000 less fortunate fellows.

The clergy nominally ranked higher than the noblesse since the affairs of God took precedence over the dignities of man. Rather less than half of the clergy were "regular" — that is monks and nuns under the monastic "rule"; the majority were "secular," bishops and parish priests mingling with the laity, and having the "cure of souls." These two branches of the clergy had a well-defined organization; sending deputies to an assembly which met every five years to deliberate on the interests of their order, and to vote "free gifts" to the King in lieu of ordinary taxation. The clergy, too, if involved in the courts, were entitled to a judgment by their own ecclesiastical tribunals. They were of course in theory subject to the Pope, but actually — in view of the Concordat of Francis I and the vigorous assertion of the "Gallican liberties" under Louis XIV — a wise Pontiff would let the affairs of the French Church pretty strictly alone; and the King was more influential in most ecclesiastical matters than the Holy Father.

The Crown was justified in taking a keen interest in matters religious. It was reckoned that one fifth of the whole soil of

France belonged in one way or another to the Church. In the province of Artois the clergy controlled three quarters of the entire real estate. Besides the regular revenues of these wide lands, the Church received a "tithe" on all agricultural products everywhere;[1] also the income from many "feudal rights" levied upon the inhabitants of the Church estates. The whole revenues of the French Church in 1789 are set at over $100,000,000 modern money.

Some of this huge income was indeed spent on hospitals, orphanages, the upkeep of churches, and legitimate alms to the poor. The "free gifts" of the Church to the King, and such other taxes as the clergy were willing to bear, came to about $6,000,000 (30,000,000 francs) per year. The rest of the revenues were distributed far otherwise.

Splitting the French Church asunder, in a manner ruinous to all its spiritual weal, was the division between the higher clergy and the lower clergy. The higher clergy were recruited almost exclusively from the noblesse. The younger son of a ducal house would seek a bishopric while his elder brother took the family château. The archbishops, bishops, abbots, canons, etc., reckoned together about 5000 or 6000 persons. They monopolized by far the greater share of all the Church revenues. Few bishops struggled along in "apostolic poverty" with less than $50,000 (250,000 francs) income per annum. Many were far happier. The Cardinal-Bishop of Strasbourg enjoyed $300,000 per year. At his palace at Saverne he could entertain two hundred guests at once. One hundred and eighty fine horses champed in his stables. The greater abbots were sometimes more lucky than the poorer bishops. The Abbot of Clairvaux displayed his monastic indigence by taking an income of $190,000 per year. Very few members of this "higher clergy" were not of noble birth. It was almost impossible for a base-born monk or priest — whatever his learning, practical abilities, or devout piety —

---

[1] In theory, a tenth sheaf, pig, chicken, etc., but the tithe was usually commuted according to local custom into a fixed money payment.

to cross the magic line which admitted him to the great dignities of the Church.

Under this higher clergy were at least 60,000 poor *curés* and "vicars," recruited from the Third Estate. Often, indeed, the nominal occupancy of the parish would belong to some absent ecclesiastic of rank, who was perhaps busy pushing his fortunes at court. The regular parish duties would be discharged by some humble assistant who received a mere fraction of the income wrung out of the neglected tithe-payers. The legal pay of these parish priests was pitiful — $350 (1750 francs) for the *curés*, $175 (875 francs) for the still less exalted vicars. Even these poor stipends were not always paid completely. The upper clergy mulcted them at every turn, and threw on them the greater share of the "free gifts" and other payments of the clergy to the King. Between the *curé* and the bishop there was therefore little love to be lost. When the Revolution came and the Church was to need the support of all its sons, not merely was the *curé* to be found refusing to sustain his old superiors in their privileges: it would be lucky if he were not egging on the peasants of his parish to some gross act of insurrection.

In this French Church there were many devout and pious souls in whom burned the spirit of true Christianity. But they were not in power. There were almost none of them among the higher clergy. Worldliness, irreligion, if not downright infidelity were the order of the day among the luxury-loving bishops and abbots who fluttered around the court, and who seemed to differ from the secular noblesse only by a variety in their gorgeous costumes and an inability to have *legal* wives. The Huguenots had been reduced to a persecuted minority, but it had never come home to the complacent French churchmen that while driving out the demon of heresy, their idle and utterly "secular" lives were giving room for the seven greater devils of open hostility to all forms of religion whatever. French Christianity to this day is paying the penalty for the utter lack of spirituality in its life during the eighteenth century. Louis XVI once feebly protested, when asked to name a certain candidate as bishop, that "He thought a bishop should really believe in God!" And when the bishops as a body were urging a revival of the anti-Huguenot laws, and a well-informed Paris ecclesiastic was asked, " did they really believe the doctrines they were insisting on?" he promptly replied, "There may be four or five [out of one hundred and thirty-one]."

Such a Church, wealthy, socially divided, and deliberately ignoring its divine mission, was to prove veritable dry tinder for the flame of Revolution once the latter was started in France.

The noblesse were less hypocritical, but not less vulnerable than the high churchmen. They were, in the first place, subdivided into the two great fractions of the "noblesse of the sword" and the "noblesse of the robe."

The noblesse were all of them exempt from the ignoble *taille*, the chief direct tax. As already seen, they were partially exempt from the other direct taxes. Also, although they had lost all their political power as feudal lords, they had kept the right to make certain levies upon the peasants upon their former dominions: thus they could hold the peasantry to tolls for the use of bridges and roads which the lords were supposed once to have constructed for the benefit of the community; and for the privilege of using the local grist-mill, which at one time every lord had built to grind his peasants' meal. They had frequently the "right of the dove-cote" — to keep swarms of pigeons — which the peasants could not shoot however much they devoured the crops, and the "hunting right" — that is, of following the fox, with hounds and horses, over a wide range of country to the infinite ruin of the standing grain.[1] All of the order had thus certain general rights; but above the run of the "nobles of the

[1] What made these privileges the more obnoxious was that the nobles did not always exercise them themselves, but sublet their privileges to greedy speculators who exploited their rights mercilessly.

sword" was the "high noblesse," numbering not over one thousand persons who were far more honored.

The "high noblesse" were the descendants of the once mighty feudal lords who had measured strength with the King. Since Louis XIV's time they had lived almost exclusively at the court, "in ruinous luxury and idleness." A few bearers of great names lived, indeed, in their ancestral châteaux and tried to take honest care of their great landed properties — but they were very few. Only when poverty-stricken or under royal displeasure would a great nobleman, as a rule, quit Versailles. They were the companions of the King and had to live on a corresponding scale. Many of them were accordingly deep in debt, even if their master awarded gifts and steady pensions. We hear of a Prince of the Blood who had a nominal fortune of $28,000,000, but who actually owed more than half of this. One could therefore prosper only by constant intrigues for royal favor. The King's bounty would rescue the mortgaged domains! The higher noblesse, therefore, stood as a rule for the perpetuation of all the old abuses in the government.

This upper nobility was none too well liked by the less fortunate lower nobility, not to mention the bourgeoisie and the peasants. The insatiable demands for money by life at Versailles made the great lords merciless in enforcing payment for the rents, feudal dues, etc., on the country estates which they seldom visited, and if they "farmed out" their rights to speculators, they, of course, became still more unpopular. There were, indeed, some great nobles who held very enlightened views, patronized the "philosophers," and assented to proposals for "a new order." The Marquis of Lafayette belonged to the gilded circle itself. Nevertheless as a class the great noblesse were among the most vulnerable defenders of the Old Régime.

Under them, were about 100,000 "noblesse of the province." These were country gentlemen, often with meager incomes down to $600 to $800 per year. They had large families, and since in France every son and daughter of a lord was "noble" also (and the younger did not become a mere commoner as in England), the task of providing for them so that they could live without vulgar trade was often a sore problem for their parents. In some regions, especially in the West of France, these lesser nobles treated their peasants well, and tried to improve the condition of the countryside. They were therefore fairly popular. Elsewhere they were merely grasping, discontented lords of the manor, anxious to sweep in enough money to be able to depart and push their fortunes at Versailles — hated by the peasants and deserving the hatred. In the main, however, being in closer touch with the lower classes, they were as a body less outrageous landlords than the great noblesse, and more open to liberal suggestions. Between the great noblesse and this "noblesse of the province" there was all the jealousy between rich and poor cousins. When the crash came, the dukes and marquises were to look in vain for real aid to most of the country barons and "sires"; although the latter were, as a class, profoundly loyal to the Church and to the person of the King.

Besides these two great sections of the "noblesse of the sword" there stood the "noblesse of the gown." They reckoned about 40,000. They were looked down upon by their nominal equals, because many of them had struggled up from the bourgeoisie and in almost every case they had owed their status originally to wealth and not to ancestry. They were men who themselves (or their forbears) had won the various official posts which carried with them "nobility" — membership in the King's councils, "presidentships" in the law courts, and other governmental positions — positions which (as seen) were often hereditary. Besides, a very rich and successful bourgeois could often invoke enough influence at Versailles to get some kind of a patent of nobility. Many of these "nobles of the robe" were arrogant, self-seeking, and grossly incompetent in the public offices to which they clung: as a class, however, they were far more enlightened than the old-line nobility, more willing to dabble with "philosophy" and to praise the daring of Voltaire and the violent theories of Rousseau. When it came to actually surrendering some of their beloved privileges, however, these nobles of the courts and "parlements" were hardly less obstinate and pigheaded than were the princes and dukes who snubbed them. The French reformers in the end were to owe them very little.

To sum up the noblesse, it should be said that a French nobleman of the eighteenth century was likely to be a man of charming social manners to his equals, much personal intelligence, chronically in debt, extremely lax in personal morality, though with a high sense of "honor" in such matters as cheating at cards. He had, indeed, a keen contempt for physical danger whether on the battle-field, or, in days to come, before the guillotine. But taken as a class, from him was to come not one constructive idea for the salvation of France, and very little willingness to sacrifice his privileges for the general public weal. He was the ornament of his royal master's court, but a great nation was not to be saved by faultless bows and delicate compliments to high-born ladies. The noblesse did little else beyond these to justify its existence, and it shared the speedy ruin which was to sweep down upon enfeebled King and degenerate Church.

The bulk of the nation was comprised in the "Third Estate." This great mass of people was, of course, split up into very distinct groups. We may at once block out the bourgeoisie, the artisan class and the peasants. Each group had its peculiar problems and grievances.

The bourgeois had certainly risen and enriched themselves in the eighteenth century. Despite the misgovernment and disastrous wars of Louis XV, commerce and trade had often prospered, because of the great natural ability of French merchants.[1]

---

[1] Despite the gross misgovernment, such was the enterprise of the French trading class, that the total volume of external trade increased between 1716 and 1787 from 214,900,000 to 1,153,500,000 francs.

THE BOURGEOISIE

The gain had all been to the bourgeoisie. The King had come to depend on the great capitalists to "farm" his revenues and to advance huge loans when the revenues were insufficient. Without them he would have been helpless, and they had to be paid — indirectly at least — by honors and exemptions despite the grumbling of the old-line nobility. The rich, intelligent bourgeois, however, detested the existing system by which they were still subjected to the *taille*, and to many unfair laws, and also were still treated with social frigidity by the noblesse. They constantly dreaded lest the royal finances fall into complete bankruptcy to their own direct ruin. They were, therefore, cheerful advocates of elaborate political reforms.

These rich folk were likewise the very best pupils of the new "philosophers." Montesquieu, Rousseau, Voltaire, and the "economists" were nowhere read so eagerly as in the parlors of great bankers and merchants. The new doctrine of "equality" was also never more welcome than with persons who had the wealth, breeding, and ideas of true ladies and gentlemen, but who would be snubbed, set off at a "second table," or treated with deliberate rudeness by a bankrupt and immoral count.

Such great bourgeois, with their high claims to consideration, of course, tapered down into the "middle" and "lower middle" classes (to use an English expression) of worthy tradesmen, shopkeepers, and small manufacturers — good folk with just social pretensions enough to expect to be called "Monsieur" and "Madame" — till one reached the regular artisan class in the towns. Outside of Paris there were few sizable cities in France, and the rural element still formed the great bulk of the population; however, the artisans reckoned say 2,500,000, about one tenth the whole French nation. They were grouped in guilds and trade corporations of the mediæval style,[1] institutions which had long outlived their usefulness. It was highly difficult for any but the son, or son-in-law of a member — for example, of the wig-makers' guild — to be admitted as an

[1] See p. 79.

authorized wig-maker in a given city; and the law gave a monopoly of the craft to the guild members. They in turn were strictly prohibited from engaging in anything but a very narrow line of trade. For the "ladies' shoemakers" of Paris to have ventured to make and sell children's or men's shoes would have occasioned instant outcry and a ruinous lawsuit. Enlightened men recognized how numbing, how ruinous to the true development of industry, this régime was, which stifled competition and all kinds of initiative, but to abolish the system seemed impossible. Turgot, the great finance minister of Louis XVI, had attempted to abolish the guilds, and the turmoil evoked ruined his schemes and drove him from office, although he declared he was fighting "for the first and the most undeniable of all rights — the right to work!"[1]

The industrial class, therefore, in France was under sore handicaps and added its own problems to the general problems of the nation.

But we come at length to the *real* backbone of the French people. Nearly nine tenths of the population, over 21,000,000, lived by agriculture. About a million of these were still legally serfs,[2] but the bulk were reckoned "free." The great ambition of a French peasant was to possess unencumbered land; but only about 500,000 had reached the happy state of actual ownership. Some of the rest were "colons" engaged on the great estates by the year, in return for clothes, food, lodging, and a very small wage; some "day-workers" toiling at a pittance of sometimes only twenty-five cents per day; some *metayers* working an estate assigned them by the great owner on shares, but sharing also the taxes, which were likely to be enormous. The remainder were likely to possess little farms which, indeed, they called their own, but which paid to the local seig-

[1] See p. 237.
[2] They were mostly in Brittany, long an autonomous principality, and Franche-Comté, long under Spain. In France proper there had been general emancipation.

neur a perpetual rent, extremely heavy, in addition to the numerous, "feudal dues." These were the unlucky *cens* payers — among the most unhappy of all the peasants. As stated, the real freeholders, self-respecting farmers subject only to the ordinary taxation, were in a great minority.

According to Cardinal Richelieu the peasant was "the mule of the State!" This had been true in 1630. It remained pitifully true in 1789. Every kind of public burden was shifted upon his much-enduring back. Even the bourgeoisie and the artisans could usually throw off the brunt of severe taxes by increasing the price of their wares. The peasant was helpless. He had to pay the King, as Turgot reckoned, more than fifty-five per cent of his receipts. He had to pay his "tithe" to the *curé*, or more exactly to the Church tax-gatherer, who would probably be the agent of the distant and luxury-loving bishop. He had to pay all the aforementioned "seigneurial dues" — the "banality" (special tax) — of the mill, the olive press, etc., and to pay these even when no real service was rendered; for example, when the mill was out of order or non-existent. He had, of course, also to pay the salt tax, and many indirect taxes on staple commodities. All in all, responsible students have estimated that *eighty per cent* of the whole income of the average peasant was swept away by King, priest, or seigneur.[1] No wonder there were misery and bitterness throughout the land. The least misfortune — bad crops, sickness, or even lack of extreme thrift — meant instant ruin for a peasant family. It would have no savings, no protection. It is a witness to the plodding conservatism and inherently law-abiding qualities of the peasantry that as a rule they had suffered for generations in silence. They were, of course, in most cases deplorably ignorant. There was no free school system. In many poverty-stricken villages, the *curé* might be the only literate inhabitant. In a dumb, ignorant way the peas-

[1] Other investigators have declared this estimate excessive; there is no doubt, however, that the proportion of a peasant's income so consumed was outrageously and amazingly high.

ants might obey the outward teachings of religion, and honor the name of the King; but the sense of misery, injustice, and oppression was penetrating deep into their souls.

In 1789 conditions were peculiarly ready to produce an explosion among the French lower classes. The harvest of 1788 had been very poor. The winter of 1788–89 was unusually severe. The rivers froze. The cities had never seen so much ice. "The peasants," wrote the Archbishop of Paris, "are reduced to the last extremities of poverty." Sturdy beggars, tramps, and absolute robbers multiplied on all the roads. The population of Paris was then about 700,000; of these 120,000 were reckoned as being in direct want. Of course, much of this misery could never be abolished by merely enacting statutes, but only by a careful process of uplift and reform; yet naturally, when the peasants were summoned to tell their desires and griefs to the States General in 1789, the cry was very great. "If you could see the poor cabins we inhabit," wrote the peasants of Champagne, in one of their bills of complaint (*cahiers*), "the wretched food we eat, you would be touched — that would tell better than our words, which we cannot make more, and which we ought to make fewer."[1]

The peasants had no fine political theories: they wanted directly two things: abolition of the feudal dues and a great lightening of taxes. Behind these lay an intense desire to get direct control of more land, especially the seigneur's land and the bishop's land. The moment the opportunity was given, they were ready to strike.

The above is a very imperfect picture of some of the complex woes of the Old Régime in France. Obviously here was an enormous amount of gunpowder, bound to shake the world when once the match was applied. And yet the imminent danger was

[1] Of course some clever, small-town lawyer may be imagined as drawing up this bill of complaints for a very ignorant constituency. The *cahiers* (petitions presented by each district, listing the grievances it desired to have redressed) were a regular part of the process of choosing a States General.

WHAT THE PEASANTS WANTED

recognized by few or none. It was generally believed that there would be reforms, yes — but by very gentle and painless processes. "With no regret for the past," wrote a French nobleman, after the stunning event, "and no apprehensions for the future, we danced gayly along a carpet of flowers stretched over an abyss."

And so Clergy, Noblesse, and Third Estate came to 1789.

CHAPTER XIV
THE FIERY COMING OF THE NEW RÉGIME: 1789-92.

"No country ever influenced Europe as France did between 1789 and 1815. Impelled by two dreams — the dream of a war against kings on behalf of the people, and the dream of the foundation of an empire of the Cæsarian or Carolingian type — the French armies overran the Continent, and trampled under foot, as they went, much rank vegetation which has never arisen again." So an authoritative historian has written, and his words are entirely true.[1] Indeed, they are not sufficiently strong. There is not a single civilized man on the earth to-day whose life, thought, and destinies have not been profoundly influenced by what happened in or near France during those five and twenty years of action, wrath, and fire.

It is a matter of extreme difficulty, in a sketch of the entire story of France, to describe with any sufficient detail the events of those tumultuous years which covered the "French Revolution." An adequate record would consider the happenings, not by years, but by months and even by days: it would describe and analyze numberless personalities; it would try to disentangle extraordinarily complex forces; it would deal alike with Paris, the French provinces, and the foreign foes of the nation. Even then it would seem very inadequate. Under the circumstances it is best to confine ourselves to a very bare and jejune enumeration of the most important facts, in order to tie the story of the Old Monarchy to that of France in the nineteenth century. He who desires a vivid and truly informing narrative will, of course, turn to the many excellent special studies.

In 1789 practically the entire French nation, barring a few

[1] Lavisse: *Political History of Europe* (Eng. trans.), p. 138.

selfish pensioners, mole-eyed noblemen, and worldly ecclesiastics, was convinced that the state of the country was bad, and it was ready for radical measures and remedies. The earlier steps of reform were taken with the high consent of nearly all the intelligent men of the nation. As, however, difficulties thickened, as it became increasingly hard to translate the political theories of Rousseau into efficient practice, as the immediate effect of the first reforms was to produce confusion, poverty, and misery almost everywhere, the situation soon changed for the worse. Faction rose against faction, with a radical element always calling for more drastic remedies for the public ills. Foreign war and the threat of Germanic invasion were soon added to domestic discords, although the mere threat of foreign danger was to lead to an intensified patriotism. This led to still more pronounced radicalism, until the Government passed to an increasingly narrow circle of fanatics, who were ready to take the life of *any* man that stood in the way of that dictatorship which was "to secure the people's happiness." Then, at last, the cord snapped. The fanatics were overthrown by a return of courage to the saner part of the French nation. The foreign foe was repelled, and in 1795 France found herself, bruised, rent, bleeding, but with her mediæval king and her mediæval institutions gone, and a whole new set of institutions political and social. These did not, indeed, give her the "Liberty, Equality, and Fraternity" her patriots had demanded until after nigh a century more of weary struggles and delays, but these new institutions were after all infinitely better calculated to promote prosperity and happiness than was the rotten Old Régime.

This in a few words was what was to happen in France. The whole tumultuous process involved was the famous Revolution.

The first part of 1789 was spent in France in the novel excitement of what Americans would call a great political campaign. "Nominations" and "elections," as we understand them, were almost unknown in the country which claimed the primacy of Europe. There were very few precedents unless one delved into the musty records of 1614. The government having ordered the elections for the States General grievously failed to arrange very many details needful for the smooth working of the electoral process. The voting had to be by an indirect method, the ordinary voters choosing a smaller number of "electors" and these in turn naming the actual deputies to go to Versailles, a complicated system that could have been avoided. The nobles, clergy, and Third Estate in each district met separately, chose their own deputies and also prepared their own special *cahiers* (bill of complaints to lay before the King). It is a testimony to the solid, practical qualities of the average Frenchman that on the whole this unfamiliar process passed off quietly and successfully. When the lists were made up there were in all 1214 members: noblesse, 285; clergy, 308; Third Estate, 621. The nobles contained many ultra-conservatives, but also a fair sprinkling of open-minded, liberal men like Lafayette. The clergy were sharply divided between the great reactionary ecclesiastics, and a very strong element (205) of country *curés*, men in close touch with their parishes and very unwilling to take the law from their wealthy superiors. In the Third Estate two thirds were various classes of lawyers — of the non-privileged classes the men who had done the most reading and had enjoyed the most leisure. There were only a very few downright peasants, who hardly as yet understood what all the talking and voting was about. The States General, in short, was a most solid and eminently *respectable* body.

Louis XVI and Necker allowed this large company to assemble at Versailles on May 5, 1789, for a magnificent procession and opening session in a great hall of the palace. To the utter astonishment of many, it soon became clear that neither King nor minister had a definite programme for the States General, either as to how it was to organize or what next it was to do. The speeches of Louis XVI and of Necker dwelt on benevolent gen-

PROBLEM OF ORGANIZATION

eralities or treated the deficit as being the one thing important. The States General (it seemed) had been convened primarily to help the King escape bankruptcy by some changes in the taxation system — hardly for anything more. There was profound disappointment.

Greater disappointment and confusion followed. Was the voting to be "by order" or "by head." If "by order," then each of the three estates must meet separately in its own chamber, and legislation to be valid must be agreed to by all three, and the majority of any one chamber, say of the nobles, could block a measure on which the great bulk of the other two orders had set its heart. If "by head," then all the three classes would sit together. The Third Estate would have a clear majority and could also count on help from the country *curés*. All the liberal element obviously wanted this second solution; but the King and Necker, curiously enough, had not arranged beyond cavil how this cardinal point was to be settled. The nobles at once began to organize by themselves. The clergy hesitated; the Third Estate, however, flatly refused to organize for business, declaring it was a "mere collection of citizens" until the others joined them in one body. Thus was created a most awkward deadlock.

Presently, however, some of the *curés* began to come over to the Third Estate, whose members at last plucked up courage to declare themselves to be the true "representatives of the nation," and to announce that they would go ahead without waiting for the others, being legally (so they called themselves) "The National Assembly of France."

The reactionary nobles were now in distress. They won the King's ear, and got him to agree to put pressure on the States General to organize in three bodies. On the 20th of June the Third Estate members discovered that their hall was closed; and they were told that there was to be a "royal session" very soon. In wrath they adjourned to a public "tennis court" on a back street in Versailles and there, led on by Bailly, their president, they took a solemn and fateful oath — "They would not disperse until they had given a constitution to France!" In this exalted mood they went to the royal session on the 23d. Louis XVI had mustered up courage to read the deputies a round lecture. They must meet, he said, as three separate houses, and not meddle with questions of the feudal dues and tithes. "If you abandon me," was his warning, "alone I will work out the welfare of my people!"

The nobles and the bulk of the clergy filed out of the hall after the King. The Third Estate remained stolidly sitting. A pompous court official appeared — Brézé, master of ceremonies. "Messieurs" — he spoke sharply — "you have heard the King's orders." Then up rose a deputy, who had already marked himself as a leader, Mirabeau.[1] "Yes, Monsieur, we have heard what the King has said," rang his voice, in words that were to reëcho through applauding France, "but do you tell those who sent you that *we are here by the will of the people*, and that we will not leave our places except at the point of the bayonet!" Brézé shuffled out. The Third Estate held its ground. It would not disperse. It voted its members "inviolable" — not subject to arrest. It undertook to do business for the whole kingdom.

What was Louis XVI to do? Disperse the members by the soldiery? Perhaps the latter would have obeyed orders, but what of the uneasy, expectant nation? Where was the chance of new taxes to stave off bankruptcy? The King was too humane to enjoy drawing the sword against his own people. At the end of

---

[1] Mirabeau (1749-91) was born of a noble family of Provence and ranked as a marquis. However, he had quarreled with his kinsmen, and was charged with leading a disgracefully irregular life. Be that as it may, he became a profound student of economic and political problems and developed an intense hatred of despotism. In 1789 the noblesse of Provence would not elect him, but he was chosen (though himself a nobleman) to represent the Third Estate. During the Assembly he developed the clearest and most constructive projects of any presented. Almost alone of the French liberals he knew when to advise to halt. His ignoble past life, however, rose up to blast his influence and rob his counsels of weight; but his death in April, 1791, robbed France of probably its greatest statesman.

EXCITEMENT IN PARIS

four days he capitulated. He asked the upper orders to join the Third Estate as one body. The clergy and most of the nobles promptly did so. The National Assembly was complete. The Third Estate had, of course, the majority. The whole body at once proceeded to organize into committees, to draft the legislation which was to redeem France.

The King had yielded, but not the Queen and the court. To Marie Antoinette and her giddy, money-grasping associates the whole action of the disobedient *canaille* had been outrageous. Quick action was needful or the realm was lost. Pressure was brought to bear on Louis. Marshal de Broglie began mustering troops, and strange regiments of reliable foreign mercenaries swung into Versailles. On July 11 a royal decree suddenly ordered Necker (still counted a champion of reform) to be banished instantly from France. As for the Assembly, that was now to be scattered, or subdued by the soldiery whom Mirabeau had defied. Then it was that, almost like a bolt from the clear sky, Paris sprang to arms. The Parisian mob supplied the fighting force which saved the Assembly, overawed the King, and continued the Revolution.

The great city had been in wild excitement for several days. All sorts of rumors were flying across the ten odd miles from Versailles. The gardens of the huge building known as the "Palais-Royal" had been the center for thousands of buzzing, gesticulating young men and of sorely anxious elders. On the 12th of July came the tidings that Necker had been dismissed, the clear sign of reaction to autocracy. A young journalist, Camille Desmoulins, leaped upon a table, a pistol in each hand. "Citizens" (a new title in France!), so he called to the heaving throng, "there is no time to lose! The dismissal of Necker rings a St. Bartholomew bell for patriots! To arms!"

Paris shook herself. All the disorderly forces in a great, wicked, luxurious, turbulent city, but withal a city full of men devoted to the new ideas of liberty and human brotherhood, blazed up together. The feeble police were brushed aside. The "French

Guards" (a kind of militia garrison) fraternized with the rioters. Arsenals were broken open and supplied weapons. The "electors"[1] set up an extemporized city government, and began to enroll a "National Guard."[2] After a day of utter confusion came a kind of orderly action. On the 14th of July the armed multitude cast itself on the King's castle, the old prison for prisoners "at the royal pleasure," the Bastile. Its dungeons were no longer full, but it was the emblem of autocratic power. De Launay, the governor, had cannon and strong walls and could have held out, but his small garrison was terrified at the thousands raging before their gates. He parleyed, surrendered, and then was shamefully massacred by the mob, while his captors were haling him to the City Hall.

Messengers in hot haste carried the news to Versailles. The Duke of Liancourt broke the tidings to Louis XVI. "This is a revolt!" cried the King. "No, Sire," answered the sagacious duke, "it is a revolution." The whole plot of the court party tumbled like a house of cards. To conquer raging Paris was a very different thing from dispersing the unarmed deputies. Necker was recalled. The position of the Assembly was left stronger than ever.

Despite provincial barriers and many other lines of division, France was in one particular an extremely centralized country. Paris dominated alike the political and the intellectual life of the remainder of the nation. Organized public effort of every kind seemed almost impossible away from the great city. The ignorance and political apathy of many rural districts was extreme. On July 4, 1789, an intelligent English traveler[3] had found himself in the thriving town of Château-Thierry. He could not discover a single newspaper (then abundant in Paris)

---

[1] These were the persons chosen by their fellow citizens to make the final selection for members of the National Assembly: they could thus claim something like a popular mandate for taking power.

[2] This enrollment of the "National Guard" — a military force at the disposal of the radicals and not of the King — was a much more important step *practically* than the capture of the Bastile.

[3] Arthur Young, an observant English gentleman. The account of his travels in France during 1787-89 is one of the classic authorities for this whole period.

to inform himself about the great public events. "What stupidity, poverty, and lack of circulation!" he records. "This people hardly deserve to be free; and should there be the least attempt with vigor to keep them otherwise it can hardly fail of succeeding." But now the news of the storming of the King's grim castle spread out to all the little villages and farms. Instantly there was a muttering, then fierce action among the peasantry. No more hated "feudal dues," extortionate taxes, tyrannous *corvées*. If "rights of the people" meant anything, they surely meant that! Soon in many districts the evening skies were red with the burning châteaux of the helpless noblesse. Elsewhere with less violence the peasants simply burned the record books for the feudal dues, thinking so to abolish them.

There was disorder everywhere and the threat of things worse. The army was not to be trusted. After the 14th of July the King had capitulated. He had visited Paris and had been met at the gate by the Mayor just elected by the new city government. "Henry IV," spoke the upstart functionary to Majesty, "reconquered his capital. Now the capital has reconquered its King!" Everywhere shone the new standard and the cockade of the revolution — the famous *tricouleur* destined to fly on a hundred stricken fields in the battle for liberty.[1] "National Guards," a kind of patriot militia, were springing into being everywhere to defend what men now gladly called "the Revolution."

The Assembly for some time strove to continue its elaborate debates on the "Rights of Man" and the fundamentals of enlightened government, but on the 4th of August a committee made a more practical report on the disordered state of France: rioting and arson everywhere, murders by mobs ("lynchings" Americans would call them) very frequent, tax-collecting suspended — anarchy threatening. Instantly a liberal-minded nobleman, the Vicomte de Noailles, declared it was needful to go to the root of the trouble. Let them abolish all feudal rights!

[1] Red and blue were the colors of Paris: white (the color of the Bourbons) was added out of respect to the King.

Soon in a spirit of self-sacrificing enthusiasm nearly all the old mediæval abuses and exactions were declared ended. The clergy surrendered some of their most cherished fiscal privileges. There was a frenzy of generous self-abnegation. Louis XVI, absent and ignorant of the debate, was voted the "Restorer of French Liberty!" A vast mass of venerable iniquities *seemed* swept from the law books. There had never been a like night in French history.

Admirable it was to vote this; infinitely less easy to rebuild on the old shattered foundations and to translate fine words into performance. The difficulty was increased by the promise given that all the losers of the old feudal dues should receive compensation. Whence were to come the funds — with Necker already at his wits' end to fend off bankruptcy, now that the taxes had almost dried up? The 4th of August, 1789, is a noble date in history, but it was to be not the end, but the beginning of strife and confusion unutterable.

The Revolution had now caught its full stride. The power had rarely slipped into the hands of the bourgeois elements, the solid intelligence of the nation which was anxious for sane and enduring reforms and was epually anxious to fend off anarchy. But the lower classes were already almost unmanageable. If the court and noblesse failed to give the Revolution an honest support, the bourgeois might not control the situation and every chance would be given the extremists. The King was perhaps honestly willing to accept the new order. Not so the Queen and the vapid princes and princesses who buzzed around her. The whole situation to them was monstrous and unbearable. To preserve their escaping privileges they were willing to throw dice for the peace and safety of France. The old intrigues of July were resumed in September. Again more troops (this time they hoped reliable) were moved up to Versailles. On the night of October 1 there was a great banquet to the newly arrived officers. There was much wine and much loose talking. The Queen was there in her sparkling beauty to draw out the loyal

THE CONSTITUENT ASSEMBLY AT VERSAILLES ON THE NIGHT OF AUGUST 4, 1789

shouts of the officers. The health of the royal family was drunk amid the waving and flashing of swords, while the orchestra crashed out the royalist song, "*Oh, Richard! Oh, my King, all the world abandons thee . . . but not I.*" Then it is said that the tricolor cockade was spitefully trampled under foot, while white cockades, the color of Bourbon royalty, were distributed; and lovely ladies mingled with the officers to confirm their loyalty and pin on the white ribbons.

It was a foolish demonstration, worthy of the intelligence of the Old Régime. The men whom the court party needed to make sure of were not the officers, but the rank and file of their regiments. The tale of these doings, of course, spread to Paris with due exaggerations. Again the capital boiled. The new liberty had not brought cheap bread. Very many were hungry. On October 4 a riotous demonstration took place before the City Hall. Coarse, strong-armed market-women and, it would seem, men masquerading in dresses, led the demonstration. The new National Guard confronted them, but could hardly be relied upon to take stern action. "You'll not fire on women!" rang the cry. Then, probably to divert them from a riot in Paris, some one began pounding a drum, and shouted, "To Versailles!" Off the whole throng swept, headed by the women yelling for "bread." Lafayette, commander of the National Guard, uncertain of his men and in sore perplexity as to the whole affair, followed them with most of his force.

The King at Versailles was parleying with a delegation of the Assembly over accepting the newly drafted "Rights of Man" when the motley host swept up from Paris. At first the gates of the château were closed, and when Lafayette arrived the danger seemed over. But as the next day broke the watch relaxed. Some of the mob (the worse for liquor) forced their way into the residence, and killed several of the royal bodyguard while they were defending the chambers of the Queen. Lafayette at length rallied enough reliable men to stop the rioting, but the whole temper of the multitude (including the National Guard) was such that there could be no assurance of safety until the King consented to depart with all his family for Paris. Thither he went, escorted by Lafayette, but also by the wild throng of viragoes, tossing their arms around the royal coach and howling in glee, "We have got the baker and the baker's wife and the baker's little boy! — *Now* we shall have bread." (October 5.)

The King was lodged in the old palace of the Tuileries. The Assembly (probably not sorry to see the court thus humiliated) made haste to follow to Paris and resumed its debates in a great riding-school near the palace. Once more the Revolution had been saved from a Royalist reaction. But it had been saved at a price. The court had been constrained by no orderly process of law, but by sheer mob violence. King and Assembly alike were now in Paris, the city of a thousand passions. They were always subject, in case they resisted the gusts of popular opinion, to physical coercion by unkempt rioters. Henceforth, more and more, the extremists of the Paris faubourgs came to take the will of their own narrow circles for the will of entire France; to assume to speak for the entire nation, and, if resisted, in the name of the nation to justify every deed of blood.

These sinister elements, however, were not at first predominant. There was abundant good-will and patriotism in the Assembly, and it now at length devoted itself to the great task of reorganizing France. For two years there was relative calm, and it could even be argued plausibly that the Revolution had been accomplished with, all things considered, a commendably small amount of bloodshed. There is still great difference of opinion as to the excellence of the new institutions which the Assembly now gave to France. On the whole it may be said that considering the absolute lack of political experience hitherto permitted to Frenchmen, the blunders were by no means greater than might be expected.[1] Many of the enactments of 1789–91 remain the law of France to this day, and many of the others

[1] Comparisons of Revolutionary France with Revolutionary Russia will leave modern students very lenient in their judgments on Frenchmen of 1789–95.

probably did not deserve to perish. Nevertheless the melancholy spectacle remained of a great constitutional edifice being laboriously erected, next proclaimed as being substantially perpetual — and then vanishing in smoke and blood within a year after it had been changed from proposals to practice.

It is better to state the principal enactments of the Assembly in these years than to hint at the reasons for each particular change. There was still in France no serious movement to establish a republic. The men who drafted the Constitution of 1791 were, however, profoundly under the influence of the dogmas of Rousseau and Montesquieu. They wished to vest all the power in the people, yet they did not abolish hereditary kingship. They wished an efficient executive, but they feared still more lest the executive should encroach upon the popular rights. They were also in great dread lest the King should somehow ruin the new liberties by corrupting or cozening the national legislature. The result was a constitution which, despite much that was excellent, failed to function properly the minute it was put in practice and thereby exposed to inevitable criticism and opposition.

If liberal intentions could make a great nation prosper, the Assembly could easily have put France upon the highroad to happiness. All the old restraints on commerce and industry were swept away. The Huguenots and Jews were given complete toleration. Primogeniture and such other rights of inheritance as tended to perpetuate an aristocratic society were abolished. All titles of nobility were also abolished, and priests were reduced to the mere status of public functionaries. The death penalties for many crimes were removed. All Frenchmen were declared equal in legal privileges, in liability to taxation according to their ability, and in their rights to public employments. The old provinces had been serious promoters of isolation and particularism and local pettiness. They were now done away. In their place France was divided into eighty-three "departments," about equal in size, and named after their rivers, mountains, etc. The departments were subdivided into "districts," these into "cantons," and these in turn into still smaller "communes," the primary units of the country, 44,828 in all. France thus became a highly articulated nation organized upon a uniform plan, with everything radiating from the nerve centers of government at Paris.

The inefficient old law courts were likewise abolished. A supreme Court of Cassation for the entire country was set up, with a system of local courts tapering down to the justices of the peace in the cantons. The magistrates were to be elected by their fellow citizens for ten years, and the great safeguard of jury trials was instituted for the more serious criminal cases. The Assembly also voted that a uniform civil code of laws should be compiled — a great task only to be executed by Napoleon. The ancient abuses in taxation were cancelled in their turn. The provincial customs barriers perished with the old provinces. The other taxes were simplified and put on a reasonably scientific basis. Schemes were set on foot for a general system of education. In short, the Assembly was entitled to high credit for much eminently successful or promising legislation along social, economic, or administrative lines, and a great fraction of what it accomplished in these directions was destined to endure — and to endure because it was worthy.

Probably the members took the highest pride (and very rightly) in their solemn pronunciament, "The Declaration of the Rights of Man," the seventeen articles of which became the veritable *Credo* of the Revolution. Although couched in terms instantly reminiscent of Rousseau and Montesquieu, few genuine Americans will quarrel with its main principles. "Men are born and remain free and equal in rights," ran Article I. "Social distinctions may be founded only upon the general good."[1]

---

[1] This Declaration was very far from being a radical document. It expressed the moderate good sense of the bourgeoisie. Article XVII expressly said,

It was in devising the political machinery which was to insure the smooth working of all these desirable laws or theories that the Assembly made its most serious blunders. Truth to tell the situation would have been immensely improved could the legislators have had to deal with a different type of king. Louis XVI did not frankly reject the Revolution and trust himself to the risks of a civil war, nor did he with dignity abdicate. He never, however, clearly and unfeignedly accepted the New Order which took away from him all rights to make laws and merely left him the honor of being the chief functionary in the State. He made concession after concession, but never in a manner that convinced his contemporaries that he was glad to pass from the giddy honors of autocracy to the safer life of a hereditary president. He was simply a well-meaning, much-bewildered man driven from point to point by an overwhelming situation. Worst of all, he never gained the courage to silence his wife in her openly reactionary counsels. He gained the ill-will of many powerful leaders he should have conciliated, and he could not conceal his disgust at many innovations he was powerless to prevent. From his great nobles and even from his own brothers he gained little enough of support and sage promptings. They were openly angry at his unwillingness to resist with force the popular demands. The best chance for Louis would have been to have taken the lead openly in championing the New Order, to have constituted himself a real "Citizen-King," champion and "tribune" of the people. All elements would then probably have rallied to him and his personal position would have been secure. But no such boldness was possible for the dull, kind-hearted individual who had inherited the titles of Louis XIV.

However, in any case the Assembly prepared a constitution for France whereof the working would have been hard, even for a very able King-President. There was to be only one cham-

---

"Property is an inviolable and sacred right," and not to be tampered with except the owner be "previously and equitably indemnified." Ultra-radicals could hardly accept this doctrine to-day.

ber in the Legislature, partly out of real detestation of a House of Lords, and partly it would seem because of a deliberate desire not to seem to imitate England. This united body was to be elected for a term of two years by the votes of all citizens aged twenty-five who paid a direct local tax equal to three days' work.[1] The King could not dissolve it or coerce it in any way. As first proposed, the King was not to be allowed to have any effective veto. On the other hand, he was supposed to choose the ministers to execute all the laws and to be responsible for the smooth working of the government. It was directly forbidden the King to take his ministers from among the members of the new "Legislative Assembly." Even under the circumstances, it is amazing that the majority of the constitution-makers did not see how such an arrangement was adapted to promote endless discord between executive and legislature, with no way out of the difficulty save a new revolution. Mirabeau did, indeed, understand matters clearly and uttered his warnings, but the radicals were already counting him "too moderate." They marched onward to disaster.

But the heaviest handicap for the New Order came by the gratuitous act of the Assembly in picking a quarrel with the Church. The deficit had not been met. Necker was more desperate than ever in seeking funds. Without counting all the inevitable cost, in 1790 the Assembly ordered the "nationalizing" (that is, the practical confiscation) of the ample Church lands. The clergy were, indeed, promised remuneration for the incomes they thus lost, but the immediate effect was to enable the Assembly to embark on the issuance of *assignats* (paper money secured by the expected sale of the Church lands), at first in moderate amounts, but then more and more until France was involved in all the perplexities and sorrows of an extremely depreciated paper currency.

---

[1] The sum involved would vary according to local custom. This discrimination against the very poor ("passive citizens") was bitterly resented, and helped to make the new constitution unpopular.

This act, of course, made every churchman anxious. It was speedily followed by something worse. The "Civil Constitution of the Clergy" was enacted. All priests were obliged to take oath to obey it. The Assembly undertook to reorganize the French Church as if it had been directly authorized to do so by the Pope. Instead of one hundred and thirty-five bishops there were to be only eighty-three (one for each department), and these and the parish *curés* were to be chosen by the same electors that chose the secular officials. The number of convents was reduced; the taking of monastic vows made difficult. No attempt was made to define points in theology, but the whole effect of the law was to make the "Catholicism in France different from that in Rome, at least in respect to discipline, canonical institutions, and spiritual jurisdiction."

The result of this unhappy law was soon evident. The Assembly surely had enough secular problems to settle without embroiling itself with the Catholic Church. Hitherto most of the *curés* and some of the worthier bishops had sided with the New Order. Now nearly all who were not worldly time-servers obeyed the Pope when he forbade the taking of the required oath (1791). They quitted their bishoprics and parishes, ejected by the less worthy remainder who, as "sworn" or "constitutional priests," usurped rectories and churches. The ejected clinics became instantly a dangerous dissenting element, venerated by the pious laity and a standing source of great danger to the whole work of the Revolution. Above all, the King (a very pious Catholic) was outraged and angered almost beyond reconciliation. The "Civil Constitution of the Clergy" was the greatest single blunder of the Constituent Assembly.

In April, 1791, Mirabeau died, the sanest leader of the Revolution, and one who, in 1790, had vainly tried to hold back the extremists and come to a fair understanding with the King. With him passed the only prominent man who understood just whither France was drifting. Louis XVI was now desperate. He had consented to the new Church laws only because he considered himself coerced and unable to resist. His brother, the Count of Artois, and many "emigrant" nobles had already fled abroad and were stirring up the rulers of Austria, Prussia, Spain, and Savoy to intervene in behalf of a brother monarch whose subjects were teaching to all the peoples of Europe daily lessons in disloyalty. Louis and Marie Antoinette were alike in a mood to call in foreign armies to prop up the throne of the once arrogant Bourbons. What a throne maintained by such humiliating means would have been worth, neither King nor Queen seemed in a mood to answer.

On June 21, 1791, Louis XVI and the Queen escaped from Paris, Marie Antoinette disguised as a Russian lady and her husband as her valet. They were headed toward Lorraine where there was supposed to be a loyal general and army, and whence in any case they could easily flee over the border. The whole flight was one series of blunders. The royal party delayed matters by insisting on traveling with considerable state in a lumbering coach with much impedimenta including the Queen's bathtub. Had they been willing to fly post-haste, they could doubtless have got away safely. As it was the alarm was given. At Varennes the party was halted and arrested, held prisoner ignominiously over a grocery shop, and then driven back with every humiliation to Paris. The flight had failed. The true sentiments of the King had been revealed. He stood branded before all the world as being out of sympathy with his people. The capital received him back with "reproachful silence" as ominous as open threatenings, while the Assembly suspended him from office.

The situation was such that nothing but abdication or downright deposition ought to have awaited Louis XVI. But the Assembly was very loath to turn the power over to his brother, the reactionary Comte de Provence, himself an "emigrant" who would logically have become regent for the very young Dauphin. It was still far from willing to proclaim a republic.[1]

[1] An agitation to remove Louis was actually conducted by Danton, already

Intelligent men realized that Louis's position deserved sympathy as well as blame. The King on his part, in a very chastened mood, showed himself willing to ratify the new Constitution. At last a solemn truce was arranged. On September 14, 1791, Louis XVI wrote to the Assembly: "I accept the Constitution. I engage to maintain it at home, to defend it from all attacks from abroad, and to cause its execution by all the means it places at my disposal." Under these circumstances the King was reinstated in power. On the 29th of September, he closed the Assembly amid congratulations, expressions of good-will and applause, after a friendly speech "worthy of Henry IV," as a voice cried across the hall. It was an enthusiasm which events were not to justify.

"The Revolution," announced Robespierre, of whom the world was to hear more hereafter — "the Revolution is finished!" These words were spoken September 29, 1791. The next day amid great rejoicings the Constituent Assembly broke up. Its members had redeemed the Oath of the Tennis Court. They had given a constitution to France. Some of their work was admirable, some was very faulty. Much of it was to crumble instantly. Intentions had been of the very best, but the subsequent history has justified the verdict of a sane and clear-minded Frenchman: "The Constituent Assembly would have done better to have suppressed royalty outright, and to have made a republican constitution. Unfortunately, despite its defiance of Louis XVI, it was profoundly monarchical in many of its tendencies. The men of 1791 thought they were creating a monarchical constitution. They actually made one that was neither monarchical nor republican. It was not even a parliamentary constitution." [1]

The "Constituent" Assembly dissolved. Its creation and becoming a power in Paris; but it was suppressed. The bourgeois National Guard was still opposed to a republic, and Danton and his fellow radicals were temporarily silenced.

[1] Malet.

child, the "Legislative" Assembly, which was to enact the ordinary working legislation of France, met immediately. The earlier body had committed one crowning blunder. Despite much of error and mediocrity, the "Constituent" had come to contain many men well experienced now in public affairs. These members should have undertaken to govern the country, but on the unhappy proposal of Robespierre the "Constituent" had passed a self-denying ordinance. None of its members were to be eligible to the new "Legislative." The latter body, when it convened, therefore, October 1, 1791, was made up entirely of untried men who knew little of the legal instrument they were expected to work. This blunder was equivalent to a lost battle for French liberty.

In October, 1791, however, what the men of 1789 had fought for appeared to have been won. The grievances of the Old Régime were vanished. A constitution that seemed to satisfy the national demand had been granted. The average Frenchman, tired of the unfamiliar excitement and confusion of politics, desired nothing better than to return to his civil occupations. Despite the flight to Varennes, the great majority of the people still desired to keep Louis XVI, and they certainly did not desire the bloody adventure of a great foreign war; but the foreign war came in April; the King was a helpless prisoner in August; and France was formally proclaimed a republic in September. Seldom had there been such a rush of capital events.

The Legislative Assembly met immediately after its parent, the Constituent, disbanded. It was a lumbering, over-large body of 745 members — very inexperienced, as has just been stated. In the election many moderate, substantial citizens, who might have taken a leading part, had become weary of the scramble of politics, and stood back to let inferior men be chosen. It is also charged that the radicals in many districts resorted to various forms of coercion to get extremist members elected. In any case the "Legislative," along with not a few honest patriots, contained many small-caliber adventurers who

THE MOUNTAIN AND THE GIRONDISTS 287

were quite willing to urge "change" merely for the sake of self-advertising.

Soon well-defined parties showed themselves. There was the respectable party of "Constitutionalists," friends of the New Order, but who desired to go no farther. They might have held their own had they been heartily supported by the old court element. The Royalists were impotent to defend themselves, but they were quite able to dream of a reaction, and to undermine the influence of any party that stood for the hated compromise of 1791. A considerable body of deputies had come to Paris frankly without a fixed programme; they were amiable opportunists willing to let things drift. But there was a still more formidable body of radicals, who (thanks to the very numbness and genteel inertia of their opponents) were soon able to dominate the "Legislative." These radicals fell roughly into the groups of the "Girondists" and of the "Mountain."[1]

The "Mountaineers" were the true ultra-radicals, whose leaders were presently to dominate France. The Girondists, who took their name from the Department of the Gironde whence came their most prominent leaders, were hot-blooded, clever, generous-hearted young lawyers, full of Plutarch and Rousseau, very ready to imagine that what was good for Athens was necessarily good for France, and frankly anxious to substitute a moderate republic for even the denatured Monarchy left in power. Some of their members — for example, Vergniaud, Brissot, etc. — were persons of remarkable eloquence and equally lofty ideals, but one of their chief guiding spirits could not sit in the "Legislative"; she was Madame Roland, "a bright ambitious woman, with a touch of genius, a taste for clubs, and a great fondness for attending to her elderly husband's business."

These nimble-witted persons were not, however, the extreme men of action. Already we meet the influence of the famous

[1] So called from the location of the high tiers of seats which they occupied in the hall of the "Legislative."

"Jacobin" Club,[1] which had begun in Paris in 1789 as a legitimate debating society with many very conservative members, but which, by 1791, had become the center for all the radicalism of the capital, with a very great influence upon the unwashed masses of the great city. From the pulpit of the Jacobin Club endless daring theories could be ventilated that would be suppressed in the Assembly or the "Legislative," and under the stimulus of this irresponsible theorizing, it was easy for one proposition to lead, with stern fanatical logic, onwards to another. The Jacobin Club, therefore, in time became the center for the propaganda of the extreme Rousseau doctrines, with the genuine propagandist's corollary, that since the doctrines were *true*, all means were lawful in giving them effect. Three men of historic fame were the soul of this Jacobin agitation — Marat, Danton, Robespierre.

Marat was a physician and scientific man of some attainments. In 1789 he began an agitation of the utmost virulence, not merely against the King, but against all the more moderate Liberals like Lafayette. He constituted himself the champion of the lowest classes — the "proletariat," to use a recent phrase, as opposed to the bourgeoisie. His paper, "The Friend of the People," became the oracle and the inspiration of all the lewd, loose spirits in Paris. He excelled in coarse invective, and seemed to delight in appealing to the most sinister passions. Against all constituted authority he had the animosity of a tiger. It would not be fair to call him an anarchist. He seems to have had his dreams of an orderly elysium — but only after the ruthless destruction of nearly everything which men had hitherto honored or called lawful.

Danton was a far less repellent figure. He was a young Paris advocate of remarkable eloquence and no slight practical ability. He had at first welcomed the Revolution of 1789, but its changes had not been radical enough to please him. Soon the Jacobin

---

[1] The name came from the old convent of the "Jacobin" monks (Monks of St. James) in which the meetings of the club were held.

MARIE ANTOINETTE

ROBESPIERRE

MARAT

DANTON

Club was accustomed to ring with the great voice of this tall, brawny man, of harsh and daring countenance, and beetling black brows, as he thundered against "the aristocrats." Danton exercised extraordinary power over what may be called the more respectable elements in the Paris mob, even as Marat was the darling of the basest. Danton wished to establish a republic and he was ready for very drastic means to gain his ends, but as events were to prove he was no friend either of needless bloodletting or of anarchy. He was by all odds the worthiest leader of the Jacobins.

Robespierre was another advocate, not however from Paris but Artois. He had served in the "Constituent," and then, when that body disbanded, he shared with Danton the honors of chief orator at the Jacobin Club. He was a "precise, austere, intense, mediocre little man whose life had been passed in poverty and study." No other leader of the Revolution ever accepted the teachings of Rousseau more implicitly than he. Probably with perfect sincerity he claimed and boasted himself to be "virtuous and incorruptible." The multitude believed him, and he gained all the prestige and following that always comes to a leader widely accepted as being unselfish and good. Robespierre was, indeed, more a man of talk than of action. Very likely from the first he was being thrust forward by others who arranged the deeds and needed a mouthpiece. He was destined, however, to become the most notable single figure in all the fiery second stage of the Revolution.

The Girondists, in short, were amiable theorists willing to see the King overthrown and a republic established, but they were incapable of fierce action and willing to let matters somewhat drift. The Jacobins were equally theorists, but they were not so amiable. They were ready and willing for action, and did *not* intend to let matters drift. No prophet was needed to tell with which faction lay the future.

With such members it did not take the Legislative Assembly long to pass first to pin-pricks and then to drawn daggers with the King. The deputies abolished the use of the terms "Sire" and "Your Majesty" in addressing royalty. There were other small matters of friction, but the first real issue came when the "Legislative" undertook to consider the foreign dangers now confronting the nation. Ever since 1789, now singly, now in scores, the great nobles of France had been packing their jewels and fleeing the realm. Both of Louis's brothers by this time were across the frontier; and at Trèves and Mayence in Germany a small army of these highborn "emigrants" had been collecting. The noble exiles were loud in their boasts and threats of bloody return and vengeance. They were using all their personal influence to get the Emperor of Austria and the King of Prussia to intervene in arms. In August, 1791, these two monarchs had issued the non-committal "Declaration of Pilnitz," announcing that they considered the cause of Louis XVI the cause of all the crowned heads of Europe. Nothing had followed, but how soon might not a foreign army strike? In view of the flight to Varennes how far were the French King and Queen to be trusted not to welcome an invader? To all the privileged classes of despot-ridden Europe, the Revolution was coming to be simply an outrageous thing, a menace to every man of wealth and coat-armor. If the nation that had posed as the intellectual leader of civilization could reduce its king to a position of little more than hereditary high-sheriff, could destroy all the rights of the nobility, could put a bargeman politically on a level with a Prince of the Blood, what would be the effect of the example upon the peasants of Prussia, Bohemia, Tuscany, and a dozen regions more? The undeniable excesses of some of the Revolutionists, of course, kindled hotter the flames of indignation. There was genuine sympathy for the plight of the beautiful Queen held prisoner in the Tuileries. There was anger, especially in Germany, over the abolition of feudal dues in certain parts of Alsace, the financial claims upon which had been retained by various German princes when they had relaxed their political dominion.

The situation was full of menace, especially as it was well known that the discipline of the French army and navy had been utterly shaken by recent events. Matters came to a climax in the spring of 1792. The attitude of the Austrian Government had seemed so equivocal that the "Legislative" had addressed it a formal demand to state its intentions. The answer came from the young Emperor Francis II, the nephew of Marie Antoinette,[1] who sent a flat demand for indemnity to the offended German princes (who claimed certain feudal rights in Alsace) and for a reëstablishment of the Old Régime, on the basis proposed by Louis before the fall of the Bastile. After that, indeed, there was only one answer for France to make, unless she was to confess that her domestic broils had removed her from the list of the great nations of Europe. On April 20, 1792, Louis XVI appeared before the deputies and asked for a declaration of war on Austria, and it was at once voted with only seven voices opposing; and so began a struggle that was to last, with short intervals of truce rather than of peace, three and twenty years till Waterloo.

There had been two French parties in favor of the war — from very different motives. Marie Antoinette and the court party seem to have been reckoning that either the public enemy would march to Paris — in which case the Revolution would collapse — or at least a victorious war would bring such prestige to the King that his position would become more endurable. The Girondists also favored the war. They believed, and rightly, that the foreign struggle would bring about such a domestic reaction as to sweep away the Monarchy. Only the extreme Jacobins had argued for peace. A war was likely to give the King a kind of dictatorship, and the burdens would all fall upon the lowly. "Who is it that suffers in a war?" wrote Marat; "not the rich, but the poor; not the high-born officer, but the poor peasant."

[1] He was genuinely concerned for his aunt, and anxious to save her from a most humiliating and dangerous position, but he took the worst possible means to accomplish his end.

Already there were abundant signs of a complete schism between the King and his legislature. The "Legislative" passed a bill ordering banishment for priests who refused to take oath of allegiance to the New Order. The King had vetoed this act — as under the Constitution he had the right to do.[1] The proposed law had certainly been harsh, possibly cruel; but popular belief made the "non-juring" priests so many agents of sedition. The Queen was accused of stopping the legislation, and loud were the curses in Paris against "the Austrian" and "Madame Veto." Louis also struggled vainly, in an effort to find ministers who would be acceptable to the dominant factions in the "Legislative" and could at the same time give France orderly and firm government. Such men were not to be found. If they were agreeable to the majority of the deputies, they could not really sustain the Constitution. If they failed to sustain the Constitution, they of course were intolerable to the King and let the land drift off into misrule. The treasury was in a worse plight than ever. Necker had long since retired hopelessly discredited. Probably there would have been an explosion in any case; but the foreign war assuredly hastened it.

Prussia had made prompt alliance with her old foe Austria. Truth to tell, though there was much cursing of the Revolution in Vienna and Berlin, and many commiserations for Marie Antoinette, there was also a keen appreciation that France, the nation which had once dominated the Continent, was in such grievous agony that a smart military blow might end the menace to her rivals forever. The French army was in an utterly deplorable state. In all 300,000 men had been reckoned for it on paper, but the bands of discipline had been loosed. Many officers had been cashiered or had fled the country. The men were sorely out of hand. Not more than 82,000 men were avail-

---

[1] By the Constitution of 1791 the King had finally been given the "suspensive" veto; the right to halt the enactment of a proposed law until it had been passed again by two successive Legislative Assemblies — that is, to delay the measure for four years.

able as mobile field armies. Against these the Duke of Brunswick (reputed an able general of Frederick the Great) prepared to move a considerably larger force of excellent troops. Fortunately for the French, the Allies advanced very slowly, and instead of striking boldly at Paris, they were anxious to reduce the frontier fortresses, but in practically every engagement the French were worsted. In some cases they were not merely defeated, but fled in disgraceful panic. Everywhere, in the army, in the provinces, in Paris, spread the desperate cry, "We are betrayed!" The Jacobins roundly declared that the courtiers in the Tuileries were praying to see the Allies enter Paris, bringing back all the "emigrant" nobles with their schemes of vengeance, and freely it was suggested that these disloyal monarchists were not confining their treasons to wishes and prayers. This military failure destroyed the last real chance for preserving the Monarchy and the Constitution of 1791.

The story of the last days of the Monarchy need not halt us long. As the military situation grew worse, the position of Louis XVI grew increasingly impossible. His Queen, at least, was a traitress. In March, 1792, she had sent to the Austrian court a memorandum of the French plan of campaign. As the news of disaster drifted into Paris the excitement of the city increased. On June 20 there was a riotous demonstration before the palace. It ended in a mob of the most sordid elements forcing their way into the royal apartments, thrusting the red "liberty cap" upon Louis's head, and offering gross familiarities to the Queen and Dauphin. The royal couple carried themselves with courage and dignity, and so averted deeds which might have ended with a lynching. There was a momentary reaction among the better elements in favor of the King. Honorable and moderate men realized that the whole country was in danger of anarchy if its rulers could thus be insulted. Lafayette came back from the army and demanded punishment of the Jacobin agitators. But Marie Antoinette and the court nobles were apparently anxious to hasten their own way to the scaffold — they could not forgive Lafayette and his fellow Liberals for assisting in the original Revolution of 1789. His offers of assistance were haughtily waved aside. Lafayette thus was left a discredited, nigh powerless man, hated by the Jacobins and rejected by the Royalists. He returned sorrowfully to his army and let matters take their course.[1]

The Girondists were now thundering in the "Legislative" that the King ought to abdicate. Why were the Austro-Prussians advancing? "Because," cried Brissot from the tribune, "a man — one man — the man whom the Constitution has made its chief, and whom perfidious advisers have made its foe [has paralyzed it!] . . . You are told to fear the kings of Hungary and Prussia: I say, the chief force of these kings is at the court, and *there* it is that we must conquer first! . . . This is the secret of our position. This is the source of the evil, and here the remedy must be applied."

Under such promptings, on the 11th of July, the "Legislative" solemnly voted the declaration — "Citizens — the country is in danger!" and attempts were made at a levy *en masse*, to hold back the invader. There were also clear indications of organizing armed action in Paris, for fighting foes much nearer to the King's residence than were the foreign armies. But the deadliest stab against the Monarchy came from a nominal friend. On July 28 the Prussian army began its advance from Coblenz. In a moment of utter folly, its leader, the Duke of Brunswick, published a manifesto in the name of Austria and Prussia.[2] He announced that he was entering France to rescue its King from captivity; that the inhabitants of towns who "dared to stand on the defensive" should be instantly punished as rebels and their houses burned; that martial punishment would be meted

[1] When the Monarchy was overthrown on August 10, 1792, Lafayette was at Sedan. He attempted to rally his army to uphold the Constitution of 1791 and to fight the Jacobins. When his attempt failed, he endeavored to flee to America, but was captured by the Austrians and held prisoner several years.

[2] It is alleged that the document was really by a French "emigrant" noble, but Brunswick signed and published it, possibly against his better judgment.

out to all members of the National Guard if the city of Paris did not restore to the King full liberty; and finally that if the King's palace were attacked the invading princes would make an example by "delivering Paris over to military execution and total destruction."

Such a manifesto was enough to drive every Frenchman to desperation. As was written by a historian whose parents lived through these days of wrath: "There was but one wish, one cry of resistance from one end of France to the other: and whoever had not joined in it, would have been looked on as guilty of impiety toward his country and the sacred cause of independence."[1] From the moment that copies of this woeful declaration reached the capital the only question was — how would the Monarchy fall?

Some of the Girondists were probably still willing to trust to "moral suasion" to induce Louis to abdicate, but not so the more ardent of their faction, and not so the robust Jacobins. On July 30 there swung into Paris a swart, grimy column, five hundred and thirteen men "who knew how to die," tugging two guns. They were the "men of Marseilles," volunteers of the National Guard from the southern seaport, who had in four weeks trudged up to the capital to save the nation and end the rule of "the Austrian woman." They were singing a hymn that had really been composed in Strasbourg as the "Song of the Army of the Rhine," by Rouget de Lisle, but which now was caught up by these stark, determined men as their battle-song. Soon all Paris, then all France, was singing this "Marseillaise" — the most passionate, soul-stirring of all national anthems, the best of all fighting songs to make strong men march onward to win or to die. Before this arrival the "Legislative" had been tossing about the question of some peaceful means to end the Monarchy. Now the radicals forced the issue.

The Marseilles volunteers made the nucleus for a fighting force. Danton and his friends were indefatigable in the lower

[1] Mignet.

quarters of Paris. A large part of the National Guard had been won over. Pétion, Mayor of the capital, was on the insurgents' side. There were still very many respectable men who wished the King well; who preferred in fact that he should be kept in power; but very few of these worthy people were anxious to die in behalf of a very discredited Monarchy. They were paralyzed also by the rumors (not unfounded) that there was treason within the palace, and the clearer knowledge that the foreign foe might soon be marching upon Paris. Against them were the radicals, sure of their goal and without fear or scruple.

On the 10th of August the plot was sprung. The city government (commune) of Paris was in the hands of the Revolutionists. The commander of the palace, Mandat, was a loyal defender of the King, but outside of the royal Swiss body-guardsmen (some 800), he had very few troops on whom he could rely. Just as matters were coming to a climax, Mandat was first kidnapped by the insurgents, then brutally murdered. The King's weak forces were left thus without a commander. Soon after dawn a threatening crowd was before the Tuileries. For safety's sake the King and royal family took refuge in the hall of the Legislative Assembly and spent a most unhappy day in the small "reporters'" room. Then, in his absence, the Marseilles battalion forced its way into the palace court, followed by the other insurgent elements. The Swiss Guards were foreigners, without interest in French disputes, but honorably loyal to their good paymaster the King. Soon a volley rang out. The Swiss were trained infantry. They cleared the palace courtyard, and then maintained a deadly fire from the windows. A young officer was spectator of the fighting. His judgment was that if the Swiss had been properly led and allowed to keep up their resistance, they would have snuffed out the whole insurrection — at least for the instant. His judgment was worth heeding, for his name was Napoleon Bonaparte. But the sound of the firing was terrifying to Louis. He had no confidence that the Swiss could resist, and his heart was torn at the thought of shooting down his fellow countrymen. He sent orders to the guardsmen to stop firing. Some of the Swiss made a safe retreat. Some were separated from their comrades and massacred as the exultant Revolutionaries swarmed back into the palace. So fell the Bourbon monarchy. It did not even honor its end by an heroic resistance to the last cartridge.

All through the firing, the royal family and the Legislative Assembly had shivered together. Might not the unpent insurgents involve King, Queen, and deputies in one common massacre? Now, as the musketry ceased, deputations of angry, imperious men came thrusting into the great hall with demands rather than petitions. The Paris Commune required the instant deposition of the King. The deputies hesitated to take so heavy a responsibility, but Vergniaud, leader of the Girondists, mounted the tribune. "I am to propose to you," spoke he, "a very vigorous measure. I appeal to the affliction of our hearts to judge how needful it is to adopt it immediately." His motion, which was unanimously carried, was to dismiss all the royal ministers, to suspend the King in office, and to convoke a new national convention which was to give yet another constitution to France. So ended this memorable 10th of August, 1792. Louis XVI ("Louis Capet" as they were already beginning to call him) was transferred to the Luxembourg Palace, where at first he was treated with decent consideration.[1]

Feudalism had seemed to go in 1789. Monarchy had gone in 1792. The question now was were the respectable bourgeois, the men of education, honest substance, and moderation, who had overthrown the Old Régime, to be themselves engulfed by the rising spirit of the lower classes, the *sans-culottes*, the "men without short breeches," who did not dress as gentlemen, whose hands were grimy and horny, whose heads were full of wild passions and equally wild dreams of happiness supplied them by Danton and Marat? Twentieth-century Americans who have

[1] He was later removed to more prison-like quarters in the "Temple" on the pretext that at the Luxembourg he might be attacked by the mob.

witnessed the fate of Russia after the collapse of czardom, know the modern equivalent of Jacobinism — Bolshevism: the turning of all political and economic power over to the unkempt proletariat with no preliminary attempt to make the new master worthy by careful education. The sequel was to show how much more heroic before a Teutonic peril, were the followers of Danton than the followers of Lenine.

Be that as it may, the overthrow of the Monarchy was to cut the last lashings holding France to her historic past. The "Sovereign People," extolled for their natural simplicity and innocency by Rousseau, had at last come fairly into their own. Wild scenes there were in the narrow streets and in the wineshops of Paris those days in 1792; excited men and brawny women joining in headlong demonstrations.

"Dance we the Carmagnole!" ran their song. *"Hurrah for the roar of the cannon!"*

The cannon were to roar in France all that year, and the next, and the next. We reach the second: the more lurid stage of the Revolution.

CHAPTER XV
THE YEARS OF BLOOD AND WRATH: 1792-95

FRANCE, as already observed, was a highly centralized state. Seven hundred thousand Parisians, affecting to speak for the entire nation, had accomplished a new revolution without pretending to consult the wishes of their 24,000,000 fellow citizens in the departments. When the news spread of the downfall of the King, the rest of France received it dumbly. Many of the more radical were, of course, glad to have Louis go, out of mere hatred of monarchy. The bulk of the peasantry would doubtless have been pleased to have matters quiet down, so that they might live peaceably on their little farms. But the foreign foe was advancing. Would not the feudal dues and the hated taxes return if the Prussians took Paris? Would *any* of the newly won personal liberties then be secure? With the nation in tumult, with the foe advancing, with everything, public or personal, that was precious at stake, what was there left but to accept a republic and to arm for the great emergency? That was the spirit of France in August and September, 1792. It was practically impossible to refuse to be a radical, because the radicals were the only people that had a programme which promised safety for the nation.

While the election to the new "Convention" was taking place, the old "Legislative" continued nominally in power-ruling France by means of an Executive Council of Five, but it was speedily evident that the real disposing power lay with the Commune of Paris,[1] men of ultra-Jacobin stamp, that speedily

[1] These "representatives" of the twenty-eight sections of the city had forced the original legal representatives to resign, and thrust themselves into their places without the slightest warrant save that of mob rule.

showed intense jealousy of the more moderate Girondists who seemed to represent the departments rather than the turbid capital. There was no time for petty bickerings, however. At the mouth of the Loire the pious peasantry in the Vendée district had taken arms, mainly because of the laws against the non-juring priests. The Prussians were pressing forward. Longwy was taken; then came the fell tidings that Verdun, already one of the keys to an advance on Paris, had surrendered. The news stirred the capital to frantic energy. There were hasty levies and military preparations, but the Jacobins feared an attack from the rear no less than from the front. The King and Queen were helpless, but not so the thousands of Royalists and upper bourgeoisie who might be praying for reaction. Late in August the gates of Paris were closed, and the whole city searched by detachments of the National Guard for suspects and sympathizers with the fallen régime. Soon three thousand-odd persons were in the overflowing prisons, but Danton at least was not satisfied. "To stop the enemy," he said bluntly, "*we must make the Royalists fear.*"

Danton in fact was working himself and his followers up into that heroic condition of mind which presages great victories or overwhelming defeat. Even across the century sounds his voice, as it trumpeted in the "Legislative" on September 2. "The signal-gun thunders! It sounds the charge upon the enemies of France! Conquer them! *Boldness, and more boldness, and ever more boldness, and France is saved!*" This was an appeal which sent the blood of his countrymen tingling, and caused the "Legislative" to vote that every man who could not march to the frontier should give his weapons to one who could, or be branded forever as infamous.

But Danton and Marat (then his coadjutor) knew well how "to make the Royalists fear." Possibly the actual deed of blood was without Danton's instigation. Marat was certainly more able to manage such a project. We do not know just how the acts which followed were organized. The fact is that between

September 2 and 7, a band of three hundred assassins, the scum of humanity, directed and paid six francs per day by the Commune, proceeded from prison to prison. They dragged out the political prisoners, gave them the barest travesty of a trial, or no trial at all, and then slaughtered the victims in cold blood. A very few prisoners were spared by some caprice or a flash of mercy, but eleven hundred persons thus perished in Paris. The rage of the murderers went out particularly against the priests. Two hundred and fifty of them were slaughtered. Moderate men in the "Legislative" wrung their hands, but were helpless. The soldiers would not defend the prisons when the band of assassins drew nigh. The Jacobins had ended the danger of a Royalist uprising in Paris for a surety!

The slaughter ceased on September 7. On September 20 was fought a battle which terminated the last hope of rescue and vengeance for the shivering survivors of the Old Régime. It was not a mighty battle as battles went, even in the eighteenth century, but its importance was to outlast that of scores of other more extensive passages-at-arms.

The new Republican rulers of France had found a fairly capable general — Dumouriez. He hastened to the front and held council with the officers of the nigh demoralized army that was trying to halt the Prussian advance from Verdun. Many opinions favored a hasty retreat to Reims, north of the Marne. This would have saved the army, but it would have uncovered the road to Paris. Dumouriez was resolved to risk a battle, and saw the great possibilities of the Argonne Forest in checking an attack from Verdun. With thirteen thousand men he took his stand at Grand-Pré where one hundred and twenty-six years later other Republicans were to grapple with other Prussians. He sent a grandiloquent dispatch to the War Minister at the capitol: "Verdun is taken: I await the Prussians. The camp of Grand-Pré is the Thermopylæ of France, but I will be more fortunate than Leonidas!"

The Duke of Brunswick, however, presently pushed forward

and turned his flank, and Dumouriez fell back rather ingloriously from Grand-Pré without a battle. His policy, nevertheless, was not an absolute failure. The Prussians had believed that they had only to advance and enter Paris without resistance. They had brought very scanty provisions. It was raining incessantly. The bad roads were knee-deep in mud. Dysentery was ravaging their files. Besides, all was not well between Prussia and her "dear ally" Austria. There was grievous friction in the East over the spoils of unhappy Poland.[1] The Duke and King Frederick William II his master had not the least desire to be chivalrously rescuing Marie Antoinette, while Francis II was taking a firm grip on Warsaw. Catherine, the mighty Czarina of Russia, was also making every sign of willingness to take advantage of the fact that Prussia might be tied up in a serious war with France. Every day, therefore, that the French blocked the road diminished the chance of getting to Paris. So it came to pass that, on the 20th of September, Brunswick tried out the French lines to see if there would really be serious resistance — and learned to his satisfaction.

About six miles east of Sainte-Menehould on the present railway from Reims, going to Verdun, there is the small village of Valmy. Here Brunswick found the heights lined with the battalions of Kellermann, Dumouriez's most efficient lieutenant. There was a brisk cannonade with the old-style six- and nine-pounders. Then the Prussian infantry swung forward with the rhythmic step and discipline made famous by Frederick the Great. Kellermann's men waited their coming steadily, never answering the musket-fire until, when close at hand, they charged forth with the bayonet, and for perhaps the first time upon a stricken field rang out the battle-cry of the revolution-

[1] The final dismemberment of Poland was largely connected with the French Revolution. France had been friendly to Poland. The minute it was evident that France was too distracted to intervene in Poland's behalf, schemes were pushed for the "second" and then the "third" and final partition of that unhappy country between Russia, Austria, and Germany. The "second" partition took place in 1793, the "third" in 1795.

ary, militant France — "Vive la nation!" The Prussian lines recoiled. Brunswick hesitated to press home a second do-or-die charge. The cannon boomed till dusk, but the infantry fighting was over. An indecisive repulse for the Prussians: that seemed the whole of the matter.

But in fact the Duke had found the answer to his question. The French had not fled. To get to Paris he must fight a great decisive battle, which, if lost, might leave the Prussian army so shaken that the Austrians could strangle their hated rival.[1] Brunswick halted, negotiated. The French "emigrants" vainly urged another advance, but he had learned how they could lie to him in saying that Paris could be reached without a desperate effort. He vainly offered to retire if the French would restore Louis on the basis of the wrecked Constitution; but the stern word came back from Paris, "that the French Republic [just officially proclaimed] could listen to no proposition until the Prussian troops had entirely evacuated French territory." And the Prussian promptly bowed to the order! Truth was he was only too anxious to quit a losing game. On September 30, the formidable army that was to have "restored the Bourbons" was in full retreat. It did not even try to hold Verdun and Longwy. The frontiers were cleared of the enemy — and so the Republic won its first great triumph.

As might be imagined, considering the time when the elections were held, the balloting (open to practically all Frenchmen over twenty-five years of age) sent to the Convention an even greater number of radicals than those in the "Legislative."[2] The new body that was "to give happiness to France" contained 782 members. Of these, 75 had been in the "Constitu-

---

[1] The alliance of Austria and Prussia was extremely unnatural, and sure to break down. "Oil and vinegar: fire and water: Prussians and Austrians are united to carry war among 26 millions of men!" So wrote Arthur Young sarcastically in 1792.

[2] It was claimed that owing to the turbulence of the times, intimidation, etc., only a small fraction of the total number of voters (but that of the most radical) got to the ballot boxes.

ent" and 183 in the "Legislative." Among the members were not lacking a decidedly large number of men of moderate views and with no cast-iron theories for exploitation, but these deputies were not organized and therefore they were at the mercy of a compact, aggressive minority. Besides, the members from the departments were frequently weakened and intimidated by the atmosphere of Paris — the eagerness of the leaders of the capital for a régime of "thorough" and their equal willingness to carry their end by very brutish physical means.

The Girondists numbered about 120. They were full of zeal for a Republic, but it was to be a well-poised, reasonable Republic, restrained from flying off into social and economic vagaries. The Jacobins could not count on more than 50 reliable members, whereof 24, however, came from Paris. They desired a far more complete overturning of the world and "breaking of fetters" than did the Girondists. Had passions been less deep, and blood been cooler, the Girondists and Jacobins would have discovered that they did not differ so violently in theories but that they could reach a fair compromise. The gulf betwixt them was really personal and temperamental. The Girondists were amiable idealists. The Jacobins, with all their sins, never left the earth for the clouds. While Vergniaud was saying, "I would conquer the world by love," Robespierre was expediting schemes for the prompter use of the guillotine.[1] The Girondists, however, far outnumbered the Jacobins. They could also make the better appeal to the unattached majority of moderates; but the Convention, for its sorrow, met in Paris, and the Commune and mob of Paris, affecting to speak for the masses of France, could give the Jacobins the persuasive support of muskets and pikes when their projects needed a majority. This great fact explains much which followed.

[1] This famous instrument for execution was invented (or rather revived from mediæval models) by a "Dr. Guillotin," who suggested it to the government in 1789 as a more merciful way of ending criminals than the old hangman's rope or headman's axe. There is no doubt that it was swift and practically painless.

THE TRIAL OF THE KING

The Convention met on September 21, 1792. It at once confirmed the proclamation of the Republic. It then devoted its whole energies to the great project for rebuilding France on a completely democratic basis. "To make the people" was the phrase of Camille Desmoulins, Danton's clever friend. When, however, the crude theories of Rousseau were rigidly and mercilessly applied by inexperienced men, what could follow but a heinous form of despotism?

The Girondists at first seemed to have the upper hand. They had the habits of gentlemen, preferred clean linen, and did not appreciate Marat's sordid rags or the obscenity of Hébert, darling though the latter was of the dregs of the Paris populace. They were soon at odds with the Jacobins before whose savage attacks their power drifted away, although for a while they kept control of the public ministries.

The "Mountain" (that is, the Jacobins and their allies) now determined to press for the trial of the King. The Girondists realized that Louis was largely the victim of his rank and of circumstances, and that the Republic would gain by a show of mercy, but Saint-Just, Robespierre's especial admirer, and a very ardent Jacobin, spoke thus for his party: "The death of the tyrant is necessary to reassure those who fear that one day they will be punished for their daring, and also to terrify those who have not yet renounced monarchy." And Robespierre himself uttered the accepted philosophy on the case: "When a nation has been forced into insurrection, it returns to a state of nature with regard to the tyrant. *There is no longer any law but the safety of the people.*"

The unfortunate King was therefore tried before the whole Convention. He was charged with "conspiring against the public liberty and an attempt against the general safety." In other words, he had not faithfully accepted the Constitution of 1791, and had not done his best to resist the Austrian. Probably these charges were true; but wise statesmen would have said that to have punished Louis XVI for swerving from the path of technical duty in 1792 was cruelty merely disguised as legal justice. The Jacobins were determined to have his blood, both because they hated him and still more because they wished to discredit the Girondists. The latter knew that the King ought to be acquitted, but they made only ineffective efforts to save him. The Jacobin shouters and rabble packed the gallery of the Convention, cheered the prosecution, howled and threatened when words were said in defense. Nevertheless Louis was given the forms of a fair trial.[1] He was skillfully defended by his old minister Malesherbes. There is little doubt that the Convention rendered a *legally* just verdict when it unanimously declared Louis "guilty." The real question came on the penalty. The Jacobins clamored for blood. The Girondists made frantic appeals for moderation, but could not set themselves effectively against the shoutings and coercion. On January 20, 1793, Louis was ordered immediately to the scaffold by a majority of *one* vote. The clamor of the galleries had affected the nerves of enough Girondists to decide the issue.

The King was guillotined publicly on January 21, dying bravely, and spending his last hours in a manner worthy of a monarch and a Christian — thus effacing much of the evil impression he had given the world during the last troubled years of his reign. The Jacobins openly rejoiced at the tragedy. "Your party is ruined!" Danton told the Girondists, and more openly he defied the hostile Powers of Europe, proclaiming, "Let us fling down to the kings the head of a king as gage of battle"; while Marat exulted because "We have burned our ships behind us."

Already, before this tragedy, the actions of France had driven the old monarchies of Europe to a frenzy. The Convention openly advocated carrying the blessings of Republican freedom to every other nation. On November 19, 1792, Danton

[1] He was treated much more fairly and was executed with far more attention to the outward forms of justice than the unfortunate Nicholas II of Russia seems to have been dealt with before his reported execution in 1918.

had persuaded it to decree that France would grant "assistance and fraternity" to all peoples who wished to recover their liberties. What was that but a direct invitation to the subjects of every king to revolt? It had been issued at the very minute when, by a reversal of previous fortune, the valiant young armies of the Republic were driving the Austrians out of Belgium, following an amazing victory at Jemappes near Mons. The seizure of Antwerp, a city which England could never tolerate in the possession of a powerful maritime rival, forced Britain into war (February 1, 1793). The order-loving English people and ministers were already horrified at the steady trend of the tidings from across the Channel. Spain, Holland, and all the lesser States of the German Empire now made haste to imitate the greater Powers, and by their hostile attitude forced the Convention to declare war upon them.

By the middle of March, 1793, France was at war with practically every important state in Western Europe. While the Republic was thus ringed around with foreign enemies, the peasants of the Vendée were likewise in dangerous insurrection. Promptly on the heels of these serious tidings came actual reports of disaster. The French army, that had penetrated into Belgium, was driven thence with heavy loss. Mayence, which had also fallen into French hands, was retaken by the Germans. Worst of all, Dumouriez, the best general of the Republic, turned traitor and went over to the Austrians. The situation was in some respects more serious than just before Valmy.

Once more it was Danton who rose to the crisis. No demagogic leader ever carried himself more dauntlessly than did he in the face of the crowding perils. His opponents had made bitter attacks upon his character. Disdainfully he swept all these aside. "What matters my reputation," said he on March 10. "May France be free, and my name forever sullied. . . . We must break the situation by a great effort. Let us conquer Holland. Let us reanimate the Republican party in England. Let us make France march forward, and we shall go down glorious to posterity. Fulfill your great destiny. No more debates! No more quarrels — and the nation is saved!"

To meet the emergency Danton and his fellow Jacobins forged a terrible weapon — a multi-headed dictatorship. It was the famous "Committee of Public Safety," at first of nine, then of twelve members, clothed with almost autocratic power to crush all foes of the Republic without and within. Marat summed up its theory in a word: "We must establish the despotism of liberty to crush the despotism of kings."[1]

The Girondists were still nominally in power, appointing the ministers and otherwise conducting the Government. The Committee was now set over regular ministers, and was allowed to send commissioners to each of the armies to supervise and spur to activity the generals, and summarily to remove and punish the inefficient and treacherous. Once a week the Committee was supposed to report to the Convention, but its own deliberations were secret. The checks upon it were very slight. "The Convention soon became the slave of the Committee. As for the Ministry, it was left with a mere shadow of authority."

Working with this all-powerful executive committee was its counterpart the "Committee of General Security," a secret body which controlled the police, drew up lists of suspects, and sent the accused before the terrible "Revolutionary Tribunal." This was a standing court martial, whose judges and juries dealt out wholesale penalties to practically all the unfortunate Royalist aristocrats and reactionaries, or even "moderates," haled to its judgment bar. Soon the public executioner began to work with increasing frequency. "France," ran the saying, "was becoming Republican to the strokes of the guillotine."

The Committee of Public Safety and its adjunct committed crimes the record whereof abides through all history, but this

[1] Modern readers will not fail to note the similarity of this sentiment to those used by the Russian Bolsheviki in 1917–19 to justify their class tyranny. The Jacobins of 1793 seem, however, men of much greater physical courage than the doctrinaires who cringed before Germany in 1918 in the Treaty of Brest-Litovsk.

awful body can plead at least one great merit — *it saved France*. With astounding energy the new dictators plunged into their work. Danton had done much to get the Committee initiated, but he declined a position upon it. He was a master agitator rather than a great executive. The Jacobins forced the Convention to choose persons of practical ability rather than glib talkers. Robespierre was elected, but he and his devoted follower, Saint-Just, were the only members who can be put down as steady orators in the Convention, except possibly the slippery Barère. Only one of twelve could claim anything like genius, but he was of sufficient ability to make up for much patriotic mediocrity — Carnot, who took over the special charge of the army, and who was to become the "Organizer of Victory" and a real savior of France.

But while the Committee summoned the nation to arms and bade every Frenchman brace himself for the national emergency, the Jacobins had their grim reckoning with the Girondists. These clever idealists were still talking much and doing little. They denounced the September massacres and the politicians who were responsible for them; but they let the King be done to death, though they knew that the act was one of cruelty, and they were unable to enforce any steps whereby new massacres might become impossible. The majority of the Convention was still under the spell of their oratory, but coming as they did nearly all from the Southern Departments, they had little influence over the Commune of Paris and its mob. On June 2, 1793, the Jacobins and the Commune deliberately surrounded the hall of the Convention with a pack of hired ruffians, and held all the deputies prisoner until they would consent to order the arrest of thirty-one members, for the most part prominent Girondists. "You see, gentlemen," announced the radicals' spokesman ironically, "that you are respected and obeyed by the people, and that you can vote on the question which is submitted to you. Lose no time, then, in complying with their wishes!" The Convention was helpless. It had no armed force to rescue it from the mob. The thirty-one were ordered suspended, and by this one stroke the Jacobins had completed their triumph. All the other deputies understood *now* who were the masters of the situation.

So in Paris, but not in France. In some respects the contest was one of the departments against the capital. Already not merely in the Vendée, but elsewhere, were the Royalists showing their heads. There was grave discontent at the proceedings in Paris. Many Girondist deputies now fled to their home districts and endeavored to commence an insurrection against the capital and its despots of the Commune. Had there been a common organization and rallying-place for the insurgents, they might well have succeeded; probably they commanded much more than half of the population and good-will of France. But they were scattered, ill-organized, and lacked all first-class leadership. The Jacobins accused them of coquetting with the Royalists, or with a scheme to make the regions of France into a loose "federation" as opposed to "the Republic, one and indivisible," and in view of the crowding foreign peril many patriotic men, naturally merciful and reasonable, saw nothing to do but to sustain the Paris dictators.

The Jacobin Committee crushed this spasmodic insurrection which flared up in many districts, with all the ruthlessness of fear and anger. Lyons which had risen, mainly at the Girondists' behest, was captured by the Republican army, and a solemn decree of the Convention ordered, in the words of Barère, "Lyons warred against liberty. Lyons exists no more." It was directed that the city should be actually destroyed. In practice only about forty houses were demolished, but a great number of the unfortunate inhabitants were put to death, not by the guillotine, but by grapeshot. At Nantes, where the Royalist Vendéans had had sympathizers, the notorious Carrier rejoiced in wholesale executions of the well-born and bourgeoisie, as well as of less genteel victims. Some hundreds were shipped to Paris for trial before the Revolutionary Tribunal, but at least eighteen hundred prisoners were shot by firing squads without any trial; and then to complete the work Carrier ordered wholesale "drownings" in the Loire, "Republican marriages" — men and women bound together and sunk in the current. This was an extreme case. But there were hideous scenes at Marseilles, Bordeaux, Toulon, and other cities that had dared to show favor to the Girondists. The whole attempt to defy the Paris Government was thus stifled in blood.

While the Committee was thus handling a desperate internal situation, it was performing an even greater work upon the frontier. The war had become almost a death-grapple between all the old monarchies of Europe and the young Republicanism of France. Hitherto armies had almost invariably consisted of professional soldiers, slowly enlisted, slowly drilled, and their numbers strictly limited to those which a given king could conveniently pay, outfit, and ration. A general levy of the masses would have been abhorrent to the average monarch. It would have taught his peasants the use of arms which they might speedily turn against authority. No such scruples held back the Jacobins. A levy *en masse* was decreed at first of 300,000, then of more, until by the end of 1793 France had at least 750,000 men under arms — a prodigious number considering the difficulties then of transport, commissariat, and munitions. Church bells were cast into cannon, every available workshop became a weapon factory. Carnot, the war minister, displayed an amazing genius in overcoming all the practical difficulties in maintaining so great a host.

The new levies were often very ill-trained, but they had a passionate courage, a willingness to die for France and the "Rights of Man" beneath their beloved tricolor, which made them terrible foes to the mechanically disciplined mercenaries sent up against them. In the days before machine guns and barbed wire there were few battle-lines that could be held against a bayonet charge of reckless enthusiasts who cared not if they fell provided their comrades behind could carry on the flag to victory. It was this dashing ardor of a people just learning to be free that decided many a stricken field. Another very decisive factor was the admirable, tough physique and the sustained marching qualities of the French peasants, who, man for man, probably constituted far better fighting material than part at least of the larger, bonier Northern soldiery pitted against them — even as the *poilus* of France were to teach the world again in 1914.

Bravery, enthusiasm, and stamina could not do everything; above all they could not give the French generals skill in the technique of war. This was the weakest link at first in the national armor. The old officers from the noblesse were dead or in exile. The new officers — traders, tapsters, and ploughman's sons perhaps — had yet to learn a great deal. But under the whip and spur of circumstance this corps of new and very young officers developed rapidly. The Central Committee was ruthless in weeding out mediocrity and in punishing incompetence. With every army went at least two "deputies on mission" from the Convention, to see everything, to report everything, above all to suspend the commanding general if he showed any signs of incapacity. "The generals of the raw levies knew that they must win if they must live. Failure was interpreted by the deputies and the Revolutionary Tribunal to mean treason, and not a few officers, like Westermann and Gustine, expiated their defeats on the scaffold."

The effort of this army of liberated France, the most intelligent, devoted national army which the modern world up to that time had ever seen, was bound to produce enormous results. The kings and the comfortable military bureaucrats of Europe were confounded at this advent of a new force, as much moral as it was material, which met their well-trained but rather apathetic "regulars" in battle after battle. During the greater part of 1793 the French held their frontiers only by the most desperate exertions, but in the autumn the struggle definitely shifted in their favor. The English and Hanoverians were forced to raise the siege of Dunkirk, the Austrians were defeated at Wattignies (near Maubeuge) by Jourdan, one of the most competent leaders discovered by Carnot,[1] and at Weissenburg in northern Alsace the Austrians were hurled back beyond the confines of France. Likewise in December, Toulon, the great southern naval port, which had gone over to the English, rather than submit to the Jacobins, was retaken — thanks to the skill of a young artillery officer named Bonaparte. "Better that 25,000,000 human beings should perish than the Republic, One and Indivisible!" had been the saying during these months of crisis — and the Republic had *not* perished.

While thus the spirit of a great ideal, the ideal of a world emancipated from slavery and dedicated to liberty, fraternity, and human happiness, was animating the youth of France to fight and suffer on the frontier, their masters, the Jacobins, were more grimly holding their own and trying to execute their programme at Paris. The Revolution had, of course, been accompanied by widespread economic prostration. Factories lacked alike customers, raw material, and workmen. Peasants were hesitating to till their farms and to dispatch their grain to market. Paris grew increasingly hungry and therefore dangerous. The *assignats* were depreciating to a point almost equal to that of the Confederate currency in America in 1865. The Convention and the Committee fought against this crisis with weapons condemned by every modern economist, but they were used not wholly in vain. Speculators in corn and *assignats* found themselves often and very suddenly before the dread Revolutionary Tribunal. A drastic "Law of the Maximum" regulated the price for grain and flour, and fixed the death penalty for transgressors. Farmers and dealers who refused to open their stores at legal prices were arrested wholesale. Owing to the good fortune which sent a very fair harvest in 1793, and to the inherent ingenuity of the French lower classes in

[1] Jourdan, it is interesting to observe, seems to have served, when he was only sixteen, in the French forces sent to help Washington in America.

meeting trying conditions as well as to these Draconian edicts, this year was tided over without unbearable suffering. Economic conditions continued bad until well after 1795, but they were by no means so intolerable as in Russia in 1917 and 1918. The French bourgeoisie and peasants (even the most doctrinaire of their leaders) were to prove far more practical and intelligent than the Russian soviets, bolshevists, and mujiks in the first two years of their national reconstruction and agony.

Paris, therefore, lived her life, while the Convention listened to endless speeches, while the Committee and the Tribunal met for their grim work, and while Carnot organized his fourteen armies. The theaters were open, there were innumerable newspapers, mostly devoted to violent personal politics; and all the little wine-shops buzzed and sometimes thundered. But the entire time the fear of the "Republican razor" lurked in the heart of every man. After this epoch was over, it was asked of a prominent member of the Convention, Sieyès, what he did during those years? "*I lived,*" came back the brief but sufficient reply. For these were the years of "The Terror."

Even despite the clangor without and the tension within, the Convention found time to give serious attention to permanent questions of reform. By no means was all the legislation then enacted bad. A new system of weights and measures was introduced — the famous metric system — so excellent that presently it was to be adopted by nearly all civilization outside of the English-speaking lands. A special committee worked bravely on a sagacious scheme for national education, with primary schools, central schools, and a normal school to equip competent teachers. A second committee wrestled with the question of a codification of the Civil Law — a problem not to be solved till the days of Napoleon. Less commendable was the attack of the old established "slave style" calendar, with its names and divisions recalling Roman despotism ("July," "August") and Christian holy-days and festivals. In its place

ATTACK ON CHRISTIANITY

came a "natural" calendar conceived in the very spirit of Rousseau. The new era was made to date from the establishment of the Republic, September 21, 1792. Then began the "Year I." Within the reformed year were twelve months, with new names,[1] and divided, not into weeks, but into "decades" of ten days each. The initial day of each decade was a holiday for the celebration of the "Republic virtues," to the complete abandonment of Sunday with its reminiscences of "superstition."

Everything else connected with the Old Régime seemed on the point of being consigned to the rubbish heap. It was no longer patriotic (or therefore safe) to address a person as other than "Citizen" or "Citizeness." The royal tombs in Saint-Denis were violated; the dust of the kings who had made France great was flung into a ditch. The Christian religion was not formally proscribed, but only the services of the time-serving schismatic clergy, who would take the oath of obedience to the "civil constitution" for the Church, were permissible — a fact which put all the more upright and devout of the priesthood under the ban. The piety of the "constitutional" priests may be judged by the fact that in November, 1793, Gobel, the Bishop of Paris, and other prominent churchmen came before the Convention and seem to have openly disavowed Christianity. The churches, in most parts of France at least, were being changed into "civil temples," their altars pillaged, their glorious stained-glass windows smashed to bits[2] as reminiscent of superstitions and slavery which Republican enlightenment had abolished.

As to what was to be put in place of the Church, which was become almost as objectionable now as the Monarchy, good Republicans were divided. Robespierre and the more consistent followers of Rousseau's theories were quite sure there ought to

[1] These months began with September 22. They were named for their characteristic climate; for example, *Nivose* (snow month), *Floréal* (flower month), etc. The five extra days in the year were holidays.

[2] As a consequence, only here and there was the fine old stained glass to be found in French cathedrals; for example, in Reims until the new Barbarian invasion of 1914.

be a "pure" cult of the "Supreme Being." The grosser Jacobins of the Commune of Paris, led by their chief spirit Hébert, wanted only an atheistical worship of "Reason"; and on November 10, 1793, the Convention declared this last to be the official cult, marching as a body in red liberty caps to Notre Dame, while an unprudish actress sat upon the altar as "The Goddess of Reason," and even coarser women danced the *carmagnole* under the gray vaulting of the nave. Elsewhere in France there were even less edifying spectacles — at Lyons a donkey was adorned with a miter, made to drink from the sacred chalice, with a crucifix and Bible tied to his tail. All this disgusted Robespierre, who wished to be anti-Christian without being atheistic, and some of these viler outrages were presently suppressed; but not till after 1795 was it to be altogether safe to hold Catholic worship publicly without fear of molestation.

All this, however, was mere detail compared with the great task of reorganizing France on a new basis as laid down by Rousseau's doctrine. The controlling Jacobins had perforce to divide up the management of the problems of the hour between themselves; and the main energies of Carnot, and to a certain extent of Danton, were devoted to flinging back the invader. To lesser men they left the task of making the home front safe, and insuring the coming of the longed-for Utopia. This was the prosperous hour of Robespierre. The foreign danger, the domestic peril, the fear of a Royalist reaction (which under the circumstances could not be other than vengeful and bloody), all these were reasons for hideous action, for silencing every possible dissident under the falling knife. Robespierre, with every quality of a fanatic, — intense conviction of the justice of his philosophy, equally intense conviction of the criminality of every person who could not accept its logic and dicta, — was thus to have his way; until men really abler and more powerful than himself came to feel in peril for their own lives. Then suddenly the whole bloody Terror stopped.

The earlier months of the Republic had not been stained by

EXECUTION OF THE QUEEN

many executions despite the tragedy of the King. Now, while 1793 advanced, the Revolutionary Tribunal was divided into two sections to double its speed and its victims began to multiply. The property of the condemned was confiscated to the State, which income helped to meet the deficit. "We coin money by the guillotine," said Barère cynically in the Convention. In September was voted the terrible "Law of Suspects" subjecting to arrest not merely the courtiers of the Old Régime and others who had probably a motive in halting the Revolution, but all others who were detected "speaking of the misfortunes of the Republic and the shortcomings of the authorities."

This sinister change produced instant results. The prisons, already full, now were soon overflowing. In October, 1793, twenty-two of the luckless Girondists were sent to the scaffold, the heroic Madame Roland making her famous saying, as she stood before the guillotine, "O Liberty, how many crimes are committed in thy name!" Her male comrades went also to their fate with like serene courage. "I die at a time when the people have lost their senses," said Lasource to his judges. "You will die when they recover them." And the whole band sang with perfect steadiness the "Marseillaise" while they waited their turn before the executioner.

Already a more remarkable victim had been the widowed Queen herself. Had Marie Antoinette been prosecuted for treason immediately following the downfall of the Monarchy, there would certainly have been more justice in condemning her than her unfortunate husband. It was now little less than bloodthirstiness to send her to death. A good legal charge of aiding the Austrians might have been made out, but her trial was only a farce. Like the King, Marie Antoinette died bravely and nobly, as became the daughter of the great Maria Theresa, obliterating by her courage as a condemned prisoner the memory of many of the blunders and worse things chargeable against her as a queen.

From November, 1793, onward (Barère had cheerfully put it

as early as September), "Terror became the order of the day." The Revolutionary Tribunal became increasingly busy, and the guillotine seldom missed a prisoner once he was placed before the dread judge, prosecutor, and jury. For a man once a "suspect" practically the only escape was a satisfactory answer to the question, "What have you done worthy of death if the Royalists come back to power?" After the recapture of Toulon every citizen who failed to show signs of joy fell under suspicion. It was enough merely to prove that a defendant had not been an enthusiastic supporter of the latest ukase from the Jacobin Club. There were even victims sent under the knife for being "moderates" The cold statistics of the executions in Paris in 1793–94 tell the story of increasing recklessness and fanaticism. In December, 69 perished; in January, 1794, 71; in February, 73; in March, 127; in April, 257; in May, 353; and in June and July together 1376.[1] "This sudden increase in the number of executions," it is well written, "was due to the efforts of Robespierre to establish his Utopia."

There is a difference of opinion among modern specialists as to how far Robespierre personally was responsible for the deeds which have rendered his name execrable to every honest man, and sacred to every anarchist.[2] Certainly other members of the Committee of Public Safety — for example, Billaud-Varenne and Collot d'Herbois — were no less bloodthirsty than he. However, Robespierre in any case was often their spokesman in their conventions, covered their most drastic propositions with elegant phrases about securing the public "happiness" and "liberty," and probably toward the end he was, indeed, little less than an uncrowned dictator, possessed by the horrible gospel that since he understood the sole means of securing justice and prosperity for France, whosoever failed to applaud his

[1] Some of this great increase may have been due to the closing of certain provincial tribunals and the sending of their victims for final judgment to Paris.

[2] In 1918 the Bolsheviki were charged with setting up statues in his honor in Petrograd and Moscow.

extreme doctrines was worthy of death; and he certainly was inflexible in carrying out this theory.

Robespierre rapidly divested himself of possible rivals. One coadjutor, and it might have been competitor for popular influence, had already passed away. Marat, the "People's Friend," had been murdered in July, 1793, by the heroic Charlotte Corday, striking her dagger in behalf of the outlawed Girondists. There remained two other presumptive adversaries: Hébert the brutal, obscene leader of the Paris Commune and champion of the most stalwart atheism, and the redoubtable Danton. Robespierre hated Hébert because the latter was disgracing the Revolution by his "Festivals to Reason" and also his travesty of Rousseau's naturalism by his sheer bestiality. Hébert was powerful in the Paris Commune and among the dregs of the populace, and it strained Robespierre's influence to get him at last sent before the Tribunal. Nevertheless, on March 24, 1794, Hébert, the roaring blasphemer, perished.[1] Had Robespierre stopped here, some things might have been forgiven him.

But the "dictator" turned next on Danton himself. Of all men who should have been immune before the Tribunal, Danton ought to have been the first. For the overthrow of Monarchy, the September massacres, the execution of the King, the drastic measures to beat back the foreigner, the defiance of Europe, nay, for the setting-up of the Committee of Public Safety and the Revolutionary Tribunal itself, Danton was more responsible than any other single mortal. But Danton, despite all these things, was committing a deadly crime against the "beneficial and good" theories of the Jacobins; he was becoming a "moderate."

Danton could probably have scattered all his assailants by one resolute charge had he but willed to do so; but he remained singularly passive. He was a man of spasmodic achievement, not

[1] Hébert had carried his antipathy to Christianity so far as to incite his followers to destroy all church steeples as "an insult to equality."

of continuous action. He had declined a place in the secret Committees and for a time had withdrawn partially into private life. At length he and his friends had begun to hint plainly that since the national crisis, caused by foreign foes and by rebels, was largely past, there was no need for continuing the wholesale executions. If this meant anything it meant that Robespierre was not to bring to pass immediately his Elysium, into which he evidently intended to drive all Frenchmen at the point of the sword. That was enough to settle the fate of the greatest of the Jacobins.

When told he was threatened, Danton refused to use revolutionary means (which he might have invoked) to confound his adversaries. "I would rather," he said contemptuously, "be guillotined than be a guillotiner; besides, my life is not worth the trouble, and I am sick of the world." Nevertheless, when he was arrested and placed before the Tribunal, the prosecution dared not allow him to make even the limited defense allowed to ordinary victims. He was silenced as "wanting in respect to justice" and condemned practically without a hearing on charges so ridiculous and insignificant that his condemnation sinks to the level of a common murder. With him was sentenced his friend, Camille Desmoulins, the first to raise Paris in arms before the taking of the Bastile. "Show my head to the people," ordered Danton haughtily to the executioner; "they do not see the like thereof every day." And so he passed (April 5, 1794).

It was well said that the French Revolution, like the god Saturn of ancient mythology, "devoured its own children."

Marat was gone, Hébert was gone; and now Danton also. Of the great idealists whose Bible was the "Social Contract," and who had dreamed of making a new universe according to the gospel of Rousseau, who save Robespierre and his immediate satellites remained? The dictator (it is fair now to call Robespierre that) had destroyed the Hébertists as "impure men of faction"; the Dantonists as "indulgents and men of immoral-

THE TERROR AT ITS APEX

ity." Now surely there was nothing to hinder the régime of "thorough"! By this time probably only a minor fraction of Parisians and a much smaller fraction of Frenchmen at large had anything but abhorrence for the Terrorists, yet so absolute had been the suppression of every act of resistance, so prompt the punishment even for "incivism" (that is, the least suggestion of lukewarmness) that the entire nation seemed hypnotized and helpless before an aggressive, organized, and perfectly unscrupulous minority. Robespierre's real reign dates from the 5th of April to the 27th of July, 1794. During that time he seemingly exercised a power of life and death over Frenchmen incalculably greater than that of Louis XIV. He might have continued his power longer had he possessed the wisdom not to smite terror for their own lives into men who had either been his cowardly tools or his bloody accomplices.

During April, May, and June, Robespierre and his ever-narrowing band of prime counselors drove straight toward their mark by decree after decree calculated to silence dissenters from "the Doctrine," and to concentrate all power in Paris where "the pure" could control all public acts. All the Parisian clubs were closed except the Jacobin Club, that the others might not become centers for insurrection. All the extraordinary tribunals in the departments were ordered to stop working, and to send their cases to the greater and more pitiless central assize in Paris. When Robespierre rose to move a decree in the Convention, opposition for the nonce seemed absolutely hushed. No man knew better than he how to proclaim a policy of ruthlessness and to cover it with words dripping with philanthropy and idealistic benevolence. The Terror was blandly advocated as a necessary expedient to introduce the reign of "virtue"; the guillotine was for "the amelioration of souls." His coadjutors were more frank. "The dead alone do not return," said Barère, while Collot d'Herbois cynically declared, "The more freely the social body perspires the more healthy it becomes."

Robespierre himself was now, of course, the subject of the

grossest flattery. "The great Incorruptible" was everywhere praised for his virtue, his genius, and his eloquence. The apogee of his career came on June 8, 1794, when, at his instigation, an enormous festival was held "in honor of the Supreme Being," on which day the Convention proceeded in high procession to the garden of the Tuileries, with Robespierre walking fifteen feet ahead of his insignificant colleagues, attired in all the brave dress of a dandy of the period, and carrying an offering to the Deity of flowers and ears of corn. Then, after burning three huge effigies of "Atheism," "Discord," and "Selfishness," this high-priest of the new Deism delivered a pompous speech, containing the ominous words: "People! Let us to-day surrender ourselves to the transports of pure delight. *To-morrow we will renew our struggle against vices and against tyrants!*"

Two days later Couthon (one of the dictator's spokesmen) imparted to the Convention what Robespierre had had in mind. The Revolutionary Tribunal was not working fast enough. There was still some small loophole for the defense. Hereafter the court was to sit daily, and the process of bringing indictments was greatly expedited. No counsel was to be allowed the accused, and "moral proofs" could suffice for a conviction. All "enemies of the people" (a frightfully indefinite phrase) were liable to prosecution, and the jurors need not follow the law, but "only their own consciences" when they voted. Possibly the Convention would have authorized all this without a whimper, but hitherto, to get the arrest of an accused deputy, it had been needful to ask the consent of a majority of his fellow members. This had been a considerable safeguard. Now the deputies themselves could be put on trial on a mere order from the terrible Committee. In substance this was asking every member to look to the safety of his own neck. The weakest animals will turn at bay. Such a request was therefore a grievous blunder.

Robespierre committed a second great blunder when (challenged in the Convention) he refused to name the deputies

OPPOSITION TO THE DICTATOR

presumably to be accused. "I will name them when it is necessary," he announced loftily: words which set every member who had ever crossed his path to trembling. In "profound silence" the new decree was passed. From this time the "Terror within the Terror" became more direful than ever. Executions took place in large batches. Often fifty wretches were sent under the knife per day. But the end was drawing nigh.

With all his fanaticism, the dictator hated corruption, immorality, and such forms of cruelty as he had not himself authorized. Powerful and wicked men, high in the Government, who had misused their opportunities had come to fear him. At least three members of the great Committee, including the mighty Carnot, were beginning to oppose him. His attempt to manufacture a new religion was laughed at by presumable supporters. "Your Supreme Being begins to *bore* me!" sneered Billaud-Varennes. Robespierre had still a great following among the Parisian lower classes, and the reorganized Commune of the capital was devoted to him, but things were obviously moving to a straining point. Late in July the cord, long under tension, snapped.

As things neared a climax the dictator became morose and distrustful. Sturdy Jacobins with clubs accompanied him as a bodyguard. His denunciations became ever more ominous.[1] "All corrupt men," he declared, "must be expelled from the Convention." Who were these corrupt men? Out of despair for their lives, the members who felt themselves threatened made ready to pull the tyrant down. Robespierre knew that there were murmurs and combinations against him, but on July 26 he harangued the Convention in his usual mood: "There exists a conspiracy against the public liberty, that owes its strength to a criminal intrigue within the very heart of the Convention.

[1] The battle of Fleurus (June 26), a great French victory over the Austrians in Belgium, really cut the ground from under the dictator's feet. Why any need now of the Terror? Robespierre realized this, and is charged with giving orders to suppress or minimize the glad news of the military success as much as possible.

... Punish the traitors! Purify the Committee! Crush every faction, and establish upon their ruins the power of justice and liberty!" Instead of applause he met flat opposition. Cambon (a brave man) said openly: "It is time to speak the whole truth. One man paralyzed the resolution of the assembly. That man is Robespierre."

The debate ended with a flat rebuff for the dictator. The next day each side having mustered its partisans, he endeavored to face the rising storm, but he was howled off of the tribune by the yells not merely of the moderates, but by most of his old Jacobins. "Let the veil [of restraint] be wholly torn aside!" thundered Tallien. "Down with the tyrant!" reëchoed from the members. Robespierre tried vainly to get a hearing. "Pure and virtuous men!" he pleaded, holding out his arms to his one-time laudators — and was met with stony looks or shrill hootings. "Wretch," some one called from an upper bench, "*the blood of Danton chokes thee!*" With an approving shout the Convention voted the motion that Robespierre, his brother, and three adherents, notably the wild and eloquent young Saint-Just, should be put under arrest. "The Republic is lost, the brigands triumph!" groaned the deposed leader as they dragged him out.

But all was not quite over. The Commune was still on Robespierre's side and controlled the Paris prisons. None of the jailers would receive him. A band of municipal officers took him from his guards and brought him in triumph to the City Hall. "Long live Robespierre!" rang in the streets. A band of armed men, led by the notorious desperado and agitator Henriot, put themselves at his disposal. For some hours the Convention was in agony. Was it not about to be attacked by the mob and all its members massacred? However, the National Guard, after some wavering, decided to support the Convention and not the Commune. The Government's troops, therefore, closed around the City Hall, and seized the band that had already been declared "outlaws." Robespierre shattered his jaw with a pistol while trying to commit suicide. He was still alive, when on the famous "10th of Thermidor" (July 28, 1794) at 5 P.M. he rumbled in the death-cart along the streets, through a crowd that cheered, raved, and screamed for his blood. Twenty-two of his friends mounted the scaffold and then the dread "dictator." When his head fell, the air shook with the applause.[1] The Terror was ended.

The men who had pulled down Robespierre were many of them no more pitiful or scrupulous than their enemy; but they had gained immense popularity by seeming to stop the Terror, and they dared not endanger their position by renewing it. The long intimidated Convention reasserted its liberty of action. The surviving Girondist deputies returned from exile. The Jacobin Club was closed. The worst abusers of justice in the Revolutionary Tribunal were executed themselves. A great many political prisoners were released; the remainder were in no danger of death without fair trial. France, and particularly Paris, shook off the incubus of fear that had brooded over it. Not merely was there a reaction toward moderation; there was even a reaction in favor of Monarchy, especially as it was believed that the kings could be brought back upon conditions that would insure the preservation of the great liberties won in 1789. The Royalists were weakened, indeed, by the report that in 1795 the unlucky Dauphin, son of Louis XVI (a frail boy bereft of parents or decent guardians), had died in prison, apparently by the sheer neglect or worse of his brutal keepers.[2] The heir to the Bourbon claims was now the late King's brother, the Comte de Provence, in exile and notorious as a reactionary. However, the Royalist feeling grew. The bourgeois elements in Paris had reasserted themselves, and supported the reaction.

[1] There is a story that just as the fallen tyrant was bound to the plank, a voice from the crowd shouted, "Yes, Robespierre, there *is* a Supreme Being."

[2] This is no place to discuss the stories that the Dauphin really escaped, was taken to America, and there lived and died in an obscure private station. These reports cannot be set aside, however, as nothing more than improbable fabrications. They deserve serious consideration.

In 1795 there was even a Royalist outbreak that came close to succeeding.

In 1793 the Convention had adopted a constitution of an ultra-democratic nature, strongly tinctured with Jacobin views. It had never actually been put in force and the moment Robespierre fell it was disregarded altogether. In 1795 the deputies produced another constitution which was an honest, if not wholly successful, attempt to avoid the mistakes of the 1791 arrangement, and to set up a Republican Government which should alike steer clear of ultra-radicalism and of Monarchy. There was a much-needed list of the "duties" as well as the "rights" of citizens, and a more debatable effort to exclude the lowest classes, by giving the vote only to men who had lived a year in one place and paid a tax. Such voters could choose "electors," who in turn chose a legislature of two houses, a "Council of Five Hundred" to initiate laws, and a "Council of Ancients" (two hundred and fifty older members) to revise and accept them. For executive the Convention set up neither President nor King, but a five-headed commission. Five "Directors," controlling the ministers, the diplomatic policy, and the army and administrative officers, were to be chosen by the Councils for terms of five years,[1] with one Director retiring annually. Three Directors could speak for the whole. In this way it was hoped that a firm executive was to be created without fear of a dictatorship.

Such a system was in fact too artificial to work well even in peaceful times and with a friendly and submissive citizen body, but the Convention now passed a measure sure to make the new scheme unpopular. The members, especially those who had voted for the death of Louis XVI, were in mortal fear lest the elections should give the Royalists a majority in the newly constituted legislatures. So great was the disgust at the Terror, so great the desires of Frenchmen to settle down in peace after the

[1] At the beginning, of course, all five Directors were chosen and it was then determined by lot in what order they should retire.

ROYALISTS ATTACK THE CONVENTION 327

years of confusion, that such a reaction was extremely probable. The Convention, therefore, in self-protection decided that two thirds of the new legislatures must be elected from among the members of the retiring Convention, thus making sure that the Royalists, at least for a few years, should not be more than a minority.

The respectable element in Paris had now completely gained the upper hand over the Jacobin lower classes, and it was driven to fury by this plain undertaking of the hated radicals to perpetuate their power under a new guise. The National Guard, as reorganized, was at the disposal of the reactionaries, and on October 5, 1795 ("13th of Vendémiaire"), some 40,000 armed Royalists were marching on the hall of the Convention to attempt by violence a change in the Government, thus using a method well taught them by Danton and Marat.

The position of the Convention was serious. It had now decidedly few friends in the city, but the regular army (devotedly Republican) was on its side, and the rather small garrison present was enraged at the idea of recalling the hated Bourbons. The deputies appointed as their leader the energetic Barras, who in turn selected as chief lieutenant a young artillery officer who had won success at the siege of Toulon and who was now waiting idly in Paris — one Napoleon Bonaparte. The latter promptly seized all the artillery at the Sablons camp, and posted it with his 6000 to 7000 men to good advantage around the Tuileries where the Convention was in session. The Royalists marched up to the old palace boldly, expecting to prosper even as had the Dantonists in 1792; but Bonaparte and his artillerymen were not as Louis XVI and his Swiss Guards. The Royalists were met by a deadly cannon fire, which raked the quays by the Seine, and their columns were literally mowed down by the "whiff of grapeshot." After a vain attempt to rally, the insurgents broke, fled, and the battle was over.

The Convention was nominally the victor. The real victor was the army. Bonaparte had arbitrated between legislators and citizens with his cannon. From this time onward until 1815 the army is the true disposing body in France. It was to remain loyal the longest to the Republic, and when its allegiance changed, it was not to be to the Old Monarchy, but to a new Cæsarism.

In October, 1795, the new directors took over the Government. The "Directory" lasted until November, 1799. It is not needful to trace its annals. The real history of France from 1796 onward was to be written in great battles in Italy and then in Egypt by the young officer who had aided Barras. As for the Directors, nearly all of them were mediocre men, however often their personnel changed: they could wrangle much, though accomplish relatively little. Law and order returned in a tolerable extent to France in 1795, although there was still much persecution of the old nobility and of the Catholic clergy. The admirable practical talents of the French people brought back a fair degree of economic prosperity. As early as April, 1795, Prussia had withdrawn from the war in disgust at her Austrian ally, and her Hohenzollern king had made peace by the Treaty of Basel with the radical Republic. The decrepit despotism of Spain had made peace the same year. England, Austria, and Sardinia still continued the war, but they could not really threaten the integrity of France or the fruits of the Revolution.

As might have been expected, the five directors (chosen without the slightest attempt to select persons likely to work together) presently quarreled among themselves. They also wrangled with the legislature, whose relations to the executive had been very poorly adjusted by the new Constitution. In 1797 three Directors combined against two, charging them with "reaction," and with the aid of the army they drove the minority from power. In 1798 and 1799 Bonaparte, who had already overshadowed completely the five little men in Paris, was fighting in Egypt. In his absence the Directors mismanaged affairs outrageously. By the valor of Bonaparte, France had made a victorious peace with Austria in 1797 (Treaty of Campo-

FRANCE RETURNS TO MONARCHY

Formio). The Directors now became involved in a second war with the Austrian Emperor, and when Bonaparte returned from Egypt in 1799, they had little to report to him but defeats in Italy and Switzerland and even a renewed danger to the frontiers. Under these circumstances it was perfectly easy for the scheming and ambitious "Little Corporal," already the darling of the army, to pull down the luckless Constitution of 1795. On November 9, 1799 ("18th of Brumaire"), by a bold stroke of state, aided by the soldiery and by three of the Directors, Bonaparte chased the other two Directors from office, and dispersed the Council of Five Hundred. At the roll of the drum the grenadiers marched into the building of the legislature, and "advancing slowly across the wide width of the hall, presented their bayonets."

What Louis XVI dared not accomplish following the defiance of Mirabeau after the "royal sitting" in 1789, had been dared and done by the man from Corsica. France had again a monarch, albeit a very different kind of a monarch from Louis XVI. Bonaparte proposed to reorganize the government with a very firm executive of three "consuls." His colleagues, provisionally, were to be the supple politician Sieyès and another ex-Director, Ducos. When the trio then gathered for their first session, Sieyès asked mildly, "Who will preside?" "Don't you see," answered Ducos, "*the general is in the chair!*" There was nothing more to be said.

From this time onward, even more than from 1796, the history of France and the biography of Napoleon Bonaparte are absolutely intermingled until the greatest of all adventurers crashed down at Waterloo.

CHAPTER XVI
NAPOLEON BONAPARTE, AS MASTER OF EUROPE

THIS volume is a history of France. It is not a biography of Napoleon. It is not a history of the wars and diplomacy of Europe between 1796 and 1815. To write the first without the other two things is, however, a matter of extreme difficulty. The wisest policy is to state a few threadbare facts about the life and personality of the Corsican, then to give a very thin outline of his more important wars and international policies. In more detail we can next explain what he did for France, and show that his restless genius by no means confined itself solely to military achievements. Finally we can trace over the story of his last years of power and of downfall, when, as a result of his personal catastrophe, France was obliged to remould her constitution and to take back for a while the outcast Bourbons.

It is useless to try to write anything new about Napoleon Bonaparte. It is unavoidable also not to restate facts contained in the most meager work of reference.

The future confounder of Europe was born at Ajaccio, Corsica, in 1769, the son of a "typically poor but noble family." His father, Charles, was of Italian extraction and was by profession an assessor for the local royal court. The young Napoleon must therefore be thought of as an Italian in birth and early breeding. His genius, virtues, vices are nearly all of them Southern. If he became a Frenchman, it is only one by adoption, however completely for a time he dominated the sympathies and enthusiasms of the entire Gallic race. In 1779 he was sent to the Continent to the military school at Brienne. In 1784 he went to the military academy at Paris. In 1785 he was commissioned sub-lieutenant in the artillery. A shy, ill-dressed lad, who did not speak French over-well, he was not particularly popular with his comrades or his teachers; although one of the latter at Paris made a note that "He will go far if circumstances favor him." He was only the forty-second in his class when he received his commission. During the Revolution he presently became possessed with an honest or affected enthusiasm for Jacobin theories and was made a captain in 1793. He achieved his first reputation at the siege of Toulon by his skill in planting a battery which drove the British fleet from the harbor. He was made brigadier-general when he was only twenty-four, but was practically dismissed from the army after he refused to command an infantry brigade against the insurgents in the Vendée.

Then by a turn of Fortune's wheel, in 1795, Barras suddenly summoned him to defend the Convention against the Royalists. His well-aimed cannon-shots alike crushed the chances of a reaction and put his superiors under a heavy obligation to him. He was given command of the "Army of Italy," the most important force at the disposal of the Directory, always excepting the great armies on the Rhine. He was at once hailed as one of the rising men of the hour, and before he left Paris he was able to marry the beautiful creole widow Josephine de Beauharnais, one of the central spirits of fashionable life in the capital. Ten days after the wedding (March 11, 1796), he left his bride to assume his new command in the South, and within a month after his arrival with the Army of Italy, he was able to report very important victories. A new era had dawned not for France only, but for all Europe.

The young man who was now to send terror down the spines of all the Highnesses, Serenities, and Majesties in Christendom has of course become a familiar figure, thanks to hundreds of authentic portraits. When he began his career we may think of him as distinctly "Southern" in aspect, an Italian rather than a Frenchman, "small, of poor physique, with long, lanky, dark hair, but with deep-set eyes and a pale, impressive face, set over a shabby uniform." Later he was to become stouter, and his valet was to provide him sometimes with a costume befitting his rank, but he was never to develop an imposing stage presence.[1]

Upon his appearance with the Army of Italy he was not enthusiastically welcomed. Many of the under-generals were men of longer service and of much greater years than he. They treated him with half-concealed sneers and almost latent insubordination. It took him an amazingly short time, however, to fascinate them all by the magnetism of his presence. "I'm afraid of him," confessed Augereau, one of his chief lieutenants, "and I don't understand his ascendancy over me, so that I feel struck down just by the flash of his eye!" In a word, Bonaparte in 1796 took a discouraged, poorly disciplined, and miserably equipped and provisioned army of 37,000 men, flung it over the Alps, and in a few weeks' time began to report back to Paris a series of victories such as no general had ever reported to Louis XIV. "The First Italian Campaign" (if he had fought no other) was sufficient to establish Bonaparte among the world's great captains. When after the desperate charge over the bridge of Lodi (May 10, 1796), a deputation of sergeants of the grenadiers waited on their general in his tent and informed him that he had been elected a "corporal" in their corps, they were simply anticipating the opinion of every student of military history. "The Little Corporal" was to make a name beside those of Alexander and Julius Cæsar.

And yet Bonaparte was no magician who with a stroke of a wand called up for himself obedient and irresistible armies. On the contrary, he could never have gone far had not the Revolution presented him with one of the most formidable fighting machines in the world. The machine was nearly ready. It needed only the master-engineer to perfect and direct it. The force that had cast back the Prussians and Austrians after Valmy, that had justified Danton's call for "boldness," that had already wrested the whole western bank of the Rhine from the then

[1] See p. 368.

tottering German Empire and taken Belgium from Austria, had been one of the fairest products of the Revolution. In the "Army of the Republic" genuine patriotism and love for the new-found liberty had burned the keenest, along with a passionate willingness to die for France or to conquer, as well as to convey the blessings of the "Rights of Man" to less fortunate nations. In the army there had been as a rule little opening for the sanguinary contentions between Girondist and Jacobin, Dantonist and Robespierrean. The *one* thing the army was resolved upon was that the Bourbons should not return — and it had therefore been the bulwark of the Directory in the days of Royalist reaction. It was to desert the Directory in 1799 and overthrow it because of the widespread feeling that the inefficiency of that five-headed executive was ruining France and thereby insuring the return of the hated kings. The soldiery in that year honestly believed that their idolized general would reëstablish in some better form their beloved Republic. They were mere wax in the Corsican's astute Southern hands.

But the Republican army was more than intensely antiroyalist. It was a magnificent fighting force. It was composed, or at least dominated, by men who were not professional mercenaries earning the pay of a king, but devoted patriots battling for an ideal. Hitherto, in the average battle, two long lines of carefully deployed infantry approached each other slowly; when within easy musket-shot they fired on one another till the weaker side — perhaps after hours of this exchange — broke under the volleys and let its enemies march deliberately forward. This traditional battle order was cast to the four winds by the new armies of France. The superior courage of their volunteers enabled their generals to form them in headlong columns and fling a regiment like a solid battering-ram against the enemy. The van of the column might perish. The rest would charge through to victory. In general also the new French armies were in no wise hampered by the traditions and rule-of-thumb methods which were the delight of the mediocre old-school martinets.[1] We are told that the French battalions often were in rags, that they marched with a long, slouching step — unlike the smart movements of the Austrians; that even their officers sometimes lacked boots — that their generals failed to carry themselves with top-lofty dignity. But the great fact remained that repeatedly on decisive fields they had defeated these same mechanical Austrians, and men remarked on "the fierce, swaggering spirit and patriotism that went far to explain their success."

The Revolution, under whip and spur, had produced several very competent generals; for example, Hoche (whose early death in 1797 rid Bonaparte of a dangerous rival), and Moreau, who was to win Hohenlinden in 1800 and next to win Bonaparte's deadly jealousy; but now this splendid fighting instrument was to fall into the hands of an incomparable military genius. No wonder he was to go far!

Bonaparte's military methods were extraordinarily simple when stated: it was their just application which made him a giant among the captains. He took advantage of the admirable physiques and marching qualities of the French peasants, and drove his men to the limit. The movements of his columns were infinitely more rapid as a rule than those of his foes. He depended on requisitions upon the country, and was not tied to a distant base by an uncertain supply train. When it came to battle, his invariable principle was to leave small forces containing or hindering the minor detachments of his enemy, then, by a swift concentration of his full fighting strength, to fall suddenly on that division of the foe which he had selected as his prey. Infinite study of the maps told him when to strike where the enemy would be most divided, and the French the most concentrated; and also where, with a victory once won it

---

[1] It is said, too, that partly because of the experience of some of their officers in America under Washington, the French adopted sharpshooter tactics, the use of trees, rocks, hedges, etc., as shelters, and other devices which scandalized the old-school tacticians — and won many victories!

NAPOLEON IN BIVOUAC IN THE VALLEY OF THE GRAND-SAINT-BERNARD

BONAPARTE'S EXCELLENT LIEUTENANTS 335

could be exploited to best advantage. This principle of rapid concentration, rapid attack, and making everything bend to catching the enemy piecemeal, marked all his campaigns from 1796 to 1814.

Bonaparte was, of course, greatly aided by most efficient lieutenants. Like Julius Cæsar his personality was so dominant, his presence so ubiquitous, that even his most capable generals had their faculties for initiative somewhat numbed, and were at a loss when offered independent commands far from their great taskmaster's eye. But given his presence within the range of a fast courier, and not a few of the Corsican's subalterns could show themselves tacticians of a very high order. Augereau, the son of a Paris fruit-vender; Davout, Bonaparte's fellow pupil at Brienne; Lannes, the gallant son of a provincial stable-keeper; Ney, the son of a poor cooper of Saarlouis; Soult, the son of a Southland notary; and finally Murat, the son of the Cahors innkeeper — such were the leaders whom their chief was to make marshals, "dukes," and "princes," or even "kings" [1] in the days of his prosperity, and who, by their rise to glory, proved the saying that in the new army "every private carried a marshal's baton in his knapsack." They were nearly all of them great captains, who have written their names with honor into military history. Bonaparte also was extremely fortunate in possessing a very competent chief-of-staff almost down to the time of his downfall — Berthier; an officer whose keen intelligence and great precision in preparing orders relieved his superior of infinite vexatious detail.

But in the last analysis it was the rank and file which was to give the Corsican his glory. How the *poilu* could fight was to be rediscovered by Europe in 1914; and the men of the Marne were after all the great-grandsons of the men of Lodi, of Rivoli, and of Austerlitz. Even with a less gifted generalissimo great victories were possible with such divisions as Masséna's in the

[1] Murat, Napoleon's brother-in-law, was made King of Naples in 1808 — "King Joachim I."

1797 campaign, when the troops fought a pitched battle on the 13th of January at Verona; marched over snow-cumbered roads all the following night — twenty full miles — till the next morning they were on the plateau of Rivoli; fought again victoriously the same day (14th); set forth again that night; marched all the next day (15th), covering then nearly forty-three miles in thirty hours; and on the 16th came up in time to decide the battle of La Favorita. Sixty-eight miles of marching and three battles in four days! While the "Army of the Republic" and its traditions lasted, what wonder that its beloved general went forth conquering and to conquer?

That the continuity of events may not be forgotten, the military annals of Napoleon Bonaparte must be stated thus very succinctly. When he took command at Nice in 1796, the French held all Belgium and the western bank of the Rhine, but they were still at war with England by sea and at war by land with all the minor States of Italy and with Austria. On the German battle-line the contest with Austria had practically reached a deadlock; but in Northern Italy there opened unlimited prospects of attack and manoeuver once the initial advantages were gained by the French. Bonaparte began his attack on the allied Austrian and Sardinian forces in April. Almost immediately he won his first victory at Millesimo. Two weeks later the terrified King of Sardinia desired an armistice. Bonaparte then invaded the Austrian province of the Milanese. He won the notable battle of Lodi in May and entered Milan, and soon began the siege of Mantua — the key fortress to all Northern Italy. Four times the Austrians strove to relieve that stronghold. Four times they were utterly repulsed. The last battle of Rivoli (January 14, 1797) was decisive. Mantua surrendered, and Bonaparte was threatening to cross the Alps and enter Vienna, when the Hapsburg government hurriedly negotiated for peace. In April, 1797, it signed the humiliating treaty of Campo-Formio, by which it was agreed that France

BONAPARTE IN EGYPT

should keep Belgium and the western bank of the Rhine, and also that the "Cisalpine Republic" (under French protection) should be set up in Northern Italy. Austria herself was allowed to annex the neutral and decrepit Republic of Venice — an act of sheer spoliation in which the old Hapsburg Monarchy and the new French Republic alike iniquitously joined.

Bonaparte was now the darling of the French people. The Directors could not honor him too highly, but, small men that they were, they felt oppressed at his popularity and his influence in Paris. They were relieved, therefore, when he undertook to defeat England by winning the back door to India — Egypt. In 1798 Bonaparte sailed away on a prodigious Oriental adventure — with an armament carrying 35,000 seasoned French troops, headed for Alexandria. He took Malta *en route*. He landed safely in Egypt, routed the Mameluke armies, ruled in Cairo like a Moslem emir, but had his schemes nearly paralyzed by the destruction of his fleet at Aboukir Bay [1] by the English Admiral Nelson. Bonaparte, however, made a bold incursion into Palestine and defeated the Turks there, though not decisively. The loss of his fleet in any case made his whole position precarious. He feared to be cut off in the East while great things were happening in Europe. When he learned that Austria, Russia, and various lesser states had renewed their alliance with England and were again attacking France, he deserted his army in Egypt. None too magnanimously, he loaded with the pick of his officers one of the frigates he had left, and escaped through the British cruisers.[2] The political situation in France was such that so far from blaming him for deserting his men, all the numerous critics of the Directory rejoiced at his coming. As already stated,[3] he promptly overthrew the Directors and

[1] "Battle of the Nile," August 1, 1798.
[2] The French force in Egypt, thus left isolated and without reinforcements, was presently attacked by an English expedition and forced to surrender. Speculation exhausts itself over the question of what would have been the history of Europe if Bonaparte's frigate had been taken by the British and he had spent the next few years in a prison camp.
[3] See p. 329.

became "First Consul" just thirty-two days after his arrival in France.[1]

Bonaparte now became practically a dictator. The new "Constitution of the Year VIII" is described elsewhere.[2] It was not much more than a clever method for concealing the return of Monarchy. The Corsican always contended that the French were not really profoundly devoted to a Republic and "liberty" so much as to the essence of "equality"; they wanted chiefly a firm, efficient administration, economic prosperity, a chance for men of talent to rise on their merits, a scope for the daring and ambitious, and above all "glory" and a flattering of their national pride. All these things Bonaparte felt well able to give.

The Directors had bequeathed him a new war with Austria and Russia. In 1800 he was again in Northern Italy and won the battle of Marengo. A little later his general Moreau won the very decisive battle of Hohenlinden in Bavaria.[3] Austria again made peace[4] by which the Campo-Formio arrangements were in the main confirmed, French domination over the minor Italian States was extended, and the old "Holy Roman Empire" (that is, the loose federation of Germany under the presidency of Austria) was formally put in liquidation. The dissolution of mediæval Germany was to be substantially completed in 1803, and in 1806 the Hapsburg Monarch was to drop his claims to being the successor of Cæsar and Charlemagne, and to call himself simply "Emperor of Austria." If Bonaparte had perished at this time, he would probably have died followed by the blessings of subsequent historians. He had destroyed much that was rotten and had rendered an improved organization of Europe inevitable. He had not yet begun, to any large extent,

---

[1] "Coup d'État of the 18th Brumaire" — November 9, 1799.
[2] See p. 350.
[3] Bonaparte did not enjoy this victory by a subordinate. Moreau became the victim of his master's jealousy, was charged with conspiracy, and was banished to America. After a residence in New Jersey, in 1813, he entered the Russian service against Napoleon and was killed in the battle of Dresden.
[4] Treaty of Lunéville, 1801.

to violate strictly national rights or to play the insatiable aggressor. But henceforth "glory" led him on.

England still held out doggedly. Her blockade was cramping the economic life of France and was cutting off the French colonies. But deserted by her allies England made the Peace of Amiens in 1801, on terms which practically left France dominant on the Continent while her rival retained her vast sea-power. It was really a truce, however, between two irreconcilable forces — free Britain and a restless Southern despot. In 1803 there were new quarrels, nominally over the questions of Malta and Hanover which had been seized by the English and French respectively. The "peace" ended in a little less than a year, and the war was renewed with full energy on both sides.

The English fleet could cripple the economic life of France, and the "Grand Army" of the First Consul seemed helpless. In 1803, indeed, Bonaparte concentrated a great force of veterans at Boulogne, ready for a great scheme to cross the Channel in flatboats when for a few days the British armadas had been chased away. But that moment never came. The "wooden walls" of England were too formidable to be stormed by the many times conqueror.

In 1804 came the political change which any keen observer might well have predicted as inevitable since 1799 — Napoleon Bonaparte, the son of the poor attorney of Ajaccio, became Napoleon I, Emperor of the French. There was a certain amount of grumbling among sundry generals who had not forgotten 1793, but the more vehement were silenced with punishments, and the more reasonable were stifled with honors. The real fact, of course, appeared patent, that Napoleon had founded a despotism, albeit an infinitely more efficient, intelligent, and therefore tolerable despotism than that, say, of Louis XV. However, the avowed theory of this despotism was that France had chosen out the best of its citizens, as a great tribune of the people, to embody in his person the championship of her honor and the advancement of her prosperity. The Emperor's nephew, destined himself to sit upon an uneasy throne as Napoleon III, was to describe his uncle in a book as "the testamentary executor of the Revolution" who had hastened the reign of Liberty; and then next was to state, "Now the nature of democracy is to personify itself in one man." Views like these were doubtless what Napoleon I desired Frenchmen to hold of his power. Yet he had too firm a grasp on the realities not to know that nothing in this world succeeds like success. If he could give prosperity, glory, and honor to France, there would be plenty of his subjects ready to explain that they were "free" albeit under a Cæsarian despotism.

The precise nature of this new "Empire" and of its glittering officials and court is recounted in another chapter.[1] The thing to notice now is that on December 2, 1804, "the new Charlemagne" was consecrated with imposing ceremonies at Paris, by none other than Pope Pius VII himself, although to prove that he held his power by no priestly authority, Napoleon ostentatiously set the crown with his own hands upon his head.

Hardly was this ceremony completed before the Emperor was resuming the congenial task of marshaling his legions to war. His assumption of the crown, a crown won for him solely by the sword, sent new terror into all the old-line hereditary monarchs of Europe. What manner of man was this who had risen from nothing and who was now overshadowing them? England had been long ready with her subsidies; Russia, Austria, and Sweden had now joined in another great coalition. Only Prussia (among the great Powers) held equivocally aloof. The Emperor Napoleon made haste to teach the world that the touch of the crown had not spoiled the professional cunning of the one-time General Bonaparte. The great camp at Boulogne was broken up, and the army streamed away toward Southern Germany.

Of all Napoleon's campaigns this of 1805 perhaps won him the most satisfaction. His "Grand Army" was now completely

[1] See pp. 364, 369.

developed as a war-machine. It had not yet suffered such terrible losses of veterans as to lose efficiency by dilution with raw levies. In several converging columns the great masses of French swept into Southern Germany. In October, the Austrian General Mack, a very ordinary drill-master pitted against a great captain, surrendered at Ulm with 30,000 men. Napoleon marched straight onward over the mountains, and led his hosts in triumph through Vienna. On December 2, 1805, he won the most famous of his victories at Austerlitz in Moravia, when with 65,000 men he met some 85,000 allied Austrians and Russians, and drove the survivors of them in rout from the battle-field. Twenty-four days later Francis II, the terrified Hapsburg, signed the peace of Pressburg, by which Austria practically resigned all her claims in Italy, leaving the French to reorganize that peninsula as they listed; ceded likewise to France Istria and Dalmatia — the old Venetian lands along the Adriatic — handed over the Tyrol and many adjacent districts to Bavaria, Napoleon's ally, and finally recognized Bavaria and Würtemberg as independent kingdoms. For practical purposes Austria was henceforth obliged to wash her hands of both Germany and Italy and to let the terrible Corsican mould them as he willed. The famous "Third Coalition" against France had been smashed to pieces. Russia still continued nominally in the war; but young Czar Alexander I was very far away from Central Europe and could hardly send an army against Napoleon without crossing neutral territory. No wonder the cathedrals of France were ordered to reëcho with Te Deums!

There was a fly in this ointment of happiness. Four days after Mack surrendered at Ulm, the English Admiral Nelson had caught the allied French and Spanish[1] fleets at Trafalgar off the Spanish coast. Twenty-seven British ships-of-the-line were arrayed against thirty-three enemies. However, the Spanish contingent had been very ill-found. The French were brave, but the

[1] During most of this period Spain had been in half-hearted alliance with France, giving her little aid save for some blundering attempts with her navy.

best blood and intelligence of France in that day was going into the army, not into the marine. Nelson fell, but not before his dying ears caught the shouts of the victory. The Franco-Spanish fleet was practically destroyed. Henceforth the tricolor was hardly met upon the seas flying from any save light cruisers and privateers bent on commerce-destroying. The British blockade closed down upon the ports of France and her allies tighter than ever. Napoleon could dictate terms of peace to the Hapsburg, but so long as he was nigh helpless upon the ocean what real hope of realizing his grandiose schemes of world dominion? Against the almost intangible influence of British sea-power the Corsican was to beat himself quite as furiously and ineffectively as did the Hohenzollern in 1914–18.

Hardly was the ink dry upon the Treaty of Pressburg before the Prussian monarchy came close to committing suicide. That kingdom had stood ingloriously neutral since 1795. Napoleon had cozened its ruler, Frederick William III, into refraining from joining the Third Coalition, holding out vague hopes of great reward if the King would keep the peace at a time when one more potent ally for Austria might have ruined France. Now, when Austria was beaten and helpless, in a spirit of utter folly Frederick William took umbrage at various diplomatic insults and declared war, with hardly an ally save distant and ineffective Russia. Prussia's provocation was great, for the moment the need of cajolery had passed Napoleon dropped the mask and showed himself ready to outrage the Hohenzollern's dearest interests. But the military odds were now so heavy against Prussia that her action seemed very reckless. Few men, however, realized how feeble could be her fight, and how completely the famous army of Frederick the Great had been wormeaten by traditional methods and the senile inefficiency of its generals.[1] In the double battle of Jena-Auerstadt, October 14,

[1] One of these superannuated worthies is alleged to have boasted, "His Majesty the King [of Prussia] has several generals far superior to *Monsieur* Bonaparte."

1806, the Prussian war-machine was not merely defeated — it was smashed to fragments. The great Prussian fortresses made indecent haste to surrender at first summons. By 1807 Frederick William was a refugee at Memel in the extreme northeastern corner of his dominions.

Czar Alexander I tried, indeed, to come to his rescue. The Russians fought an indecisive battle with the French at Eylau — and an indecisive battle against Napoleon was ranked by his foes as a victory. A little later, however (June 14, 1807), the French defeated the Russians unequivocally at Friedland. Alexander was near the end of his fighting strength. On a raft in the river Niemen he held a conference with Napoleon. The Corsican's stronger personality easily cast its influence over the impressionable and none too steadfast Czar. Russia and France were to make close alliance, and divide the empire of the world. Alexander was to adopt Napoleon's scheme for a "Continental Blockade" of the English and to allow Prussia to be reduced to a third-class power; in return he was given great, if vague, prospects of conquests in the East. As for Napoleon, he was now free to deprive Prussia of nearly half of her territory; lay on her a crushing indemnity, and force out of her a pledge to keep an army of only 42,000 men. Austria seemed already helpless. Prussia was now helpless. Russia was an ally. Nowhere on the Continent could Napoleon meet a rival. This Treaty of Tilsit, concluded in July, 1807, in many respects marks the apogee of his career.

Only England with bull-dog tenacity defied him. The economic strain of the war upon the Britons was great; the taxes were heavy, the chances of winning a peace which did not leave Napoleon the dominator of the entire Continent seemed slight enough, but the islanders held grimly on. Helpless to scatter their blockading squadrons, the Corsican struck back by his famous "Continental Blockade." By his "Decree of Berlin," issued in that conquered city in November, 1806, he declared the British Isles under blockade, and prohibited the least commerce between them and France *and all the latter's allies.* To refuse to accept the blockade, to allow the least intercourse with Britain, to decline to declare British goods confiscate and subject to destruction, was practically to invite war with Napoleon. What Continental prince dared risk it? "I desire," announced the Emperor, "to conquer the sea by the power of the land!" [1]

To enforce such a drastic decree was, however, impossible even for the victor of Austerlitz and Jena. A great fraction of all Oriental wares and of all manufactured goods had come into Europe either by way of England or direct from English looms and forges. The profit from smuggling was enormous. Indeed, Napoleon's own high officers sometimes connived at it and took bribes for looking the other way.[2] The docks of the great commercial cities were idle. Powerful mercantile classes were alienated. Factories stood silent for want of raw material. Despite the unpopularity of the decree, Napoleon adhered to it and sharpened it. Russia, Austria, Prussia, and Denmark all kissed the rod, and joined the "blockade" of Britain. When Napoleon's own brother Louis Bonaparte (whom he had made King of Holland) refused to ruin his subjects by a strict application of the system, the Emperor forced him off his puppet throne and annexed Holland to the already swollen Empire of France (1810). Earlier he had laid a like hand on Italy, and in 1807 had overrun Portugal, because that weak kingdom had vainly talked of "neutrality."

By 1808, however, there had begun to be signs that the clear, hard intellect which had carried the sublieutenant of

[1] The Corsican, in his efforts to circumvent the pressure of sea-power by means of irregular and unusual devices, was only anticipating the more desperate expedients of Germany (1915–18) with her "unlimited" submarine policy. It is fair to assume, however, that Napoleon would never have embarked on such a policy unless he had been far more assured of the practical efficiency of the submarines than were the Germans. Napoleon was seldom cruel unless he was very sure his cruelty would win success.

[2] It is alleged that even the Emperor himself had to wink at certain forms of smuggling.

artillery up to a new throne of the Cæsars, had begun to be warped by unbroken successes. Spain was now a crazy and utterly decrepit monarchy that for some years had been trailing along in helpless alliance with France. She seemed an easy prey. Her great American colonies had not yet become independent — they might serve a lofty purpose once under the power of France! With absolute lack of scruple and with not the slightest real pretext, Napoleon took advantage of a family squabble in the Spanish royal house; bullied the execrable old Charles IV into abdicating; extracted a second abdication out of the Crown Prince Ferdinand, and then openly sent a French army into Spain to put in his own brother, Joseph Bonaparte, as the crowned successor of Ferdinand and Isabella.

Hitherto Napoleon had had to fight only against *kings*. He had found them very easy prey. Now to his amazement he had to collide with *peoples*. The results were not as he expected. The proud Spanish nation rose almost as one man against the aggressor. It was not difficult for the disciplined French troops to defeat the hasty levies of the Spanish patriots, but Napoleon was soon to learn the truth of the saying, "Spain is an easy country to overrun; a hard country to conquer." The Spaniards were past-masters in guerrilla warfare: skirmishes, raids, attacks on convoys, petty sieges. A vast number of French troops were immobilized holding down the peninsula — and yet "King Joseph" had never a comfortable minute on his throne. An English army under Sir Arthur Wellesley (later the Viscount, then Duke of Wellington) came to the Spaniards' aid. At first it was barely able to save itself from being driven into the sea by the superior hosts of the French, but, for all that, the drain upon Napoleon's resources caused by this unhappy Spanish venture continued. He could not subdue the entire country. He could not withdraw from Spain without great loss of prestige. And at this juncture he had yet another war with Austria.

The Hapsburgs had reorganized their army. They now (1809) called on all the German people to imitate the Spaniards and to rise against the oppressor. The attempt was premature. Prussia was helpless and only stirred ineffectively. The South-German kinglets cheerfully followed their French master. Only in the Tyrol was there a brave but abortive uprising under Andreas Hofer, the innkeeper. Napoleon promptly invaded Austria, took Vienna a second time, but at Aspern, on the Danube near the capital, he had an astonishing experience: he met with an undeniable defeat. It was not a decisive disaster, however. The excellent French war-machine was still functioning. The Emperor declined to retire from Vienna, held his ground, and on July 6, 1809, retrieved his tarnished glory by an old-form victory at Wagram. Austria had not been badly worsted. But no allies had joined her; she could endure the strain of the war no longer. In 1809 Francis II again consented to peace. By the Treaty of Vienna Austria ceded fully 32,000 square miles, mostly to Napoleon's ally Bavaria; and gave up the last districts which connected her with the sea. She meekly reëntered the Continental System. The prestige of the Corsican seemed higher than ever.

In 1809 Napoleon had divorced Josephine.[1] She had borne him no children, and his position would be strengthened if he had a son to succeed to his power. After vain negotiations for a Russian princess, the diplomats arranged an alliance with Maria Louisa, daughter of Francis the Hapsburg himself. The Archduchess was sent with due ceremony from Vienna to Paris, and on the 1st of April, 1810, the Emperor and she were married in Notre Dame. The train of the cloak of the new Empress was borne by *five* queens. In March, 1811, Napoleon seemed more fortunate still — he became the father of a son, the ill-starred "Napoleon II," never destined to reign, who, in his very cradle, was given the soaring title of the "King of Rome."

[1] There is no doubt that the putting aside of Josephine was a cold-blooded act of state policy. Nevertheless her conduct when her husband had been absent in Egypt (1798–99) had been so scandalous as to give good grounds for a divorce. At that time, however, Bonaparte consented to a reconciliation. This fact mitigates the blame for his later conduct, but does not excuse it.

EUROPE IN 1810, SHOWING NAPOLEON'S POWER AT ITS HEIGHT

HEIGHT OF THE EMPIRE

The year 1811 seemed to present Napoleon still at the summit of his prosperity. If there were murmurs in France at his autocratic government, if Te Deums were becoming wearisome in the churches, if the Continental blockade seemed ruining French commerce but not coercing England into peace, if the remorseless conscription for the army was awakening deep resentment throughout the nation, the fact nevertheless remained that the Corsican's power seemed more imposing than ever. One of his brothers, Jerôme, was King of Westphalia in Northwestern Germany; Joseph was King of Spain, thanks to French bayonets; Louis had, indeed, refused to play the puppet in Holland and had just renounced his regal honors, but that simply meant that his brother had annexed the old "Dutch Republic" to France itself. In Naples, Murat, the Emperor's brother-in-law, and his most dashing cavalry general, was reigning in the room of the exiled Bourbon dynasts. The minor States of Germany were organized into the "Confederation of the Rhine," helpless under the "protection" of the Emperor. Prussia appeared crushed and passive. Russia seemed still to be an ally. The Emperor of Austria was now the Corsican's father-in-law. As for France herself, her boundaries grew monthly by ever fresh decrees of annexation. Besides Holland and the western Rhinelands and Belgium,[1] new "departments" were now being organized clear across the northern coast of Germany, including Bremen and Hamburg, even to the Trave. In Italy a portion of the northeastern regions had been organized into the new "Kingdom of Italy" with Napoleon himself as "king," although ruling through a viceroy. Murat, of course, kept his Neapolitan kingdom in the South. But Piedmont, Genoa, most of Tuscany, and a strip of western coast including even Rome itself was annexed outright to the "Empire" — governed by French prefects and taking the law direct from Paris. The Pope in person was a political prisoner in France.[2]

[1] The Rhinelands and Belgium, of course, had been annexed under the Republic.
[2] See p. 375.

The army still appeared the perfect war-engine of ten years earlier, although the battle of Friedland had cost Napoleon a pitifully great number of veterans, and the ceaseless Spanish campaigns were a constant drain upon the military reserves and budget. Despite all his court ceremonial at Paris, when Napoleon was with his troops he often seemed the "Little Corporal" again, able to catch their imaginations by his fiery proclamations, and to command their implicit loyalty by such acts as mingling among the grenadiers in their bivouacs, tasting their soup, calling out by name and decorating brave privates with his own hand, and manifesting intense interest in the welfare of "his comrades." Each soldier, in short, believed himself in the confidence of the Emperor, and that the Emperor's eye was personally upon him in all that he did. To the veterans who had followed him all through his wars, loyalty to the Emperor had passed from a duty to a religion. "I cannot tell Your Majesty," wrote a marshal in 1813, "how much my men love you; and never was one more devoted to his wife than are they to your person." As for the "Old Guard" that surrounded the Emperor in all his campaigns, in 1815, after Waterloo, when all was over, one of the officers was to lament openly, "You see that we have not had the good fortune to die in your service."

Such seemed the position of Napoleon and of his Empire at its height. After such successes it is not unreasonable to say that he might not merely have consolidated all his vast dominions, but have added others also, even to the establishment of a new Roman Empire, had he learned moderation in the hour of greatest triumph. Unfortunately for him, however, even in 1811 his ruthless aggressions were enkindling so much resentment from outraged nations — Spain, Prussia, etc. — that the Emperor's position was probably less secure than it seemed.

Before, however, stating very briefly how "glory and madness" led to his abject downfall, it is needful to examine with some care the less dramatic, but more lasting, work of civil reformation which he brought to France.

CHAPTER XVII
THE NAPOLEONIC RÉGIME IN FRANCE THE CONSULATE AND THE EMPIRE

NAPOLEON BONAPARTE is usually thought of solely as the resistless "man on horseback" who for nineteen years hypnotized France and intimidated all the world by military achievements which probably surpass those of Alexander, Hannibal, or Julius Cæsar. Or if not as the master of armies, he is studied as the supreme disposer of thrones throughout Europe, the creator and re-creator of all boundaries, the wizard at whose summons kingdoms appeared and as quickly vanished. His permanent work is sometimes imagined to be solely that of the "Destroyer," who shattered so completely the effigies of mediævalism on the Continent, that not all the malign genius of Metternich, and of his fellow reactionaries who watched the Corsican's downfall, could halt the march of mankind toward relative efficiency, happiness, and liberty.

All these things concerning Napoleon's foreign activities are true, but when we look solely at France it is important to realize that his universal genius allowed him to be a great civil innovator at home as well as a conqueror abroad. To Napoleon, France owes many peaceful institutions which were to endure a century after his victories and blood-stained "glory" had vanished into the cupboards of history. The "Kingdom of Westphalia" and the "Confederation of the Rhine" are dead forever. The Code Napoléon is still the law for many millions of enlightened Frenchmen. Therefore we devote this chapter, not to the details of military achievement, but to an examination of the Napoleonic Régime in France under the Consulate and the Empire. There is the more excuse for this because relatively few popular histories dwell on the achievements of the Corsican as a civil ruler.

The Consulate, established after the revolution November 9, 1799, lasted until the 18th of May, 1804. In this period Bonaparte, as "First Consul," gave to France her fourth constitution, the "Constitution of the Year VIII," and followed this with a complete administrative, judicial, and financial reorganization of the nation. The Constitution then adopted, and partially modified in 1802 and again in 1804, lasted only to the downfall of the Empire in 1814; but the administrative, judicial, and financial organization exists to-day in France at least in its essential characteristics: its details are therefore far from possessing merely antiquarian interest. Such achievements and creations were of far greater moment than many of the Corsican's famous battles.

France at the time of the *coup d'état* of 1799 was again, thanks to the unrepaired mischief wrought by Revolutionary violence and the inefficiency of the Directors, partly submerged in anarchy. In appearance, she presented, according to reliable witnesses, "the aspect of a country devasted by a long war or abandoned after a number of years by its inhabitants." In the south the districts, painfully redeemed from the marshes, were again covered by water. In the east the port of Rochefort was blocked up with sand. In the north the dike which at Ostend protected a part of Flanders (then annexed) from the sea threatened to collapse. Everywhere the roads were practically impassable for want of repairs. In the environs of towns and villages the pavements even had been torn up by the inhabitants, who used the stones to repair their walls. In the open country the roads were also cut up by bogs where carriages were engulfed and sometimes ran the risk of disappearing. Bridges were collapsing everywhere.

The lack of public security and the general lawlessness was even more deplorable. Bands of brigands, particularly in the east, the center, and the southeast (where they were recruited from deserters), succeeded in rendering traveling nigh impossible. They pillaged the government strong boxes and halted the stage-coaches. The public coach from Nantes to Angers was once held up five times in a single journey in a distance of forty miles. The bandits robbed the travelers, kidnapped well-to-do peasants, whom they held to ransom, and attempted to storm isolated houses. In the east the brigands — the *chauffeurs* (firemen) — singed the feet of their prisoners to force them to reveal the hiding-place of their silver plate. At certain points, for example, in the Dordogne districts, even as more recently in Albania and Macedonia, travelers bought a safe-conduct in cash from the chiefs of the band. In the departments of Var, of the Lower-Alps, of the Mouths of the Rhone, and elsewhere the Directory, again like the Turkish Sultan, had to furnish to important travelers armed escorts in order to guarantee their safety.

Industry and commerce seemed practically ruined despite a certain recuperation. At Paris there could not be found in the workshops one eighth of the workmen employed before 1789. At Lyons the number of weavers in silk had decreased from eight thousand to fifteen hundred. At Marseilles the number of commercial transactions did not equal in one year the number of like exchanges in six weeks before the Revolution.

The power of the State was anything but respected. Taxes were not paid or were paid very slowly. On the day Napoleon seized power there were only 187,000 francs ($37,000) in the public treasury. Two years' arrears were owed to the national bondholders and pensioners. Patients died of hunger in some of the hospitals; in the hospital at Toulouse there were only seven pounds of food a day for eighty patients. The soldiers were receiving neither proper food, clothes, nor pay; they deserted by the thousands, or, while still in France, conducted themselves as in conquered territory. In the newly created departments of Belgium and in the borders of the Rhine they treated the inhabitants, according to an official report, "not as their fellow citizens, but as enemies disarmed or as prisoners." In these regions, too, the population, in all its prayers invoked its "liberators," that is, the Austrians. In a large number of the departments the conscripts refused to join their regiments. The Vendée and Brittany were again urged to insurrection in the name of Louis XVIII, and in Central France insurgent "Chouans," grouped into small armies under regular leaders, seemed virtually the masters.

Among the majority of the population there was a universal sense of weariness, of disgust for politics and the turbulence thereof, and of indifference even to startling news coming across the frontier. "It seems that in reading the account of our own battles we are reading the history of another people," an official report states. "The changes in our internal situation did not arouse much emotion." After ten years of convulsion the French, beyond anything else, felt the need of order, security, and repose. This disposition on the part of the public mind rendered more easy, however, the unescapably difficult task which the three provisional Consuls, Bonaparte, Sieyès, Roger Ducos, had assumed — a task in which Bonaparte, a man of genius in war, revealed himself a great statesman and a powerful civil organizer.

The Consuls and the parliamentary Commission appointed on the evening of the last *coup d'état* to draft a new Constitution set about their work without delay. Their deliberations lasted a little more than a month, and the Constitution was in the last analysis the personal work of Bonaparte. At the beginning it was thought that Sieyès had a project all in readiness. But he produced only two drafts which were decidedly confused, or, according to Bonaparte, he contributed "only shadows, the shadow of legislative, of judicial, of executive power." Bonaparte rejected them. He did the same with the two projects prepared by the assisting Commission because these seemed to him embarrassing to his ambition. In the end he himself dictated the principal clauses of the draft to which the commissioners were forced to acquiesce, and which became the "Constitution of the Year VIII." This Constitution was published December

24, 1799, and was immediately put into effect, without awaiting the results of the plebiscite — that is, the vote of the people, prescribed by the Constitution. This plebiscite only took place February 7, 1800. Less than sixteen hundred voters in all France voted "No," while the new Constitution was accepted (so it was announced) by more than three million votes. For the moment there could be no doubt of its success.

This "Constitution" was a document all in favor of the coming autocrat. The difference between avowed monarchy and "liberty" became faint, indeed, but the time was not quite ripe to cry "*Vive l'Empereur!*" and Bonaparte prudently waited. Under this new type of "Republic" there was an executive of three "Consuls," but only the "First Consul" had genuine power. He, indeed, practically controlled the entire government and appointed and dismissed all important officials. The "Second" and "Third Consuls" were to be merely consulted by him in important matters: final decision lay with him alone. All three held office for ten years and then could be reëlected by popular vote.

Under this uncrowned autocrat there was a three-headed legislature — Council of State, "Tribunate" and "Legislative" body — pretentious assemblies, but with highly conflicting prerogatives and unable really to handle a single question not first submitted by the First Consul. There was, too, a pompous "Senate" to be the "Guardian of the Constitution." The French people did not have even the privilege of electing this weak and cumbersome legislature. The voters could only choose, by indirect and clumsy processes, a hierarchy of "notables." From this decidedly large number of "notables" (of various grades and distinctions) the First Consul selected, virtually at his own sweet will, the members for the legislative bodies, the Senate, and for the numerous government offices. Thus Bonaparte practically chose his own legislature. And yet Robespierre was barely six years dead! The "constitutional power" of the First Consul hardly fell short of the "divine power" of a Louis XIV.

This resemblance to the days of royalty was made clearer by the reorganization of the local administration of France in 1800. The local elective officers of 1790 were replaced by appointive officers named by the Central Government. Over the department was now set the ubiquitous prefect, with the sub-prefects and communal mayors beneath him. Even the local councils were named by the central power. Thus was created a vast swarm of functionaries — agents and creations of the Paris Government, instantly removable by it, and completely subservient to its wishes. Prefects and sub-prefects had replaced the submissive intendants and sub-delegates of the Old Régime, their direct heirs in authority, allegiance, and servility. The Consulate thus restored the highly centralized form of government which the reformers of 1789 had labored to destroy. This bureaucratic, ministerial-controlled system has been maintained by all the Governments which have succeeded the Consulate. Amended somewhat after 1870 and under the Third Republic it still exists even in our own day.[1] For no slight reason, therefore, we have dwelt on this great administrative change by Napoleon Bonaparte.

The reorganization of the judiciary closely followed the administrative reform (March 18, 1800). There, too, the electoral system was abolished except in the case of the justices of the peace. All other judges were named either by the First Consul or by the Senate. To assure their independence and self-respect, however, in the face of the Government, there was established in the beginning the just rule that they were irremovable, except for crime. Like the administrative machinery, this judicial system substantially exists to-day. Again the Corsican was building something more permanent than many of his ephemeral kingdoms.

It was the same with the financial organization and the system

[1] There is very bitter criticism of this centralization by Frenchmen; the reorganization of the administration of the Third Republic, involving the granting of greater *local* liberties, was one of the problems confronting the Republic at the end of the Great War in 1918.

for the collection of taxes. Here Bonaparte's quick intelligence produced prompt results even before the new Constitution had been drafted. He knew how wretched had been the financial plight of the Convention and the Directory and that this distress had been caused not only by the enormous expenses of the war and the depreciation of the paper *assignats*, but also by the poor system for the collection of the taxes. The task of assessing and of collecting these had been entrusted by the Constituent Assembly to the administrators of the communes and of the departments, who had utterly neglected their tasks. Here, as everywhere, Bonaparte substituted for these feeble bodies, elected by the citizens, agents named by himself. His power gained and also the comfort of all honest Frenchmen.

Thanks to the reforms of the Consulate the national finances were put on a firm foundation and the taxes collected in a way to be no menace to the country's prosperity.

The Constitution, the administrative reorganization, the judicial and the financial reforms were the labor of the first four months of the Consulate. These permitted the prompt reëstablishment of order throughout the entire country and, therefore, the rapid revival of France. All these things were put in force under the constant and active direction of Bonaparte with his selected officials. The civil officials the First Consul had recruited without concerning himself with their political theories, present or past, or whether even they had been Royalists or Republicans, considering only the services which they were capable of rendering the State; his ambition, as he stated much later, being only to impel into the service of the country all its talents.

Two other measures of great consequence mark the later history of the Consulate: the signing of the Concordat with the Pope and the drawing up of the Civil Code.

Since he was anxious to restore internal peace to France, Napoleon could not neglect to terminate the religious crisis so unfortunately provoked by the "Civil Constitution of the Clergy." In spite of the persecutions, which were brutally renewed by the Directory after the year 1796, the majority of the people were probably still attached to the "non-juring" clergy and to Roman Catholicism. Therefore, one of the first acts of the Consul was to revoke the decrees of banishment against the priests and to assure them entire freedom of worship.

But more than this, Bonaparte was convinced that religion was the most valuable element of order. Concrete theological beliefs of his own, he hardly possessed; unless it were a blind faith in his destiny. He is alleged to have spoken respectfully at times of Jesus Christ, and it is not proper to call him an atheist. But as the ruler of France he went at the religious problem from a strictly utilitarian standpoint. The Church properly handled would serve to strengthen the new autocracy he was founding; therefore he must patronize and control it. "A society without religion is like a vase without a bottom," he said. "It is only *that* which gives to a state a firm and lasting support." The clergy, preaching love for all that is good and hatred for all evil in the name of the God of eternal justice, seemed to his mind the safest guardian of the public peace. He therefore undertook to order about priests just as he ordered about gendarmes.

To achieve this it was necessary to treat with the Pope, since the attempted organization of a national Church by the Revolutionists had failed disastrously. Pope Pius VII, a man of conciliatory spirit, favored *rapprochement* on his own side. The negotiations were commenced immediately after the signing of the Peace of Lunéville (February, 1801) through the mediation of Abbé Bernier, a Vendéan priest who before, at the beginning of the Consulate, had already negotiated and procured the submission of the insurgents of the Vendée and Brittany (January, 1800). These negotiations were carried on laboriously at Paris and finally ended on July 15, 1801, with the signing of the Concordat.

By this treaty "the Government of the Republic recognized that Catholicism was the religion of the majority of the French people." It promised to insure its free and public exercise. On the other hand, the Church agreed to the reduction of the dioceses, which the Constituent Assembly had claimed the right of enforcing on its own authority. These were now set at only sixty, including ten archbishoprics. The Pope also consented, "for the sake of peace," to recognize the "assumption" by the State in 1789 of the property of the Church. In return the French Government promised, as it already had solemnly done through the Constituent Assembly, to assure adequate salaries to the bishops and the curés, and to authorize an endowment for the benefit of the Church.

As for the nomination of the bishops, this would be done jointly by the French Government and by the Pope. The Government would appoint them, the Pope would then "invest" them with their spiritual power, without which they had no authority in the eyes of the Church. They would be obliged to take an oath of allegiance to the head of the State. They could in turn nominate the curés of the canton without the assent of the Government. The nomination by the State, the salaries, and the oath transformed the bishops into public functionaries and practically placed them in the hands of the Government. So long as a Napoleon Bonaparte ruled France, the Papal control of the French Church, whatever the letter of the treaty, was almost insignificant.

The Concordat went into effect in April, 1802. It was destined to govern the relations between Church and State for more than a century, up to 1905. It was received with real satisfaction by the majority of France, and met with disfavor only among the old politicians of the Revolution and in a part of the army, where the prejudices and passions of 1793 were still strong.

Immediately after he had thus reorganized the State, the First Consul turned his attention to completing and solidifying the social work of the Revolution, by embodying its entire achievements into a single great "Code"; that is, a collection of the laws which governed the relations of individuals in the new society. The preparation of a code had, indeed, been ordained in 1790 by the Constituent Assembly and by the Convention, while the Council of the Five Hundred under the Directory had prepared several plans, none of which had materialized. But in August, 1800, Bonaparte appointed a commission of six members with Tronchet, the President of the Court of Cassation, as its chairman. In four months the Commission decided on a new project. This was first submitted to the legal bodies for examination and later was reviewed by the Council of State, where, according to Cambacères, the First Consul took the most active part in the discussion and often amazed the jurists by his strictly juridical viewpoints and by his real understanding of law. The various parts of the Code were then successively submitted to the Tribunate and voted on by the Legislative Chamber. The "Civil Code," inspired by Roman law and the royal ordinances as well as by the enactments of the Revolutionaries, was concluded on March 21, 1804. It later received, and the title was regularly applied to it abroad, the name, "the Napoleonic Code." It is in force in France to-day, and has been imitated or at least has had an important influence upon the legal systems of the majority of European States.

The political and administrative institutions, the Concordat, the Code, were only a part of the work accomplished from 1800 to 1804. No government, in fact, has abounded in more activities than that of the Consulate; and no other period in French history has been marked by so many lasting achievements. To mould future civil officials the First Consul went on to reorganize secondary education in the *lycées* (or high schools), providing them with numerous foundations for the maintenance of poor scholars. As a means of rewarding public services he instituted the Legion of Honor (1802), organized in military fashion and divided into cohorts with a hierarchy of knights, officers, commanders, and grand officers. To aid in the reconstruction of industry and commerce, a group of bankers, yet again on the initiative of the First Consul, founded the Bank of France (1800) whose bank notes were soon on a par with gold and silver money, and which later became, save possibly the Bank of England, the most powerful financial establishment in the world.

These were not all of the First Consul's schemes and projects; he was tossing about great plans for public works and the encouragement of industry and commerce when the renewal of the wars diverted all the energies of France.

At the time of his seizure of power the Royalists fondly imagined that Napoleon would work for the return of the Monarchy and would be glad to play the part of Monk who reëstablished Charles II in England. "Louis XVIII," at the time a refugee in Poland, had also written to the First Consul asking his support and offering to let him fix his own reward (1800). Far from dreaming, however, of restoring the Bourbons, Bonaparte was already aiming to perpetuate his own power and to create a dynasty in his own name. He reached this goal in two stages; in August, 1802, he succeeded in having himself appointed Consul for life; in May, 1804, he was named Emperor of France.

After being elected "Consul for life," by a plebiscite of all French voters (3,600,000 "yes" against only 9000 "no," said the official announcement), the Constitution was immediately modified. To the former powers of the First Consul was now added the right to sign treaties with no other counter-sanction than that of a Privy Council named by himself. The lists of "notables" were abolished and replaced by equally dependable "electoral colleges"; supposed to be elected by cumbersome indirect processes by the citizens. The legislative bodies (especially the "Tribunate") were shorn of part of their already very limited powers. On the contrary, the numbers of Senators and their influence were increased. The Senate henceforth had the right to "interpret" the Constitution and to govern by decrees called, according to the old Roman expression, "Senatus consultum." This increase of power was bound, of course, to profit the First Consul, especially as he received the right to nominate directly one third of the members of the Senate, and could in any case count on a devoted majority of this pretentious body.

The establishment of the Life Consulate ruined the hopes of the Royalists. Already, after Napoleon Bonaparte had refused to assist them in the restoration, certain "emigrants" had essayed to slay the usurper. One evening in December, 1800, at the time when he was on his way to the Comédie Française, they had attempted his life by means of a barrel of powder concealed under a hand cart and thrust in the way of his carriage. The recollection of that attempt did not prevent the First Consul, however, from attempting to win over those of the old nobility who were in Paris. He went farther; he abrogated the Revolutionary decrees against the "emigrants." They were permitted to return to France on the condition that they take an oath of fidelity to the Republic, and the Consul caused such of their property as had not already been sold to be restored to them (April 26, 1802).

All this could not conciliate the extremists, however. In August, 1803, a group of "emigrants" living in England, among whom was the notorious Polignac, formed an elaborate conspiracy; the English Government furnished the funds for the execution of the plot. An old leader of the Royalist insurgents (*Chouans*), George Cadoudal, at the head of a resolute band, was to attack and kill the First Consul in the very midst of his bodyguard. Under cover of the disturbance caused by the death of the Consul, General Pichegru, who had gone over to the side of the Royalists in the days of the Directory, was prepared to restore the Bourbons by a military revolution. To accomplish this, Pichegru invited the coöperation of Moreau, another distinguished general who was at personal variance with the

First Consul. Moreau declared himself ready to assist in the overthrow of Napoleon; but he refused to work for the restoration of Louis XVIII, preferring to play somehow for his own hand.

The plot was uncovered in January, 1804. Moreau, Pichegru, and afterwards Cadoudal, who concealed themselves in Paris for several months, were successively arrested (February 15, March 7, 1804). Cadoudal confessed that he had been awaiting, before attempting his crime, for the arrival in France of a Prince of the royal family who was to be promptly on hand as soon as the First Consul had been disposed of.

A fatal concurrence of circumstances, a report of the police pointing out the mysterious journeys of the Duke d'Enghien (which reached the ears of Bonaparte at the same time as the confessions of Cadoudal), led the Consul to imagine that the Prince whom Cadoudal had expected was the selfsame Duke d'Enghien, son of the Prince of Condé. This exiled nobleman lived just across the Rhine from Strasbourg, at Ettenheim, in the Duchy of Baden. The Corsican's rage was furious. "Am I then a dog whom one can beat to death in the street?" he exclaimed. "I shall not allow myself to be killed without resistance. Verily I will cause those people to tremble and teach them how to hold their peace!"

In spite of the remonstrances of Cambacères and Lebrun, he had the Duke d'Enghien kidnapped from Badenese territory by a detachment of dragoons. The prisoner was transferred to a fort at Vincennes, where he was immediately brought before a court martial for having borne arms against France — a fact in which he gloried. He was condemned to die at midnight and was shot immediately in the moat of the citadel. His execution naturally terrified the Royalists and snuffed out the entire conspiracy. A little later Cadoudal was guillotined; Pichegru was strangled in prison; Moreau was banished. But the 'scutcheon of the conqueror was eternally stained by the death of d'Enghien who was nothing less than murdered.

The conspiracy of Cadoudal hastened the transformation of the Consulate into an hereditary Monarchy. Several days after the arrest of the conspirators, the Senate at the suggestion of an old Jacobin Terrorist, Fouché, now the obsequious tool of the new "Cæsar," had requested that Napoleon, *le grand homme,* "should complete his work by rendering it as immortal as his glory!" A tribune put this request into more intelligible language; he demanded that Napoleon Bonaparte be proclaimed the "Emperor of the French" and that this imperial dignity be declared hereditary. Carnot, the old Terrorist war-chief, alone had the courage to resist this motion. It was adopted by the Senate that issued a "Senatus consultum" on the 18th of May, 1804, by virtue of which "the government of the *Republic* was entrusted to the *Emperor* Napoleon." The imperial title was hereditary, from father to son in the order of primogeniture in the Bonaparte family. In default of direct descendants, the brothers of Napoleon, Joseph and Louis, were named to succeed him. This new modification of the "Constitution of the Year VIII" was submitted to a plebiscite and was ratified by more than three and one half million votes; while not three thousand were officially counted as opposing it. France was, indeed, then completely hypnotized by the adventurer from Corsica. It was in a mood to vote him anything.

And so the wheel of fortune had completely turned. After the Old Monarchy, the Limited Monarchy of 1791; then the Radical Republic of 1793; then the Conservative Republic under the Directors of 1795; then the Dictatorship (for such the Consulate was) of 1799; and now a Monarchy again, with a ruler more masterful and powerful than Louis XIV. Surely in the Under-World the shades of the Bourbon monarchs must have indulged in ghostly laughter! It was a monarchy very different, however, from that of the Sun King which Napoleon I was founding.

The Empire lasted ten years — from May 18, 1804, to April 6, 1814. In so far as foreign affairs were concerned, they were ten years of continuous warfare. They opened with the French armies occupying the majority of the European capitals, they closed with the defeat of France and with the abdication of Napoleon, vanquished by Europe, at the castle of Fontainebleau. At home Napoleon, who had retained the institutions of the Consulate, completed the centralization of his absolutist government. He created, however, a few new institutions, whereof the most important and the most characteristic was the "University," founded in 1808.

The suppression of all political liberty and of all forms of popular control, and the return to the arbitrary rule of the Old Régime detached from Napoleon the support of the wealthy educated bourgeoisie. The violence of his measures against the Pope, caused by foreign political factors, added to the religious complications within France and detached from the Imperial Government the support of the clergy and the Catholics. The ceaseless levying of conscripts at last alienated even the masses of people, the artisans and the peasants, who had, nevertheless, remained faithful for a long time, because Napoleon maintained civil liberty and equality and assured them of the tranquil possession of their farms — in their eyes the most important acquisitions of the Revolution. By the time this internal revolution in public opinion was completed, the disaster of 1814 was of course near at hand. Napoleon was at length defeated because France had reached the limit of her willingness to make sacrifices for him.

The transformation of the Consulate for life into an hereditary Empire necessitated modifications and amendments to the "Constitution of the Year VIII." These changes had for their goal the surrounding of the new autocracy with all the external pomp and ceremony of the Ancient Monarchy, as well as that of increasing still more the powers of the sovereign. The Constitution, nevertheless, continued to be called the "Constitution of the Year VIII," albeit all its "Republican" reminiscences had almost vanished.

The Emperor, like Louis XVI, received a civil list of twenty-five million francs ($5,000,000). The Constitution created an imperial family and gave the title of French princes and princesses to the brothers and sisters of the Emperor. The Emperor, like the vanished kings, was surrounded by a hierarchy of august personages whose titles had been for the most part borrowed from the old court: the grand dignitaries, the marshals of France, the colonels-general, the grand officers of the Crown, etc. There were six "grand dignitaries": the Grand Elector, the Arch-Chancellor of the Empire, the Arch-Chancellor of the State, the Arch-Treasurer, the High Constable, the High Admiral — all these enjoyed glittering distinction. The marshals and the colonels-general were chosen by the Emperor from among the most illustrious generals of the Revolution. The grand officers of the Crown were known as the Grand Chaplain, the Grand Chamberlain, the Master of the Hounds, the Master of the Horse, the Grand Master of Ceremonies, and the Grand Marshal of the Palace. The royal residence under Louis XIV had not been more complete or more brilliant. Several of the grand officials were in fact men of the old court; the Grand Chamberlain was the former Bishop of Autun, Count Talleyrand, already Minister of Foreign Affairs; while the Grand Master of Ceremonies was the Count of Ségur, former Ambassador of Louis XVI to the court of Catherine II of Russia.

The Senate under the Empire lost the most important of its prerogatives, the right to pronounce on the constitutionality of laws. Its decisions in other like matters were only valid after ratification by the Emperor. As a result the Emperor henceforth had as much legislative as executive power: "Cæsar" would do everything!

All things considered, Napoleon has been the most formidable and commanding figure of Christian times. Outside of Julius Cæsar, there is almost none to be reckoned his compeer in all human history; whatever be the estimate put upon his character, "A man of mammoth proportions, fashioned in a mould apart," according to the description of Taine, "he could not be described, according to the remark of one of his enemies [Madame de Staël], in the words which have been accustomed to serve our purposes."

At the time of his taking the throne he was thirty-one years of age; and his genius and character had attained their full development. His striking characteristics were power of intellect and imagination, a passion for glory and power, combined with an extraordinary capacity for work.

His prodigious intellect, as spontaneous and lucid as it seems possible for a mortal to possess, was regulated and disciplined in a remarkable fashion. "Various matters," he said candidly, "are arranged in my head as in a cupboard. When I leave off *one* affair, I close its drawer and open up that of another. These do not become confused one with another and they never bother nor tire me." The intense objectivity of his spirit, always predominant, could not endure mere theories or theory-makers; such men he heartily detested, calling them, "Ideologues — a mere rabble!"

Nevertheless, his imagination was as remarkable as his intellect. "I never see more than two years ahead," he remarked, but it is evident enough that he had plenty of dreams and cherished visions. His reign was in large part consecrated — his enemies furnishing the pretexts and occasion — to the task of giving life to these children of his imagination. These dreams, revealed by him in various conversations, were to make of the French Empire "the mother country of other sovereignties." Napoleon, the heir of Charlemagne, the supreme ruler of Europe, was to distribute kingdoms among his generals, and he would even condescend to retain the Pope as his spiritual lieutenant. Paris was to become "the one and only city" (*la ville unique*), where the chief works of science and art and all those things which had rendered preceding centuries illustrious were to be treasured; she was to become the capital of capitals and "each king of Europe was to be forced to build a great palace," where he was to dwell on the coronation day of the Emperor of the French.

To this inordinate imagination was added the passion for glory and power, a passion so inordinate that it caused Napoleon to regard Europe as a "molehill" where nothing could be accomplished on a large scale. He openly regretted that "he had come too late" and that he had not lived in ancient times when "Alexander, after he had conquered Asia, announced to his people that he was the son of Jove, and was proclaimed to be such by the entire Orient." This power, which he desired in its entirety, was incapable of division; Napoleon never dreamed of having a colleague, or even a junior regent to share his vast responsibilities; everything must be done by him, even as all the nations must be bent under him. This passion for omnipotence increased ceaselessly up to the final catastrophe. Moreover, notwithstanding the fact that in the earliest stages of his career he had endeavored to surround himself entirely with men of merit and had solicited their counsel, from 1801 onward, he would allow no real advisers. In all of their activities he desired his subordinates to be simply his submissive servants, incapable of initiative, blind executioners of his wishes; as a result, he gathered all too many men of mean talent, and toward the close of his reign in the truest sense he was governing alone over half of Europe.

He performed this colossal task gracefully, as a result of that capacity for work such as has never perhaps been equaled by any other man, Colbert excepted. Louis XIV, the industrious king, when compared to Napoleon, seems almost a dilettante. "Work is my element," the Emperor remarked, and added that he had never realized "the limit of his capacity." He rarely labored less than eighteen hours a day, nearly always without any relaxation. He toiled everywhere and anywhere; while dining, during the fifteen minutes which he allowed for his meal, while walking, at the theater. He had the singular faculty of awaking and sleeping at will, and at night he would often interrupt the three or four hours which he devoted to slumber, by rising and resuming the endless reading and answering of dispatches. The task which occupied him for the moment absorbed him completely, to a point where he could forget everything else and render himself during such hours quite insensible to fatigue. Only *he* could have made the time suffice for all the multifarious things which he had to do; yet that he knew remarkably well how to distribute the precious hours was the testimony of those who worked with him. One of these helpers confessed admiringly that the Emperor could "accomplish more at governing in three years than the old kings in a hundred!"

Once a week on a fixed day Napoleon assembled all of his ministers. Each one gave an account of the affairs of his own department. No one could come to a decision on his own authority. Likewise all of the correspondence of these ten ministers was submitted daily to the Emperor. In fact, the ministers were reduced to the rôle of mere bureau chiefs, expected simply to present questions and to transmit commands. The Emperor dictated his orders in a conversational tone, while pacing to and fro in his cabinet, without ever repeating a word, and talking so swiftly that the expert secretaries — for he dictated several orders at the same time — sometimes had trouble in copying down one half of what he said. One can understand what a prodigious amount of labor Napoleon accomplished by merely considering that twenty-three thousand articles of correspondence in thirty volumes have been published, and that nevertheless there still remain, scattered about in the archives, nearly fifty thousand letters of his dictation.

The character of Napoleon explains alike the institutions and the collection of governmental measures which constitute the Imperial Régime.

His powerful imagination and, on the other hand, his conviction which laid hold on men, especially in France, by reason of personal vanity, urged "His Imperial Majesty" to surround himself with pomp and magnificence; therefore, he reconstituted the court and created a new nobility.

Jealous despot that he was, Napoleon would support nothing in the present which could threaten to become an obstacle in the future. He suppressed the Tribunate, developed the police system on a tremendous scale, reëstablished the state prisons, and abolished the freedom of the press. Henceforth he wished to be master of men's minds as well as their bodies, and therefore to mould their intellects to suit his own convenience. It was to this end that he created the "University."[1]

The Emperor personally was very simple in his tastes. He lived like a high-rank officer, whose thousand military duties did not allow much personal nonsense. He was always in a uniform, usually the somber costume of a colonel of the light cavalry (*colonel de chasseurs*) — a green coat with white trousers. The soldiers saw him go about as one of the most shabbily dressed officers in the army. But those around him, the officers and members of the court, were decked out with plumes and bedizened with gold and embroideries. At the Tuileries, the ordinary residence of Napoleon, to a large extent, there had been reëstablished around the Empress Josephine, the ceremony of Versailles. The costume of the ancient court, the coat, the trousers, the sword, the shoes with buckles, the long-trained robes, were again in vogue. And, just as in 1789 there had existed in addition to the palace of the King, the palaces of the Queen and of the King's brother, so now in 1804 besides the Imperial palace there were those of the Empress, of the mother of Napoleon, and of the brothers and sisters of the Emperor, the Imperial Princes and Princesses. Nevertheless, there was no genuine return to the worst abuses of the Ancient Régime. Most vital fact of all, there was this profound difference between the royal and the imperial courts — the latter did not have any political importance and neither women nor mistresses had the slightest influence over the Government.

[1] See p. 372.

GREAT DIGNITARIES

After the triumphs at Austerlitz, Jena, and Friedland, and the defeat of the Austro-Russian and Russo-Prussian coalitions (1805–07), Napoleon in 1807 established an imperial nobility. The origins of this new noblesse often, indeed, could ill bear peevish scrutiny. We have seen[1] the humble birth of some of Napoleon's most distinguished generals who now stood on the very footsteps of the throne. Of course many of the old nobility, who accepted the new régime, were welcomed to places of dignity; none the less the new court was really a court of parvenus. But these parvenus, as so often elsewhere, stood stiffly for their prerogatives and honors. It takes little time to create a pretentious "aristocracy" under an efficient and rewarding autocrat.

This nobility was one made up of officials. Just as in the famous *tchin* established by Peter the Great in Russia, there was a hierarchy of titles corresponding to the hierarchy of offices. The ministers, the Senators, the Councilors of State, the archbishops, various members of the Institute, and certain favored generals-of-division received the title of "count." The presidents of the High Court of Cassation, and of the various courts of appeal, the bishops, the presidents of the electoral colleges, and certain mayors rejoiced as "barons"; while the members of the Legion of Honor were made "knights." The titles of count and baron could under certain conditions be rendered hereditary in favor of the eldest sons of the original holders — thus perpetuating an aristocracy.

In the same manner the Emperor bestowed the titles of "dukes" and "princes" on many of the marshals and certain of the grand civil dignitaries. These titles awaited the marshals as a reward for their most illustrious services under the Republic and the Empire. Thus Kellermann, the old sword of the Jacobins, was made the "Duke of Valmy"; Augereau, the "Duke of Castiglione"; Lannes, "Duke of Montebello"; Ney, "Duke of Elchingen," and later "Prince of Moscow"; Davout, "Duke

[1] See p. 335.

of Auerstadt," later "Prince of Eckmuhl," etc. Among the civilians, Talleyrand, Minister of Foreign Affairs, received the title of "Prince of Benevento"; Fouché, the adroit and utterly unscrupulous Minister of the Police, that of the "Duke of Otranto." To each of these hereditary titles the Emperor added pensions, often decidedly large; Davout, for example, received nearly one million francs ($200,000) a year. Some of these pensions were still paid by the French Government to the heirs of the original holders until comparatively recently.

At the same time that he created an imperial nobility, the Emperor suppressed the unlucky "Tribunate" because in that assembly, Napoleon said, there were still evidences of "that restless and democratic spirit which so long had agitated France!" The fifty tribunes were seated in the Legislative Chamber. Later that Assembly too was practically destroyed; the duration of its sessions was reduced to a certain number of weeks, and there were even certain years in which the Legislative Chamber was not convoked. Napoleon then illegally demanded of the Senate, which was very subservient, the ratification of various acts, such as the levying of conscripts, the establishment of a budget, etc., for which, according to the Constitution, the vote of the legislative deputies had been indispensable. The Emperor also proceeded, in 1813, to draw up the budget himself and to establish new taxes on his own authority, in the precise manner of Louis XIV. Thus disappeared the most important of the political liberties acquired in 1789; the right of the people to determine for themselves their expenses and receipts. It would have been better to have abolished the pretense of a constitution altogether.

Under such a system, individual liberty was of course no longer respected. An enormous police system, so numerous and so active that a special minister had been instituted to direct it, held Paris and the departments in its clutch. The official agents, the "commissioners," in all the villages, and the "secret agents" everywhere, inspected, spied upon, denounced to the courts, and arrested luckless folk suspected of being hostile to the Empire. The state prisons were therefore reëstablished and citizens were interned without regular trial, "as a measure of safety," on a mere order of the Emperor, executed by the police, just as the subjects of the King before 1789 had been flung into the Bastile by virtue of a "*lettre de cachet.*" In 1808, Napoleon issued an order to the Minister of Police, Fouché, to prepare for the sending of a certain number of young boys "whom their parents, former emigrants, maintained in vexatious idleness," to the military school of Saint-Cyr. "If any one makes objection," the Emperor added, he should make no other response than "this is His Majesty's good pleasure." That was almost exactly the formula of Louis XIV and the Absolute Monarchy.

The same "good pleasure" suppressed the freedom of the press, just as it had suppressed the men of the Terror and of the Directory. Many newspapers had been seized at the beginning of the Consulate. Over seventy-three political journals were appearing in Paris in 1799; sixty were immediately silenced. Of the thirteen others, four alone, in 1811, were authorized to continue their issues. Moreover, their editors-in-chief were named by the Emperor, and no article could be published without first having been submitted to a censor named by the Minister of Police. Outside of Paris, journals could be published in only eighty cities, and only one in each place. This solitary journal, likewise, was published under the surveillance of the prefect of the department and could insert only official announcements, various harmless items of news, accidents, fires, etc. Free discussion, even in a perfectly loyal spirit, was rigidly discouraged.

Books and printers were treated no better than newspapers and editors, and here again the Emperor restored the usages of the Absolute Monarchy. He established a censorship (1810) which even prohibited the publication of a translation of the Psalms of David, because, the censors said, "certain passages could be found in them which contained prophetic allusions to the conflict between Napoleon and the Pope." As for the printers, their number was limited. No one could become a printer without a license, that is, an imperial authorization. The Press, Napoleon frankly declared, is "an arsenal which must not descend to the level of the whole world, but only to those who are in the confidence of the Government." This was again going back to the days preceding Voltaire.

Napoleon desired above all things, however, that in the future the Government should have the confidence of the majority of Frenchmen. To accomplish this the Government must needs have control of their intellects, and must mould the same to its own good pleasure, taking charge of its citizens from their infancy by means of an elaborate system of education.[1] This was a new idea which Napoleon had borrowed from the Assemblies of the Revolution. Under the Ancient Régime, in fact, the King had not interested himself in the education of his subjects. Practically all education worthy of the name was in the hands of ecclesiastics, frequently Jesuits; and a great fraction of the lower classes had been pitifully illiterate. The men of the Revolution and their leaders occupied themselves with preparing a scheme for instruction by the State. Napoleon built upon their work and attached the utmost importance to the development of this type of instruction, because "he wished to form," he declared, "a block of granite on which to build the strata of the new society." As Consul he had organized the high schools (*lycées*). As Emperor he established the "University."

The Imperial University was founded (March 17, 1808), in order, the decree stated, "to assure uniformity of instruction and to mould for the State citizens devoted to their religion, their prince, their fatherland, and their families." It was to teach "faithfulness to the Emperor and to the Imperial Monarchy, the guardian of the prosperity of the people."

Under the direction of a "Grand Master," who ranked among

[1] A somewhat similar idea seems to have actuated the German Government in its control of education during the generation preceding 1914.

EDUCATION A STATE MONOPOLY

the principal dignitaries of the Empire, and who later became the Minister of Public Instruction, the University comprised a graded system with three types of instruction — primary, secondary, and higher. For the sake of administration it was divided into academies, each supervised by a Rector. This hierarchy of instruction and administrative organization exist to-day just as they were established by Napoleon.

Primary education was not, indeed, organized by the State. The Emperor entrusted it to the care of the "Brothers of the Christian Faith." They received an annual subsidy of only 4250 francs. This was the entire budget for primary instruction! All this meant that elementary instruction, too elementary to convey any political knowledge, was turned over to the Church and its charities. So far as Napoleon was involved, it did not greatly matter if ploughmen and vine-dressers remained illiterate.

Secondary instruction, however, was organized with great care, because it was to mould the future military and civil officials through whom the Emperor was to control France. This instruction was given in the colleges and high schools (*lycées*). The programmes were stripped almost completely of all those studies which might tend to create or develop the critical spirit: philosophy and history, etc. The professors and pupils were subjected to military discipline. The ordinary high schools were governed by a uniform regulation, where their entire programme was carried out to the tap from the drum, and had all the aspect of military schools.

Higher education was given in the "Faculties" (*Facultés*) — the faculties of theology, law, medicine, sciences, and literature. In all of these the instruction was of a purely practical character. The aim was to fashion not only men of science, capable of contributing to the progress of human knowledge, but also specialists — magistrates, advocates, physicians, professors — fitted to carry on their professions. The specialized establishments reorganized or created by the Revolution (the Collège de France, the École Normale) for the preparation of professors of the sciences and literature were also skillfully woven into this great centralized system. It is idle to deny that, whatever Napoleon's motives, many of these arrangements for the highest learning were to prove of great utility to France and to all civilization.

Secondary and higher education thus became the monopoly of the State; they could be given only in government establishments taught by government professors. The pupils of the lower "free schools" were constrained to follow the course of study of the high school if they hoped to continue their programme. This monopoly by the University was to be maintained for almost half a century, clear up to the Second Republic and the Law of Falloux (1850). It greatly affected the life and thought of France, but of course military disasters had toppled down the Empire long before all educated Frenchmen had been drilled to believe that "Napoleon the Great" was their only possible ruler.

Napoleon essayed to make the Church as useful to him as the University for controlling the minds of the younger generation. The catechism, alongside of the "duties owed to God," enumerated those also due to the Emperor, and stated them to be: "love, respect, obedience, fidelity, military service, and the taxes imposed for the preservation and the defense of the Empire." "Those who disregarded these duties to our Emperor," the catechism stated, invoking the authority of St. Paul, "resisted the order established by God himself and rendered themselves liable to eternal damnation." The doctrine was plain that the conscript who refused to join his regiment, the merchant who would not pay for his license, exposed themselves forever to the torments of hell!

However, it was not merely the French clergy ("his clergy" according to Napoleon's own expression), but the Pope himself, whom the Emperor endeavored to harness into the service of his statecraft. As a result there was a conflict between Pius VII and Napoleon which commenced in 1806 and lasted down to the end of the Empire and which reveals with remarkable vividness the despotic instincts of the Emperor and the brutality of his character.

When the war against England recommenced, Napoleon treated the Pope, an independent sovereign, as he treated his own prefects. He enjoined him at first to expel the English who were living in the Papal States, and later he ordered him to close his ports to all forms of English merchandise (November, 1806). To justify himself for this high-handed procedure, Napoleon referred to Charlemagne, "his august predecessor," the donor of the patrimony of St. Peter, and supreme master of Rome. "Your Holiness is the Pope of Rome, but, as for me, *I am the Emperor*," he wrote to the Pope. Pius VII affected to remain neutral, whereupon Napoleon first occupied the Pontifical States (1807); later he annexed them outright to the Empire (May, 1809). The Pope excommunicated him, upon which act the Pontiff was immediately arrested and transferred to Savona. He was there treated as a criminal; he was deprived of everything with which to write and a police officer posted to guard him day and night.

These events had their reaction on France. The Pope, while prisoner, refused to give spiritual investiture to the bishops appointed by Napoleon and twenty-seven dioceses were therefore vacant. The Emperor attempted to induce the French bishops to forego their Papal investiture. In spite of his threats, however, and the imprisonment of several bishops in the dungeon at Vincennes, they all, even the most devoted and obedient to Napoleon, announced that their highest allegiance was to the Pope. Napoleon attempted to break that allegiance by a great struggle. In 1812 he transferred Pius VII, then in very frail health, to Fontainebleau. Through deception he wrested from him a new Concordat (1813) which reduced the authority of the Pope to nothing and made him, now formally domiciled in France, merely a kind of spiritual lieutenant of the Emperor.

But the aged Pius VII recovered his physical strength enough to disavow the signature which had been forced from him during his illness. As for the rest, successive military defeats shortly forced Napoleon to restore the Pope to liberty (1814) and Pius VII promptly retook possession of Rome. In 1815 he magnanimously offered an asylum to the Bonapartes who had been forced to flee from France, and a little later he intervened among the allied sovereigns to obtain a mitigation of the sentence which banished Napoleon to St. Helena. This was a Christian vengeance worthy of the heir of St. Peter.

This religious struggle had its political consequences. The clergy and the Catholics who were favorable to "Napoleon, Restorer of the Faith," speedily became hostile to "Napoleon, the Persecutor of the Pope." The fear which the Corsican inspired to the very last of his reign prevented that hostility from manifesting itself in public acts. But the clergy were already reconciled to the recall of the Bourbons, and the royal restoration in 1814-15 found among its ranks most devoted partisans.

The Imperial Government ended at last with discontent spreading widely among the majority of the French people. About 1809, scarcely five years after the establishment of the Empire, practically all classes of society began to detach themselves from the selfsame Napoleon, who had been so popular during the time of his Consulate. This disaffection lasted pretty generally up to his actual overthrow in 1814. The suppression of all political liberty, the elaborate system of inquisition by the police, the despotism which claimed the right to rule even the thoughts of men, encountered the intense dissatisfaction of the educated bourgeoisie. The Continental Blockade paralyzed commerce on a large scale, and if it favored the development of industry, it also favored immoral speculation. As a result in

1811 there was a terrible economic crisis, numerous bankruptcies, with general dissatisfaction in all circles, especially of manufacturers, shipowners, and merchants.

On the other hand, the Government of the Empire never ceased its aggrandizements and ended by comprising one hundred and thirty departments with sixty million inhabitants, until by constant annexations of very alien lands it stretched from Rome to Hamburg, from Brest to Ragusa on the eastern Adriatic. The cost of maintaining the Empire was enormous even though expenditures were very carefully regulated. Likewise, although the immediate costs of the wars were largely imposed upon the vanquished, the cost of constantly equipping new armies could not but react terribly upon the imperial budget. The amount which direct taxes yielded speedily proved insufficient, and the Government sought new resources. As a result a system of indirect taxes was established; in 1805 France found herself under heavy imposts on liquor, on cards, and on vehicles; in 1806 appeared an impost on salt, and in 1811, a monopoly on tobacco. The revival of these taxes abolished by the Revolution, the return to the old "aides," and especially to the salt tax, the very memory of which was odious, irritated all those who were put under the burden.

But the principal and most general cause of the dissatisfaction was the continual levying of conscripts, made necessary by the incessant wars. Conscription was unpopular from the beginning, because all danger of invasion appeared now to be very remote, and consequently the necessity for military service was not understood in France. At the time of the Consulate, Napoleon had attempted to make the burden lighter by not levying more than a small part of the entire contingent, some 80,000 men from a total of 200,000 or 250,000 nominally available. He established a lottery system under which all those conscripts drawing the "lucky numbers" — that is, the highest numbers — were freed from service. Presently, too, he authorized substitutions; that is, he permitted a wealthy conscript to "buy a man" to serve in his place. But at the beginning of 1805 the disadvantages of this system were evident. The contingents which had already been levied were increasing annually and the levies became more frequent. The Emperor decided not only to take men by entire groups, but also to recall conscripts previously discharged and to levy the various classes one and even two years in advance of the legal age. The levies in 1813 amounted to very nearly twelve hundred thousand men. As early as the beginning of 1808 young men by the thousands attempted to escape service either by mutilating themselves or by fleeing into the mountains or the forests. Quite futilely Napoleon endeavored to make kinsmen responsible for deserters; he fined them severely — in a single year 170,000,000 francs ($34,000,000) — or he quartered soldiers among them who were to be maintained at their expense, billeting the gendarmes and bailiffs upon the offenders, even as Louis XIV had coerced the Protestants. In spite of all this, there were 160,000 refractory conscripts in 1810, and 55,000 men, organized into small columns, were employed to chase them down. In 1813 in Paris, while Napoleon was walking along in the suburb Saint-Antoine, a conscript insulted him; and women attacked the agents of the police who arrested the offender. Complaints were arising on all sides, and everywhere the antipathy had penetrated. Men flung at the Emperor the epithet of "The Ogre." It took the cruelties committed by the Allies when they invaded France in 1814, the national humiliation of the first Treaty of Paris, and the blunders of the Bourbons after the first Restoration to make Frenchmen forget their hatred and to restore Napoleon to his former popularity.

The Emperor, however, was at no time entirely the despot. He continued very energetically the reorganization of France which he had projected during the Consulate. In the matter of legislation he added to the Civil Code a Code of Civil Procedure (1805–07), a Commercial Code (1807), a Code of Criminal

GREAT PUBLIC IMPROVEMENTS

Cases (1808), and a Penal Code (1810), all of which, in their essential character, are still in force.

Likewise, even more than under the Consulate, he now proffered encouragements to industry in the form of bonuses to inventors and to manufacturers, or of profitable orders to stimulate them, or even at times of direct financial assistance. For example, he lent a million and a half francs ($300,000) to Richard Lenoir, who established the cotton industry in France; and during the commercial crisis of 1811 he secretly advanced the salaries of their workmen to the master weavers of Amiens. The Continental Blockade, as a matter of fact, created a need for such benevolence; the entrance of English products into France was prohibited, and France was forced to provide herself all kinds of manufactured articles, a good share of which she had formerly bought in England. The old woolen and silk manufactures as well as the new cotton, iron, and beet sugar industries, in particular, were aided by the Government. Napoleon not only desired France to be self-supporting, but he wanted her to provide all the manufactured articles required by Europe. It was all part of his scheme for world empire.

Lastly the Emperor carried on the great public works which he had inaugurated during the Consulate. At Paris there was, for example, the opening up of the Rue de Rivoli, the construction of many noble bridges over the Seine, the building of the "Temple of Victory" — to-day the church of the Madeleine — of the Bourse, of the Arch of Triumph, the completion of the passage from the Louvre to the Tuileries, and the erection of the Vendôme Column made from the bronze of the cannon captured at Austerlitz. In the departments there could be reckoned the embellishing of Lyons, the completion of the Canal de Saint-Quentin, and also of the canal from Nantes to Brest, and from the Rhone to the Rhine; likewise the large additions to the ports of Brest and Cherbourg, and other great havens. To the public works in France were added the public enterprises in Italy: in Milan, Venice, and Rome and on the Adriatic even beyond Dalmatia. Nor can any deny that wherever the French rule spread it brought with it good roads, elegant public buildings, the sweeping away of feudal abuses and inefficiency, and the advent of law and order.

The methods of Napoleon's proconsuls and generals were not always nice, but they did not come solely as plunderers and destroyers. To many regions of wretched Italian or Germanic peasants French administration often meant the first just and efficient rule the subject population had ever known. All these were the achievements of less than ten years; enterprises, too, that were undertaken amid constant wars, when the Emperor was spending his major energies in violent campaigning and preoccupying diplomacy. Consequently these great public works, more than anything one can write, are the tangible proofs of the Corsican's prodigious activity and of the abounding versatility of his genius.

When touching upon Napoleon, whether for praise or for blame, almost perforce one must write in superlatives.

CHAPTER XVIII
"GLORY AND MADNESS" — MOSCOW, LEIPZIG, AND WATERLOO

IN 1811, thanks to his ruthless policy of aggression, Napoleon was towering above the common rulers of Europe, terrible as the Miltonic Fiend. He had never lost a campaign, very seldom had he lost a battle. He still kept his grip on struggling Spain. There were signs that, thanks to the Continental Blockade, England was suffering economically and was becoming very weary. Had the Emperor merely kept the peace upon the mainland and maintained a resolute front toward England, he might presently have forced the latter into a compromise treaty which would really have been a victory for France. Wisdom in any case dictated that he take on no new enemies. As just stated, his autocracy was becoming very unpopular at home; the Continental Blockade was proving even more severe economically upon France than upon England; the blood tax of conscription was setting every mother of a growing son against the Emperor: and even some of his stanchest lieutenants were growing weary of war. They had been well fed with rewards, and wished quiet and leisure wherein to digest their honors and pensions. In short, there had been a surfeit of "glory" for all France, save only for its never-resting master.

The most serious situation of all was really in the imperial armies. There were still an abundance of competent officers, but the rank and file, the veterans of the old Republican victories, of the First Italian campaign, of Austerlitz, and of Jena, had left their bones on a score of battle-fields. The young conscripts were not their equals. Napoleon was, indeed, using his vassal allies wherever possible — Italians, Bavarians, Hollanders, Westphalians; even Prussians marched now in great numbers under his standards. These troops were not unfaithful so long as things went well with him, but they would make no great sacrifices for the French cause, and a few defeats would be sure to shake their loyalty. Napoleon simply could not continue flinging the youth of Western Europe, like tinder into the furnace of his incessant wars, and expect his supply of man-power to remain unexhausted. Neither could he expect France and her dependencies to undergo unnecessary agonies merely to gratify his restless ambition. Probably it is true that his position at home would have become an uneasy one, had he frankly said "Enough!" when urged to new conquests, and had settled down as the peaceful regenerator of France. The demand for civil liberties would have been instantaneous the moment the pressure of war conditions had been removed, and although one can imagine Napoleon doing many things, it is hard to imagine him for any length of time as the strictly constitutional sovereign of a limited monarchy, conscious of his people's rights and respectful toward opposition.

After Tilsit the Emperor had for some time worked in real harmony with Czar Alexander I; but the friendship had presently cooled. Napoleon thwarted the Russian schemes for the conquest of Turkey — already he had marked Constantinople as his prospective prey. He had also angered the Czar by dethroning the German Duke of Oldenburg, to whom Alexander was related. The Russians again saw their commerce being ruined by Napoleon's insistence upon their enforcement of the Continental System. In 1812 the two great Empires of Eastern and Western Europe exchanged defiances, and Napoleon led forth again the "Grand Army" — its van headed toward Moscow.

There is little doubt that the Emperor was showing himself the spoiled child of fortune. His campaigns were not being planned with the same concentration upon all-important details. He was trusting too much to spontaneous strokes of genius. He was too willing to assume that because his intuitions had been right in the past they would therefore always be right in the

THE DISASTROUS MOSCOW CAMPAIGN 383

future. It is probably not true that he was suffering from a disease that weakened his faculties, but he possibly had lost much of that physical alertness which made men marvel during the first campaign in Italy. But all these things were only to be appreciated after the great event. What Europe knew in June, 1812, was that with over 553,000 men — very many of them Italians, Poles, and Germans as well as Frenchmen — he was marching into the heart of Russia.

What followed taught the nations that the Corsican was a *man*, and not a perfectly functioning and pitilessly intelligent mechanism. The story of the Russian campaign is one of the most familiar in all history. In June Napoleon had crossed the Niemen with the "Grand Army" and was headed for the heart of Muscovy. On September 7 he had won the battle of Borodino, the most sanguinary struggle in all his wars.[1] Seven days later he marched into Moscow, and made his headquarters upon the deserted Kremlin. But his main army had already shrunken to 95,000 men. Not all the rest had perished, of course, but his numbers had been terribly drawn upon by the need of keeping open a perilously long line of communication. From September 15 to 19, Moscow was burning, it is needless to question now whether by accident or by deliberate Russian design. Napoleon's position was obviously uncomfortable. He expected the Czar to sue for peace, but Alexander sued not. The imminence of the Russian winter was ignored, until by October 19 the situation was so critical that the Emperor evacuated Moscow, and gave the unfamiliar orders to retreat.

Early in November the terrible Northern cold settled down. One disaster followed another as the starving, freezing "Grand Army" trailed its way toward Poland. At the crossing of the Berezina, the French were nearly cut off, and were only saved by the valor of Ney and Oudinot. From that time the retreat of

[1] The French lost 32,000 and the Russians 47,000. These casualties, great as they of course are, have lost part of their grimness since it has been possible to compare them with the hecatombs of 1914–18.

the invaders degenerated into what was little better than a rout. Had the Czar's Cossacks been ordered to push their attacks more resolutely, probably the entire host of their enemies would have been taken or perished; but toward the end the victory seemed so complete that they let Napoleon and his last remnants escape. At last, near the Prussian frontier, the Emperor "decided to leave the army for Paris, where his presence was urgently demanded." A great calamity could not be concealed or denied, but by the famous "Bulletin No. 29" the main blame was cast upon the severity of the winter. About 20,000 men straggled over the frontier in an organization somewhat resembling an army. Of the remainder of the invading host many were prisoners in Russia, others had made their escape in small detachments; but a conservative estimate is that to France and her allies the lives of 300,000 able-bodied young men had been lost. When before had there been a like military disaster?

It was a great misfortune for his foes, however, that the Cossacks had not pressed Napoleon harder. He had lost nearly all his rank and file, but the remnant of the French that escaped included a very large proportion of his best officers; men whose professional abilities made them worth their weight in gold. Given time and raw material he could thus hope to rebuild new armies. Time he could scarcely have; for the instant the news of the great defeat was spread, Prussia made haste to throw off her chains and to rally not merely her own people, but many other North Germans to arms, also to make prompt alliance with the victorious and advancing Russians. England would again furnish subsidies to maintain a great coalition against her arch-enemy. Austria still talked "neutrality," but was not to be relied upon by Napoleon — she was merely waiting her chance.

The Emperor returned to Paris, however, in anything but a crestfallen mood. For the first time the dice had fallen against him, but he had still plenty of stakes to lay against Fate. Once more by a remorseless conscription, levies of almost every able-

PYRRHIC VICTORIES AND THE ARMISTICE 385

bodied man and boy in France were hurried to the colors. The Emperor accomplished prodigies in securing the arming and uniforming of these new forces. The conscripts were brave and although their parents cursed the relentless policy that dragged their sons away, the young troops acquitted themselves loyally like Frenchmen in the ensuing battles. But no good-will could make them into hard-bodied, experienced veterans. Napoleon entered his last campaign in Germany with infinitely poorer human material sustaining him than in any previous adventure with Destiny. He committed also the serious blunder of trying to hold too many of the North-German fortresses — Danzig, Stettin, Küstrin, Hamburg, etc. — placing in them some of his best troops. These garrisons were presently blockaded by groups of Prussian local militia, and thereby immobilized and rendered useless in the open campaign. With their numbers added to his field army Napoleon had a chance of victory; without them, it turned out that he had none.

So the campaign of 1813 began with one arm of the Corsican tied behind his back. He was weaker than before and his foes, as he ruefully confessed, had learned much of his own military art. In May he defeated the allied Prussians and Russians at Lützen (near Leipzig), then again at Bautzen. But these were anything but decisive victories. Then in June he committed another grievous blunder. He granted an armistice (June 4 to August 10, 1813) nominally to let Austria mediate and patch up a peace; actually to allow both sides to secure reinforcements. Austrian "mediation," however, was very insincere, and the Emperor had fewer reinforcements to bring up than his enemies. Napoleon's marshals were becoming very anxious that the war should cease. If the Empire went down, where would be their own fine principalities and emoluments? But their moderating counsels weighed little with their master. Up to the last he protested that the French would never endure him if he once made public confession of defeat by consenting (as his foes now demanded) to relinquish a large share of his former conquests:

and he kept a dogged confidence that by some lightning military stroke he could still recover everything.

The crisis came at Dresden, June 26, when Metternich, the astute Austrian prime minister, had his famous interview with the Emperor, vainly urging a spirit of reasonableness. Napoleon was in an entirely arrogant mood. He had learned nothing from adversity. "So you want war," were his words: "well, you shall have it. I have beaten the Russians at Bautzen: now you wish *your* turn to come! Be it so, the rendezvous shall be in Vienna." Vainly Metternich reminded him that his army was depleted; that his troops were not men, but boys; to which the great egoist tossed back: "You do not know what goes on in the mind of a soldier: a man such as I does not take much heed of the lives of a million men" — and he threw aside his hat. Metternich did not pick it up. Thus the interview ended stormily. When the Austrian minister went out, the French generals in the anteroom crowded up eagerly, hoping for a report of real peace negotiations. "Were you satisfied with the Emperor?" anxiously asked Berthier. "Yes," came back from Metternich. "He has explained everything to me: *it is all over with the man.*"

Manifestly for the safety of the world, this colossal vampire, who despite a thousand admirable qualities was literally sucking away the best blood of France no less than of all Europe, must be flung from power. In August, 1813, the war was renewed, after Napoleon had proved utterly unconciliatory. Austria joined his other foes. For the first time since 1795, Prussia, Russia, Austria, and England were all at war with France, and all fighting heartily in alliance: the struggle was now for life and death. The old cunning had not deserted Napoleon. He held out for more than two months in Central Germany, defending the line of the Elbe. He repulsed the first attacks, and even won a great battle at Dresden (August 26); but the numbers against him were too great.[1] Sweden was joining the coali-

---

[1] Napoleon's blunder in making his generals almost completely dependent upon his direct orders now cost him dearly. They lacked proper initiative when

DESPERATE SITUATION

tion, and on October 16, 17, and 18, the Allies at last bayed the terrible lion at Leipzig. Here in a three days' battle ("The Battle of the Nations" the Germans called it) 150,000 French stood against 300,000 Russians, Austrians, Prussians, and Swedes. The young conscripts fought bravely, but they were being asked to achieve the impossible. On the 19th Napoleon was obliged to order a general retreat toward France. The losses in the battle and in the subsequent hasty flight across Germany were terrible. With barely 70,000 men, none too well organized, the Corsican found himself again behind the Rhine.

The situation was now, from a military standpoint, all but hopeless. The veteran field army was gone; the new conscript field army was almost gone. The garrisons were being starved out one by one, in the now distant and isolated German fortresses. The good-will of France had been alienated by the Continental Blockade and the blood tax. The English were sweeping Napoleon's generals out of Spain and crossing the Pyrenees. The South-German vassal states were all making their peace with the victors. Nevertheless the Allies would probably have left Napoleon his throne and a territory much larger than that of Louis XVI in 1792, had he promptly and sincerely treated for peace. He would not do so. Even when the Allies were crossing the Rhine in great force, he fought against the inevitable. He sent delegates, indeed, to a Peace Conference at Châtillon (on the Seine), but allowed his representatives only to play for time. And so he went on to the end.

Napoleon's campaign of 1814 was in some respects his best — considered merely from a military standpoint. He had barely 50,000 mobile troops left. The French nation would not rise against the invader. The old fires of 1792–93 had burned out. There was, of course, some anger at the cruelties inflicted by the conquering Allies, but, compared with 1914, the invaders of 1814 seem to have been fairly humane and loath to stimulate

he was absent. The French were now beaten almost everywhere, save for long at the point where the Emperor led in person.

French patriotism by a policy of *schrecklichkeit*. With all these handicaps, with odds three and four to one against him, the Corsican fought brilliantly; hurling himself now against one, now another of the columns advancing on Paris, and repeatedly he won temporary victories which brought the whole Austro-Prusso-Russian advance to a stand. But in the end the attempt was impossible. The army became weary of its hopeless struggle. The masses of the invader were too great. On March 31, in the absence of Napoleon — after the Allies had stormed their way to the very gates of Paris — Marshal Marmont, commandant of the capital, capitulated and the victors marched in triumph into the city from which, after Valmy, Brunswick had turned back twenty-two years before.

Napoleon could still muster 50,000 men around him at Fontainebleau. Many of the privates and lower officers seem to have been willing to keep up the struggle, such was their devotion to the leader who would have sacrificed them with scarcely a sigh. But the marshals and upper officers recognized that the game was up; to fight longer meant their personal ruin, and they desired neither poverty nor exile. In Paris, the Allies were forming a provisional government presided over by an ex-minister of Napoleon's, the supple, immoral, and infinitely clever Talleyrand, who now cheerfully deserted his master, proclaimed that the Emperor had forfeited his throne, and who hastily prepared for the restoration of the Bourbons. Under the pressure of his old comrades, on April 4,[1] Napoleon signed a formal act of abdication. The Allies, with a magnanimity they doubtless regretted a year later, consented to assign him the small island of Elba in the Mediterranean as a "sovereign principality," and permitted him to keep the poor consolation of the formal title of "Emperor."

Napoleon was very unpopular at this time in France. The nation longed for peace, and his ambition had seemed alone to

[1] Napoleon then abdicated in favor of his son. That compromise being rejected, in a few days he abdicated unconditionally.

stand in the way of checking the public ruin. When he traveled through Languedoc and Provence he was cursed to his face and stones were flung at his carriage, while mobs howled after the "Hateful tyrant, punished at last!" and at Orange and Avignon there were even fears of a lynching. The fallen despot, much cowed possibly for the moment, was taken to Elba, and there he was to wait ten uneasy months — while many things happened in France.

Louis XVIII, the eldest of the brothers of Louis XVI, had been placed on the throne by the Allies, not because they had any great love for him personally, but because they were resolved to have an end to "Bonaparte" and his family, and they objected heartily to a Republic. To recall the old dynasty then was really the only thing possible. The conquerors assigned to France slightly larger boundaries than she had in 1790, before the beginning of the great wars, and they imposed no indemnity upon her. They also compelled Louis XVIII to give his subjects a kind of a constitution and to guarantee that the great social and personal liberties won in 1789 should not be abolished. This was worldly wisdom — the Allies feared to drive the French people to desperation. Then the main interest of the world shifted from Paris to the Congress of Vienna. At the Austrian capital, under Metternich's artful presidency, the diplomats met in the famous peace congress to quarrel, threaten one another, but presently to agree on the territorial and other arrangements which, it was fondly hoped, would last for many generations; and which were, indeed, to cast their shadow over Europe till 1914.

Meantime France, chastened, economically smitten, invaded, cut short, bereft of the flower of her youth, was flung back very unhappily upon herself. The character of the new King, and the Restoration, and its political institutions will be stated later, it is enough to say here that the new Government was soon extremely unpopular with influential classes. When the peace was made, all the captive officers and veterans of course came back from Russia and Germany. They were outraged at finding a new and unwelcome King in Paris, and the Bourbon white flag with its lilies flying in the place of the beloved tricolor of Lodi and Marengo. Instead of public thanks and triumphs, they received black looks and distrust from the new masters of the Tuileries, and no better material rewards than being put on the retired list on half-pay. The professional army, in short, speedily became intensely dissatisfied at the whole situation, and the bulk of the people were soon displeased enough with many acts of the new dynasty to lose much of their recent hatred for the Corsican[1] — all of which facts competent agents promptly brought to Napoleon in Elba.[2]

On March 1, 1815, the Emperor landed at Cannes with fifteen hundred troops he had been allowed to take with him into exile. On March 20 he entered Paris, while King Louis XVIII had made a hasty exit to Ghent.

"I shall reach Paris without firing a shot," Napoleon had said, as his small vessel approached the French coast. Near Grenoble a battalion of the now "royal army" had been drawn up to halt his advance. The Corsican had come forward in the face of the leveled muskets. "Soldiers," said the well-known voice, "if there is one among you who wishes to kill his Emperor he can do so. — Here I am." "Long live the Emperor!" burst from the ranks, and the whole force went over to the returning leader. Marshal Ney, who had turned against Napoleon in 1814 with peculiar bitterness, marched out with six thousand troops from Besançon to "bring him back in an iron cage." His troops began to desert. Ney's loyalty for the Bourbons oozed out, and he called his officers around him and again proclaimed the

---

[1] A very serious factor was the fear of the peasantry, lest the Bourbons disturb the titles to the real estate confiscated from the Church and the noblesse in 1789-93, and give the property back to its former owners.

[2] He was also greatly encouraged by report of the serious discords between his late foes now at the Congress of Vienna. Russia and Prussia seemed on the point of crossing swords with England and Austria. The discords were, indeed, violent, but they were not quite serious enough to prevent all four Powers from uniting to attack him the minute he returned from Elba.

Emperor. It was amid vast rejoicings by the army and all the jubilant half-pay officers that the returned exile swept into the Tuileries. For an instant it seemed as if the whole effect of the disasters of Moscow and Leipzig had been undone.

But Napoleon did not conceal from himself the fact that while the army was delighted to have him return, the rest of the nation was more or less indifferent to his prospects, although without the least enthusiasm for Louis XVIII. "My dear fellow," said the Emperor to an intimate, "people have let me come just as they have let the Bourbons go." Probably, other things being equal, the bulk of Frenchmen greatly preferred Napoleon to the restored Royalists, but other things were not equal. Frenchmen were terribly anxious for peace, and the Emperor announced (perhaps with sincerity) that he intended to try to keep the peace and not to make any attempt to restore the swollen boundaries of France in 1812. But no sooner had the news of his landing in France reached Vienna, than the allied diplomats dropped their serious squabblings and united in a general decree of outlawry. Russia, Austria, Prussia, and England joined in declaring that "Bonaparte" had broken the compact which established him at Elba, and "placed himself outside the bounds of civil and social relation" and was to be punished as "an enemy and disturber of the peace of the world."

So the Emperor stood again with all the other great Powers embattled against him, and not a single ally. His only chance lay in the enthusiastic support of the entire French nation. He endeavored to conciliate public opinion by announcing liberalizing changes, technically known as "The Additional Act," in the former "Constitution of the Empire." These changes on analysis, however, did nothing to weaken the Emperor's autocratic disposal of the entire State. Intelligent Frenchmen were angered at being obliged thus to continue under the absolutist régime; and all Frenchmen, outside the army, were aghast at the prospect of the renewal of desperate war. It is not surprising then that almost the whole of Napoleon's famous "Hundred Days" were spent in hurried preparations and in intense anxiety.

Attempts to get the great Powers to keep the peace having completely failed, the Corsican once more threw dice for the supreme stakes in war. He had, indeed, an admirable army — so far as it went: 180,000 veteran troops devoted to him; men who had been shut up in German fortresses in 1813 or had submitted unwillingly in 1814. His foes were concentrating infinitely greater numbers, but he had the bare chance of crushing their armies piecemeal before they could effect a junction. To this end he flung his main forces into Belgium in June, 1815, to strike the Prussian Blücher and the English Wellington before the Austrians and Russians could bring up their myriads.

The master of legions had not lost his old-time cunning. On June 15–16 he fell on the Prussian army of Blücher at Ligny and he roundly defeated it. The first misfortune came when the Emperor was led to believe that Blücher was much more badly beaten than was actually the case, and that the victors were free to turn elsewhere. As a matter of fact the Prussians, though worsted, were able soon to halt their retreat, while Grouchy, the French general ordered to pursue, lost touch with them. On June 18 Napoleon then smote against the Duke of Wellington with his mixed English, Dutch, and North-German force at Waterloo. The French had about 70,000 men, Wellington rather less. What Napoleon did not know, however, was that Blücher was drawing nigh with 30,000 men to reinforce Wellington. The battle that followed almost resulted in a French victory, thanks to the splendid charges of the imperial cavalry; but the Emperor, who had never really fought against the English before, was astonished at the stubborn resistance of the hostile squares. Outnumbered, and the non-British part of his troops of very mediocre quality, Wellington hung grimly on, praying for "Night or Blücher!" And at length, when the fight was practically at a deadlock, Blücher came. A last charge by the imperial

"Old Guard" was driven home heroically, but broke down with sanguinary losses. Then the whole English line advanced, and realizing the hopelessness of their situation, the bulk of the French army scattered in rout.

One or two squares of the Guard made off the field in the semblance of order, but there was no chance to stay the panic. Never was there an overthrow more complete than Waterloo. Seven times the fugitives paused to make their bivouac. Seven times they were driven on by the pursuing cavalry. "Cowards! Have you forgotten how to die?" Ney is said to have called to his men. The taunt was unjust. The French army had done for the Corsican more, perhaps, than any other army had ever done for a leader. His restless ambition had created a situation in Europe by which there could be no peace for the world nor for France if he were to keep the throne. Even had he won Waterloo, the Russian and Austrian hosts were drawing nigh. The only result would have been a new vista of great wars. The French leader himself did not court a soldier's death. Dazed by the rout, he fled with the foremost fugitives. When he reached Paris on June 20 he found his case was hopeless. No one would fight for him. A provisional government, headed by his old minister Fouché, provided a kind of order until the Allies arrived to restore the Bourbons.

Once more Napoleon abdicated "in favor of his son." He fled to Rochefort on the seacoast hoping to get ship for America,[1] but the English cruisers were blockading him, and the case being hopeless he went on board a British man-of-war and cast himself on the magnanimity of his oldest and most constant foes. What was then done with him has been often criticized for its severity, but it must be realized that this fugitive and prisoner had caused nigh twenty years of capital warfare and the

[1] Speculation easily exhausts itself considering what the Corsican might have done had he reached America. His fascinating personality might easily have won a following, and he would speedily have compromised our relations with all Europe.

death therein of some millions of human beings.[1] After the escape from Elba the statesmen of the day felt it to be criminal negligence to risk allowing this firebrand to enkindle the world again. As all men know, he was sent by the British on the ship-of-the-line Bellerophon to the island of St. Helena in the South Atlantic; and there he remained an unhappy and quarrel-seeking prisoner until his death by cancer in 1821. When the news of his passing spread, many Frenchmen mourned, but all over the world there was a general relief that the arch-destroyer could threaten the nations' happiness no more.

After reviewing the deeds of Napoleon Bonaparte, it is impossible to resist the conclusion that had Heaven given him a modicum of unmixed humanity and patriotism and of real unselfishness, he could have approached the very limits of human achievement. As it was, despite the service he rendered mankind in destroying the decrepit institutions all over Europe, and in creating various admirable civil institutions for France, the latter part of his career was calamitous to the world, and most calamitous of all to the great nation of which he boasted himself to be Emperor.[2]

The Corsican could fascinate the planet by his brilliance, but it was the brilliance of Satan arrayed as an angel of light.

[1] Readers of the present age, familiar with the problem of the disposition of the German Kaiser William II, after his downfall in 1918, and with the general exasperation of the world against him, will be lenient in their judgments upon the statesmen of 1815 in their treatment of Napoleon.

[2] Of course it is possible to credit Napoleon with many charming acts of geniality, comradery, or even of magnanimity: but hardly with *one* which, on close analysis, seemed to involve the unselfish sacrifice of a keen personal ambition.

CHAPTER XIX
THE RESTORED BOURBONS AND THEIR EXIT

Louis XVIII returned to Paris in 1815, not because the French nation wanted him, but because the bayonets of the victors of Waterloo imposed him on his not very willing subjects. A second time foreign armies marched into the great city by the Seine. Nevertheless France was not grievously depressed. There had been no anxiety to make costly sacrifices for Napoleon. The enthusiasm to carry "liberty, fraternity, and equality" to the ends of the earth, the ardor that had kindled the young armies of the Republic, had been burned away on a hundred battle-fields. A new generation had grown up which knew not Rousseau, and which was very anxious for peace and for solid bodily comfort. The great estates of the Church and of the old noblesse had been redistributed, and their new owners, men of short pedigrees but often of large fortunes, desired static conditions. The mothers of tall sons rejoiced at the end of conscriptions; and men who had been Jacobins in their youth were willing to shudder at the excesses of the past five and twenty years and thank Providence that they had emerged from them all safe and much wiser.

After the great days, great passions, great crimes of the Revolution, after the colossal Cæsarism of the Empire, it is a more petty and infinitely more prosaic France which we encounter. Most of the heroes of 1789-93 were dead. Lafayette, indeed, was still alive; we shall meet him again, but the guillotine, as it worked up to 1795, and after that date the blood tax of the Napoleonic wars, had robbed the nation of a great proportion of all the keenest intellects which might have built for the future. The terrific drain of the battles is even said to have pulled down the physical stamina of the country. It is alleged that the physique of the average young Frenchman of 1815 was poorer, his stature shorter, than that of his father in 1789. In any case, France was a terribly disillusioned nation. From being apparently on the point of founding an empire greater than the Roman, she had beheld her soil twice overrun, her capital occupied, her ruler dethroned by foreign armies. True, the very circumstances of the defeat were somewhat flattering to French pride. To overcome her all the rest of Europe had had to form a common league against her; it had almost been France against the world. But that did not obliterate the great fact that the end of all the Napoleonic "glory" had been a smashing military defeat.

The Allies had treated France with comparative generosity in 1814. In 1815 when they brought back Louis XVIII the second time, they were thoroughly exasperated and imposed harsher terms. France was given the boundaries, not of 1792 (as in the first treaty), but of 1790. Thus she lost various fortresses on the frontiers of Alsace-Lorraine, and ceded back to the King of Sardinia the province of Savoy. She had also to pay a war indemnity (huge for the day) of 700,000,000 francs ($140,000,-000) and submit to the military occupation of some of her border towns until the sum had been discharged. These terms were not crushing, but they were humiliating. They served to start Louis XVIII upon his renewed lease of power with very little glory.

France was still a very great nation, but she hardly held even her old position before 1789. British sea power had seemingly given its possessor a strangle hold upon the commerce of the world, and British industries were incomparably more developed than those of any rival. The most powerful politician in Europe was not at Paris; he was at Vienna, and he was the clever absolutist Prince Metternich. The greatest military power seemed to rest with Czar Alexander I, who was now notoriously at Metternich's beck and call. France was thus thrown back upon herself. Most of her colonies had been seized by the

English. The treaty of peace returned to her only a few small islands in the West Indies and some trading factories in Africa and India. The great colonial empire which had existed before 1760 had, of course, vanished much earlier. The second great colonial empire, which was to cover Northern Africa before 1900, was not yet even planted. Frenchmen had therefore few outside problems to take their thoughts away from their home troubles.

The France of 1815, nevertheless, was very far from being the France of 1789. The Jacobins had decidedly failed. Their despised and berated predecessors, the men of 1789, had largely succeeded. The "privileges" and most of the other gross abuses of the Old Régime had vanished never to return. There were no privileged "classes," and property was widely divided among a large fraction of the population: all Frenchmen were equal in the eyes of the law and had, theoretically, equal claims to public office. The Church had been shorn of its overweening prerogatives. The national finances were in relatively good order. There was pretty complete religious toleration. In short, in 1815 "the nation was already provided with its social and administrative organization; it remained — as it still remains — a democratic society, whose affairs are managed by a centralized administration. *The mechanism of the central government, was not, however, yet constructed* France has labored to establish it: she has spent the nineteenth century in making herself a political constitution." [1] The importance of this statement can be realized only if it is understood how completely the Government in Paris dominated the entire life of the nation. America and most British communities would remain essentially democratic and liberal even if the National Government were suddenly to become non-liberal; local autonomy is so strong. But there was and still is (to American thinking) very little local autonomy in France. The Paris ministries extend their power to the obscurest commune. Therefore our gaze is continually upon the capital.

[1] Seignobos.

In 1815 the great bulk of the French nation was not, it should be said, profoundly interested in politics. The population had risen, despite the long wars, to some 29,000,000. The great majority of the people were still the peasants. The Revolution and its destruction of the estates of the noblesse and the Church had brought to many of these their heart's desire — a solid little farm with a modest competency. They constituted, on the whole, the most thrifty, self-respecting, stable, home-keeping peasantry in the world: with a deplorably high element of illiteracy and superstition, indeed, but comparing very favorably with those of any other country. They were the real strength of the nation. The Revolution and the Empire had done more for them than for any other class of Frenchmen, but they cared relatively little who was their ruler so long as he gave them peace, good order, and prosperity. Again and again the peasantry of France were to redress the blunders of the more obvious parts of the nation: to repress revolutionary excesses; to pay enormous war debts and indemnities; and finally, in 1914–18, to supply the great majority of those sturdy, indomitable *poilus* who were to be the living bulwark of the freedom of the world.[1]

In the cities there were, of course, considerable industrial classes, but French cities were, by present comparisons, neither numerous nor large. Outside of Paris, probably only Lyons had over 100,000 inhabitants. French manufacturers were by no means so far developed as were the English. A very large fraction of these artisan classes were, of course, in Paris, the seat of government. On several occasions a sudden uprising by them was therefore to have extremely serious political consequences: for their fingers were always close to the administrative windpipe of France. Ten thousand howling working-men in Paris

[1] As is well known, a great fraction of the "defeatist," "Internationalist," pro-German propaganda which threatened to ruin France in 1917–18, at the height of the struggle with Germany, found its best reception among the industrial elements in Paris. It made relatively little head among the peasantry.

could accomplish far more in the way of a revolution than 100,000 malcontent peasants scattered through the departments. But when the revolution had once been accomplished, its cheerful acceptance by all the rest of France could by no means be assumed. The peasantry could more slowly, indeed, but none the less emphatically, express their dissent. This was to be peculiarly true in 1848.

Above peasant and artisan was the great class known as the bourgeoisie — property-owners of more or less social pretension, public officials, great and small, professional men, etc. They were charged with being intensely conservative, leading "a simple, quiet life, the life of a small town — monotonous, without comforts, without amusements, without intellectual activity, a slave to public opinion." They were also accused of having almost as few political ideas as the peasants, and with being grossly selfish in their efforts, especially in those to prevent the artisans from bettering their wages and conditions of labor. The sodden state of French public opinion is testified to by the extremely small number of newspapers in circulation. True, under the "Restoration" there was, most of the time, a severe press censorship and a tax of ten centimes (two cents) on every copy, also a very heavy postage; still it is an amazing fact that an official report of 1824 makes a formal estimate that there were only 55,000 copies of papers with political articles circulated in all France. These papers it must be admitted were usually stupid and unenlightening enough — but the public for the while seemed hardly eager for anything better.

Of course there was a saving minority in the nation that looked intelligently toward the future — that planned for a better day. These men were as a rule members also of the bourgeoisie, or were scions of the old noblesse who had enlightenment enough to stop plotting reaction and forget their pedigrees. Yet in the main it may be said that what spurred enough Frenchmen to accomplish political changes between 1815 and 1848 were these four factors: (1) The fear lest a complete reaction of the Old Régime (as seemed repeatedly threatened) would upset all the fortunes and property-titles established since 1789; (2) a demand from the property-owning classes that the Government should be efficient, and give stable conditions calculated to promote profitable commerce and industry; (3) a demand from the Parisian industrial classes that *something* should be done to mitigate their grievously unfavorable conditions of labor; and then (4) a gradual return to the ideas and idealism of a former generation, with the demand for genuinely liberal institutions and a realization of the theories of democracy. All these things combined at length to pull France out of the soulless mire into which she seemed to have been cast in 1815, and to set her on the way to nobler things.

Louis XVIII, installed in 1814 and reinstalled in 1815, had been placed in power by the Allies, because Metternich and Czar Alexander could not find any other possible monarch for France, and they abhorred the idea of admitting that the people could choose their own government. "It would be," affirmed Metternich, "a new breaking forth of the Revolution [to do this]. Besides what question is a [popular] assembly to decide? The legitimate King is here."

Louis XVIII [1] had been nominally "king" since 1795 when his nephew, the luckless "Louis XVII," the unhappy Dauphin of the French Revolution, had died in captivity because of the brutality of his keepers.[2] He had lived weary years in exile, mostly in Russia and England, hoping against hope for the ruin of the Corsican and a return to France. Now at last fortune had favored him. The Great Powers twice placed him on the throne. Truth to tell he was not a very majestic substitute for the "Little Corporal." A portrait, published with official consent, shows him fat, gross, and with hands and feet deformed with gout. He was sixty years old in 1815. In 1789 he had been notoriously a champion of absolutism and reaction, but fortu-

---

[1] The former Comte de Provence, eldest brother of Louis XVI.
[2] See p. 325.

nately in his exile he had absorbed not a few useful ideas. He realized that much had happened since he had fled in disguise from France in 1791. As a contemporary well says, "he had in him a very firm desire *to die* upon the throne"; and obviously the only method by which he could fulfill this wish was by accepting all the more significant innovations which had commended themselves to the nation. During his reign from 1815 to 1824 he showed considerable intelligence and firmness in his policy, and on the whole he left a worthy memory. To the best of his ability he endeavored to unite the champions of the Old Régime and of the New, saying that "he did not wish to be king over two peoples," and that "the children of one fatherland should be a people of brothers."

If, however, Louis XVIII realized that the only condition on which he could remain in France was to recognize what had happened since 1789, very few of his family and personal associates did this. In 1814–15 a great swarm of "emigrant" noblemen had hastened back to Paris. Exile proverbially makes men warped and bitter. The returned outlaws, whose kindred very likely had died under the guillotine, could see nothing good in anything the New Régime had accomplished. They clamored for vengeance, for the return of their lost estates, for the upsetting of every enactment since the good old days of Calonne's and Marie Antoinette's garden fêtes at Versailles. Professing extreme loyalty to Louis XVIII, they were soon disgusted because the King did not at once embark on a policy of extreme reaction. In this they were supported by the King's brother, the Count of Artois, who (since Louis lacked a son) was obviously to be his heir as Charles X. Artois was full of the most absolutist notions conceivable. "He would rather," he later averred, "saw wood than 'reign' in the fashion of a king of England!" On the day Louis XVIII proclaimed a new Constitution (the "Charter"), Artois feigned illness that he might not have to swear fidelity to it. His palace was the constant center for Ultra-Royalist intrigues. The King realized that his brother's influence was malignant and would ruin the dynasty, but for the sake of family peace he often yielded to him. Considering, therefore, the kind of man the future Charles X was, it is perhaps slight wonder that the Bourbon régime lasted as long as 1830.

The European Allies had brought back the Bourbons, but they did not try to bring back Absolutism. Metternich wished to have no constitution in his own Austria, but he assented to the suggestion that if France were forced back under a purely autocratic rule, there would soon be a new revolution which would menace the peace of other countries. Louis XVIII was therefore very strictly compelled to publish a constitution for France, as a condition to being set upon the throne. This Constitution was the once famous "Charter." Circumscribed as it now seems, in its day it gave France, on the whole, a more liberal government than that of any other kingdom except England, and it was very decidedly more liberal than the system in France under Napoleon.

From 1815 to 1848 France was governed by this "Charter," although very important changes were made in that document in 1830. Since nearly all public life in that time revolved around the attacks upon or the defense of the document, we cannot avoid discussing its main provisos.

Louis XVIII claimed to reign "by the grace of God" even as had his unlucky brother, and the Charter was declared to emanate "from the free exercise of the royal authority." It was therefore in theory the gracious concession of an autocrat, not the expression of the popular will. Also it was dated from "the nineteenth year of the reign," as if Louis XVIII had been a ruling monarch since 1795 when his nephew died. The theory of the Charter was thus wholly illiberal. Yet in its text are contained clauses that made it possible to argue that France was a somewhat limited monarchy; and the chief flaw in the letter of the document was not the great powers granted the King, but the great powers it granted the wealthy classes.

The King was, of course, the head of "the executive power."

He led the armies, declared war, made peace, signed treaties, and (an ambiguous clause destined to work mischief) "made the regulations and ordinances necessary for the execution of the laws and the safety of the State." He named all the public officials, and governed through "responsible" ministers. If the latter misbehaved, they could be indicted by the lower house of the legislature and tried before the upper house.

The "legislative power" was shared by the King with the "Chamber of Peers" and the "Chamber of Deputies." The King initiated the proposal of laws. They had to be discussed and ratified by the two Chambers, then the King promulgated them. The "peers" seem to have been an obvious imitation of the British House of Lords. They were at the outset all named by the King from among the great personages, marshals, civil notables, etc., of France. Some were appointed simply for life. Others could transmit their honor by hereditary succession. The "deputies" were elected for a term of five years, one fifth of the Chamber to be chosen annually so that there should not be too many sudden changes. No tax could be established or levied without the consent of the Chambers, which consent must be annually renewed; and this in theory should have given the new parliament a very heavy hand upon the Crown: but all this apparent evidence of liberalism was vitiated by the one important fact that only the well-to-do and wealthy were allowed to vote for members of the Chamber of Deputies.

To be an elector a Frenchman must be thirty years of age and must pay a direct tax of 300 francs ($60).[1] To be eligible to be chosen a member of the lower House himself, he had to be forty years old and to pay a direct tax of 1000 francs ($200). Under such a franchise, to be known as a "voter" would be a somewhat conspicuous honor: in a rural community probably it would come to only two or three of the most important landowners. There were in 1815 in all France only above 90,000 ordinary

[1] Of course a much greater sum relatively then than to-day: say two to three times as great, all changes considered.

electors, and of these less than 12,000 were qualified to be sent to Paris. A new kind of privilege was thus arbitrarily created: one of the most obnoxious varieties and sure to awaken heart-burnings — the privilege of wealth.

Apart from this great error the Charter contained many excellent provisions. The judicial organization of the Empire was maintained and the judges were given self-respect and proper power by their irremovability save for direct crimes. Individual liberty was guaranteed, as well as religious liberty, although Catholicism was declared the religion of the State. Also liberty of the press was affirmed, provided it "conformed to laws which should repress the abuse of that liberty" — a qualification destined to breed much woe.

No property was to be seized without compensation, and as a concession to the popular feeling which had helped to pull down Napoleon, conscription for the army was abolished. Special laws were to provide for military reorganization.

In spite, then, of many limitations and of one grand fault, the Charter was a document which, if handled and developed in a proper spirit, would have given France contentment and prosperity. The essential conquests of 1789 had been preserved, liberty, equality in all private rights at least, and the theoretical right to a share in the government. The practical effect of the Charter was, of course, to entrust the franchise to the upper bourgeoisie, usually landowners, but also often mill-owners and bankers. These men were naturally devoted to the "rights of property," but they were no friends to the claims of the noblesse who talked wildly of reëstablishing the Old Régime. They were not inaccessible to new ideas, and small a fraction as they were of the total manhood of France, they were presently to show themselves conscious of the drift and force of public opinion. The result was that following 1815 we have something very like a real limited monarchy, with parties, programmes, an "opposition," elections, etc., although the whole scheme of government was anything but democratic.

The "Restoration" had not lasted long before three parties were developing rapidly in French political life: (1) the Ultra-Royalists; (2) the Independents; (3) the Constitutional Royalists. The first element was frankly reactionary. It regarded everything that had happened since June, 1789, as a crime, and the granting of the Charter as a direful blunder. This was the party of the returned exiles, and its whole ambition was to turn back the clock of history just as far as possible. The Independents also regarded the Charter with extreme dissatisfaction. It did not grant enough of popular liberties, and the Independents nursed the secret desire of sending the Bourbons again upon their travels. This party was, of course, the child of the old Republicans and the father of the later Republicans. With it lay the future; but for the moment it was very weak. The whole current of the reactionary epoch was against it. Midway between these disturbing elements were the Constitutional Royalists. They believed the Charter presented a good working scheme calculated to satisfy France, and they were resolved to keep it in operation with practically no changes. Whether they could succeed or not, largely depended on the support they might receive from the King.

If Louis XVIII had been left to himself there is little doubt he would have tried earnestly to make the Charter a success. He had found the throne "a most comfortable easy-chair," and wished to do nothing to send himself on another flight to Ghent, chased out by a new uprising. But he found poor enough allies in the returned "emigrants," the "Ultras." More absolutist than the King, these noblemen who surrounded him, and whom he could not disregard, avowed they wanted an Absolute Monarchy — then they could get whatever they wanted. They demanded a complete "purification" of the civil and military service, the dismissal of all the parvenu Napoleonic prefects, generals, etc., and their replacement by aristocrats who suffered poverty and exile "for the good cause." They demanded, too, huge indemnities for their lost estates. The press and education were likewise to be entrusted only to reliable Royalists, or to their very ardent and reliable helpers, the clergy. When the King failed to endorse these projects, the full acceptance of which would have cost him his throne, they wrathfully drank to the toast, "The health of the King *in spite of everything*," and hopefully looked ahead for the day when the Count of Artois would take the royal seat.

When after the "Hundred Days," the Chamber of the new legislature assembled, it was speedily evident that in the confusion attending the fall of the Empire the Ultras had won a great majority among the deputies. In the South Country the Royalists were conducting wholesale rabblings and lynchings of their opponents in a regular "White Terror." At Paris the new Chambers were hardly less ardent for swift and bloody revenge upon the men who had again set up the hated Corsican. Everything in France was to be "purged"; and as Louis XVIII angrily declared, "If these gentlemen had their way completely, they would end even by purging *me!*" The King strove to moderate them, but he could not save some of their victims. Marshal Ney had earned their particular wrath because he had deserted to Napoleon after promising the Bourbons to arrest him. When the Royalists returned to Paris, Ney failed to take warning promptly and to escape. He was seized, to the great disgust of the King: "By letting himself be caught, he has done us more harm than he did on March 13 [when he deserted]," exclaimed the Monarch testily. But Louis could not rescue Ney. The "Bravest of the Brave" was dragged before a court of generals who were completely intimidated by the cries for blood rising from the salons of the noblesse and from the Chambers. Ney was convicted of treason, and was shot on December 7, 1815, in the Luxembourg Gardens. Thus ended the career of one of the most distinguished officers who ever fought for France. His fate left a stigma upon the Restoration that did nothing to lessen its unpopularity; and for this stigma not the King, but his "loyal" nobility were responsible.

Truth to tell the Ultras were without the least rational political programme, and after having thus destroyed Ney and certain other objects of especial vengeance, they made haste to weave their own rope. They foolishly rejected the budget, thus striking fear into every wealthy magnate interested in French financial stability. The King promptly dissolved the Chamber, and the electors, terrified at the storm of sanguinary passions that had been loosed, returned a "moderate" majority. France was thus saved from another spasm of revolution, with possible foreign intervention.

Although Louis's ministers had had to wrestle with this intractable element, they were not unsuccessful in handling the grave problem of rehabilitating the nation. Once again the enormous practical genius of the French people asserted itself. Mere conditions of peace, law and order, gave back a large measure of prosperity. The heavy indemnity due to the Allies was paid off steadily, and in 1818 the last of the foreign armies of occupation quitted French soil, instead of going in 1820 as had been originally expected. "I can die in peace," said the King, "since I shall see France free, and the French flag floating over every city of France."

Another problem not unwisely handled was that of the army. The Napoleonic conscription had been abandoned, and the magnificent fighting machine (or rather all of it that had survived Waterloo) was being allowed to dwindle away. But the nation could not hold up its head again in Europe without an efficient military force. There was nothing for it but to go back to a form of conscription. As many troops as possible were to be recruited by volunteering; then for the remainder all the young men of twenty were to draw lots, and those receiving "bad numbers" (a small proportion) were obliged to serve six years with the active army and six years more in the reserve. In this way an army of about 240,000 was provided, nearly all of them long-service, professionalized soldiers. Compared with other European armies, this was a sufficient force; but it was very easy for a young man of good family to avoid this kind of conscription,[1] and the bourgeoisie usually hated military service. France thus drifted onward, almost until 1870, with the bulk of her youth untrained, while Prussia was making "universal service" a reality. This danger, however, did not become pressing until the 1860's. What awakened controversy at the time was the proviso in the new law that promotion and appointments as officers were equally open to all classes. This blasted the Ultras' hopes of monopolizing again the officers' corps in the army, and drew their violent though useless protest. The measure passed in spite of them, and another rock had been set in the path to reaction.

The thing which did, however, for the moment tend to promote reaction was the evidence that the "Independents"— the radical party which talked of the tricolor flag and even of a republic — were again becoming a serious factor in the Chamber of Deputies. In 1817 they had had only 25 voices out of 258; in 1818 they had had 45; in 1819, at least 90. One of their leaders was the notorious Grégoire; a bitter foe of the Catholic Church, an ardent old-line Jacobin and member of the Convention, who had said that "kings were to the moral world what monsters were to the physical." Even the moderate "Constitutionalists" joined with the Ultras in voting to banish him from the Chamber. On top of this excitement came the murder by an isolated fanatic of the Duc de Berry, the son of the Count of Artois, and a presumable heir to the crown. The Republicans had had no part in the crime, but of course they reaped in full its unpopularity. In 1820 there was another inevitable Royalist reaction, which Louis XVIII could not withstand. "It is all over with me," remarked the King gloomily, meaning that he could no longer hold back the pressure of the Ultras. The result was ten years of steady tightening of autocracy, and then the cord

[1] The purchase of substitutes was not unknown. The Government did not dislike this. With the extra money could be hired professional soldiers far more efficient than young bourgeois gentlemen serving against their will.

snapped: France escaped to a somewhat more liberal régime by the bloody road of revolution.

Just before 1820 there had been signs of a gradual liberalizing of the Government. In 1819 a law had been passed permitting trial by jury for press cases, and doing away with the censorship, although newspapers were still subject to a heavy tax and had to make a deposit of money ($40,000) as security for good behavior. Now all this came to an end. The Ultras reëstablished the control of the press, and then proceeded (1820) to juggle with the organization of the deputies to their own great advantage. The membership of the lower Chamber was increased to 430. Only the original 258 could be voted for by the ordinary 300-franc taxpayers. The remainder, 172, were to be chosen solely by the ballots of the 1000-franc taxpayers who were themselves eligible as legislators. This practically gave a double vote to the very rich. The new elections (November, 1820) rejoiced the Ultras with an enormous majority. The Independents (the "Tricolor Party") sank to a helpless handful in the Chambers. The Royalists, of course, were enchanted. They seemed to have crushed opposition. As a matter of fact the radicals — denied now the ordinary means of pressing their cause — fell back on good revolutionary expedients — secret societies, intrigues, and presently on downright conspiracies. In 1830 they were to show their power at the barricades.

Surrounded by such reactionary influences in 1823, Louis XVIII was induced to intervene in Spain to overthrow an attempt of the Liberals in that much-vexed country to compel their tyrannous King to establish Constitutionalism. It is true Metternich would have probably induced some other autocratic power to intervene if France had hung back, but it irked patriotic men sorely that the country, which in 1793 had endeavored to carry liberty to all the oppressed lands of Europe, should now seem the servile gendarme of Absolutism. In 1824 the Ultras had such success in a new election that there were only 19 Liberals in the entire Chamber, and the majority openly entertained schemes to reëstablish a landed aristocracy and the authority of the clergy. The Royalists were thus in a mood to disregard jauntily the warnings of such old but still venerated leaders as Lafayette. In 1824 that famous general revisited the country where he had first drawn the sword for liberty, America, and was received with unparalleled honors and rejoicings. To his American friends Lafayette spoke his mind very freely: "France," he declared, "cannot be happy under the rule of the Bourbons; and we must send them adrift!"

Lafayette's desires were greatly promoted that same year by the death of Louis XVIII and the accession of his brother as Charles X (1824-30). The new King never attempted like his predecessor to steer a middle course between the Moderate Royalists and the Ultras. Charles was always avowedly an Ultra. He hated Constitutionalism and doubtless would have restored the Monarchy of Louis XIV the instant that it might have become possible. He was also an extreme partisan of the Church. It was to this Prince "who never learned anything and never forgot anything," that there was very largely due that fatal alliance of "the Altar and the Throne" which was to afflict alike French political life and the Catholic Church of France down to the very eve of 1914. For practical purposes, after 1815 the ecclesiastics of France had entered into a working agreement with the Ultras. The churchmen were to do everything possible to promote a return to Autocracy. The Ultras were to secure to the clergy a complete control of education, and to get back for them, if possible, all the wealth and influence they had possessed before 1789. Charles X, as Crown Prince and as King, never concealed his intense sympathy with this movement.

The new King, indeed, at his accession announced his intention to "maintain the Charter." Political prisoners were released, even the press censorship was for a little while reabolished. Every sovereign is naturally gracious and popular the week after he comes to power; but Charles soon showed his hopelessly mediæval temper. In 1825 he had himself crowned at Reims with all the elaborate ceremonial used before 1789, and in the precise costume of the ancient kings — tunic, dalmatic, golden scepter, and the rest. Frenchmen had a keen sense of the ludicrous. It did not add to the prestige of the Monarch in the nineteenth century to have himself "anointed on seven parts of his person with sacred oil, 'miraculously preserved,' and dating from the time of Clovis." Nor did many of Charles's subjects take seriously his claim to heal the sick "by the King's touch." Such proceedings only moved the godless to laughter, but there was worse than laughter when this "Son of St. Louis" undertook to urge his ministers to execute a violently reactionary political programme.

The returned noblemen had long demanded compensation, if not actual restoration, for their confiscated estates. This was now done by voting them 1,000,000,000 francs indemnity; but to raise the money the interest on the earlier public debt was "converted" from five per cent to three per cent. The numerous and powerful bondholders were enraged at the change, and were more distrustful of the Restoration than ever. The ecclesiastics everywhere showed their hand in the Government. The death penalty was established for stealing sacred vessels from churches. The number of bishops increased. The teachers in the State educational system were put under the supervision of the Church authorities, and there were general dismissals of civil officials who did not show zeal for the new policy.

Inevitably all these undertakings raised up enemies right and left. The electoral body in France had been a small enough part of the nation in any case; now even the electors began to desert the Government. To the Liberals were joined many great manufacturers and bankers — wealthy, powerful men despite their short pedigrees, who were furious at the way things were going. An attempt to carry a law reëstablishing primogeniture in the transmission of large estates, a necessary preliminary to reëstablishing a privileged aristocracy, broke down in the Chamber of

Peers.[1] Another attempt to carry a press law, which would have required every newspaper to deposit with the Government the manuscript copy of every issue *five* days before publication, was similarly thwarted.

In anger the Ultra prime minister Villèle proceeded to swamp the Liberal majority in the Chamber of Peers by getting the King to name 73 new peers from among picked reactionaries. But the Government went on to dissolve the lower Chamber and precipitated a new election (1827), hoping to get a wholly tractable parliament. Instantly it was discovered how utterly out of touch ministers and King had become with even the most privileged classes in the nation. A strong anti-Ultra majority was returned, despite the very limited franchise. To Charles's open sorrow Villèle resigned, and the King in order to do business had to take the Moderate Martignac as his prime minister.

But Charles hated the Martignac policies and he quickly showed his hand. The last thing he desired was to play the part of a genuinely constitutional king. In 1829 he deliberately dismissed his Moderate ministers and gave the power to a personal friend, the "emigrant" Count Polignac, who was to help him most admirably in pulling down the dynasty. He was a narrow-minded Ultra, "with the fatal obstinacy of a martyr, and the worst courage of the 'let the heavens fall' sort."[2] Minister and King charged cheerfully ahead, confessing that a majority of the Chamber was now against them, but resolved to let nothing swerve their purpose. Such statesmen seldom fail to precipitate revolutions.

The great weakness of Polignac's position was that he could not legally collect taxes without the consent of the Chambers. Men began to talk of "legal resistance." The Liberal *Journal*

[1] The "peers" under the Restoration were sometimes more liberal than the "deputies." The "peers" contained a large sprinkling of intelligent magnates taken over from the Napoleonic régime.

[2] A fair sample of his "liberality" was his refusal in 1814 to swear allegiance to the Charter because it guaranteed freedom of worship to Jews and Protestants.

des Débats, in August, 1829, flatly said, "The people will pay a thousand millions to the law: they will not pay one franc to the ordinances of a minister"; and wound up its warning article with "Unhappy France! Unhappy King!" [1] The minister and the Monarch, however, seem to have hugged the delusion that since only the well-to-do and wealthy could vote for deputies, the rest of the nation had no interest in how the administration might coerce the parliament. As a matter of fact, serious schemes were now on foot for effecting a radical change in the Government, and the rights of the deputies were being generally felt to be identical with the rights of the people. Associations began to be formed to resist the payment of taxes in case the ministers should try to collect them illegally, and to one of these bodies joined the famous historian and "Constitutionalist" Guizot, possibly the leading literary man of France, who had been dismissed from the University because his lectures had not been reactionary. Lafayette made a tour of the South Country. The acclamations which greeted him showed how numerous were the Liberals and the violently anti-clerical Free Masons. In Paris the hitherto feeble little Republican clubs took courage and began to form schemes to throw up barricades. The clever young political writer Thiers also lent his pen to an organized attack on the policy of the Government. And so Polignac and Charles X marched onward to their fall.

In March, 1830, the deputies by a formal vote declared their lack of confidence in the Polignac Ministry. Charles retaliated by dissolving the Chamber and ordering a new election. "This is not a question of the Ministry, but of the Monarchy," he said bluntly. Hitherto it had been possible to claim that the King was merely the victim of bad advisers. Now he invited all criticisms directly upon himself. The King himself went into the political lists to get a favorable majority. "Perform your duty," he told the electors, "and I will do mine." Louis XIV had been

[1] The author of this article was prosecuted and condemned, but the courts finally acquitted him on appeal.

charged with saying, "I am the State." Charles X was practically saying, "I am the Ministry."

The instant the election was held, the eyes of the Ultras should have been opened. Public opinion had the few electors in its clutches. In place of a majority of 221 against Polignac in the Chamber, there was now one of 274. Talleyrand, the time-serving minister of Napoleon, who had done so much to secure the recall of the Bourbons and who was now shrewdly watching events in retirement, summed up the situation very crisply. "In 1814 the return of the Bourbons secured the repose of Europe. In 1830 or 1831 their departure will secure the repose of France." But the King and his myrmidon did not allow matters to drag out until 1831.[1]

The last events in the Bourbon Monarchy were so inevitable they need not detain us long. Only with the aid of a great and loyal army could Charles X have adhered to his policy and kept his throne. On the strength of a vague clause in the Charter which gave the King power to issue ordinances "for the safety of the State," on July 26, 1830, Polignac suddenly placarded Paris with four "ordinances" that changed the fundamental laws of France. The first ordinance completely suppressed the liberty of the press. The second dissolved the Chamber just elected. The third modified the electoral law so drastically that practically only great landed proprietors could vote, barely leaving some 25,000 "electors" in all France. The fourth ordered new elections and the convocation of a Chamber elected as prescribed in the third ordinance. Four days later the Government and the dynasty had been overthrown by armed insurrection.

The fighting was confined to Paris, and its episodes can be omitted. It was merely a case of spontaneous combustion.

When the unconstitutional ordinances were issued, the editors

[1] Czar Nicholas, an extreme Absolutist, advised the King to be cautious, for nobody wanted to plunge France in revolution, but Charles X doggedly replied "Concessions ruined Louis XVI."

of the liberal papers of Paris issued a protest. "The Government has violated the law. We are under no obligation to obey. ... We shall resist [the Government]. It is for France to judge how far the resistance shall extend." The editors by themselves were, of course, physically helpless, but now, as in 1789, the populace of Paris came to the rescue with a fighting force. The "Party of the Tricolor" arose. Its leader, Cavaignac, the son of a member of the Convention, wished clearly to establish a republic: many who followed him had no exact programme, but "hatred of the Bourbons and love of the Tricolor flag kept them together." Not more than 8000 to 10,000 men took arms against the Government at first, but physical conditions in Paris greatly favored them.[1] Many of the wards of the capital formed labyrinths of crooked lanes lined with tall old houses. A few paving-stones, an upturned cart, some chairs flung into the street with their legs pointing outward, made a formidable barricade. It was before the days of machine guns and shrapnel. The soldiers could use little except their muskets in forcing their way down streets cut up, block by block, with barricades, and with the insurgents pouring in flanking volleys from every window. Marshal Marmont, who commanded the King's troops, was very unpopular in Paris. He had commanded in the city when it was surrendered to the Allies in 1814. He had only 14,000 available men. The troops were neither cowardly nor mutinous, but they had no such love for the Bourbons that they would make reckless sacrifices to aid them, and they hated to fire on the beloved Tricolor flag which the insurgents everywhere hoisted. The result was that while Charles X complacently played cards at his suburban palace, the capital and then the throne was lost to him.

On the 26th of July, 1830, had appeared the illegal ordinances. On the 27th the barricades were springing up over Paris by

[1] Modern readers, recalling the street fighting in Berlin in 1919, can rather easily picture the struggle in Paris, taking, however, into account the existence of very crooked, difficult streets.

magic. On the 28th the insurgents held the City Hall and Notre Dame and were yelling, "Down with the Bourbons!" Marmont's men were being driven out of the east of the city and were taking refuge near the Louvre. On the 29th the insurgents were on the offensive, and an executive committee in the City Hall was organizing again the "National Guard," to protect life and property, and was putting it under the command of its old leader Lafayette. As for Charles X, he was at last terrified enough to dismiss Polignac and to announce that the fatal "ordinances" were repealed. When his envoys reached the City Hall they were not received. "Too late," was the answer, "the throne of Charles X has already passed from him in blood."

The moment the Republican insurgents had sent Marmont's legions skulking backward the liberal Royalists acted. They had taken possession of the Chamber of Deputies and affected to represent legal authority. They had a candidate for the throne of a strictly constitutional monarchy, Louis-Philippe, Duke of Orléans, of whom more hereafter. A proclamation, drafted by the skillful Thiers, was posted, urging all Frenchmen to compromise on the Duke. "He awaits our call. Let us issue this call, and he will accept the Charter as we have always wished it to be. It is at the hands of the French nation that he will receive his crown."

The Duke of Orléans took possession of the royal palace, although for the moment he only affected to be "Lieutenant-General of the Kingdom." He made the famous promise, "The Charter shall henceforth be a reality."

Cavaignac and his Republican committee still held the City Hall. They had wished, not for a better king, but for no king at all; however, it was clear enough that they only represented a minor fraction of the nation. Louis-Philippe rode across the city to their stronghold, praised and cajoled them, embraced Lafayette, and stood out with him upon the balcony of the City Hall, draped in the Tricolor and receiving the applause of the people (July 31). The Republicans perforce made the best of the situation. As Cavaignac said frankly: "You are wrong in thanking us [for retiring]: we have yielded because we are not ready for resistance."

The rest of France cheerfully accepted the decision of the capital. Charles X vainly tried to abdicate in favor of his grandson, but the Chamber promptly declared Louis-Philippe "King of the French" (August 7, 1830). The deposed monarch then retired wearily to England and ended his days in exile, dying at Goritz in Austria, in 1836. No king was ever more clearly the author of his own troubles than he.[1]

And so the nation was to have another government and another dynasty. Louis-Philippe, "the King of the Barricades," was to substitute for the rule of the Ultras the reign of the bourgeois.

[1] An opinion worth quoting is that of Queen Victoria of England who wrote in a letter to King Leopold I of Belgium in 1836, that Charles X "from his despotic and harsh disposition upset all that the other [Louis XVIII] had done, and lost the throne."

CHAPTER XX
THE "CITIZEN-KING" AND THE RULE OF THE BOURGEOIS

THE "July Revolution" of 1830 caused a great rumbling and tumbling in Europe. It seemed as if France was about to start again on her old path of being the trouble-maker for the world. Almost before the tidings of the new king in Paris had become cold, the report spread of the outbreak in Brussels (August 25, 1830) whereby the Belgians declared their independence and put an end to their uncomfortable union with Holland. In November was to come a revolt in Poland against Russian authority, and before the year closed there had been also movements in many of the smaller German States aiming to wring constitutions from their unwilling rulers. Early in 1831 there were new uprisings of Liberalists in several of the wretched little Italian principalities in a vain effort to get better government and less tyranny. For all these upheavals, which threatened to wreck the whole precious system laid down in 1815 at Vienna, the autocrats of Austria, Russia, and Prussia, and their second cousins the Tory party in England, were prone to blame Louis-Philippe. Would France fly off at a tangent? Would she quickly degenerate into a new Jacobinism at home, and encourage every kind of disturbing propaganda abroad? There was a serious possibility that German, Austrian, and Russian armies might even, at Metternich's behest, invade France again, to restore the Bourbons as a preventive of a new spread of Revolutionary heresy.

All these fears were in vain. The whole history of the reign of Louis-Philippe is one of dull anti-climax. The new régime was very little different from that of the Restoration. The real change consisted in giving power to a new set of men. Instead of the Bourbons, tied by tradition and obligation to the old noblesse and the clergy, there was the Orléans family, half bourgeois and "Voltairean," and forced to lean on the semi-liberal middle classes. Theoretically, indeed, this "July Monarchy"[1] represented the acceptance of the sovereignty of the people. Thiers in a proclamation said, "It is from the French people that he [Louis-Philippe] will hold his crown." Guizot, another promoter of the new dynasty, announced, "He will respect our rights, for it is from us that he will hold his own rights." The new ruler himself declared that he was "King of the French by the grace of God and the good-will of the nation"; and he took particular pains to swear allegiance to the Charter. It was written into the law that the Charter was not merely granted by the Monarch, but handed down by the nation and agreed to by the King; also that the King had no power to issue ordinances which suspended or altered the regular statutes. So far all was excellent. France was to become a limited monarchy in fact as well as in name. But although the King was to be "limited," he was nevertheless still a king. The question of his personality and policy became all-important.

Louis-Philippe was the son of a Duke of Orléans who in 1789 would have possessed a clear title to the throne had anything cut off the reigning family of the Bourbons. The elder prince had been on very uncousinly terms with Louis XVI, had pandered demagogically to the Revolutionists, had called himself "Philippe Égalité (Equality)" when the old titles were shipped overboard, and had finally been elected to the Convention and actually voted for the execution of the King.[2] Citizen "Égalité" himself fell under the guillotine in 1793. His oldest son was Louis-Philippe. That heir to a great title spent a wandering and

[1] The French, as the reader has of course noted, delight to describe political institutions, etc., from the *date* which saw their birth. The "July Monarchy," of course, originated with the revolution of *July*, 1830.

[2] This truckling to the mob did not win him the least respect from the more honorable Jacobins. One of them declared he would vote to acquit Louis XVI, and not to convict (as he had intended), "that I may not tread in the steps of the man who voted before me."

poverty-stricken youth. He taught mathematics in Switzerland. For a little while he lived as an exile in the United States near Brooklyn; then he drifted back to England, the Government whereof gave him a pension. He married the daughter of the King of Sicily and in 1814 came back to Paris with the Bourbons. His kinsmen naturally detested him, and gave him just as little favor at court as possible, but he recovered most of his family property, and made himself very popular by his democratic habits — walking the streets under his green umbrella, talking and rubbing elbows with working-men, sending his sons to the same schools as did well-to-do bourgeois, and welcoming to his palace artists and literary men who were of avowedly "liberal" tendencies. His habits were those of a jovial English gentleman rather than of a French *grand seigneur*, and when in 1830 it became needful to make a hurried dispatch of the Bourbons, no candidate for the throne seemed more likely to meet the requirements than he. He would steer France to liberty, it was said, without plunging her on the rocks of Jacobinism.

Nevertheless this "Citizen-King," who even after reaching the throne seemed so delightfully democratic in his habits, was as a matter of fact intensely tenacious of authority, anxious to dictate to his ministers, and almost as obstinate as Charles X. He had a large family. He devoted a large part of his energies to the eminently "bourgeois" pursuit of marrying off his children advantageously and adding to the great personal wealth of the Orléans princes. He took pains not to violate the terms of the Charter as it was revised in 1830–31, but he set his face like flint against any proposition to amplify the modest liberties therein granted. He knew the other Great Powers regarded his advent with distrust if not with aversion. He carefully discouraged, therefore, any proposal by the French liberals to carry diplomatic and military aid to the struggling revolutionists in other countries. His private life was virtuous and dignified, but he never was guilty of constructive statesmanship, and he hugged the delusion that by playing for the favor of a single influential

THE NEW NATIONAL GUARD

class of the nation he could avoid the need of conciliating all the rest. This delusion was the final cause of his downfall.

The Charter had presented certain features which even the most moderate Liberals in 1830 demanded should be altered. Of course the Republicans desired universal suffrage. They were told in substance to be content with their beloved Tricolor flag and a very modest enlargement of the electorate. By the new law of 1831 the double vote for the very rich was suppressed. For the electors, the legal age was lowered to twenty-five, and the tax rating from 300 to 200 francs ($40). Certain professional "capacities" — lawyers, judges, professors, physicians — were allowed to vote even if they only paid 100 francs. To be a candidate for the Chamber of Deputies one had to pay 500 francs tax, not 1000 as formerly. This raised the whole electoral body to about 190,000 out of a population of 30,000,000. The 190,000 were known soon by an arrogant name, insulting to the rest of the nation; they were the *Pays légale* ("the country before the law"), as if the rest of their fellow citizens counted for nothing!

To defend this aristocracy of wealth the ruling powers now proceeded to reorganize the National Guard, and make it into a really formidable fighting force. Its purpose, however, was not so much to defend the frontier against a new Prussian or Austrian invasion as to defend the July Monarchy against the assaults by the radicals. Pains were taken that only reliable bourgeois should be enrolled in the lists of the new "legions." The reorganized militia found in truth that its task was no sinecure. It had to handle serious riots and even rebellions. In the first years of Louis-Philippe more than two thousand Guardsmen were killed or wounded fighting insurgents. The Corps was in short the bulwark of the Orléanist régime. While it was faithful the Constitutional Monarchy held its own. When it deserted, in 1848, Louis-Philippe fled quickly into exile.

So then we have a fairly complete and formidable personal monarchy "veiled under a middle-class disguise." Just as Augustus Cæsar called himself, not "king," but "first citizen," to hoodwink his fellow Romans as to the true nature of his government, so Louis-Philippe erased the royal lilies from the panels of his carriages, and on reception days caused the doors of his palace to stand open to almost any decently dressed citizen who cared to come in and shake hands with the head of the State. But the true philosophy of his government revealed itself in the speech of his prime minister, Casimir-Périer, in March, 1831, "France has desired that the Monarchy should become national: it does not desire that it should become powerless."

No recent period of French history is so exempt from striking episodes as this reign of Louis-Philippe (1830–48). There were no serious wars except in Algeria — a colonial conquest to be discussed later, no important crisis in the Government, absolutely no important political reforms. The Church now paid the penalty for the much-vaunted alliance of "the Altar and the Throne" under Charles X. Without being actually persecuted and deposed as a State religion, the Church party was made to feel clearly enough that the new Government owed it little and loved it less. On the other hand, the Republicans, without whose brave if undisciplined fighting behind the barricades the overthrow of the Bourbons would have been impossible, were soon angry and vengeful. They had dreamed of some kind of a return to the brave days of 1792–94: and behold, the new rulers of France were barely adhering to the most essential things won in 1789! The result was a series of insurrections by the working-classes bent on completing the task they had dropped in 1830. There were two days of fierce street fighting in Paris in 1832; while in 1834 in Lyons the ill-paid silk-workers rose in insurrection giving the city over to a five days' riot, and only succumbing to a serious military effort.

These attempts should have been a warning to Louis-Philippe and his "Liberal" ministers that a genuine attempt should be made to conciliate the lower classes, both by enlarging the electorate and by legislation calculated to improve the economic condition of the industrial elements. Nothing substantial was done except in the way of repression. The courts were clogged with prosecutions of Republican newspapers, and the *Tribune* (a leading radical organ) was prosecuted 111 separate times, and condemned to fines in the aggregate of 157,000 francs ($31,400). The hatred for the King grew: between 1835 and 1846 six distinct attempts were made to murder him. The 1835 attempt was especially diabolical. A Corsican, one Fieschi, manufactured an "infernal machine" with a hundred gun-barrels, which were fired simultaneously at the King when he rode with his suite through a street in Paris. Louis-Philippe and his sons all escaped: but twelve other persons perished. The natural answer to such a deed was more repression. Special courts were set to handle offenders attacking the security of the State. Convictions could be given by a mere majority vote of the jury, seven out of twelve.[1] Exceedingly heavy penalties were provided for all "excesses" by the press; for example, it was forbidden to publish the lists of jurors; and if a newspaper was fined, it was forbidden that sympathizers of the editor should take up a subscription to discharge his penalty.

There seemed now as little real liberty in France as in the palmiest days of the Ultras. Louis-Philippe was thus subjected from both sides to the most biting manner of criticism; the friends of the Church and of the old Bourbons (still to be reckoned with) of course would have none of him, and as most unnatural allies they now had the Republicans. These elements of dissatisfaction continued to grow until the new explosion of 1848.

The one class the King *did* stand well with was his sworn partisans, the upper bourgeois. This was an age for stock-jobbing and expanding commercial enterprises. France was prosperous, although it was not a prosperity that was shared fairly by the artisan classes. Wealth was creating a host of pre-

[1] Note, however, French law at that time did not require unanimity in a jury to convict: eight out of twelve could bring in an adverse verdict.

tentious parvenus who found the prevailing atmosphere of Paris much to their liking. Thiers and Guizot, the most important of Louis-Philippe's ministers, were nothing if not ardent defenders of "the rights of property." The novels of Balzac, written in this period, give typical pictures of the spirit of sordid acquisitiveness which seemed to dominate the life of the nation: a spirit whose loftiest gospel was that "honesty is the best policy," and which often seemed to treat bankruptcy as a less pardonable offense than murder. With lighter and more romantic touch, the elder Dumas, in his "Count of Monte Cristo," gives a commentary upon the "higher circles" of this period — the great financiers who think in terms of millions, the vulgar scrambling for wealth as the key to power, the sham aristocrats who boast their nobility while they conceal a very recent family skeleton: the willingness of great and small to cringe before any adventurer who seems to have a vast banker's credit. It was as if the nation that had given the world the theology of Calvin, the philosophy of Rousseau, the heroic idealism of the Girondists, was running to seed in an inglorious commercialism which made wealth the superior of breeding, intelligence, and religion. This was not so, but it was certainly true of the men who seemed leading the policy of France for these monotonous eighteen years.

While Louis-Philippe maintained pretty stiffly his personal control of the Government, he did not make the mistake of trying to do without real ministers. On the contrary, by using competent administrators he boasted that he alike confirmed his own power and satisfied the "country-before-the-law." He was obliged repeatedly to use as prime minister Thiers, one of the Liberals to whom he largely owed his throne in 1830. But Thiers was not sufficiently subservient. He held that the King should choose his ministers from the party predominant in the Chamber and then let them govern in their own way, until they lost the confidence of the deputies. That, however, was far too "constitutional" for Louis-Philippe. He desired to choose his

LOUIS-PHILIPPE

NAPOLEON III

ADOLPHE THIERS

LÉON GAMBETTA

own ministers, and mark out for them a policy of his own selection, leaving to them the task of manipulating the Chamber so as to avoid friction, and getting it to ratify cheerfully the propositions submitted.

Thiers was a personage of very high ability, who was repeatedly summoned to power prior to 1840 because the King could find no other man able to handle the Chamber, but in 1840 there came a crisis over foreign matters. England, Austria, and Russia were interfering in the affairs of Egypt, whose viceroy, Mehemet Ali, had placed himself under French protection. Thiers was willing to risk even a war with England to vindicate French interests in the Near East, and he urged a bellicose policy. Louis-Philippe understood clearly enough, however, that his beloved bourgeois wished for anything sooner than a capital war. At best, it would interrupt speculations and dividends; at worst, it would see France invaded by a new coalition. He dismissed Thiers from office, pocketed the national pride, and summoned as prime minister Guizot (another Liberal of 1830 fame), who by a somewhat inglorious surrender of French claims in Egypt tided over the crisis. At last the King had found a lieutenant after his own heart. Guizot and Louis-Philippe remained in close working alliance from 1840 to 1848 when they suddenly and simultaneously had to take the road to exile.

Before Thiers left power he had apparently, with the hearty consent of the King, taken a step which was to have important consequences. Ever since 1815, the Napoleonic legend had been growing and gripping the imaginations of the rising generation of France. The Corsican was no longer the pitiless "ogre" of the conscription; he was the peerless champion of France against her old enemies, the hero of Lodi, Jena, and Moscow. Thiers had himself greatly contributed to this rehabilitation of the Emperor's memory by his literary efforts,[1] he being already one

[1] His famous *History of the Consulate and the Empire*, however, did not appear until after his retirement from office in 1840.

of the most famous historians as well as politicians of France. Napoleon had expressed a wish in his will to be buried on the banks of the Seine, "in the midst of the French people I have loved so well." In 1840 the Government sent a frigate to St. Helena, and Louis-Philippe's third son, Prince de Joinville, honored the famous dead by commanding this vessel that brought the casket homeward. In December, 1840, Paris went into extravagant excitement over the most magnificent State funeral which the capital had ever seen. As the catafalque passed under the Arch of Triumph the old cry once more rang out — "*Vive l'Empereur!*" The numerous veterans of the great captain dissolved in tears. And so the procession swept on to the Dome of the Invalides.

This funeral was undoubtedly a serious political blunder. It seemed to revive and to stimulate the "Napoleonic legend" — the belief growing in the hearts of all too many Frenchmen that the Emperor had been a true patriot who had been overthrown only because he had defended the honor and liberty of the nation. Within less than ten years the friends of the July Monarchy were to lament this celebration in their exile, and yet in 1840 the proceedings seemed harmless enough. If there were dangers to Louis-Philippe were they not from the old Bourbons or the new Republicans? As for the Bonapartist pretensions, the leader of the party was a certain Louis Napoleon, son of the one-time "King of Holland." He was considered a very impractical adventurer. In 1836 he had attempted a filibustering raid upon Strasbourg. It had failed comically. In 1840 he had just attempted another raid upon Boulogne. It had failed even more comically, and this time its leader had been lodged tightly in prison. The King and his ministers had more dangerous foes to dread.

Louis-Philippe had had ten prime ministers in the ten years preceding 1840: now he was to have only one for eight years. François Guizot was frankly a Monarchist. "The throne," as he put it, "was not an empty armchair." He was a native of

INERTIA OF THE GOVERNMENT 427

Nismes in the South Country and was born of a Protestant family at a time when to be a Protestant meant public disfavor if not regular persecution. He had been professor of modern history in the University of Paris,[1] but in 1822 the Ultra ministers found his teachings "too liberal" and suspended him. From that time until 1830 he had been one of the leading defenders of constitutionalism against reaction, and he might have been expected to go on and advocate a progressive régime under the "Citizen-King." This was not to be. As he had opposed anything *less* than the terms of the Charter before 1830, so after 1830 he opposed the slightest enlargement of its very narrow "liberties." Constitutionalism to him meant the rule of the upper bourgeoisie — the only part of France educated, but not mediævalized. He was entirely willing, with all his Calvinist tenacity, to put his talents at the disposal of Louis-Philippe. He had been first tried in lesser positions. Now he was made prime minister. The King was delighted with him, declaring, "He is my mouth!"

This last phase of the July Monarchy is extremely uneventful. The Government had neither a reform programme nor even one of deliberate reaction. Its sole ambition was for the static prosperity of the dynasty and of the favored classes. There were no serious wars (save in Algeria), and Guizot deliberately endured the taunt that he was "for peace at any price" in his foreign policy. Louis-Philippe continued to play the "Citizen-King," although after the Fieschi affair in 1835 he no longer dared to walk along the Paris streets, and when he drove out he sat with his back to the horses, as being thus a less exposed target for assassins. Thirteen times in all he is alleged to have been shot at, and it must be admitted that the King faced with considerable bravery the constant chance of being murdered; but he never seems to have endeavored to make his existence safer by conciliating public opinion with liberalizing reforms.[2]

[1] His printed lectures on *The History of Civilization* are epoch-making in the new scientific study of history as it developed in the nineteenth century.

[2] Louis-Philippe and his Queen, Marie Amelie, seem to have kept up all their

The brilliant orator Lamartine summed up the situation when in 1842 he said of Guizot and his master, "A stone post could carry out their policy!" And in 1847 another protesting deputy cried, "What have they done in seven years? — *Nothing, nothing, nothing!*" To all of which criticism Guizot calmly replied that his aim was "to satisfy the general body of sane and calm citizens" rather than "the limited body of fanatics" affected with "a craze for innovation."

And yet this was a strictly constitutional régime. The minister and the King could declare they were living up to the precise letter of the Charter. Not merely did Guizot have a majority in the Chamber in 1840; it was increased by the elections of 1842 and of 1846. How, therefore, could it be truthfully said that the policy of the Government defied public opinion? As a matter of fact the ministers, with admirable adroitness, had made themselves very secure with the "country-before-the-law." The body of electors was so small that it was possible for the Government to offer direct inducements to their disposing fraction to get it to select deputies who would be after the "Citizen-King's" own heart. Readers familiar with the means whereby Walpole in eighteenth-century England retained his majority in the House of Commons will have a keen idea of the methods of Guizot. The average "electoral college" contained such a number of public officials (who owed their positions to the good-will of the ministry) that the Government could count on a solid block of devoted friends in every district. Petty governmental favors — for example, patronage with licenses to sell tobacco, opportunities for good speculations in the new railways, and actual gifts of Government contracts, etc. — would secure the votes of more waverers. After a deputy had been elected, it would be lucky if Guizot did not soon have him bound hand and foot. There were no salaries to the mem-

bourgeois virtues to the end. Shortly before 1848 an American lady in Paris was visiting a prominent dressmaker. Observing an old black silk dress hanging over a chair she remarked, "I did not know you would fix over old dresses?" "*I do so only for the Queen*" came the prompt answer.

bers of the Chamber. The Government would offer them all kinds of chances to get railway franchises, and what was worse, downright official positions. Presently about 200 deputies, nearly fifty per cent of the entire Chamber, were holding Government offices and drawing Government pay — which they were naturally loath to forfeit by unfriendly votes and speeches! "Corruption" (the name was almost openly used) thus became a regular system of government, and the numerous scandals, revealed in 1848, proved sufficiently that the subalterns practiced the system as well as the austere prime minister.

"What is the Chamber?" cried a deputy in 1841 — "A great bazar, where every one barters his conscience, or what passes for his conscience, in exchange for a place or an office."

There was, indeed, an opposition to Guizot that vented itself in protests about his inert foreign policy and in demands for electoral reform. It was only a helpless minority. Part of the protests came from sincere liberals, who desired either an orderly republic, or at least a monarchy with infinitely greater popular rights than existed under the "Citizen-King." There was rising, however, a party of protest which aimed for *economic* as well as merely political reforms. French industry was developing. The factories were increasing in size. The use of the steam engine and of the new machinery was driving out the old hand work.[1] Labor conditions were bad, the hours long, pay pitifully small, and the legitimate grievances of the working-class many. The bourgeois administration met the rising industrial discontent with few concessions, almost no intelligent reforms and much repression. Better working conditions implied, for the moment at least, smaller dividends for the great manufacturers who swore by Guizot. It was well known that the Paris industrial quarters were full of socialist theorizing and that a very clever author and thinker — Louis Blanc — was

[1] Steam stationary engines came into France much more slowly than in England. They were hardly used in industry prior to 1815; in 1810 there had been only 15 or 16, employed solely for pumping. In 1830 there were still only 625: but in 1850 these had risen to 5322.

advocating not merely a democratic republic, but the creation of "national workshops," owned by the State, controlled by their workmen, and suppressing, or at least gradually succeeding, all private industrial establishments. As early as 1842, an acute German observer, Stein, asserted, "The time for purely political movements in France is past: the next revolution must inevitably be a social revolution."

The King, the Prime Minister, and the bourgeoisie heeded none of these things. Guizot met the demand for an increase of the voting body with arrogant disdain. " Work and grow rich!" he declared. "Then you will become voters!" — although his whole policy toward the artisans made it practically impossible for the average Frenchman even to hope to "grow rich." [1]

There were, indeed, certain desirable changes made by the July Monarchy. Some of the terribly severe penal laws were modified. An honest attempt was made to introduce better primary schools. Hitherto elementary instruction for the chilren of the poor in many communes had been simply a farce. Henceforth the communes were required not merely to appoint a schoolmaster, but to provide him with a lodging, a schoolroom, and a fixed salary. These primary schools, however, were not strictly free, and this fact put them still at a heavy discount. It was to be a good while before the French school system was on a satisfactory basis.

The July Monarchy was thus mainly a period of shams, sterility, and growing discontent. Nevertheless Louis-Philippe did witness *one* great change for France which was to react mightily upon her future and, one may say, upon the future of other nations, especially that of the great continent of Africa.

In 1815 France had possessed one foothold on African soil,

[1] He had also said, "This world is no place for universal suffrage, *that absurd system* which would call all living creatures to the exercise of political rights." This from a leader who had suffered much for liberalism under the Bourbon Monarchy!

the insignificant trading post of Senegal. In 1914 she was to possess nearly one third of the entire African continent, acquiring this by one of the most important feats of colonial expansion in the history of the world. The foundations for this amazing success were laid by the otherwise inglorious monarchs Charles X and Louis-Philippe.

Algeria was one of the Mohammedan North African States between Tunis on the east and Morocco on the west. Since the Arabs had conquered the country in the seventh century, sweeping out the remnants of Roman and Byzantine power, the country had lapsed back into semi-barbarism. The native Moors had become completely Mohammedanized, and under Islamic conditions the country, which had given to the Christian world St. Augustine, was as lost to progress as if sunk in the bottom of the sea. The government had been nominally under a "dey" supposed to be the vassal of the Turkish Sultan, but his authority over the interior tribes of "Arabs" and "Berbers" was very uncertain. It became still more uncertain when, beyond the heights of the Atlas Mountains, Algeria wandered off into the limitless sands of Sahara. Under good government, however, Algeria was capable of great fertility, and was one of the most promising lands not yet occupied by Europeans.

In 1815, Algiers, the chief city, was still the center of a lawless piratical power whose ships were the terror of Mediterranean waters. Most Americans know that in 1815 the United States declared war on the Dey, and sent a squadron under Commodore Decatur which avenged the depredations against American commerce and forced the Corsairs to promise good behavior for the future. There were also English demonstrations against the Dey in 1816 and 1819, but nothing real was accomplished. Oriental promises are easily broken, and the Algerine pirate chiefs were irresponsible and incorrigible. In 1827, however, a dispute arose between France and Dey Hussein over a commercial matter. The local despot lost his temper during a discussion and struck the French consul in the face with his fly-flapper. This was a direct insult to Charles X's Government which could not be overlooked unless the French wished to lose all prestige before Orientals. French warships blockaded Algiers Harbor, and in 1829 the corsairs added to their insults by firing on a French vessel carrying a flag of truce. The Paris Government was now compelled to very resolute action.

A regular expeditionary force was sent to Algeria, the Dey was attacked by land and sea, and on July 5, 1830, the city of Algiers surrendered. This act was almost simultaneous with the July Revolution. The victory came too late to prop up the prestige of the tottering Bourbons, and Louis-Philippe found himself faced with the question of following up the conquest or at once evacuating the country. In France there were soon two parties. The majority of the Chambers favored letting Algeria alone. To the average bourgeois elector the region seemed far away, with only remote commercial possibilities, but with a very great certainty of being a heavy drain on the taxpayer. Popular sentiment, however, was decidedly in favor of pursuing a conquest fairly begun. With characteristic sluggishness the July Monarchy decided merely to occupy the chief harbors and "to await events." The natives, however, provided the "events" themselves. They made formidable attacks on the French troops and it was needful to take the offensive to avenge the outbreaks.

Nevertheless, the French hold on Algeria for long was confined merely to the coast. For several years only the towns of Algeria, Oran, and Bona were occupied by garrisons, although some attempts were made to negotiate with the local "beys" of the interior (former dependents of the "dey"), that they should put themselves under French protection. While matters were in this inchoate state, however, the Moors found a redoubtable leader: the Emir Abd-el-Kader, "a man of rare intelligence, a fearless horseman, and an eloquent orator." This gallant chieftain, a veritable new Jugurtha on the old Numidian soil, united the scattered tribes under his sovereignty, and for fifteen years waged fairly even warfare with the whole power which France could send to Africa.

For Louis-Philippe to have evacuated Algeria now, in the face of such an attack, would have shaken the prestige of his Government alike in all the Levant and in France itself. This became increasingly true after 1835, when the Emir defeated General Trezel in a regular battle on the banks of the Macta. Abd-el-Kader continued to fight so successfully that in 1837 the French were fain to make a treaty with him by which, in return for a vague acknowledgment of "French sovereignty," the whole of western Algeria was resigned to his direct rule. But the Emir looked on this treaty only as a truce preparatory to a regular *Jidad* ("Holy War"). He devoted his great energies to organizing a formidable army partly on the European model, and assembled not merely field artillery, but a park of siege guns. It was claimed that 50,000 cavalry and a still larger body of footmen would answer his summons. He prepared arsenals, powder factories, cannon foundries, and posts for supply along the probable strategic positions. When he believed that all was ready, in 1839 he broke the truce, and drove his attack up to the very gates of Algiers, burning the farms and massacring the unlucky French colonists who fell into his hands.

There was nothing for it now but for Louis-Philippe to send a really formidable army into Algeria. General Bugeaud was given first 80,000, then 115,000, men to handle a decidedly serious military situation. He made a deliberate change in the French system of warfare in Africa. Hitherto the invaders had held on to the coast towns, but had made no effort to grasp the hinterland. Bugeaud lightened the equipment of his regulars, used small cannon that could be carried by mule-back, and multiplied the number of his swift, mobile columns. By this principle of the "resolute offensive" Bugeaud carried the war into the western Oran district, whence Abd-el-Kader drew most of his resources, captured his strongholds and magazines one by one, and by 1843 he had chased the Emir and the remnant of his forces into Morocco. This was not quite the end, however. Islamic fanaticism made a supreme effort. A devotee, Bu-Mazu (the "Goat Man"), called the faithful again to arms and Abd-el-Kader appeared again in Algeria. But by this time the Berbers and the other Moorish elements were splitting into parties. A strong faction had come to regard French rule as a lesser evil than that of falling under the despotism of the Emir. Finally, in 1847, Abd-el-Kader surrendered to the Duc d'Aumale, a son of Louis-Philippe (Bugeaud having recently retired), and the period of conquest was over.[1]

The French had still, of course, their problems in Algeria. To handle the warlike and fanatical mountain or desert tribes required much firmness and very much tact. There was to be a spasmodic insurrection in 1864, and a decidedly serious one in 1871, when the prestige of France was everywhere lowered by the defeat by Germany, and when the restless Moors were fain to believe that her power was broken. They learned to their cost that Frenchmen could still fight, although it required a bitter struggle to reassert European authority at a moment when the home Government was sorely beset with many nearer problems.

By 1890 the French hold on Algeria was so consolidated that the attempt could be begun to reach out across the Sahara and to couple up with the French post developing in the great region of the Niger and the Senegal. Finally in 1914 the relations between European and Algerine had become so mutually trustful that France was able, not merely to withdraw a large fraction of her entire army of occupation to meet the German crisis but to recruit many tens of thousands of fiery Berbers to fight valiantly and loyally for the cause of the world's freedom on the fields of Picardy and Champagne.

[1] Abd-el-Kader was sent (contrary to the terms of his capitulation) to France, and there held prisoner until Louis Napoleon came into power. The latter gave him a pension and allowed him to retire to Damascus in Syria. He died there in comfortable exile in 1883. One of his grandsons seems to have been an officer in the French army in 1914.

The surrender of Abd-el-Kader was only two months, almost to a day, before the downfall of Louis-Philippe. The July Monarchy continued apparently prosperous and pretentious up to the very end. The suddenness of its downfall indicated how rotten had been its foundation. Its prestige and popularity had been, indeed, undermined by the notorious "Spanish marriages," wherein the King had clearly shown his willingness to advance the private interests of his family even at the expense of the general interests of France.[1] The downfall of Louis Philippe had, indeed, been foreseen for years by many shrewd observers. Metternich, who (with all his narrowness) was no fool, remarked early in the reign that the Orléanist régime rested neither on popular enthusiasm, the authority of a plebiscite, the glory of a Napoleon, nor the sanction of a "legitimate" dynasty. "Its durability rests solely upon accidents." That it lasted as long as it did was mainly due to the inherent conservatism of the French masses outside of Paris, the sordid worldly wisdom of the King's bourgeois politicians, the generally peaceful state of Europe, and to a large amount of mere good luck. In February, 1848, that good luck suddenly deserted.

Year by year the demand for "reform" — mainly electoral reform — had been rising. Even with the very limited franchise there was a respectable amount of protest in the Chamber. Outside of the Chamber there was still more protest. In 1847 there began to be a series of "reform banquets," as a substitute for parades and for regular public meetings which the Government resolutely discouraged. The participants in these banquets often claimed to be loyal to the King, but that they were simply desiring a wider franchise. Sometimes the agitators, however,

[1] The details of this rather sordid family plot need not be discussed. The essential fact was that Louis-Philippe arranged for the marriage of one of his younger sons to a Spanish princess who was likely to inherit the throne of Spain. This marriage enraged the English, who believed the King had broken a pledge given to them in the matter; and it did France no good whatever. It merely enabled Louis-Philippe to provide for an unattached member of his own family, while embittering relations with a great foreign power.

expected something more. There began to be "Republican" banquets at which the Monarchy's right to existence was at least indirectly criticized. Nothing was done to meet the demands of the moderates, so it was not surprising that the radicals made headway. It could not be denied that the existing franchise made the Chamber a mere "club of capitalists"; and when charges of corruption were hurled against the body, Guizot felt it enough to ask his own nominees in the deputies whether they felt themselves corrupted? The whole situation was summed up in the striking assertion of Lamartine, "*France is bored.*"

Omitting picturesque and merely personal incidents the overthrow of the July Monarchy came briefly thus: on the 22d of February, 1848, the Opposition elements in the deputies resolved to hold a grand banquet of protest against the "do nothing" policy of the Government. The authorities, however, foolishly prohibited the banquet. The original holders thereof peaceably decided to give it up, but the news of its abandonment was not spread in time. There was excitement and expectancy of a clash, and on the 22d many Parisians were on the streets. Turbulent elements were soon shouting recklessly, "Hurrah for reform!" All day there were petty riots and some gun-shops were plundered. The police, however, seemed to have the situation well in hand.

The leaders of the radical movement considered the case unpromising and did not issue a summons to arms, but on the morning of the 23d unattached bodies of working-men began casting up barricades. The Government then called out the National Guard. That body, however, "bourgeois" as it was, was disgusted with the ministry. Many of its members in turn began yelling, "Hurrah for reform!" — often adding, "Down with Guizot." This defection of the Guard shook the resolution of King and premier. Guizot resigned and the word spread that there would be a "reform ministry" and a genuine recasting of the Constitution. What more was there to fight for? That night all respectable middle-class Parisians first illuminated their

THE RADICALS CALL FOR A REPUBLIC 437

windows and then quietly went to bed. The victory was won and the crisis seemed over.

But the crisis was not over for the Republican radicals. They realized that there was no time like the present, when barricades were up and arms were still in the hands of the industrial element. In front of the Foreign Office a body of anti-monarchists was fired upon by the police. Placing several dead bodies on a cart and parading the same by torchlight through the artisan quarters, the radicals called the people "to arms!" The Monarchy had been slaughtering the people; now let the people turn out the Monarchy. On the 24th the cry was no longer for "reform," but, "Long live the Republic!"

Vainly Louis-Philippe now began announcing concession after concession. The soldiers, as in 1830, proved none too valiant when fighting for a Government highly unpopular. The eastern quarters of the city were soon held by the insurgents. Everywhere were the placards, "Louis-Philippe massacres us as Charles X did; let him follow Charles X!" The elderly King showed considerable energy in exhorting the National Guard to resist the radicals, but when he heard discordant shouts from its ranks he returned discouraged to the Tuileries and hastily abdicated in favor of his young grandson, the Comte de Paris. Under a popular regent for the lad the dynasty might be saved.

But no such eleventh-hour subterfuge could deliver the Orléanists. At 4.30 P.M. on that turbulent 24th of February the mob forced its way into the Tuileries. The Chamber had in the meantime proclaimed the young Comte de Paris as king. The lad's "reign" lasted only a few minutes. The mob surged into the hall. The Republican fraction of the deputies hastily took charge of the situation and proclaimed a provisional government to rule France until a more regular executive could be chosen. The last relics of royalty vanished. At the City Hall a still more radical body of "Democratic Republicans" had also proclaimed a new government, but the two factions presently reached a compromise by which the conservative Republicans took most of the governmental portfolios, and the radical leaders were put in as "secretaries" to the various ministers.[1] The next day the new provisional rulers sent out their proclamation, "The Republic is the Government of France!" A few days later they decreed the convocation of a national convention to draw up a constitution. Meantime the Orléans princes were fleeing, not very heroically, across the Channel to join their Bourbon cousins in dreary exile.

Old Louis-Philippe died in England in 1850. He had been neither a knave nor a fool, but by his sordid, self-centered, obstinate policy he had destroyed the chance that France could find a peaceful happiness as a democratic government with an hereditary president as in England. Needless to say his opinions of the acts of his countrymen remained bitter unto the end. "All is possible," said he, to a visitor in his exile — "all is possible to France — an empire, a republic, the [Bourbon claimant] Chambord, or my grandson; but one thing is impossible — that any of these should last. *The nation has killed respect.*"[2]

This judgment was, of course, harsh and untrue. But it was quite true that an insurrection by only a limited fraction of Paris had overthrown the Government and substituted another without making the slightest attempt to discover what kind of a reformed régime would be most welcome to the rest of France. The departments had accepted the new revolution in a kind of stupor, unprepared, unconsulted, unorganized for prompt action and confronted with a completed deed. Speedy developments, however, were to show the great gulf fixed between the

[1] Modern readers will not fail to see the similarity to the case of the "Majority" and the "Independent Socialists" when the German Monarchy was overthrown in Berlin in November, 1918.

[2] Louis-Philippe's Prime Minister long survived him. Guizot escaped to London in 1848. In 1849 he returned to France, but soon found that chances of restoring the Orléans Monarchy were hopeless. He then retired definitely from politics, and devoted himself with dignity and success to literary work. His old age, when he was recognized as a national "sage," went far to redeem the blunders of his ministry. He was a devout Protestant, and took a distinguished position as a leader of the French non-Catholics. He died in Normandy in 1874.

explosive faubourgs and the conservative solid peasantry. As a very competent judge (Jules Simon) thus sums up the 1848 Revolution: "The agitation, set on foot by certain Liberals, resulted in the Republic which they dreaded, and at the last moment, universal suffrage, set on foot by certain Republicans, resulted in promoting the cause of socialism which they abhorred."

Aspects of French Life under the Restored Monarchy: 1814–1848

Despite the fact that this is mainly a political history, certain phases of French life, the development of conditions in Paris, etc., have a considerable importance in illustrating the conditions under which the events of 1814 to 1848 were possible.

The revolutions of 1830 and 1848 were both largely of Parisian manufacture, and to understand them a certain understanding of affairs in the capital is highly necessary. French society in this period reflects the general state of transition from the days of the Old Régime to the Modern France of to-day, and like every era of social transition it presented various phases which have to be accounted for in ordinary history.[1]

French society has never seemed more refined than during this period when the nobility, who had profited by recent adversity, and the bourgeoisie, who had never forsaken their habits of cold restraint, set their stamp upon society. It is true, however, that there were now political dissensions which gave rise to at least two political parties, and we no longer find a single, unified upper society as in the France of the eighteenth century. On the one side were the salons of the Royalists; on the other, those of the Liberals. When the Chaussée-d'Antin or the Faubourg Saint-Honoré entertained and held their revels, it might safely be concluded that the Faubourg Saint-Germain was depressed and had no interest in the lists of invitations and in the succeeding festivities.

Royalists and Liberals alike, however, shared a predilection for unostentatious elegance, took a keen delight in the life of the salon, and enjoyed the society of elegant women. The old type of French conversation, with its deference and spirited gallantry, was revived. The polish

---

[1] The following is largely adapted from M. Alfred Rambaud's excellent *Histoire de la Civilisation Contemporaine en France*, pp. 491–515.

and the etiquette peculiar to these circles have in fact never again been witnessed since their decline after the year 1848. In the salons of 1820 and 1840 there lived again that same ingenious type of conversation with its clever retorts, its pleasantries and witticisms; even the very madrigals and other poetic affectations of the *Ancien Régime*. Politics, philosophy, art, literature were discussed, but just as in the period before the Revolution, much less mention was made of natural science because the interests of the people were essentially literary. The dramas of Victor Hugo, the works of Ingres or of Delacroix, the lyrical compositions of Meyerbeer or Berlioz held a much more prominent place in conversation than the discoveries of Ampère the electrician, or of Arago the astronomer.

The influence exerted by the ruling classes on the life of society had not yet been menaced by the counter-influence of the lower classes. It was rarely that any person of social pretensions allowed even a single word of "slang" to intrude into his conversation. Nor had society as yet been affected by those stormy petrels of the middle classes, the artists or the "daubers," the *litterati*, or above all the literary "bohemians." The ideas, the manners, the artistic and literary tastes of these parvenus in letters and in learning, were still simply the occasion for jests and caricatures on the part of good society; and to stamp a thing as "bourgeois" was to damn it as equivalent to all that was hopelessly out of date.

Society, however, had its caprices; for example, about 1820 it suddenly became completely infatuated with the poetry of Byron, with Goethe's "Werther," with "René." by Chateaubriand; and as a consequence of this mania it became actually fashionable to look "dispirited" and "weary of life." "The younger set, who were usually in the best of health, posed as consumptives." The seraphic poetry of Lamartine was popular with large coteries of ethereal and fragile ladies who, with their eyes lifted to heaven, "affected to live on nothing else than the perfume of roses!"

Very little is heard of the court of Louis XVIII; the King, who was of a studious nature, a scholar and a classicist, in short, an urbane old gentleman who recited Horace and who made really clever jests, was infirm and afflicted with gout, and had no fondness for society. When his daughter-in-law, the Duchess de Berry, ceased to do the honors of the court after the tragic death of her husband, very little entertaining was indulged in except at the residences of the Duke and Duchess of Angouleme or at the Pavillon de Marsan where the Count of Artois, the heir-presumptive, held his state. Under Charles X these receptions were limited to a small circle of Royalists of good

THE ROYAL COURT

standing, or to such individuals as had given proof of their loyalty to the Monarchy. Under the Orléans régime there was of course a decidedly marked change.

Louis-Philippe, who held his throne as a result of the combined efforts of the Paris masses and of the bourgeois, had caught the allegiance of the former by singing the "Marseillaise" on the balcony of the Tuileries, of the latter by his practice of admitting them freely to his salons. The first receptions given by Louis-Philippe at the Palais Royal were in fact a curious spectacle. By the indulgence of the King practically any orderly person who desired was allowed to attend, and the officers of the National Guard from the market districts and from the suburbs arrived in full dress, their wives on their arms, to pay their compliments to the "Citizen-King."

The personal virtues of the King and Queen and the simple, unaffected manners of the entire royal household naturally delighted the bourgeois. They were gratified when the King authorized them to promenade in the Garden of the Tuileries under the very windows of his apartment, which was in turn thrown open to them on certain days. Visitors were impressed, while passing through the salons, and even the bedchambers of the royal couple, to see everywhere evidences of good management in both the public and private life of the court. They enjoyed and appreciated the familiar sight of the King going about with his green umbrella, an act and article which was to the average bourgeois a symbol alike of economy and of foresight. They were also greatly impressed on learning that the King like themselves carved his own fowl at table even in the presence of ambassadors.

The sons of the King received the same education as the sons of the bourgeoisie, and attended the public lycée; when they had finished the general course there, a reception was held at the Tuileries to which their comrades were invited. And in fairness it should be said, that notwithstanding all the charges hurled against the July Monarchy, no Prince, even under the Old Régime, has been more lamented than was the Duke of Orléans after his tragic death in 1842.

In literature the bourgeois had abandoned the drama of the "Boulevard" to the people and had been shocked from the very first by the invasion of Victor Hugo at the Comédie Française. The favorite authors were Scribe and Musset. They were by no means averse to certain types of gayety; even in the best homes of the bourgeois after a particularly good dinner it was the custom to remain around the table and sing the songs of Béranger, the refrains whereof were sung in a chorus.

The best society attended the masked ball at the Opéra; here everybody danced together, met the leaders of feminine society, and learned the methods of polite intrigue. As the population of Paris grew, the originally modest character of these balls vanished. More and more they were attended by adventurers and strangers. The management began to hire professional dancers; Musard with his brass band, strident and roisterous, with his symphonies of pistol shots and falling chairs, and with his infernal "gallop"; Chicard, with his gauntlets, his helmet, and extravagant plumes, took possession, and one by one the respectable people deserted these heterogeneous fêtes.

The Restoration had retained the State lottery which had been suppressed in 1793 and reëstablished in 1797. It had an enormous fascination for a certain type of people; they attempted to divine the winning numbers, to see them in dreams, to obtain them from fortune-tellers or from clairvoyant mediums. There were five lottery bureaus — respectively at Paris, Bordeaux, Lille, Lyons, and Strasbourg — and there were five "drawings" per month. There was also a system of public gambling which was highly popular. It was played at Paris under the patronage of the State, just as later it went on at Baden or Monte Carlo. Even this, however, did not drive out private gambling-houses, and during a spasm of public righteousness in 1836 both the private and the public establishments as well were ordered suppressed. In 1839 the lottery was likewise forbidden as "immoral." It has been calculated that these two institutions cost the French nation very nearly four hundred million francs annually ($80,000,000).

Social customs were borrowed wholesale from England in this period, despite the alleged national antagonism. One of the most important and desirable of these usages, introduced following 1814, was that of personal hygiene. People began to pay more attention to cleanliness than they had during the preceding twenty-five years of military campaigns, bivouacs, and nomadic life. "They began to use perfume less and water more." In their homes they devoted less attention to elegance and thought more of "comfort," a word which was English both in spirit and in form. British cooking, which was wholesome and simple, also largely replaced the super-refined dishes of the French chefs. Even in France they came to know thoroughly the meaning of "a good beefsteak."

At first there was a rage for the woven fabrics, for the steel, and for the thousand and one little knick-knacks which England could supply; a passion held in check only by very stringent customs duties. "Coats, shoes, needles, razors, in fact there was nothing that was good, beautiful, or convenient but what came from across the Channel."

The word *mode* was replaced by that of "fashion" and every one prided himself on being "fashionable." People spoke glibly of the "courses," "horses," "Irish banquets," "the steeple-chase," the "turf," "jockeys," "starters," and quite after the English fashion, of "bets" with "bookmakers." Horses, and even in fact strictly French songs, were given English names.

The Second Restoration excited the most intense hatred because of the harsh treatment it awarded the leaders of the Napoleonic army, whereas the ruthless slayers in the "Massacres of the Midi" (South Country)[1] were treated with extreme indulgence. The alliance between the Royalists and the invaders[2] was an additional cause for disaffection.

Among the elements which proved most irreconcilable to the Restoration were the officers of Napoleon who had been put on half-pay, whereas the State had lavished military promotions on the detested "emigrants" who had flocked back with the Monarchy. Some of these unhappy officers had gone to Texas under the leadership of General Lallemand to establish a military colony called the *Champ d'Asile* (the "Place of Refuge") which was supported in France by a national subscription (1819). It was given the name of the *Canton de Marengo* and its chief town was *Aigleville* ("Eagle-town"). Other retired half-pay officers, riding-coats buttoned up under their chins and with their hats, ornamented with the rosette or red ribbon, cocked over one eye, contented themselves with assisting in the instruction of recruits on the parade grounds, an act which irritated many of them, however, because of the consciousness of their own inaction and unmerited disgrace. Still others mixed in regular conspiracies and became the chief source of danger to the dynasty.

The Café Valois was the rendezvous of the peaceful Legitimists, the old "emigrants" who were called the *voltigeurs* of Louis XVIII. The Bonapartists frequented the Café Lamblin. When the bodyguards announced their intention, in 1814, of coming thither to set up a bust of Louis XVIII, three hundred officers of the Empire garrisoned the

---

[1] Marshal Brune had been assassinated by a Royalist mob at Avignon in a most dastardly fashion; General Ramel was slain by another at Toulouse. The excesses of the "White Terror" recall those of the Terror of 1793.

[2] France's enemies, not her friends, were officially her allies at this time. "Long live our friends the enemies," Béranger ironically remarked. A captain on half-pay was arrested for calling his horse the "Cossack." The magistrate who examined him asked him how he dared give his horse a name which was dear to all good Frenchmen!

place to protect it, and even the intervention of the authorities failed to prevent bloodshed.

After the return of the Emperor in 1815 the Café Montansier at the Palaise-Royal became the headquarters of the Imperial officers. They converted the stage of the music hall into a political rostrum, substituted themselves for the actors, and uttered the most abusive tirades against the Bourbons. After the second return of the King the royal musketeers and the bodyguards in their fury for reprisal took this café by storm, shattered the glasses and dishes, and hurled the silver and furniture out of the windows.

In the provinces the old *seigneurs* of the village, who were very often in league with the parish priests, disturbed the purchasers of "national property,"[1] treated the mayor and the municipal council with contempt, and maintained that they still had the right to sit in the old seigneurial pew and to receive the consecrated wafer in church before the rest of the congregation. These pretentious country squires soon became the victims of open satire and caricature, and stock figures for the jests of the Liberals.

It was as if in France two nations, two armies, stood facing each other. Liberals and Bonapartists at this time held common cause. In a thousand ways, some of them quite absurd, the antagonism between them and the Legitimists showed itself. The Royalists punned on the two words *libéreaux* and *libérés* (that is, "returned convicts"), they more seriously distributed pious books and "Legitimist" pamphlets. The Liberal publisher, Touquet, retaliated by multiplying the editions of Rousseau and Voltaire which were sold in all sizes and at all prices. This same Touquet also sold Liberal snuff-boxes under the cover of which was concealed the text of the Charter. The Royalists adopted this same device, substituting the will of Louis XVI or the portrait of their "martyr king." In 1819 canes were manufactured with adjustable heads, which revealed, when opened, a statue of Napoloen. The fad was also conceived of selling tricolored braces and of manufacturing alcoholic beverages which were called "*Liqueur des Braves*" or "*Larmes* [tears] *du Général Foy.*" In 1815 the clergy refused burial in the church of Saint-Roch to an actress, Mlle. Raucourt. Incensed by this insult, the Liberals forced the doors of the church, broke down the gratings, and deposited the coffin before the High Altar. Louis XVIII indulgently dispatched a chaplain to repeat the last rites over the dead and the threatening mob subsided. In 1817 the Liberals and Royalists crowded

---

[1] This comprised the Church lands and estates of the *noblesses* confiscated during the Revolution.

into the Théâtre-Français for a presentation of "Germanicus" by a mediocre tragedian Arnault who was famous solely because of his well-known fidelity to Napoleon. On both sides officers drew their swords in the riot which ensued, and it was necessary to call out the gendarmes. The epilogue was a half-dozen of duels on the morrow!

Dueling, indeed, had never been so common as during the first years of the Restoration. Every morning (reports had it) the officers of the old Imperial Guard and the new Royal Guard had their combats.

There were also the parliamentary duels which followed the discussions in the Chambers, such as the duel between General Foy and M. de Corday (1820). In these encounters pistols were ordinarily used. If the first one to fire missed, the other out of courtesy would fire in the air. Of these duels the most celebrated during the July Monarchy was that one in which Emile de Girardin killed a fellow journalist, Armand Carrel; a duel which was much more famous from the uproar it created than were the principals themselves (1836).

Freemasonry, to which nearly all Liberals belonged, was not nearly so active during this period as were some other types of secret societies. On one side was the *Congrégation*, which was under the supervision of the Jesuits; on the other was the *Carbonari* (French, *Charbonnerie*) which was established by Buchez, at that time a medical student. The Carbonari, or, as the Italian word signifies, "Charcoal-burners," were organized in imitation of their fellow members in Italy. They swore over a dagger their "eternal hatred to the King and to Monarchy." Members were charged an assessment of a franc a month. They organized in groups of twenties. When numbers increased, new "twenties" were formed until they enveloped the entire country, and even the army, with a network of organizations. They were modeled like a hierarchy, and at the top was the "Supreme Council" of whose composition the thousands of members themselves, as well as the Bourbon police, were ignorant. "Carbonarism" invaded the army and the results came in the military conspiracies of Saumur and Belfort, the plot of Captain Valle, and the attempted insurrection of Lieutenant-Colonel Caron in Alsace. One of the most celebrated trials occurred at this time and ended in the execution of "the four sergeants of La Rochelle" (1822), on whose tombs the people of Paris placed flowers every year. This redoubtable association disappeared when the hatred for the Bourbons began to wear off.

Under Louis-Philippe there were, however, other societies, more or less secret; such as the "Friends of the People," the "Friends of Equality," the "July Union," the "Rights of Man" (which numbered more than sixty thousand adherents in 1833), "Action," the "Seasons," the "Families," all of which continued to organize riots and insurrections, became the subjects for judicial proceedings, and provoked the restrictive law of 1835.[1]

The new Government, following the Old Régime, had permitted a peculiar type of working-men's associations to survive when it abolished the others. The guilds which did not include "stationary workmen" — that is, laborers who settled in one place — served to gather into groups the "journeymen" who went from one town to another in search of work, or, as the saying went, who made "the tour of France." In every town of this "tour," the guild received any traveler who was a member of the "company." It attempted to secure work for him; he was entertained in their appointed tavern, and he was taken in charge by the "mother of the guild" whose members were called her "children." If he fell ill, he was nursed by the "mother," watched over by his companions, and visited by the "rouleur," one of the dignitaries of the society. If he died, his body was suitably accompanied to the cemetery, where it was buried by the members of the association.

All those who joined the guild were initiated to certain "mysteries." When two workmen encountered each other, they exchanged certain formulas and signs of recognition. A very elaborate ritual accompanied this ceremony, on account of which it became customary for members to carry canes and ribbons during public celebrations, and to hold their drinking-glasses over the table, etc. At the funeral of any member, after the eulogy had been pronounced by one of the company, the rest would utter a groan and would then pass alongside the grave, two by two, placing their canes on the ground in the form of a cross. At the corners of the grave they would place their feet in a certain manner. After the ceremony the attendant members then embraced each other.

These corporations still retained certain of the quaint vices of those of the Old Régime. The title of "journeyman" was purchased only after a long and painful apprenticeship. The apprentices were called the "aspirants," the "youngsters," or "foxes." The journeymen usually took advantage of them and harassed them in a thousand different ways. They always took the best of the work for themselves and sent the apprentices into the *broussailles* or "brambles" — that is, the suburbs or little villages. They did not allow them to sleep in the same room as they did themselves nor could the novices sit down at the same table with them at the fêtes. "Renard, fetch me my boots," a journeyman would cry and the apprentice was bound to obey.

---

[1] See p. 423.

The two most celebrated of these associations at the beginning of the century were the "Children of Solomon" and the "Children of Master James." The former claimed that their society had been established by Hiram, the architect of Solomon, who had been assassinated in the original Temple by three traitors to whom he had refused to reveal the secrets of the guild. The latter prided themselves on being able to trace their society back to their master, James, a Provençal architect who had been a colleague of Hiram, and had been murdered by a jealous enemy after his return to Provence from Jerusalem.

The "Children of Solomon," who asserted that they were the older organization, were extremely arrogant. Their rites had been communicated to only four guilds: the stone-masons, the locksmiths, the carpenters, and the joiners. These received workmen into membership without any religious distinctions, and as a result recruited members very largely from among the Protestants. The "Children of Master James" were more hospitable and had confided their mysteries to a large number of guilds, but they received only Catholic journeymen into membership. They styled themselves the "Companions of Duty," or the "Dutiful."[1]

These companies were jealous of one another and treated each other with downright hostility. The locksmiths of "Solomon" would have nothing to do with those of "Master James" in the village where they happened to be working. Frequently scrimmages arose between these *gavots* and *devoirants*. At Sens in 1842, a *devoirant* ("Master James" member) conceived the idea of mounting an ass and riding past the shops of the locksmiths of the rival association crying "Gee-up, Gavot" ("Solomon" member). The result was a bloody quarrel. In 1845 at Nantes the bakers prepared to celebrate the feast of their patron saint with the insignia of the regular "companies" — the canes and ribbons. Infuriated by this usurpation, the journeymen fell upon the procession and a regular riot ensued.

These "associations" very frequently lost sight of their real object. Their affection of the "mysteries," the oppressions of the journeymen over the apprentices, and the constant warfare and bickering naturally prevented mutual assistance. The Old Régime had tried to proscribe the guilds and the Constituent Assembly renewed this proscription by its restrictive law of 1791. Nevertheless, among the laborers of lower capacities and more quarrelsome natures, with whom this system had become entrenched, the companies long survived.

---

[1] There were also other associations like the "Children of Father Soubise" and the "Good Cousins," but these two mentioned above were the most important.

In 1823 the apprentices revolted against their masters and established the *Société des Independants*. In 1839 another revolt produced a new and better type of association. It was at this time that preparations for the expedition to Algeria were under way, and were attracting a large number of working-men to the southern seaport of Toulon. The "mother" of the company proposed that the journeymen allow the apprentices to occupy the same rooms. They refused, and were offended by the proposition, whereupon they deserted the "mother" and ordered the apprentices to follow them. The Juniors, however, refused in turn, threw off their signs of bondage, and established the *Société del'Union*. They no longer made use of insignia such as the canes and ribbons, had no password, no rallying cry, and no martial hymns. The society had a single purpose, that of mutual aid and succor. This was, of course, the legitimate type of labor organization which in the end prevailed. Little by little the old system of guilds therefore fell into disuse.

The growth of national activities and of national wealth was beginning at this time to be realized in Paris, a growth which Napoleon had succeeded in stimulating only by despoiling the entire world for his own personal "glory." Paris was now developing rapidly. In 1816 it numbered 710,000 inhabitants;[1] in 1826, 800,000; in 1836, 909,000; and in 1846 more than a million (1,053,000).

Under the Restoration the Pont des Invalides, the Pont d'Arcole, and other bridges were built across the Seine. The statue of Louis XIII. by Cortot and Dupaty, was erected in the Place Royale, that of Louis XIV by Bosio, in the Place des Victoires, and in 1818 was set up that of Henry IV by Lemot, made of the bronze in the statues of Napoleon and Desaix. A system of gas lighting was introduced during this period, an omnibus service was developed, and an efficient police system established.

Under the July Monarchy Paris owed a great deal of its development to the efforts of the Prefect of the Seine, Rambuteau. It was he who at this time constructed the bridge of Louis-Philippe and the Pont du Carrousel. The Rue Rambuteau was laid out, and the Place de la Concorde, with the Obélisque de Luxor surrounded by the eight statues representative of the eight principal cities of France, was planned. The column in honor of the July Monarchy (Colonne de

---

[1] Probably its population had long been stagnant. It was very hard to feed an inland city of more than a certain size, before the development of modern transportation methods.

APPEARANCE OF PARIS

Juillet) was also erected, the Arc de l'Etoile finished, and the two marvels of mediæval Gothic architecture, Notre Dame and the Sainte-Chapelle were restored. Among other things which were completed, were the Church of the Madeleine, the Panthéon, the Palais Bourbon, and the Palais de Quai d'Orsay. The School of Fine Arts (l'École de Beaux-Arts), the school of medicine (l'École de médecine), and the normal school of the Rue d'Ulm were likewise built. The squares of Louvois and Saint-Sulpice were laid out, the latter with its beautiful fountains of Visconte.[1]

Finally, Thiers and Guizot gave to the capital the system of barriers which surround it, and the detached forts (1841) which the Opposition press denounced at the time as no better than "prisons" the despotism of the Government was arming against Paris, but which were to prove of great value in the siege of 1870.

At this period Paris was far from presenting the appearance which it does to-day. In the center of the capital the most important streets were, as at present, Saint-Denis and Saint-Martin. At this time the Avenue de l'Opéra, the Boulevard Saint-Germain, the Rue des Écoles, and other famous thoroughfares had not been laid out. The wealthy districts lay along the boulevards, Malesherbes, Haussmann, and Pereire, and the Avenues de Villiers and de Courcelles, or along the broad streets which radiate from the Arc de Triomphe. The thickly crowded districts and the slums along the northern and southern boulevards were not yet in existence. Paris included only a dozen *arrondissements* (wards) instead of as to-day twenty, the last eight having been formed later by including within the city the suburban communes. When vaudeville actors wished to poke fun at illegitimate love-affairs, they spoke of them as the "marriages performed in the town hall of the *thirteenth* ward!"

There were still a number of inextricable labyrinths of narrow streets in Paris, with high old houses on either side, naturally very damp because the rays of the sun rarely penetrated thither. It was these rows of houses that gave excellent vantage to the barricade fighters, in the various revolutions that racked the city in 1830 and 1848 as well as during the less successful uprisings. One of the most famous of these

---

[1] Louis-Philippe, who was accused of avarice because he was so economical, levied on his own "Civil List" for thirty millions of francs, which he used for the restoration of the châteaux at Versailles, Fontainebleau, and Pau, which were not inhabited by the court at this time and which he generously opened up to the public.

labyrinths occupied the space which lies between the Arc du Carrousel and the old Louvre. Along these narrow streets were to be found the huts where the dealers in parrots and other exotic birds had set up their shops. Many of these huts almost seemed to hem in the Tuileries.

During the Restoration very few of the streets in Paris had sidewalks. In 1830 there were in all only 16 kilometers (about 10 miles) of such footways. The July Monarchy did much to remedy this evil state and increased the sidewalks to a total of 195 kilometers (about 140 miles). At best, however, these sidewalks were narrow and uneven. Pedestrians could protect themselves from passing vehicles only by hugging the walls or by stepping upon the doorsteps of the houses. The dwellings in turn were usually small and narrow although with oftentimes five or six stories, with tiled roofs which were very steep and with gutters which often disgorged rainwater in torrents on the heads of passers-by. Many streets, so far as they were paved at all, were made of limestone blocks, very irregularly and poorly laid, and were so much ready material for the master-builders of the barricades during the insurrections. Macadamized paving, invented by the Scotch engineer, John Loudon MacAdam who died in 1836, was not used in Paris until after 1849. The system of sewerage was likewise very inadequate. In 1806 there were only 24,297 meters (say 75,000 feet) thereof. The Government of Louis-Philippe, especially during the prefectureship of Rambuteau, increased this number to 78,675 meters (over 240,000 feet). Subterranean Paris, however, dates especially from the Second Empire.[1] "Conveniences" were still being installed in the houses of Paris before 1848 precisely in the manner they exist in rural French communities to-day. What wonder that the cholera epidemic of 1832 had so many victims!

The streets, instead of being raised in the center as at present to assure the drainage of water, were deliberately made on two planes with a depression in the center of the street which formed a gutter. To cross from one side of the street to the other after hard rain-storms was like crossing a veritable torrent. On occasions like these, enterprising fellows would place a board across the gutter and would assist pedestrians across dryshod in return for a fee of a sou. Carle Vernet has depicted this popular scene in one of his engravings entitled "Pass, Pay" (*Passez, payez*). In the middle of the street at regular intervals there also were openings into the sewer. They were covered, indeed,

---

[1] The development of the sewers under the engineer Belgrand was so great that the extent was then increased to 772,846 meters.

with an iron grating, but clumsy vehicles often shattered them to the great detriment of goods or passengers.

The population of the capital was so congested that there was not a square where people could go for a breath of fresh air even in the heat of summer. To mention another nuisance, the water of the Seine was practically never fit for drinking purposes but provincial visitors who were not so aware of this fact as were the Parisians, often were not sufficiently careful and had to pay the penalty by all sorts of plagues and epidemic diseases. There was no more thought then of having water in the houses than of having gas on every story. Water was drawn either from wells or "water posts," or it was carried into the house by water-carriers. Some of the more prosperous of the latter had a two-wheeled cart drawn by a horse and went from door to door. All Parisians of this period could recall having seen these lusty "auvergers"[1] (so-called because nearly all of the water-carriers came originally from Central France) who climbed the stairs every morning with two buckets of water hanging from a yoke across their shoulders, and from which they served their customers. One bucket cost a sou or even more. Nothing was more astonishing to visitors than to find that in Paris *water* like everything else had to be paid for.

Markets and market-places were not very numerous. All the provisions for ordinary households were bought from small merchants who passed from house to house, pushing their hand-carts before them. These were called the "merchants of the Four Seasons" and preserved the tradition of the "criers" of old Paris.

Shop-fronts, which were much less numerous and less elegant than they are to-day, were not closed at night by metal gratings locked by some mechanical device, as is now the case in most European cities. Instead the shopkeeper would have to unlock, one after another, the eight or ten shutters which protected the shop-front, and which were fastened at the top by a hook and at the base by a latch. It was not unusual, after he had unlatched the narrow entrance to his place of business, and was passing along with his shutters on his shoulder, to knock violently against some unsuspecting passer-by. The basements of the shops were reached by means of trap-doors which opened out upon the street and were consequently another source of danger to the pedestrian.

All these things indicated how tenaciously "the good old ways"

---

[1] The "auvergnat" water-carrier, the charcoal merchant, the vender of fagots, and the errand boy were types especially dear to romance, song, and the vaudeville at this time.

still hung on the French capital. Nevertheless the period of the restored Monarchy was undoubtedly a time of progress in the aspect of Paris as in so many other things. For example, the lighting of the city streets was vastly improved. In 1848 there were still 2608 old-style lanterns, but there were also no less than 8600 of the far more efficient new-style gas lamps.

Such were some of the social customs and physical conditions of the France and of the capital, which bridged the gap from the Old Régime to the Third Republic we know to-day.

CHAPTER XXI
RADICAL OUTBREAKS AND THE REACTION TO CÆSARISM
THE SECOND REPUBLIC: 1848-51

NEVER had the fact that all governmental power in France was centralized in Paris reacted more decidedly, and on the whole more unfortunately, upon the nation, than in February, 1848. The departments had had almost no part in the new revolution: they certainly had little sympathy with the extreme radicals who had fought the movement through to physical success. The average peasant, or bourgeois in the small towns, was only very mildly interested in politics. He wanted assured conditions for his farm or business, light taxes, personal liberty, and a government at Paris which appeared to be reasonably progressive and which would maintain for France a leadership among the nations. The country was frankly disgusted with the policy of absolute prudence (Americans would say of "safety first") in foreign affairs which seemed to make France cringe to outsiders, especially to England, lest by any show of resolution the financiers in Paris should see their bonds go down in value during foreign complications. But as for constitutional details the provincial Frenchman cared next to nothing. It is a damning indictment of the Guizot-Louis-Philippe rulers that notwithstanding this state of political quiescence, they were unable to keep their hold upon the Government. It is true, it was radical Paris which expelled them. It is also true that nowhere in the departments was there the slightest hope of any material action to prevent their expulsion.

And so France found a "republic" thrust upon her overnight. This result was accepted with reasonable submission if with very little enthusiasm. But any acute student of public opinion would have said that to make the republic succeed, it must be a very orderly, reasonable, moderate republic, carefully respecting the rights of property, and not endeavoring to produce Utopias too rapidly. This is precisely what the "Second Republic" did not do. The result was a reaction to dictatorship and then to open imperialism, on the ground that Cæsarism was far better than anarchy. The violence of the Paris Socialists in 1848 was the best argument for the founding and for the existence of the "Second Empire."

On account of its experiment with part of the programme of socialism, the Second Republic presents great interest to students of economic theory and sociology. As historical students, however, the episodes of 1848 need not detain us very long. Their main importance was: (1) to disgust the French nation with half-baked experiments of radicalism; (2) to hasten thereby the coming to power of Napoleon III, as the champion of "order."

The Republicans who overthrew Louis-Philippe were themselves seriously divided. The moderate Republicans, whereof the eloquent Lamartine was a typical leader, aimed for a *democratic* republic with the beloved *tricolor* flag. The radical Republicans, led notably by Louis Blanc, desired a *socialistic* republic with the *red* flag of extreme revolution. The moderates and the radicals at first worked together. They both wished some kind, at least, of a republic. The moderates had on the whole the upper hand in the new provisional government, but they had to make heavy concessions to the radicals who struck while the iron was hot. In March, 1848, "all citizens" were to be enrolled in the National Guard. It ceased to be merely a bourgeois affair. Soon in Paris it contained 190,000 instead of 56,000 members — most of the reinforcements coming from the industrialists. Political clubs, often controlled by the most violent type of agitators, sprang up like mushrooms. There were repeated armed demonstrations before the City Hall, where the provisional government had its seat; and the terrified administrators were driven to one concession after another.

NATIONAL WORKSHOPS

On February 25, following such a demonstration, Louis Blanc carried the decree, "The Government of the French Republic undertakes to guarantee the existence of the working-man by labor, and to provide labor for all citizens." This was soon followed by a decree ordaining "national workshops."

On February 28, following a second demonstration, the administrators created a "government committee on the laboring class with the express mission of looking after their interests." Blanc and Albert as heads of this committee took their seats in the Luxembourg. They were able to issue some useful and highly proper orders: for example, reducing the normal working day to ten hours in Paris and eleven hours in the departments.[1] All sorts of excellent schemes were mooted. The employers, however, sullenly resisted the committee. The radicals demanded that it should produce instantaneous results. The committee (with very little power to enforce its mandates) wasted its time in futile conferences, while both sides, of course, grew distrustful and angry.

Finally, on April 26, the radicals attempted to coerce the Government again. The working-men's clubs paraded *en masse* to the City Hall to demand "the abolition of the exploitation of one man by another, and for the organization of labor by association." Just what was implied by this demand was not wholly clear. Seventy-five years later the world would have called it "Bolshevism" — perhaps unjustly. But the moderate Republicans were taking fright. The east of Paris might rage for socialism, but to submit to it would be about the surest way to send the rest of France back to monarchy. Ledru-Rollin, one of the most prominent leaders in the anti-Orléanist movement, called out various reliable companies of the National Guard, which met the working-men before the City Hall with the

---

[1] Hours of labor in France had been abominably long: and in general Frenchmen seem to have been willing to spend a greater fraction of the day at work than in certain other countries. The regulation stated was a very considerable gain.

counter-cry of "Down with the Communists!" For the instant the radicals quailed and dispersed.

So all the socialistic schemes seemed to have fizzled out, save only the "National Workshops." Even these institutions were conducted, it would seem, by men who secretly desired that they should fail, although in fair truth it must be said that any such project would obviously require the most careful introduction and the working-out of details to have any hope of success; and the Socialists were demanding that the new organizations should spring up like mushrooms and function overnight. The disturbances in Paris produced an abundance of unemployed labor. There were 6000 "national" working-men early in March, 1848. There were soon 25,000; and there were over 100,000 in May. Obviously great factories could not be provided at once for all of these, without wholesale expropriations from which the Government shrank. The men were therefore employed in building fortifications around Paris at two francs (forty cents) per day. Presently to save money (the treasury was in a most sorry condition) these laborers were kept busy only two days of the week. For the other four they were left idle on only one franc (twenty cents) per day. Paris was thus full of disgruntled and often ignorant men, with all too much time on their hands and very ready to listen to extremist orators with their catalogues of grievances.

Meantime the provisional government was trying desperately to get its young republic really started. The finances were in confusion. Loans could not be floated. The only expedient was to increase the direct taxes about forty-five per cent — a proceeding which naturally made the peasants and bourgeois very angry. Under this unpleasant condition the elections were held for the Constituent Assembly which was to arrange the permanent government of France. The balloting was by universal suffrage, and 900 members were chosen from the various departments. The Assembly was to administer the government, until it completed its labors, by means of an executive committee of five. Under the circumstances the expected happened. The old Bourbons had few friends; the Orléanists were for the moment utterly discredited; the Bonapartists had had no time to organize and to lift their heads. The great majority of the Convention therefore *professed* to desire a republic. But very few Socialist deputies were elected, and a considerable number of delegates represented the great landowners and the clergy — elements still very powerful. The radicals would obviously get little comfort from such an Assembly.

It did not take long for the Paris Socialists to discover the facts of the case, and to determine that "there's no receipt like pike and drum for mending constitutions." Not to be thwarted now had they fought behind the barricades in February. On May 15 armed bands thrust themselves into the Assembly Hall, and were in the very act of declaring that the whole body was dissolved and that a new "Provisional Government" was set up, when a sudden rally of the National Guard chased them out. There was no bloodshed. But the Assembly was rendered justly fearful. It made arrests, closed the political clubs, and decided to strike at the heart of the matter by winding up the "national workshops." They were costing 150,000 francs per day, and were accomplishing little save to "tear up the paving, and to remove earth uselessly" at the Champ de Mars. Doubtless Louis Blanc's enemies were bringing this to pass in order to discredit his whole set of liberal and not wholly impractical proposals. But in any case the situation was intolerable. On the 21st of June, 1848, the Assembly ordered the national workshops closed. The younger workmen could enlist in the army; the older would be given jobs on the public works in the departments.

The Assembly thus flung down the gauntlet. The Socialists promptly took it up. They had now an elaborate organization and plenty of muskets, though they were short of artillery. All the east of Paris, from the Pantheon clear to the Boulevard Saint-Martin, was turned into an entrenched camp with over

400 barricades, often built scientifically and elaborately, with moats and battlements sometimes rising higher than the first stories of the houses. Behind these were at least 50,000 insurgents. The Government had for the moment only 40,000 troops, regulars and reliable National Guards, to send against them; but it was now a case of the working quarters of Paris against nearly all the rest of France. The bourgeois National Guards from the suburbs, and later from the out-lying cities and communities in a wide circuit, came gradually swarming in "all eager to exterminate the Socialists." The Assembly gave General Cavaignac, an old Republican agitator but no Socialist, dictatorial powers to crush the radicals. Four days long the desperate struggle lasted, bloody to the last degree. The streets of Paris were raked with artillery. The Archbishop was shot down while trying to interpose between the raging combatants. On June 26 the last entrenchments of the "Reds" were stormed in the Faubourg Saint-Antoine. How many thousands perished in these bloody "Days of June" can never be safely guessed. Eleven thousand prisoners were taken by the Government troops, and of these 3000 were exiled to Algeria without trial, by a simple decree of the Assembly.

This explosion had very important consequences. The industrial classes were crushed and beaten for the moment, but their hatred toward the bourgeois and the peasants (who had clearly sided with the bourgeois) was intense and lasting.[1] It was to mark an evil schism in France. On the other hand, the bourgeois themselves were terrified and threatened in fortune. The national bonds had sold for 116 in February. They were worth only 50 in April; the June commotions did nothing to restore their value! Many worthy merchants and small manufacturers

[1] One should observe that neither now nor later were the French industrial classes so strong as they were, for example, in England. French manufactures were very largely of objects of elegance and luxury: not coarse staples made in huge grimy factories. The proportion, in France, of small handicraftsmen working in their own shops and of thrifty peasants (always conservative folk) was very large. Outside of Paris, "labor," as we understand the term, was decidedly weak.

THE NEW CONSTITUTION

were utterly ruined by the existing business prostration. What but evil had this much-vaunted Republic brought them? Was it not better to have a "strong government" well able to assure "order." As for the peasants they found that the changed régime had merely brought forty-five per cent higher taxes, and they were led to believe (perhaps unjustly) that the execrated "Reds" intended to begin a wholesale division of farm lands. They, like the bourgeois, signed for a government that would permit none of these things.

The Assembly, however, had been elected before this revulsion of popular feeling. It continued to be mildly Republican. With much labor a new constitution was drafted which it was hoped would avoid the evils of the brave efforts of 1791 and 1795. The United States had by this time been in existence long enough to present some pretty clear examples of how to get along without monarchy. Unfortunately, however, the Assembly failed to borrow many excellent points in the American Constitution, and it woefully failed to recognize the essential difference between many things in America and in France. Briefly speaking the "Constitution of 1848" set up a President, elected for a term of four years by direct universal suffrage. He was clothed with very large executive powers, but was not eligible for reëlection immediately upon retirement. Over against him was set a single Legislative Assembly of 750 members also chosen by universal suffrage. The means for securing reconciliation between President and Assembly in case of friction were, to say the least, very scanty and imperfect. It had been proposed that the Assembly should choose the President, but Lamartine, the silver-tongued orator of the year, the historian of the Girondists and himself partaking of their Utopian spirit, had cried magnificently, "Let God and the nation speak — something must be left to Providence!" And so "God and the nation" were allowed to choose "Napoleon the Little."

"Thus," says a penetrating French historian (Seignobos),

"was the American mechanism transported from a federal government, without an army and without a functionary class, into a centralized government, provided with an irresistible army and a body of office-holders accustomed to ruling." What wonder the life of the Second Republic was a short and unhappy one!

By December, 1848, the new Constitution had been proclaimed, and France was in the throes of a presidential election. Instantly there came on the scene a man who was destined to stand in the center of the politics of Europe for two and twenty years, then to disappear amid a great national catastrophe.

Louis Napoleon Bonaparte, born in 1808, was the son of Louis, the brother of Napoleon I, who from 1806 to 1810 had been King of Holland. He, with the rest of the Bonaparte family, following 1814, had spent his life in various forms of exile. His branch of the family had had a decent private fortune, and young Louis Napoleon was brought up partly in Switzerland and partly in South Germany. There, it is said, he acquired a slight German accent which he never wholly lost. His ambitious mother did not cease to fill him with the consciousness that he was the heir to a great potential heritage. "With your name," she would say, "you will always count for something, whether in the Old World of Europe or in the New."

In 1832 there died in Austria the unfortunate Duke of Reichstadt, "Napoleon II," son of Napoleon I and Maria Louisa. The passing of this poor youth, "the Eaglet," left Louis Napoleon the best claimant in the family to the Bonapartist heritage. Henceforth he began to take himself very seriously, to gather up the loose threads of old Bonapartist plots and conspiracies, and to begin a literary progapanda in favor of a new "Empire" as the true solution for the political ills of France. He appeared to be a hopeless visionary, and the July Monarchists did not regard him as in any way dangerous, until suddenly he appeared in Strasbourg in 1836 and made a desperate

EARLY LIFE OF LOUIS NAPOLEON

attempt to seduce the garrison. He was arrested, placed on a ship bound for America, and released in New York in April (1837); but in August he slipped back to Switzerland. Later he spent much time in London. The disgust already developing against Louis-Philippe's régime prevented this pretender's claims from perishing under sheer ridicule. He gathered a certain number of ardent friends. "Would you believe it," the bluff old Duke of Wellington wrote of him, "this young man will not have it said he is not going to be Emperor of the French! His chief thoughts are of what he will do 'when he comes to the throne.'" In 1839 he published a book, "Napoleonic Ideas," to justify his hopes and propaganda. This book "a curious mixture of Bonapartism, socialism, and pacifism," represented Napoleon I absurdly enough as the supreme champion of French liberty, having been entrusted by the people with the task of protecting their freedom against reactionaries.

In 1840 Louis Napoleon strove once again to seize the throne. His attempt this time was by means of a small "filibustering" expedition across the Channel to Boulogne. The attempt failed even more abjectly than the one at Strasbourg. Its leader was held prisoner in the fortress of Ham, but in 1846 he escaped thence in a somewhat cheap-novel manner, and got back to London. There he remained two years more, still in good countenance, dreaming dreams and seeing visions. "Though fortune has twice betrayed me," he would say, "yet my destiny will none the less surely be fulfilled. *I wait.*" In 1848 he waited no longer.

After the fall of the July Monarchy he promptly turned up in France. He had influence enough, thanks to the awakening of Bonapartist memories, to get elected to the new Constituent Assembly. But he would not take his seat at first. He realized that the Assembly was likely to make mistakes and he did not wish to share the blame for them. He had thus no part in the notorious Days of June. However, in September he took a seat. When in October a law was proposed intended to make it impossible for him to run for the presidency, he made so poor a speech defending his position, that Thouret, who had made the hostile motion, contemptuously withdrew it on the ground that such a proviso was wholly unnecessary. Hardly two months later, however, this "pretender," whom shrewd politicians treated as little better than a dreamy fool, suddenly became a most formidable candidate for the presidency.

He had powerful backing. The great Church element, which had been under disfavor in Louis-Philippe's day, believed it saw in him a candidate who would put the Clericals once more into at least part of their power. The peasants were scared and angry at all that the Republican leaders had done or produced since February. The memories of the glories of the Empire had become increasingly gilded by distance. The peasants knew that above all things Napoleon I had stood for "law and order." They hated Cavaignac the "Democratic" candidate, and Ledru-Rollin the "Socialist" candidate. The Royalists of both persuasions resolved to vote Bonapartist: the pretender, they argued, would probably make a quick failure, then the Monarchists could return. The result was that nearly all the departments of France "went heavily," as Americans would say, for this obscure idealist and petty conspirator. Over 5,430,000 Frenchmen voted for Louis Napoleon; 1,450,000 for Cavaignac; only about 370,000 for Ledru-Rollin.

The new President promptly seized the reins of power. He took oath "to remain faithful to the democratic Republic . . . and to regard as enemies all who may attempt to change the form of the government." He then promptly showed his hand by naming ministers who were mostly ex-Orléanists and Catholics. The Republic was to find in him a peculiar "guardian" indeed.

From the moment Louis Napoleon took over the presidency (December 20, 1848) to the moment he overthrew the Constitution which he had sworn to defend, it was perfectly safe to predict that he would make some effort to harden into perma-

ADROIT POLICY OF THE PRESIDENT 463

nent power. Considering his Bonapartist blood and theories to ask anything else of him was unreasonable. The change, however, might have come less violently. It might also have been entirely thwarted had there been a sane and united opposition. As it was, almost everything played straight into the adroit adventurer's hands.

In May, 1849, the new "Legislative Assembly" had been elected. Anti-Republican reaction was in full swing. Over 500 of the 750 members were of one stripe or another of Monarchists. The Republican minority was not itself united; some were moderates, some "Reds." France thus faced this bizarre situation: the legal government was a Republic, but the President desired to transform the government into one form of monarchy; the majority of the deputies into still another form of monarchy. It was easy for the President and the majority to work together to make a return to radicalism impossible. The rub came when they attempted a constructive programme for the future.

The policy of Louis Napoleon from 1849 to 1851 was extraordinarily clever. He confirmed himself in the good graces of the Clericals by sending an army to Rome to overthrow the revolutionaries there, and to renew the temporal power of Pope Pius IX. He sat back while the Legislative Assembly, on its own initiative, passed laws gagging the press, suspending the right of public meeting, and finally, in May, 1850, ordering that hereafter three years' residence in a district was necessary in order to be a voter. This struck off the list over three million migratory workmen and laborers. The law was very unpopular, but the Assembly reaped all the blame. "I cannot understand how you, the offspring of universal suffrage," said a friend to Louis Napoleon, "can defend the restricted suffrage?" "You do not understand," replied the President; "I am preparing the ruin of the Assembly." "But you will perish with it," was the suggestion. "On the contrary," Louis Napoleon declared, "when the Assembly is hanging over the precipice I shall cut the rope!"

Very soon it became evident that the President's chief public asset was the fact that he had had a very famous uncle. "The name of Napoleon," he said in an address, "is itself a programme. It stands for order, authority, religion, and the welfare of the people in internal affairs; and in foreign affairs for the national dignity." Great reviews were held of the army, likewise public festivals, at which loud-voiced individuals (possibly not without monetary inspiration) would cry, "Long live Napoleon!" or even, "Long live the Emperor!" A general who ordered his men not to do this was cashiered. Around the President was soon gathering a group of short-pedigreed, bold, adroit, political and military adventurers, who saw every kind of personal profit in lifting a fellow adventurer into permanent power. The ministers and most of the public officials were completely controlled by the President. A change in the presidency would pretty plainly imply a change in all their well-paid comfortable offices. As Americans would assert, a great political "machine" was speedily in the making.

The immediate object of this machine was to insure Louis Napoleon's reëlection as President. His term would run out late in 1852. The Constitution forbade his reëlection. But the Assembly could change this arrangement by a two-thirds vote. The change was requested and was denied in a very untactful manner (July 19, 1851). The President could say that he had been chosen by the wills of the vast majority of all Frenchmen: very likely this same majority wished to reëlect him. Was the mere letter of a constitution, hastily drafted and wholly untested by experience, to set aside the deliberate will of the nation? When a political leader once abandons himself to such questionings all the rest is easy.

From 1848 to 1851 Louis Napoleon was thus taking every possible measure to transform his presidential chair into a throne. At his palace, the Élysée, he appealed to all kinds of interests. He enjoyed being called "Prince," "Highness," and "Monseigneur," but listened calmly when styled plain "Citizen." He flattered the clergy at every turn, distributed sausages and cigars to soldiers, chattered to sedate bourgeois about the need of "order in the streets," and then went out on tours in the provinces and was all friendliness and benignity to the peasants. But while the President thus pursued a course of wise modesty, his friends were acting for him. The men who erected the Second Empire were neither elegant noblemen, wild-eyed radicals, nor sword-clattering soldiers. They were men who might have felt in congenial company around a gambling table or manipulating unstable bonds and stocks. One of the President's prime counselors and men of action was his illegitimate half-brother, De Morny, "well fitted to keep secrets, to conduct plots, and to do the cruelest things in a jocund, offhand way." Another adventurer was a De Persigny who had changed his name, probably for good reasons, from Fialin. Another was Saint-Arnaud, a headlong, courageous soldier who had won a considerable fame in Algeria, where daredevil leadership counted for more against the Arabs than did textbook strategy. He also had changed his name, having once been Le Roy, and then again Florival, while he had been an actor in a small Paris theater. Saint-Arnaud was counted "an excellent administrator, a cultivated and agreeable companion, perfectly unscrupulous, and ready to assist in any scheme of what he considered *necessary* cruelty." There were other satellites of the President — De Maupas, Rouher, Magnan, etc. — all of about the same dusky character. To make Louis Napoleon autocrat meant for them, of course, incalculable personal gain.

The Constitution of 1848 had made it possible for a gang of greedy adventurers like these to conspire with the President to subvert the nation. The divisions and the utter political ineptitude of the Legislative Assembly made it possible for this conspiracy to proceed with very reasonable hopes of success.

By December, 1851, all was ready for springing the plot. The conspirators were satisfied (1) that public opinion in

France would acquiesce in the overthrow of the Assembly; (2) that the Republican movement was for the time being nearly dead; (3) that the army (carefully flattered and manipulated) could be relied upon to obey orders from "Napoleon."

To handle the army, on whose action in the last analysis everything depended, Saint-Arnaud was put in as Minister of War. Men realized something was coming. A prominent deputy declared, "When you see Saint-Arnaud a minister, say, 'Here is the *coup d'état*.'" Another congenial spirit was De Maupas, appointed now as prefect of the Paris police, a most ticklish office in the crisis. The President said to him, "Here I am on the edge of a ditch full of water. On the other side I see safety for the country. Will you be one of the men to help me across?" De Maupas was charmed at the responsibility.

However, up to the very last, Louis Napoleon hesitated to take the leap or the plunge: halting "between the desire to establish himself firmly in power without risking anything, and the fear of losing that power if he risked nothing." It was De Morny and the rest who at last overbore his doubtings, and forced him to take action. On the evening of December 1, 1851, the President was greeting casual guests at his reception at the Élysée. When the last visitor had departed, the chief magistrate of the Republic went into his smoking-room with De Morny, Saint-Arnaud, and a few others. Orders then flew fast, and everything moved like clock-work. A time schedule had been drawn up, adjusted down to minutes: at such a fixed time certain obnoxious generals were to be arrested; at such a time troops were to assume given positions; at such a time every printing-office in Paris was to be surrounded. The plan, in short, involved the arrest of practically every man in Paris prominent in politics since February, 1848, saving only the President's sworn myrmidons.

The execution of the *coup* was a masterpiece. Gendarmes seized the Government printing-office. Proclamations were set up, but the copy for each split into such short sections that no

THE CONSPIRACY

compositor could get an idea of the entire document. When dawn broke on December 2, the Parisians found the soldiers patrolling the streets and the walls placarded with the President's manifestoes. The Assembly was declared dissolved, universal suffrage was restored, and a plebiscite was ordered to be held very shortly to determine the future constitution. Two regiments of regulars held the "Legislative Palace," and soon the news spread that practically all the leaders of the deputies, Royalists, Republicans, and "Reds" alike, were safe in the Mazas Prison.[1] A wholesale arrest of journalists and unofficial agitators was going on. The President's aim was of course to deprive all the elements that might resist the coup of any possible leaders.

However, it was impossible to seize all the deputies. About two hundred of them made their way to the "Mairie" of the Tenth Arrondissement of Paris. Here they hastily organized, declared the President deposed for treason, and announced that the Assembly was still in lawful session. But theirs was merely so much empty thunder. De Maupas sent General Forney to break up the gathering, and the end of this despairing session was the departure of these last supporters of the Constitution marching away to prison between two lines of soldiers.

There was one last recourse. Victor Hugo, the famous author, Jules Favre, and other prominent Liberals tried it. The Faubourg Saint-Antoine was still the hotbed of radicalism. At the summons of the Liberals a number of the old radical fighters took up arms. Barricades rose on the evening of the 3d; but not until the 4th was there any serious bloodshed. Then Saint-Arnaud drove his troops over the barricades, and used grapeshot pitilessly even upon unarmed spectators. The resistance, that had been too much for Charles X and Louis-Philippe, and

[1] The imprisoned deputies, to get food, ordered in a luncheon from a neighboring restaurant. There were very few drinking-glasses. Royalist and radical deputies drank together. "Equality and fraternity!" cried a conservative nobleman, passing his tumbler to a "Red" fellow captive. "Ah!" was the answer, "but not liberty!"

which had almost baffled Cavaignac in 1848, had been snuffed out now by the regulars. Paris was firmly in the hands of the nephew of the Corsican.

Paris was won: but Paris was not the whole of France. As the news of the *Coup d'État* spread, there were serious uprisings in several centers of democratic sympathies; especially in the South Country and around Marseilles there was resistance which taxed the local gendarmerie. De Morny, who had been appointed Minister of the Interior the moment his half-brother seized Paris, crushed these demonstrations with an iron hand. The Bonapartists exaggerated the amount of disturbance in order to pose before the bourgeois and well-to-do peasants as "saviors of the country" from general upheaval and ruin. De Morny authorized his departmental prefects to replace all mayors, schoolmasters, and local justices, who were in any sense unreliable. Suspected persons were to be arrested instantly. On December 6 he ordered that no newspaper could appear unless one of his trusted prefects had first seen the proofs. "The Administration," De Morny proclaimed, "needed all its *moral* force to accomplish its work of regeneration and salvation." And on the 8th, he ordered wholesale arrests, as convicts and criminals at common law, of "all those rascally members of secret societies and unrecognized political associations."

Under these circumstances, bewildered, fed only with absolutely censored, and often with deliberately perverted, information, with all free agencies of opinion enchained, or at least intimidated by the military, what possible chance was there for a proper expression of national judgment when the plebiscite was held on December 20, 1851? There was martial law in 32 departments, while 26,642 persons had been arrested, and these victims were being tried by special tribunals acting without a jury. The people were asked whether they were willing to allow Louis Napoleon to draw up a new constitution. No alternative was presented. If a majority had been registered against the President, he ought logically to have retired from office and resigned the administration to sheer anarchy. De Morny used all the machinery of the Government to "insure the free and sincere expression of the will of the nation," and to insure that it expressed itself in one particular way. Every kind of expedient was to be used by the public officials "in the smallest hamlets" to get a favorable vote. "Liberty of conscience" was granted, De Morny wrote to the departmental prefects, "*but the resolute and consistent use of every allowable means of influence and persuasion is what I expect of you.*"

Such eminently practical methods produced results. Choosing between Louis Napoleon and anarchy, the French nation chose Louis Napoleon. There were cast in his favor 7,481,000 votes: 647,000 against him.[1] He promptly proclaimed himself "President for ten years," with almost autocratic powers and with a legislature entirely at his mercy. Few were greatly interested in this last phase of the "Republic" and of its "Prince President." All knew what was speedily to come.

To clear the way for the final step, De Morny, who never flinched from "dirty work," hastened the judicial forces in which prominent radicals were hurried before rigid tribunals and finally before a special Court of Justice — a kind of reversed Revolutionary Tribunal to deal summarily with political offenders. "The number of guilty persons and the fear of public strife," said De Morny in a circular, "did not admit of acting otherwise." All in all, well over 20,000 such cases found their way into these special courts. There was little to fear from the old conservatives: they were soon released. With the Republicans and even with moderate Liberals it was different. Of these 3000 were imprisoned in France, about 10,000 were exiled to Algeria, and about 6000 were allowed to live at home under police "supervision." But a very great number more, including

---

[1] It was, of course, alleged that these returns were "cooked" by the Government, but it cannot be denied that a very large majority of the votes were cast for the Bonapartists. Various footings of the election returns differ considerably, although they all agree in the general effect.

some of the most distinguished men in the nation, were in exile in England, Belgium, or Switzerland. As George Sand wrote in 1852, "When you go into the provinces and see how crushed is the spirit, you must bear in mind all the force [of public opinion] lay in a few men — now in prison, dead, or banished."

On March 29, 1852, the Prince-President solemnly proclaimed the new Constitution, announcing grandiloquently, "The dictatorship entrusted to me by the people terminates to-day." It might well terminate. A higher title than "Dictator" was awaiting him. When he toured through France he was received literally with royal honors. He made speeches clearly indicating he was soon to be a monarch, and promising how excellent would be his rule. Many conservatives had feared he would imitate his uncle and plunge France into dangerous wars. He strove hard to reassure them. At Bordeaux he made his famous statement, "The Empire means peace." Then came the climax. The "Senate," newly created by the new Constitution, proceeded to pass a decree to the effect that France was an Empire and that "Napoleon III was Emperor of the French." Again there was the inevitable plebiscite (November 21, 1852). The radicals were crushed and without heart. There was no organized opposition: 7,824,000 Frenchmen voted "Yes" to the question of the enthronement of the Bonapartist; 253,000 were allowed to be counted for "No." On December 2, 1852, the anniversary of Austerlitz and of the *Coup d'État*, "Napoleon III" became hereditary Emperor, and took to himself all the splendid trappings of French autocracy. And so the circle from monarchy to monarchy was closed.

Thus was completed one of the most remarkable personal successes in history. A man who a very few years earlier had been (to quote Queen Victoria's own words) "in exile, poor and unthought of," was now practically the autocrat of what was then counted the most wealthy and powerful country in Continental Europe.

Louis Napoleon was, during the next ten years, to become the most commanding figure in Europe, filling men's thoughts and imaginations to an extent the present age can hardly realize. But all through his days of greatness the memory of the treachery and brutality of the *Coup d'État* was to cling to him and from their exile implacable enemies were to brand him as "Napoleon the Little" and "the Pinchbeck Napoleon." In 1870 the world was to learn that these names were justified.

CHAPTER XXII
NAPOLEON THE LITTLE: HIS PROSPERITY AND DECADENCE

ONCE again a Bonaparte was in the Tuileries. But he was far from being a resolute, egotistical "little corporal." With all his sins, and they were many, Napoleon III was not without noble ambitions and humanitarian impulses. He desired to have power partly at least because he was genuinely persuaded that he could give France a good fortune and a happiness impossible under Bourbon, Orléanist, or any type of Republic. He was above all things a dreamer, and many of his dreams were worthy. His portraits show him with his clear blue eyes always gazing neither downward nor forward, but *upward*, as if in a constant reverie. His air was frequently melancholic, his personal actions usually kindly and benevolent. The man who turned Saint-Arnaud and his Janizaries loose in the Paris streets was by no means impervious when brought face to face himself with human suffering. It was his sight of the vast numbers of wounded after the battle of Solferino which went far to induce him to make a speedy peace with Austria (1859). Whether he would ever have screwed his courage to the sticking point for the *Coup d'État*, had there been no De Morny and other like spirits close at hand, is something that can never be told.

Napoleon III had boasted much of playing the part of the champion of the people. He, or his advisers, took peculiar pains that the French nation should not choose any other champions. The Constitution of 1852, under which the Second Empire was governed until 1860, was a "constitution" only because that word was written near the head of the document. Grim Czar Nicholas I, Autocrat of all the Russias, hardly exercised more complete power than his "great and good friend," [1] "the Emperor of the French."

[1] This was the title Nicholas used toward Napoleon III. The latter was

THE LEGISLATIVE BODY

The "Man of Destiny" did not, indeed, endeavor to govern without the forms of a limited monarchy. On the contrary, there was seldom a time when so much was said about "popular sovereignty" and "consulting the national will." But special care had been taken by the authors of the Constitution of 1852 that the "national will" should always coincide with the Emperor's. In his own right the powers of the Emperor were vast. He declared war, signed treaties, and appointed and dismissed all public officials. The ministers of the great departments of state were the mere creatures of his pleasure. He alone could propose new laws. Naturally, therefore, his power of sanctioning them after passage and of giving them validity by promulgation completed his grip on all legislation. The actual bills for the legislature were drafted by the Council of State (named by the Emperor), and if the feeble legislature mustered courage to make any amendments, the Council could advise the Emperor whether to accept or reject them.

The regular "Legislative Body" (*Corps législatif*) consisted of 261 deputies, elected by popular vote for a term of six years. It was completely under the rein and curb of the Emperor. It met at his summons, he could adjourn it and dissolve it. He named its president and vice-president. It could consider no bill except what was proposed by the imperial ministers, except with the special consent of the Council of State. The sessions were indeed public in that auditors were allowed in a gallery, but nothing of the debates could be published, beyond a very summary official abstract prepared by the president of the body, himself of course the Emperor's nominee and obligated to suppress any remark unwelcome to the Government. The deputies were supposed to vote the appropriation bills (budget), but if the Government desired, it could always get funds for an object by shifting them from one account to another. The deputies, in

extremely incensed because the Czar would not write to him as "my Brother." The crowned heads of Europe generally looked on Napoleon III as an unwelcome upstart with no claims to social equality.

short, did not in any real sense possess the decisive power of the purse.

In higher honor than the Legislative Body was the new "Senate" of 150 members, some sitting in "their own right," — admirals, marshals, cardinals, — the rest named for life by the Emperor. They examined the laws passed by the deputies, and no measure could be promulgated until they had given approval. Thus theoretically they had a kind of veto power, but of course they in turn were completely at the Emperor's disposal. If there were any matters in the Government not adjusted by the Constitution, they could promulgate the necessary laws — thereby practically amending the Constitution. Finally, it should be said, this very self-important body met in secret, another aid to manipulation by its lord and master.

Much was always being said by Napoleon III about the "privileges" of being a voter in France. These often-flattered voters, however, found little left to their discretion. The Government undertook to "enlighten them" (to use an official formula) how to cast their ballots. "Official candidates" favored by the Emperor were announced. Every public functionary was obliged to work for their election. Their appeals and proclamations were printed on the official white paper.[1] The departmental prefects distributed ballots for the favored candidates, and on a thousand pretexts could repress the appeals and meetings of the Opposition candidates. Ballot boxes were solely in the custody of Government officials, and very strange things doubtless happened while depositing and counting the vote.

Nominally there was no press censorship. In practice it was nigh impossible to subject the Government to real criticism. A heavy deposit (50,000 francs [$10,000] for a paper in Paris) had to be made for the good behavior of a journal. Press cases were tried in special courts without a jury. If a paper displeased the Government, it might be "warned." If there was a second warn-

[1] In France only Government placards and notices could be posted on *white* paper: all private appeals and pronunciamentoes had to be on colored paper.

ing, the paper might be suppressed outright. It was an offense to publish "false news"; and since to err in trivial matters is not an unknown newspaper error, almost any unwelcome journal could be prosecuted out of existence. The administration of these laws was often left to local officials anxious to curry favor at Paris, by showing themselves busy prosecutors. Some of the "warnings" were for utterly comical reasons; for example, two papers were admonished for printing a discussion of the value of certain chemical manures "because this can only bring about indecision in the minds of the purchasers." [1]

Never in modern France had the country been more infested with spies, "agents of police," and all the despicable small-fry of oppressive officialdom: making arbitrary arrests everywhere, and often selecting their victims out of sheer caprice. The most innocent expressions were enough to bring persons to the lockup. At Tours a woman remarked, "The grape blight is coming again." She was seized and the prefect of the department himself threatened her with life imprisonment "if she spread any more bad news."

Education was, of course, completely in the clutches of the new Government. Instructors of all classes had to take oath to the Emperor or be dismissed, and consequently many honorably resigned. History and philosophy were discouraged as studies; they might lead to dangerous political discussions and "discontent." The Minister of Education (Fortoul) undertook to reduce all the teaching in France to an automatic lifeless system, and issued the oft-quoted order that professors were to shave their mustaches "that they might drop from their appearance as well as from their manners the last vestiges of anarchy." [2]

[1] More famous even is the case of the paper which reported a speech by Napoleon III which "several times evoked cries of 'long live the Emperor!'" The paper was promptly "warned" because "this doubtful expression is unsuitable in the presence of the wild enthusiasm which the Emperor's words excited."

[2] At that time the wearing of a mustache or beard was sometimes regarded as a sign favoring Republican or radical theories. This notwithstanding that Napoleon III wore his well-known "imperial" goatee.

Under these circumstances the question, of course, is, "How could the French nation, liberty-loving, keenly appreciative of wrongs and shams, and highly intelligent, endure this régime? The first answer is that the measures of repression made any kind of resistance highly difficult. But in any case Napoleon III had three great assets: (1) The army was his. The soldiers were delighted to obey the man who promised to imitate the traditions of his mighty uncle, and who flattered and pampered them at every turn. (2) The run of the bourgeois were his. They asked only for law and order, and for steady material prosperity. The Second Empire undertook to provide them with these. (3) The clergy were at first devotedly on the side of Napoleon III. The Clericals had hated Louis-Philippe's régime. They had more or less welcomed the Second Republic. Now the Second Empire promised them honor and influence; while political conditions in Italy were such that Pope Pius IX might at any time need the support of French bayonets. In return the Clericals praised and supported the imperial régime, and (most valuable help of all) the parish priests often mustered their docile peasants down to the ballot places to vote for the "official candidates." Napoleon III was always hated by the industrial element in Paris and other sizable cities. He was irreconcilably opposed by most of the intellectual and literary leaders of the nation. But bayonets and ballots were what for the moment counted. For not a few years the Emperor could defy all mutterings of opposition.

Nevertheless, Napoleon III and the eager spirits around him never deceived themselves into believing that they were firmly rooted in power, and could remain in the Tuileries if once they became highly unpopular. To attract and retain popular imagination there must be wars, victorious, of course, and as bloodless and inexpensive as possible, but adding to the "glory" of the Napoleonic name. To satisfy the bourgeois there must also be a steady promotion of railways, steamships, commerce, etc. To conciliate the hostile industrialists, measures must be

A COURT OF PARVENUS

taken for the benefit of the working-men. The Emperor, in short, set out to play the benevolent despot, and it must be admitted that his intentions were good. He intended to make the Second Empire justify itself by the vast and genuine benefits it conferred upon France.[1]

Unfortunately, to be a successful despot one must have efficient helpers: men of probity, capacity, and self-respect. But the *Coup d'État* had made it impossible for Napoleon III ever to command the best brains of France. The men who should have been in his ministries were in exile, or at least muttering helplessly in private life. In their stead were the personages who had managed the deed of the 2d of December, and of course many other spirits like them. It was the time for every broken-down soldier of fortune, for every nobleman of tarnished title, for every reckless promoter who seemed nearest home when he leaned over the roulette wheel, to flock to Paris from all Europe and offer his "services" to the Emperor or his ministers.[2] Napoleon III created a magnificent and glittering court, an elegant nineteenth-century counterpart of the splendors of Louis XIV, but "it was composed of men and women all more or less adventurers. It was the court of the *nouveaux riches* and of a mushroom aristocracy. There were prizes to be won, and pleasures to be enjoyed, and it was 'like as in the days of Noah, until the flood came and swept them all away.'"

With such coadjutors it is perhaps a testimony to the ability of the Emperor that he was able to hold his throne eighteen years, and that the first half of this reign was on the whole a great outward success. Europe was in ferment from 1848 onward. Italy and Germany were painfully achieving their national unity. The huge conglomerate of the Austro-Hungarian domin-

---

[1] See note, pp. 494–495.

[2] It was well said that the revived imperialism of Louis Napoleon was not, like the Old Monarchy, a *cause* (to be fought and died for), but to most of its adherents, a *speculation*. They had to be attracted and held by direct hopes of personal gain: not by any appeal to their patriotism or personal fealty — rotten foundations for any government!

ions, which young Franz Josef was already ruling, was in unhappy labor. Russia was reaching out her iron hand once more toward Constantinople and the rest of the heritage of "the Sick Man of Europe." Foreign complications could hardly be avoided even had Napoleon III so desired, and how could he be a Napoleon and wish to avoid foreign complications? In the French army, fired now by careful references to the memories of Lodi and Jena, he had a fighting instrument which seemed the best in Europe until sudden collision with Von Moltke's new war-machine taught men otherwise. It is not fair to say that the Second Empire deliberately sought wars of aggrandizement as did the Pan-Germans in 1914. It is fair to say that the Emperor seemed well content when Russia and Austria in their turn took measures which enabled him to declare that "the struggle was forced upon him." Despite the famous promise, "The Empire is peace," Napoleon had to go to war with Russia in 1854, and with Austria in 1859. He won both of these wars, if not overwhelmingly, at least in a manner which increased his prestige, his hold upon France, and his claim to be the first figure in Europe.

It is no purpose of this volume to untangle the diplomatic mazes in which Europe was involved from 1848 down through 1870, and in which Napoleon III and his foreign ministers were tangled for their full share. It is needful, however, to see how his foreign policy reacted upon the prosperity and destinies of the great French people which had placed itself, somewhat reluctantly, indeed, under his leadership. In the first of his wars Napoleon III had the alliance of the old national enemy, England, against Russia. The Crimean War (1854-56) was not entered upon by France against Czar Nicholas I for precisely the same reason as by the British. The latter were fearful that the dreaded Muscovite was about to seize Constantinople as the outer door to Egypt and India. The French had long regarded themselves as the protectors of the *Latin* Christians of the much distracted Turkish Empire, and as the preferred Christian

Power in all the Sultan's dominions. Nicholas was thrusting forward the claims of the *Greek* Christians as against those of their very uncordial brethren of the West, and in the Levant was certainly overshadowing all other non-Moslem nations by his constant interference in Turkish affairs. The personal relations of the Czar and the Emperor were also very cold. Nicholas regarded Napoleon as a mere upstart with only fictitious claims to pose as a fellow monarch. The Crimean War could have been avoided in 1854, alike by England and France, if only they had been willing to treat with the Czar in a conciliatory spirit for the liquidation of the nigh-bankrupt Ottoman Empire. It is now generally agreed that the Turks were not worth saving, and that their preservation was therefore little short of a crime. On the other hand, Russian policy was certainly aggressive, brutal, and seemingly was menacing to the Western Powers. The blame is therefore fairly distributed.

This war lasted two years (1854–56). As is well known, the superior Anglo-French navies held the Russian squadrons in close blockade. The Czar's armies soon evacuated the Balkan States, and the struggle practically resolved itself into the prolonged and desperate siege of Sebastopol, the chief fortress in the Crimean peninsula. This siege began in October, 1854. The stronghold held out until September, 1855. The story of the valor of attackers and defenders — of the Alma, Balaklava, Inkermann, and the storming of the Malakhoff and the Redan, can be left to other books. As for the French part in the struggle, it is fair to say that if the English supplied the greater part of the necessary shipping for the war, the French land contingent at the siege was always the larger, and therefore did proportionately more than the English to win the open battles, repulse the sorties, and finally to force the Russians to evacuate the city. The French troops were said to have been more resourceful than the British in meeting the awful cold and hardships of the Russian winter. Their original commander had been Saint-Arnaud of *Coup d'État* fame, but he died of cholera almost before the siege was begun, and Canrobert and Pélissier carried the struggle through at last to military success.[1]

The bad roads of Southern Russia and the miserable administrative service of the Czar perhaps did more than French or British valor to bring about a victory for the Western Allies. Nicholas I had died a chagrined man in 1855. The hated parvenu and the despised English were defeating him. His successor, Alexander II, was fain to make peace, albeit on decidedly humiliating terms.

In March and April, 1856, Napoleon III had the congenial honor of entertaining the leading diplomats of Europe at the once famous Congress of Paris, which "settled" the ever unsettled Eastern Question. With the precise terms of this treaty we need not deal: enough that Turkey was given a new lease of life under the fostering protection of Britain and France, and that Russia was obliged to renounce most of her claims to meddle in Turkish affairs and even the right to keep warships on the Black Sea. The Emperor played a great part at this conference. He seemed laying the law down to obedient Europe. He dictated a settlement of the problems of Roumania that was very unwelcome to Austria. He allowed the delicate question of the oppression of Italy, and of the misgovernment of the Austro-Italian provinces, a question even more distasteful to the Hapsburgs, to be raised by Cavour, the prime minister of Sardinia. The princes of Europe recognized his great power and ceased to treat him as an upstart. The members of his family were "taken in" to the various royal houses. French pride was immensely flattered by seeing their ruler — almost as in the days of Louis XIV — treated as the first sovereign of Europe. The Crimean War, in short, had been neither very sanguinary nor very expensive and it had paid Napoleon III excellent dividends.

[1] Most Americans read of the Crimean War only in English narratives. These inevitably fail to accent the fact that the French did the lion's share of the fighting and won corresponding right to credit for the victory.

NAPOLEON MARRIES EUGÉNIE

So within five years after the *Coup d'État* the Second Empire was at its height. Paris was the center of wealth, elegance, and fashion. Never had all the questionable amusements of the glittering capital been so attractive, never had the famous city been so "gay." It was a time of sudden prosperity and corresponding profusion. If Napoleon's ministers and protégés were often adventurers, they were most interesting adventurers, who lived most admirably by their wits. The imperial court had needed a mistress in 1852. The Emperor's advisers cast eyes on a Hohenzollern princess [1] and one or two other high-born eligibles; but before 1856 the old dynasties had no great ambition to mate up with a Bonaparte. Napoleon, therefore, married Eugénie de Montijo (January 29, 1853), a young Spanish lady of fairly noble descent, whose family had been especially faithful to the cause of Joseph Bonaparte when he posed as King of Spain. The new Empress was "tall, fair and graceful, with hair like one of Titian's beauties." She made an admirable arbitress of costume and etiquette, to be copied by every robe-maker and in every drawing-room in Europe. Her personal character seems to have been on the whole benevolent and worthy, but her political views were largely limited to an intense partisanship with everything friendly to the Church and a corresponding dislike of everything anti-Clerical or Protestant. Her influence was against the Italian patriots because they were anti-Papal, and against Prussia chiefly, it would seem, because Prussians were Lutherans. On the whole, therefore, she tended to embroil her husband with elements he needed as his friends.

While the Crimean War was raging, Queen Victoria and the Prince-Consort Albert visited their mighty ally at Boulogne. The Prince was a shrewd observer and in his memoranda gave interesting sidelights upon the Second Empire and its master.

[1] She was sister to the Prince of Hohenzollern, whose candidacy for the throne of Spain in 1870 precipitated the Franco-Prussian War. Royal marriages have seldom kept the peace, but it is worth speculating, whether if Napoleon had married this princess the struggle of 1870 would have occurred — at least in the form it actually did.

"The gentlemen composing the Emperor's *entourage*," wrote the Prince, "are not distinguished by birth, manners, or education. The tone [of the circle] is rather that of a garrison, with a good deal of smoking. . . . Upon the whole, my impression is that neither in home nor in foreign politics would the Emperor take any violent steps, but that he appears in distress for means of governing and is obliged to look about him from day to day. Having deprived the people of any active participation in the government, and reduced them to mere spectators, they grow impatient, like a crowd at a display of fireworks, whenever there is any cessation of the display."

This was in 1854. In 1855 Napoleon and Eugénie made a return visit to England, and were received with magnificent hospitality at Windsor, passing through London "where seven years before he [the Emperor] was wont to stroll with his faithful dog at his heels to the news-vendor's stall by the Burlington Arcade to get the latest news." In 1856 came, of course, the Congress of Paris, and higher glories still. A little son had just been born to the imperial couple, the promise seemingly of a long and prosperous dynasty. The Heir Presumptive of Prussia came to accept the Emperor's bounty for a brief visit. With the Prussian suite was a modest officer, Major von Moltke. He had not yet risen to fame but, like Prince Albert, was well able to see under the surface. His letters home to Germany praised many things in the Second Empire, and dwelt much on Napoleon's good-humor and benevolence, but declared: "He suffers from the want of men of ability to uphold him. He cannot make use of men of independent character, who insist on having their own notions, as the direction of affairs of state must be concentrated in his hands." Von Moltke commends the Emperor, however, for not forgetting that "the French people like to see their sovereigns surrounded by a brilliant court."

So the Congress of Paris came and went: and Napoleon drifted on to his second great war — with Austria in behalf of

THE WAR WITH AUSTRIA

Italian freedom. The Emperor had been in his youth a member of a secret society for the liberation of Italy from the Austrian yoke. His generous impulses made him sympathize with the bitter complaints arising from the peninsula at the oppressions by the Hapsburgs and by the lesser princes, their dependents. His own political theories, about the right of every nation to settle its own destinies by plebiscites, inclined him also to listen favorably to the pleas of Cavour, the very astute prime minister of Sardinia-Piedmont,[1] that France should intervene in Italian affairs and should at least drive the Austrians out of Lombardy and Venetia.

Again we must turn aside from the highly interesting diplomatic story. In 1858 Napoleon made a secret alliance with Cavour and Victor Emmanuel to aid them to drive the Austrians from Italian soil. In return for great additions to his territory within the peninsula, Victor Emmanuel would cede to France his French-speaking districts of Savoy and Nice. In 1859, after a most exciting diplomatic flurry, Cavour maneuvered Austria into declaring war upon Piedmont, under circumstances which permitted Napoleon to say he was merely coming to the rescue of a weak ally. This Italian war, however, was not universally popular in France. Behind the Austrian stood the Pope fearful for his "temporal power"; consequently the Empress and the French clericals discouraged the whole undertaking. The bourgeois element too disliked the military uncertainties and the war taxation. Nevertheless Napoleon threw a considerable army into Northern Italy. Neither the Austrian nor the French generals displayed the least real capacity as strategists, but the French infantry were incomparably the better fighters, and under blundering leadership they carried the Tricolor gallantly through the two great victories, first of Magenta and soon after that of Solferino.

[1] Victor Emmanuel, King of Sardinia-Piedmont, the northwest portion of Italy, alone of all the Italian dynasts had resisted the pressure of Austria to maintain a harsh autocracy, and had allowed his people a liberal constitution.

The Austrians, nevertheless, were not yet crushed. There was danger of an unfriendly move on the Rhine by Prussia. The Clericals in France were anxious and angry. Therefore, leaving his Piedmontese ally somewhat shabbily in the lurch, Napoleon concluded peace with Franz Josef very suddenly at Villa Franca (July 11, 1859). Lombardy alone was to be ceded to Sardinia-Piedmont, and Venetia was still to lie in Austrian bondage. Since he had not completed his part of the bargain, the Emperor did not now insist on getting Savoy and Nice; but when a little later (1859–60) the Central and South Italian States themselves expelled their local "grand dukes" or papal legates, and united under Victor Emmanuel as "King of Italy," Napoleon exacted the promised districts as his price for closing his ears to the cries of the outraged Clericals at the direful curtailing of the territories of the Pope. So France gained two new departments, made from Savoy in the Alps, and also a fair city (Nice) on the Riviera, but at the expense of some decidedly ungracious bargaining on the part of her Emperor. The Italian war left Napoleon with perhaps greater military prestige than ever, but at the cost of the good-will of the Clericals, while in turn the Italians did not love him. They felt that he had left them in the lurch as to Venetia, and then had exacted an unfair price for letting them consolidate most of the rest of their country without his intervention.

Nevertheless in 1859 the glory of the Second Empire was probably at its height. France was remarkably prosperous. Great public works were undertaken to win the industrial classes. Railroads were developed. Huge stock companies were floated with more or less Government patronage. Paris had been systematically rebuilt with wide, stately boulevards by Baron Haussmann. The expense was vast, but the effect was magnificent. Paris became somewhat less picturesque, but was now more clearly than ever the superb, clean, modern capital. Another object was also gained. The wide, straight avenues could hereafter be easily swept by artillery. The elimination of the

ATTEMPTS TO CONCILIATE THE LIBERALS

crooked, mediæval-looking streets made barricade fighting a hundred per cent harder.

After 1859 it was evident that the Pope was likely to lose his entire temporal power in Rome and become, as indeed happened in 1870, the "prisoner of the Vatican." For this result the Clericals blamed Napoleon, and their support cooled. To replace them he began to favor the long-despised Liberals.

The Republicans had been suppressed with an iron hand. Prior to 1857 they had not had a single representative in the entire body of deputies. In 1857 and down to 1863 they had only five — "The Five" — chosen by districts in Paris and Lyons which even the police and the official candidates could not entirely coerce. The two brands of Royalists had been a little less persecuted, but were about equally helpless. Mails and travelers' baggage had been regularly searched at the frontiers to prevent the incoming of anti-Bonapartist literature. Now, however, the pressure was a little released. In 1860 the official *Moniteur* was allowed to reprint the full debates in the Chamber. In 1861 measures were taken to have the items in the budget voted separately, with some real control by the deputies over the treasury. The Chamber was allowed to reply with an address to the speech from the throne. The press restrictions were also partially lifted. Very moderate criticisms of the Government were permitted. In 1863 there were elected 35 Opposition members to the deputies.[1] This was a very small fraction of the Chamber (set by the Constitution of 1851 at 251 members), but it involved real debates, and compelled the Government to defend itself in a parliamentary way against a genuine Opposition. In Paris only Opposition deputies were elected. This meant that Napoleon could not count on the loyalty of the nerve-center of France, a very dangerous situation in case for an instant he lost control of the army.

[1] Many of these were, indeed, Orléanists or regular old-line Bourbons, "Legitimists;" but they merged their issues in common hostility to Bonapartism, and called themselves the "Liberal Opposition."

However, having taken the first steps toward a liberal régime, it was impossible to tighten up again. In 1864 the Emperor strove to conciliate the industrialists by a law giving the workingmen a right to form labor unions (hitherto prohibited in deference to bourgeois interests), and also, of course, to "strike" to better their condition, a measure of the greatest importance for the future economic and social development of the country. Whatever popularity Napoleon III may, nevertheless, have gained by such a step was completely offset by the loss of prestige he brought on the Second Empire by his utterly disastrous and discreditable adventure in Mexico.

The "Man of Destiny" had watched the American Civil War with cynical interest. If the great Anglo-Saxon Republic could have been rent asunder and eternally weakened, there was an end to the Monroe Doctrine, and a delightful vista was opened in Latin America for every kind of imperialistic exploitation. Probably Napoleon III would have intervened in behalf of the Southern Confederacy had he been sure of the support of England, and also of French public opinion, which may not have understood all the issues in America, but which balked at spending blood and treasure to uphold a government founded on slavery.[1] But after American hands seemed firmly tied in 1862, the Emperor determined at least to interfere in Mexico. His intervention there was the beginning of the end of the Second Empire.

Once more we have a story familiar to Americans, and only indirectly concerning the life of the French people. Mexican finances were in their normal grievous disorder, and French, English, and Spanish banking interests brought about a joint intervention by their three nations to secure the payment of the debt. But soon it was evident that Napoleon intended a direct political occupation of the offending nation. England and

---

[1] It is alleged that Napoleon III told Southern sympathizers that he wished, indeed, to interfere in their behalf, but feared that if he did so there would be riots in the streets of Paris.

Spain hastily withdrew. A French army was sent up from Vera Cruz into the interior, and after some initial defeats took Mexico City (1863). The anti-Republican clericals in Mexico now played into Napoleon's hands. They caused a monarchy to be proclaimed and offered the "Empire of Mexico" to the Archduke Maximilian of Austria,[1] an amiable prince who knew nothing of Mexican problems, and who rashly trusted to the solemn promise of Napoleon to support him with French bayonets till his new Government was well settled. In 1864 Maximilian arrived in Mexico, but the Republicans continued their resistance. The French forces sent over were not large enough to conquer the country, and the whole expedition was so expensive that the French taxpayers began to become very vocal in the Chambers. Then in 1865 the Southern Confederacy collapsed. The United States sent stern "notes" to Paris about Mexico, the Monroe Doctrine had a most ominous resurrection, and an army of Northern veterans concentrated significantly in Texas. A desperate conflict with the now armed and victorious United States was the last thing Napoleon wanted. Despite his solemn promise to the Austrian Prince, in 1867 he withdrew the French troops from Mexico and left Maximilian to his fate. How the latter remained, resisted the Republicans, was taken, and then shot is one of the best-known stories of North American history.

The Mexican affair cost Napoleon a vast deal of money; it tied up French troops in America at a time when they were sorely needed to protect national interests in Europe; it ended with the disgraceful death of Maximilian, whose friends blamed Napoleon severely for luring him to his ruin; and, of course, it brought no "glory," but only an immense onus of failure at the end. By the time it was finished, the Second Empire had lost all the splendor which had followed the Congress of Paris, and was itself obviously drifting on the rocks.

Those rocks and quicksands were now clearly lying in the

[1] Brother of the Emperor Franz Josef, who died in 1916.

direction of Germany. In 1862 Bismarck became first minister of Prussia, while Von Moltke was building that great scientific war-machine which the world was soon to learn to know so well. It had been a serious blow in certain quarters to French pride when the bulk of Italy had become united in a single powerful kingdom. Now, as by successive steps Bismarck began erecting a great well-compacted German State directly across the Rhine, the anxiety and the injured feelings grew infinitely faster. In 1864 this astute minister of King William I had induced Austria to join with Prussia in a common attack on Denmark, which was duly overwhelmed by the two Great Powers and bereft of Schleswig-Holstein. It was patent enough that the two victors in this inglorious war were bound to quarrel over the supremacy of Germany. In the issue of that quarrel France had every possible interest. If Napoleon III announced his intention of aiding Austria, all Bismarck's schemes for making Prussia dominant in Central Europe would vanish in thin air, and never did that clever Junker use his great gifts of cajolery and insinuation to better advantage than in 1865, when he visited the Emperor at Biarritz, and in several confidential interviews talked Napoleon into promising neutrality in German affairs, in return for some utterly vague hopes, and repudiable half-promises of giving France additional territories west of the Rhine while Prussia adjusted matters with Austria.

Napoleon agreed to neutrality. He did not believe that either of the Germanic Powers would be victorious promptly. The result (he expected) would be a dragging, indecisive war, into which he could presently plunge as the irresistible arbiter. So he sat back, permitted Italy to make alliance with Prussia against Austria — and waited events.

Events came with a vengeance War was declared between Prussia and Austria on June 16, 1866. On July 3, seventeen days later, the power of Austria lay crushed and nigh helpless after the great battle of Sadowa (or Königgrätz). On August 23, the final Treaty of Prague was signed, and the war was over.

VAIN ANGER OF FRANCE

Austria had been obliged to resign all interest in German affairs and to cede Venetia to Italy. As for Prussia she annexed Hanover, Hesse-Cassel, Nassau, and other German States and proceeded to organize all but South Germany into the formidable North-German Confederation — very strictly under her own leadership. Prussia had thus increased her area nearly twenty-five per cent. She had increased her power and prestige in Europe infinitely more.

The news of the catastrophe of Sadowa was hardly less terrible in Paris than in Vienna. From the French standpoint the Emperor had committed a hideous mistake. He had watched a great aggressive military power spring up on the very boundaries of France, and had done absolutely nothing to prevent a vast national danger. In vain now he tried to remind Bismarck of his alleged promises of more territories for France — the Bavarian and Hessian lands west of the Rhine? — or (no creditable proposal) the permission to seize part of Belgium? Anything in short to save the shattered prestige of the Second Empire! Bismarck, more or less bluntly, refused to remember any of his fine words at Biarritz. He encouraged the Belgian proposition only enough so that he could let it leak out in 1870 to discredit France with England. He made it very plain that Prussia intended to organize Germany in her own way, and would snap her fingers at French intervention. Napoleon would willingly have considered going to war, but the Mexican adventure had tied up part of the army, while other regiments were in Rome protecting the Pope against the seizure of the Eternal City by the Italian patriots. Even with his whole forces consolidated, competent generals told the Emperor that he would still lack strength to attack Von Moltke's terrible new war-machine. In infinite anguish Napoleon resolved to keep the peace.

One last attempt he made to solace French pride by an annexation. The Grand Duchy of Luxembourg belonged to the King of Holland. The latter needed money and took no joy in this minor principality. In 1867 it was arranged to sell the little country to France.¹ Matters seemed almost completed, when suddenly Bismarck announced that he could not consent, and informed the King of Holland if he went ahead with the sale "public opinion" in Germany might force war. Of course the King dropped the matter at once. Napoleon had again been utterly rebuffed by the Prussian, and all Europe, and especially all France, knew it.

Between 1867 and 1870 the Second Empire enjoyed its Indian summer. France was still very prosperous. Commerce and industry showed gratifying gains. The great increase of wealth enabled the munificent patronage of the fine arts. Paris was more than ever the abode of comfort, luxury, and of all alluring forms of amusement and "wickedness." In 1867 the Emperor was the host to many of the crowned heads of Europe at the Great Universal Exposition, held now a second time in Paris.² But no one could conceal the fact that Napoleon III was losing prestige. He was suffering painfully from a disease of the bladder, and was unable to concentrate his attention on public affairs. The Mexican fiasco and the full consequences of the Prussian aggrandisement both came home to the French people in 1867. As Thiers, the veteran statesman, now again in politics, bitterly exclaimed, "There are no blunders left for us to make."

In 1868 a rising journalist, Henri Rochefort, dipped his pen in gall. In his organ, the *Lanterne*, he launched attacks like this: "I am a thorough Bonapartist: but I must be allowed to choose my hero in the dynasty. As a Bonapartist, *I prefer Napoleon II*. It is my right. He represents to me the ideal of the sovereign. No one can deny that he occupied the throne, because his successor was Napoleon III. What a reign, my friends, what a reign! No taxes! No war! No Civil List! Oh, yes, Napoleon II, I love and admire you without reserve!" Rochefort

¹ The inhabitants of Luxembourg seem to have been reasonably willing for the change.
² The first "Exposition" held in 1855 had also been a great success and an excellent advertisement for the prosperity of France in the early years of the Second Empire.

paid for this utterance with prosecution and exile; but the dissemination of this "scarlet pamphlet" could not be stopped. The Second Empire was being ruinously discredited.

Under these circumstances there was nothing left for the Emperor to do save to try to regain his popularity by increasing concessions to the Liberals. An attempt was made by the Government to create the "Democratic Empire." In 1868 the press laws were still further relaxed. Political meetings could be held if they were vouched for by seven responsible citizens. In 1869 there were still more ample concessions. After some discussion the Emperor granted ministerial responsibility. Hereafter the Chamber was to have real control. It could initiate laws, demand explanations of policy from the ministers, and control its own organization. The ministers were supposed to be responsible to the majority of the Chamber, although it was not until 1870 that this last step was put in practice. In this last stage the office of premier was accepted by Ollivier, the leader hitherto of the moderate Opposition, who now announced that he intended to govern according to strictly Liberal and parliamentary views. So again the wheel had turned. From Autocracy Napoleon III was swinging over to Limited Monarchy. He boasted in 1869 that he was founding at length a system of government "equally removed from reaction and from revolutionary theories"; and he appealed to the nation: "I can answer for *order:* help me to save *liberty!*"

Whether if there had been no foreign disaster the Second Empire would have lasted is at best doubtful. The memory of the crime of the *Coup d'État* clung around it like a poisoned Nessus shirt. The Republicans lifted their heads the moment the pressure of the police relaxed. In the elections for the new Chamber in May, 1869, the Government candidates had in all only 4,438,000 votes. The Opposition had 3,385,000. The city of Paris went against the Government by 231,000 votes to only 74,000. Fully ninety Opposition deputies were chosen.[1]

[1] Or 116 if some very lukewarm "Bonapartists" be taken into account.

On the 2d of December, 1869, the date of the seizure of power by Napoleon, the Republicans held a celebration in honor of the Frenchmen who had died in 1851 defending Republican liberties. A young advocate, Gambetta, appeared to defend those who were promptly accused of "insulting the Government." His speech smote heavily upon the defenders of the Bonapartist régime. "Listen, you who have for seventeen years been the absolute master of France. The thing that characterizes you best, because it proves your own remorse, is the fact you have never dared to say, 'We will place among the solemn festivals of France, this Second of December.' . . . Good! This anniversary we [Republicans] take to ourselves. We will observe it always, without fail, . . . the anniversary of our dead, until the day when the country having become once again master itself, shall impose on you the great expiation in the name of liberty, equality, and fraternity."

After the Liberal reforms of April, 1870, notwithstanding all this, Ollivier undertook to assure the Emperor of a "happy old age." To bolster up the prestige of the new Government, another referendum vote was held. France was asked to ballot on the proposition: "The nation approves of the Liberal reforms made in the Constitution since 1860, and ratifies the senatorial decree of April 20, 1870." As might be expected, a great majority was cast in favor of the Government. The question had been cleverly worded so as not to make the voters reply whether they really liked the Second Empire, but only whether they approved the moves toward liberalism: 7,358,000 voters replied, "Yes"; 1,571,000 "No." The Republicans denounced the whole scheme as a dishonest trick. For the moment, however, the Second Empire seemed to have been given a new sanction and a new lease of life. Very possibly this referendum actually contributed to bring on the final disaster, convincing Napoleon III (as Lebon wrote later) "that he still possessed the confidence of the country, and that a little *external* glory succeeding upon so many reverses, would restore his shaken authority."

IMPERFECT ARMY REFORMS 493

In 1869 had come the Emperor's last foreign sunshine. The Suez Canal (the work of a remarkable Frenchman, De Lesseps) had been completed. Napoleon himself could not go to Egypt to attend the opening, but Eugénie went on a man-of-war, to be the guest of honor of Khedive Ismaïl and to shine as the "bright particular star" of the fête along with the Emperor Franz Josef and very many other European royalties. The international horizon seemed fairly clear in 1869 and in 1870. France had apparently submitted to the consolidation of North Germany. No great issues appeared pending. Nevertheless all men knew there was serious tension. Frenchmen talked of "avenging Sadowa" as if it had been their own defeat. Prussians talked of the need of humbling "the hereditary enemy."

In France it was keenly realized by military men that all was not well with the army. The new Prussian organization had been an eye-opener. In 1866 a genuine attempt had been made in France to reorganize the military system. The term of army service had been too long. The troops were practically professional soldiers, not short-term conscripts. There was no adequate reserve. A law of 1855 had actually allowed the payment of a money commutation for army service, and most bourgeois were glad enough to hand over the cash and to save their sons from an irksome duty. Marshal Niel proposed universal service, but the Chamber of that year (1866) had refused to listen and the Emperor had declined to force the matter through. Finally certain imperfect reforms had been voted in 1868. Had they been effected, they would have given an army of 800,000 men. For the most part, however, they were still on paper in 1870, when the great crash came. France faced Prussia in that year with her old professional army, and with practically no efficient reserves or other trained organization behind it. It was easy to be wise after the event.

Nevertheless in 1870 as in 1914 the half of the year passed with the world appearing very peaceful. The policy of Ollivier, the new Liberal prime minister, was so pacifistic, that in January, 1870, he offered to reduce the size of the French army provided Prussia would do the same. Bismarck, who knew his own plottings, waved this well-meant proposal aside. Matters thus drifted calmly on until early summer. The Second Empire seemed in less danger of foundering than at any time since 1866. Europe had quieted down. Ollivier seemed resolved to let Prussianized Germany strictly alone. It was publicly said that the international horizon was singularly clear, and many diplomats departed for their vacations. Then suddenly the great gusts blew. On July 19, 1870, war existed between France and Prussia. On September 2 "Napoleon the Little" ceased to reign.

NOTE ON THE ECONOMIC AND MATERIAL PROGRESS OF FRANCE:
1852–1870

It is idle to deny that the Second Empire contributed much to the material betterment of the nation. In fact, it was incumbent on Napoleon III and his fellow adventurers to popularize their rule by improving the condition of the masses. The Emperor furthermore had an honest love of humanity — so long as that love did not conflict with his own aggrandizement. Many Government hospitals and convalescent homes were founded, and steps taken to establish a system of public physicians and free medicines. Self-help societies were encouraged, and the Government fostered benefit funds for the relief of old men and women; also for insurance against sickness and accidents; and in 1868 there was founded the "Prince Imperial's Fund" to advance to working-men the money wherewith to buy their own tools. The commercial treaty with Great Britain (1860) was much denounced by the manufacturing interests, but it certainly aided to reduce the cost of many essential articles for the poor. The establishment of the right of working-men to organize and to strike for better conditions has been mentioned. By one of those back-washes of reaction, which are so curious, the lawmakers of the Revolution had actually made organized "striking" a penal offense. All this was now changed.

Railroad-building was pushed with energy. There had been almost no railroads in France before 1842. There were only about 2100 miles of them in 1851. There were nearly 10,000 miles in 1870.

The magnificent reconstruction of Paris by Baron Haussmann has been explained. Besides the enormous and costly changes in the boulevards and avenues, there was a wholesale erection of new churches, hospitals, theaters, markets, barracks, etc., which added enormously to the magnificence of the capital. In addition to Paris, Lille, Lyons, Bordeaux, and Marseilles were proportionately beautified.

These great public undertakings, the stimulation of commerce and industry, etc., naturally produced a corresponding development in financial enterprises. The Crédit Foncier was founded in 1852 and the Crédit Lyonnais in 1865, to advance money to agriculturists, manufacturers, and merchants. These great establishments did much to add to the stability and prosperity of France. The Government deliberately increased the public debt to find money for its numerous undertakings, but it had no trouble in floating its bonds. In 1868 it required a loan of 400,000,000 francs ($80,000,000). There were no less than 830,000 subscribers, and they together offered 15,000,000,000 francs.

It was this wealth, accumulated between 1852 and 1870, that enabled France to recover so rapidly from the terrible maltreatment by Prussia.

Tested only from a materialistic standard the Second Empire deserved well of the nation; it was a tribute to the intelligence, moral qualities, and conscience of France that she refused to be drugged into contentment by the Bonapartist adventurers.

CHAPTER XXIII
THE CRUCIFIXION BY PRUSSIA: 1870-71

It was the misfortune of Napoleon III that his Government was so unstable that the least swing of the international weather vane could create a situation in which he must either engage in a capital war or see his throne put in jeopardy provided he did not avenge "the national honor." Firmly rooted governments can do many distasteful or unpopular things: but the Second Empire was not a firmly rooted government. Hence one of the main reasons for the crisis and *débâcle* of 1870.

Why Otto von Bismarck felt that his policy for German consolidation would be advantaged by a war with France is a matter solely for German history. And as for the detailed moves on the military chess-board which registered the downfall of the Second Empire and the agony of the nation it had led to disaster, these also are outside the scope of this book. We have only to see how the gang of cheerful incompetents whom Napoleon III called his ministers plunged their country into the war, and what were the physical and moral effects of a frightful calamity upon the French nation. Few modern countries (prior to 1914) had been more tried than was France in 1870-71, and that the nation could survive the crucifixion it then suffered, and become again an upstanding power in the world, is one of the best evidences possible that the stock of the Gallo-Roman, Frank and Northman, was still productive, worthy, and strong after very many centuries of momentous history.

In 1870 Ollivier was head of the Cabinet, but he necessarily had to leave diplomatic affairs largely to the Duc de Gramont, an exceedingly jingoistic and incautious foreign minister. There were no outstanding questions which seemed to promise direct trouble, but the whole international situation was still rather turbid. Things had not changed since 1869 when General Ducrot wrote: "We are alike bellicose and pacific. We cannot resign ourselves to accept freely the situation which we created by the enormous blunders we committed in 1866, and yet we cannot decide frankly upon war. Peace rests on too frail foundations to last. Prussia may adjourn its projects but will never renounce them. In this state of transition, of friction, and of defiances, is it not clear that at any instant an unforeseen incident can bring on a terrible crisis?"

The outline of what happened, of the events which played directly into the hands of Bismarck, master of unscrupulous intrigue, and of Von Moltke, master of the legions, stands somewhat as follows: The throne of Spain was vacant. Early in July it became known in Paris that the disposing faction at Madrid had offered the crown to Prince Leopold of Hohenzollern Sigmaringen, a kinsman of William I of Prussia. Instantly the Paris press blew up in a rage. Another insult from Prussia! A Hohenzollern south of the Pyrenees as well as just across the Rhine! Would the Government endure it? etc. There was an angry "interpellation" in the Chamber. On July 6, 1870, the Duc de Gramont, "in a tone of insolent provocation," told that body that it would destroy the balance of power in Europe if one of the great kingdoms put a prince on the throne of Charles V, and in that case "France would discharge her duty without hesitation and without weakness."

Leopold of Hohenzollern promptly withdrew his candidature. King William of Prussia was not anxious for war. He did nothing to reply to the fiery utterance of De Gramont; but the latter was resolved on a public rebuff for Prussia, to make it appear that the latter had recoiled before the threats of France. The French Foreign Office therefore pressed for a formal letter from William forbidding his kinsman to renew his candidature. The King was not willing to go so far, inasmuch as the matter was now for all practical purposes closed. Then by a blunder, to be paid for by a great nation's tears, De Gramont required Benedetti, the French ambassador, to wait on William at the watering-place of Ems, on the fateful 13th of July, to demand a binding pledge from the King that the Prince should *never* again aspire to the throne of Spain. The King declined somewhat coldly to do as requested; but he parted from Benedetti on terms of perfect cordiality, and it was understood that the negotiations were to continue amicably.

"Benedetti had not therefore been insulted, nor did he complain of an insult." [1] But, as all the world knows to-day, Bismarck in Berlin deliberately gave to the press a garbled telegram from Ems representing the King as treating the envoy with gross discourtesy and "showing him the door." The great minister's motive was of course to render conflict inevitable in order to consolidate Germany after a victorious war against France.

No device of unmoral statecraft ever had prompter success than this "edited" Ems telegram. The situation at Paris had already become ticklish. Irresponsible journalists had been calling for an "energetic policy" and "for clearing the Prussians out of the right bank of the Rhine." De Gramont, however, had been sure he could obtain a great diplomatic success without fighting; and the Emperor and Ollivier, the premier, had been firmly on the side of peace. In fact on the 12th, when the order to Benedetti had been sent, the Council of Ministers had voted that whatever the reply of the King of Prussia, "the Government would content itself with what it had obtained." Now, however, the wine-glass seemed flung across the table in the face of France. The warm summer weather filled the Paris boulevards. The one roar was, "To Berlin!" For Napoleon III to have refused to answer the challenge would have cost the Second Empire the last remnants of its waning prestige. How long the "Man of Destiny" could then have kept his crown would have been a matter for nice calculation.

[1] Chuquet.

FOOLISH CONFIDENCE OF THE GOVERNMENT

The nation had been fed up on lying statements as to the efficiency of the army. In the Cabinet the war party instantly gained the upper hand. The Empress was all for action. Personal prejudices were swaying the queen of elegance and fashion. "This is *my* war!" she is alleged to have exclaimed. "We will crush those Protestant Prussians!" The Emperor was still half persuaded to peace, but he was racked by disease and overborne by the clamor. On the 15th of July, Ollivier appeared in the Chamber to ask for a credit of 50,000,000 francs for war purposes. Thiers vainly tried to pin him down to facts and discover whether the "insult" was really so deadly as represented. The premier waved him aside. In the spirit of explosive patriotism then reigning, anything like calm debate was impossible. By an enormous majority war was declared (July 19, 1870).

The leaders of the French nation were either men living in a fool's paradise, or else they were criminally leading the nation over a precipice, merely to postpone for a little interval their own personal ejection from power. Ollivier made his everfamous utterance, "I accept the challenge with a light heart." De Gramont (after the event) said: "I decided upon war with an absolute confidence in victory. I believed in the greatness of my country, its strength, its warlike virtues, even as I believe in my holy religion." But, after all, war is primarily a military undertaking. Neither the premier nor the foreign minister were military experts, and what were their military "experts" saying? Lebœuf, the Minister of War, was assuring his colleagues that "the army was ready"; and when pressed to tell what that meant, replied, "I mean that the army is perfectly equipped in every respect; that it will not need a single gaiter button for a year to come!" And so a great nation was sent down into the valley of humiliation.

The military story of 1870 has become fairly familiar now to every educated American.[1] We all understand how complete

[1] The author has contributed his interpretation of the military events in 1870-71 in *The Roots of the War* (N.Y. 1918), pp. 3-23, wherein the principal battles, etc., are outlined.

was the preparation in Prussia and her South-German allies; how like an impersonal engine of destruction Von Moltke's thousands mobilized in perfect order and with admirable equipment set forth toward the Rhine. We also know how the instant the summons came to active service, the military machine of the Second Empire displayed its complete incompetence. Of course the prime evil had been that Napoleon III in military no less than civil affairs had not been able to command the best abilities in France. His generals were mostly adventurers, downright "grafters," or at best routine-hardened mediocrities who assumed that because Napoleon the Great had defeated the Prussians at Jena, the same methods would enable "Napoleon the Little" to defeat the Prussians again, say at Frankfort. The soldiers were brave, the subaltern officers competent; but the higher command, the methods of supply, etc., were execrable. The field guns were much inferior to the Prussian, and so through nearly every detail of the service. The military reforms proposed in 1868 had been most imperfectly executed.[1] There were no adequate reserves. The bulk of the youth of France had not been trained to arms. The old professional army, in short, was practically all that could be relied upon, and up to August 1 it barely exceeded 250,000 men, to be pitted against much larger Prussian forces which were steadily augmenting. A competent critic, assessing the disaster which followed, assigned the ruin of the nation to three causes, easy to state — "inferiority of numbers, inferiority of weapons, inferiority of the higher command." More pithily still might be set down the one cause of causes — the incompetence of Napoleon III to exercise the power he had seized by a crime.

Napoleon had done more than get himself embroiled with Prussia when he ought to have known enough to keep the

[1] In fairness it should be said that Marshal Niel, a decidedly able war minister, tried energetically to reform the military system. If he had lived much might have been accomplished; but in 1869 he died. His successor, Lebœuf, was a boastful meddler, who undid most of Niel's reforms and accomplished nothing on his own account.

peace. He had also failed to make any alliance for France. Austria might have moved against Prussia, but she feared a counter-attack by Russia, and waited for "the first French victories" — which never came. Italy might have come to Napoleon's aid, but her price was the evacuation of Rome by the French troops. The Emperor was too dependent upon the Clericals to dare to leave the Pope to his fate. The French garrison remained in Rome until the situation had become hopeless in the North. France, therefore, went into the war without a friend, with an army miserably organized and equipped, and, as it soon appeared, still more miserably commanded. The result was hardly doubtful the moment the two hosts came to grips.

Even before the first defeats it began to be evident that things were very wrong. It was said that the telegraph offices swarmed with soldiers and officers all writing messages beginning, "Please send me." Reports of utter confusion came back to Paris from Metz, the grand headquarters. Nevertheless the capital continued excited and joyfully expectant. Late in July the Emperor and the young Prince Imperial took trains for Metz to join the army, leaving the Empress in Paris as regent. Father and son were never to see Paris again.

For our purposes what now happened can be stated in the briefest possible manner.

1. To satisfy the impatience of the French populace for a "victory," on August 2 Napoleon ordered an attack on a weak Prussian detachment just across the frontier at Saarbrücken. It was absurd to call it a battle. The Prussian battalion retired after a little firing. The Emperor telegraphed that the Prince had had his "baptism of fire," and the skirmish was celebrated with Te Deums as being a really important victory.

2. On August 4 an overwhelming force of Prussians surprised and defeated a French division at Weissenburg, thus winning the first serious engagement.

3. On August 6, 45,000 French under MacMahon were attacked at Wörth in Alsace by about twice as many Prussians.

After valiant resistance the French had to flee in what was little better than rout.

4. On this same disastrous August 6 the French corps of Frossard was attacked at Forbach in Lorraine. It beat off the first attacks, but finally had to retire, more as a consequence of bad generalship than of the inability of the soldiery to stop the Prussians.

5. Paris had waited impatiently for the successes promised by the Government. On the very day after the defeat at Wörth, the city was sent for some hours into a frenzied ecstasy over the false report (possibly instigated to promote stock speculations) of a great victory and the capture of the Prussian Crown Prince. Then came bulletins admitting that the enemy was across the frontier, "which fact presented us marked military advantages," and that "all could be recovered." The reaction of feeling, of course, needed a victim. Ollivier resigned. Count Palikao became head of the ministry (August 10). He was a pompous, utterly inefficient man, who continued the policy of lying about the situation, saying oracularly, "If Paris knew *what I know*, the city would be illuminated."

6. The Germans drove right onward against Metz. The Emperor abandoned the command of the main army to Marshal Bazaine (a showy, selfish individual, overwhelmed by a situation far too great for him) and got away from Metz just in time to escape being hemmed in by the Prussians. The latter forced the French forces back into Metz in a series of battles beginning on August 14 and culminating in the decisive engagement of Gravelotte (August 18). The French fought bravely, but Bazaine ruined all his chances by great sluggishness in action, and utter failure to fling in his ample reserves to reinforce hard-pressed divisions in the firing line. Soon he was blockaded in Metz, and was calling lustily for a relieving army.

7. Napoleon dared not go back to Paris with the awful tale of defeat. He took refuge in the camp at Châlons where his best general, MacMahon, was trying to organize a very heterogene-

DISASTER OF SEDAN — NAPOLEON PRISONER

ous reserve army into something useful.[1] MacMahon wished to leave Bazaine to hold out for a while, and to retire himself slowly toward Paris, exhausting the Germans by Fabian tactics. Since his was the only regular field army now available for France, this advice was the one thing really possible. But Palikao and the affrighted Empress telegraphed from Paris that if the army retreated without trying to rescue Bazaine, there would be a revolution which would destroy the dynasty. In defiance of all good strategy, MacMahon set off for the Meuse, vainly hoping to make a junction with Bazaine. With his army went the Emperor, a sad guest, a helpless witness of events he could not control. As might have been expected, MacMahon was chased down by Von Moltke, penned up by vastly superior forces in Sedan near the Belgian line, and after a brave and almost frantic struggle, he was forced to surrender on September 2, with 82,000 unwounded men, including — as the Germans gleefully reported — "one Emperor."

Napoleon III telegraphed laconically to Paris: "The army has been defeated and is captive. I myself am a prisoner." The Prussians sent him to a pleasant castle in Hesse where he remained until after the war. Then he departed to exile in England. He had done to France almost all the harm which one man could.

8. The Prussians now, of course, advanced directly on Paris. There was no longer any French field army capable of opposing them. Strasbourg and other frontier fortresses were still holding out gallantly but hopelessly. Bazaine lay supinely under the guns of Metz. By September 19 the Prussians had seized Versailles and begun the investment of the capital. They had no longer to fight against the Second Empire, but against the new "Government of the National Defense."

The moment the fell news of Sedan spread in Paris the old

[1] Despite his defeat at Wörth, MacMahon was the only one of the French generals capable of meeting Von Moltke with any show of equality. Had he been given a free hand, uninterfered with by cowardly politicians, he might have saved France from the worst consequences of the war.

bonds of authority were snapped. The lying bulletins and the creeping consciousness that the myrmidons of "Napoleon the Little" were leading the country into a frightful physical disaster had exasperated the Parisians. It speaks well for their self-restraint that there were not violent lynchings and even massacres.

On the night of September 3 the Chamber was in session. Jules Favre, a Republican leader, instantly proposed that the Bonapartist régime be considered ended and that a provisional government be set up. In the prevailing torpor, his proposal was neither rejected nor accepted. At 10 A.M. on the 4th, workingmen were parading and crying, "Downfall! Downfall!" At the Tuileries the ministers were having a last distracted conference with the Empress Regent. Palikao offered to try to hold down the mob with "40,000 men," but no 40,000 reliable troops were available. So the day passed in futile debates amid all the supposedly ruling bodies. At last, while the Chamber was voting on a motion of Thiers for a committee of national defense, the mob swept into the building. The session was broken up. The members, to please the people, withdrew to the City Hall. Here they were joined by Trochu, the military governor of Paris, a man who had the confidence of the garrison, and who had no great personal friendship for Eugénie. Trochu put himself at the head of a new provisional government. His fellow members were mostly Republicans. The most prominent were Jules Favre, who took the portfolio of Foreign Affairs, and Gambetta who became Minister of the Interior.

The crisis was not one that permitted constitutional quibbling or nice processes of adjustment and transition. Eugénie fled (somewhat beset by the mob), chased from the Tuileries by the yells of "Deposition!" and "Long live the Republic!" Thanks to the aid of her American dentist, Dr. Evans,[1] she presently, with

[1] Later-day readers will not fail to note with some humor that as William II of Prussia had his indispensable court dentist, the dapper American, Dr. Davis, so Napoleon III and his family likewise were served by a skillful Yankee, Dr. Evans.

GOVERNMENT OF THE NATIONAL DEFENCE

some adventures, escaped to England, there to enter upon a long exile. The Senate and the Legislative Chamber dispersed without much dignity. Thiers spoke the obituary words for the helpless deputies: "We can neither resist nor assist those who are fighting against the enemy. *We can only say, 'God help them!'* "

The Government of National Defense was received promptly with obedience by all France. There was nothing else to do, unless the land were to be consigned to anarchy in the face of a victorious advancing enemy. And so again France had a "republic" — but a republic handicapped by terrors without and utter demoralization within; a republic given the almost impossible task of saving the nation from physical ruin. No new government ever came into being on harder terms, yet this was to be the Government which was to emerge twice victor of the Marne, victorious at Verdun, victorious in Champagne, and through its commander-in-chief to speak for the democracies of the world in dictating the armistice to the Hohenzollern in 1918. But before that "day of glory" France was to go down into the Valley of the Shadow for many distressful years.

The new Government tried to negotiate with the Prussians. Napoleon III had made the war. Napoleon was now gone. The French people were willing to pay for peace by a heavy indemnity — so Jules Favre argued in an interview with Bismarck; but when the latter talked of annexing Alsace and northern Lorraine he met the proud answer, "Not one inch of our lands, not one stone of our fortresses." The war must go on. "We are not in power, but in combat!" announced the Republican chiefs to the country, and they called on France to defend the national integrity. Thiers was started off on a round of the European capitals, in vain quest of an alliance;[1] while all energies at home were devoted to resistance to the bitter end.

[1] He received friendly expressions of regret at the plight of France, but not one Great Power would do the only thing that might have stopped the Prussian — namely, threaten to draw the sword. This tacit permission that France should be crushed was duly regretted in London and St. Petersburg, after 1900, as the Pan-German menace grew.

If the French did not save their territory in the struggle which followed, they assuredly saved their honor. The case was so desperate that there would have been no shame in prompt surrender to the enemy.[1] Outside of the besieged garrisons of Metz and Strasbourg there were barely 95,000 regular troops (widely scattered) at the orders of the Government, and almost no dependable reserves. Of these troops about 50,000 were in Paris. The Prussians were advancing with over 230,000, flushed with victory and admirably organized.

But between September 4 and 19 (when the enemy closed in) enormous efforts were made at the capital. Heavy naval guns were rushed up from the arsenals at Cherbourg and Brest; 125,000 "Gardes Mobiles" (a kind of militia) were brought from the provinces, and a great fraction of the city folk were enrolled in the new "National Guard." In all 500,000 persons were listed for the defense of the capital.[2] Unfortunately this number was utterly deceptive. Undisciplined, without competent officers, embodied in the haste of panic, most of these troops had nothing but fervid patriotism to pit against Von Moltke's veterans. It was impossible to use the bulk of them for offensive fighting, and the Germans were, of course, too canny to try to

[1] Undoubtedly by November, 1870, the position of France and of Paris was nigh hopeless, and prudent men began to counsel capitulation. General Ducrot (one of the chief officers in Paris), however, spoke the sentiments of very many, when he told Thiers that he felt the capital should still hold out and gain time for the country to raise new armies and make another effort.

"You speak as a soldier," said Thiers, "not as a statesman."

"I speak as a statesman," replied Ducrot; "a great nation like France always recovers from its *material* ruin, but it can never recover from moral ruin. This generation will suffer, but the next will benefit by the honor which we shall have saved."

Ducrot was right. France saved her honor and her self-respect by her resistance after Sedan. Out of the agony of the winter of 1870–71 was born the spirit which led to the victory of 1918.

[2] It was afterward wisely argued that the Government of the National Defense made a serious mistake in leaving so large a garrison locked up in Paris. It could have used the troops better for relief operations from the outside. There was no danger that the Germans would make a direct assault upon the forts protecting the city.

GAMBETTA ESCAPES FROM PARIS

storm the defense system which girdled Paris. Nevertheless, this energy, plus the foresight which hurried huge quantities of provisions into the city, enabled the capital to hold out, not the four weeks that Von Moltke had reckoned, but four months.

To save Paris before provisions failed, it was needful that the departments should raise a huge relieving army and cut through the besiegers' lines. But the policy of placing so large a garrison in the capital made the prospects of the attempt very discouraging, despite the great potential resources of provincial France. The new Government remained for the most part in Paris, but stationed at Tours three delegates to organize the exterior war. They were rather inefficient men. Only 23,000 reliable troops and one battery of six guns were said to have been actually at their disposal when they began their work, but a mighty moral reinforcement was at hand.

It was before the days of aeroplanes, but the Parisians were sending up balloons (when the wind favored) to drift across the German lines. On October 9, Léon Gambetta, thirty-two years old, the same young advocate who had recently excoriated the Second Empire,[1] escaped from Paris by balloon and appeared in Tours. He now came as a "delegate" from the imprisoned Government in the capital. Soon he seemed himself the incarnation of the entire Government of France. With an energy worthy of Carnot in the original Revolution, he flung himself into the task of organizing "the nation in arms." Every able-bodied Frenchman was called to the colors. Without competent staff officers, forced to build his own organization, obeyed more because of his imperious patriotism than because of any lawful commission, Gambetta called into being vast armies. In four months he armed, organized, and sent into battle 600,000 men, fired by the lyrical proclamations which the French masses loved so well.

Gambetta's handicaps, however, could not have been overcome by a Napoleon I. He could enroll large armies, but he was

[1] See p. 492.

allowed no time to train them. He had almost no well-tested professional officers; only brave amateurs who had to learn the grim art of war by leading their fellow citizens against the most scientifically prepared army in the world. No genius for organization, no fervid appeal to patriotism could make well-intentioned bourgeois and peasants into hardened and experienced soldiers overnight. Nevertheless, Gambetta would probably have saved Paris had only he been spared a new calamity; had not the German army around Paris been almost doubled in strength.

After their first victories, the Prussians had besieged Strasbourg. On August 13 they had begun the bombardment, intending by their deadly shell-fire, aimed at private buildings, schools, etc., rather than at the forts, to induce the citizens to put pressure on the commander to surrender. In this they utterly failed. The people took refuge in cellars. Many public edifices were burned including two valuable libraries. The famous cathedral was somewhat shattered. But the citizens bore up bravely. As their commandant told them, "Your heroism, at this hour, consists in patience." The city, however, had not been properly provisioned, and on September 27 there was nothing for it but to hoist the white flag over the cathedral. Strasbourg entered upon her forty-eight years of captivity.[1]

The fall of Strasbourg, of course, released a considerable German force for use before Paris, but that was nothing to what became available a month later. Bazaine had clung around the fortress of Metz in an utterly cowardly manner. He made no resolute efforts to cut his way through the German blockade, though the besieging force was not overwhelmingly superior to his own. When news of the fall of the Empire drifted into his camp his "stupid and criminal" mind turned to politics. He

[1] By the bombardment 300 civilians, men, women, and children, had been killed, and over 2000 wounded; 600 houses had been burned. It was deeds like these which made the Alsatians very loath to be reconciled to their new Prussian masters!

would negotiate with the enemy, patch up some kind of truce, lead back to Paris the only army left to France, and reëstablish the Second Empire or some other kind of dictatorship. Bismarck spun him along with sham negotiations and half-promises until Bazaine's supplies were exhausted and the morale of his soldiers was so undermined that there was nothing possible but surrender. It was an infinitely more disgraceful capitulation than that of Sedan. On October 27, 1870, Bazaine surrendered at Metz with 179,000 men, 1570 cannon, and 260,000 muskets. His act was the last evil legacy of the Second Empire, and came just in time to complete the act of ruin.[1]

Bazaine's duty had been to try to cut his way through the enemy. Failing that, he ought to have held out to the last gasp, even if his men were starving. His mere existence in Metz kept 200,000 Germans immobilized, and consequently made the relief of Paris by Gambetta possible. Now at one stroke this whole great German force was released to aid in the blockade of Paris. Gambetta's relieving armies were just beginning to take shape and to get into action. On November 9, a fairly competent French general, D'Aurelles de Paladine, won a victory at Coulmiers (almost the first gleam of sunlight on the French arms) and retook Orléans from the Teutons. But before any use

[1] After the close of hostilities, in 1873, Bazaine was tried by court martial for gross neglect of duty in surrendering when he did. It was still left vague why he practically played the traitor, entering into a political negotiation with Bismarck, and even betraying to the Germans the all-important fact that he was near the end of his provisions. Probably he entertained some vicious notion of coming back to Paris as another "restorer of order,." He was in fact an utterly mediocre man, though typical of the kind of adventurers the Second Empire brought to the top.

During the trial he asserted in way of defense that after the capture of the Emperor and the flight of the Empress there was nothing left to fight for: "All was lost." "There was still France!" crushingly answered the president of the court.

Bazaine was sentenced to death, but MacMahon, then President, goodheartedly commuted the penalty for an old comrade to twenty years' imprisonment. In 1874 Bazaine escaped from custody and fled to Spain. There he lived in despised exile, counted by most Frenchmen as a kind of Benedict Arnold, until he died in 1888.

could be made of this success, the German besieging hosts had been so reinforced by "the avalanche descending from Metz" that the case became absolutely hopeless.

The remainder of the melancholy story is soon told. A winter of unusual severity added to the miseries of the unhappy French armies. Ill-equipped, shoeless, coatless often, unacquainted with their new and half-trained officers, the French soldiery did all that mortals might, but they could do no more. Every attempt to break through the German blockade was defeated. Every attempt (several times bravely undertaken) by the Paris garrison to break out was likewise defeated. Gambetta still toiled on; optimistic, indefatigable, willing to struggle against every adverse circumstance. The central departments of France, however, were becoming terribly ravaged by the war. The peasants were losing heart. The military men were telling Gambetta that the case was hopeless, and in January conditions within Paris brought the war to its inevitable climax.

The capital held out until the daily bread ration had been reduced to 300 grammes, and that of a "black and gluey mixture of rice, oats, hempseed, and bran." Horse meat was selling at 12 francs ($2.40) per pound (500 grammes), but a person was only allowed to buy 30 grammes per day. Rats were worth 2 francs apiece. The lions, elephants, and giraffes in the menagerie had long since been served up in exclusive restaurants.[1] Firewood and coal had become exhausted in a winter so severe that wine froze in the vats. Young children were dying by hundreds for lack of milk, and of course the mortality among the invalids and the old was frightful. The Germans early in January began also a long-range bombardment, killing and wounding in all about 400 persons, although this cannonading did little to produce the final surrender. The end came when the authorities knew

---

[1] The food situation in Paris during the latter part of the siege is well illustrated by the tale of the wealthy gentleman who sent to a butcher-shop to inquire if he could buy anything edible for his two favorite cats. The reply was that they had nothing the cats would care to eat, but they would gladly make a cash offer for the cats themselves.

that in a few days even the scanty bread ration would fail, and feared lest in that case they could not handle the inevitable rioting.

Jules Favre went out to Versailles to the Prussians on January 23. Bismarck was inexorable to pleas for mercy and on January 28 Paris surrendered, most of the regular garrison becoming prisoners of war. When the news spread to the departments, although Gambetta wished to go on fighting, the leaders of the army told him the situation was hopeless. France must make peace on whatever terms or face absolute ruin. The brokenhearted "dictator" quietly laid down his office and retired to Spain, while Favre and Thiers conducted the final sad negotiations with Bismarck. A National Convention was to be called, to give a popular approval to the treaty, and to establish a permanent government for France. The country which had seemed incomparably the first Power of Europe as recently as 1856, had now to submit to the demands of ceding Alsace and northern Lorraine (including Metz) to Germany, and of paying an indemnity of five billion francs (one billion dollars). It was only thanks to the firmness and even to the despairing threats of Thiers that the strong fortress of Belfort was not also required,[1] and six billion francs instead of five. The humiliation of the "Grand Nation" was abject and unparalleled.

The National Assembly met at Bordeaux on February 12, 1871. The circumstances under which it was elected and the character of its members will be discussed in the next chapter. On February 26 the preliminaries of the treaty of peace were drafted between Thiers and Bismarck at Versailles. There was an agonizing debate when the deputies from Alsace-Lorraine pleaded with their fellow countrymen against being handed over to the hated alien and proclaimed "their immutable will to

[1] Belfort was not taken by the Germans. It held out gallantly till the end of the war. The French were thus doubly resolved not to give it up. The dramatic interview between Bismarck and Thiers is related by the author in *The Roots of the War*, p. 21.

remain French." There was nothing to do, however, but to record their protest and sorrowfully to bid them depart. One of the dissenting and protesting minority, that declared the whole act of separation void, was a young politician, a certain Georges Clemenceau, who many years later was to ride again into Strasbourg with the Tricolor going on before him.

The cup of national sorrow was not yet full. After the slaughter of Frenchmen by Prussians must come the slaughter of Frenchmen by Frenchmen. The sufferings of the Parisian masses during the siege undoubtedly had been bitter. There had been several times, even while the investment lasted, when a popular uprising, a mad spasm of discontent, had almost overthrown the Provisional Government. On the 31st of October, 1870, a turbulent band of insurgents had tried to usurp power at the City Hall and had been dispersed only by armed force. Now the vain struggle was over. The Germans had made their brief parade through the Arc de Triomphe. The great masses of the city were left disheartened, restless, with most of them out of employment and still very unsatisfactorily fed. As Machiavelli has wisely generalized, "Almost all the great sieges known to history have terminated with seditions, for the moral and physical sufferings of the people predispose them to be influenced by agitators, while the arms with which they are unavoidably provided furnish the weapons for a rising." This was exactly the case in Paris in that most unhappy spring of 1871.

The next chapter will explain how the new National Assembly was largely dominated by partisans whom the Parisian populace considered monarchical and reactionary. The deputies first met at Bordeaux to be safe from German molestation, but on the 10th of March, as the Germans retired,[1] the Assembly departed for Versailles. This selection of the old Royalist residence town

[1] The Germans were to stay in the northeastern departments until the indemnity had been paid. They were also to remain for a while in some of the forts dominating Paris.

and not of Paris seemed an insult to the capital, a sign that the Assembly did not sympathize with the sufferings of the Parisians and would do nothing for them. Bad blood was brewing, and every radical agitator found his opportunity.

The industrial population of the eastern quarters of Paris had "gone through the siege in a violent state of exaltation, physical and moral, with diseased nerves and a distracted mind." The workers had had little to eat and had been deprived of much of their familiar light wine, but there had been an unfortunate abundance of whiskey and brandy. When the city fell, not understanding that modern warfare is less a matter of bravery than of careful, scientific preparation, they readily charged the defeat to sheer "treason" on the part of the Government. They were passionate Republicans and believed the Assembly was about to call back the kings. They had been organized as part of the National Guard, and now they clung tightly to their weapons, and refused to be deprived of some two hundred and thirty cannon which they claimed were the property of the people of Paris and not of the Central Government. While they were resentful and distrustful, and were being worked upon by the Socialist chiefs (who saw their opportunity), the Assembly committed a grievous blunder. It suppressed the pay of $1\frac{1}{2}$ francs (30 cents) per day which had been given the National Guardsmen, and which, considering the suspension of all regular industry, was the sole sustenance of many working-men. The Assembly also ordered the resumption of the collection of debts, rents, etc., which had been interrupted during the siege. One hundred and fifty thousand Parisians suddenly found themselves liable to legal process for unpaid rents. Needless to say discontent grew apace.

On the 18th of March, 1871, Thiers, now head of the new executive government set up by the Assembly, ordered some troops to seize a park of cannon belonging to the Paris National Guard. The populace resisted. The troops wavered and fraternized with the malcontents. The guns were not taken, and in the disturbance a band of desperadoes murdered the generals Lacomte and Clement Thomas. This was the beginning of a hideous civil war which lasted until May 28.

The capital now found itself in the hands of the "Council General of the Commune of Paris," made up of delegates elected by the industrial quarters alone. This Commune professed to be the regular government of the city, appointed ministers, adopted the "red" flag of ultra-radicalism, and pretended to issue decrees binding upon all France. The ruling idea, however, seems to have been to reduce France to a loose federation of autonomous communes, each working out its own particular brand of socialism. In one sense the movement represented Paris battling against the departments; the struggle of the ideals of the industrial population fighting against the ideals of the peasants and the bourgeoisie. Some of the Communist chiefs were men of sincere enthusiasms and considerable ability; some were unpoised fanatics; some were mere uncaged criminals of the most dangerous type. As the struggle went on, and tended to go against the Socialists, increasingly desperate counsels of course prevailed, and the viler elements came ever more conspicuously to the top. The Commune began then, like many another social movement, in a genuine attempt to redress undoubted wrongs and to bring nearer the Earthly Paradise: it ended with blood-stained desperadoes trying to burn down Paris to make its ash-heaps the monument to their own ruin.

Early in April the Communist troops marched out on Versailles to break up the Assembly. That body, however, had collected loyalist forces and drove them back. The Germans had now released many of their prisoners. MacMahon's and Bazaine's veterans came back from captivity, only to find France rent with civil war and threatened with anarchy on top of foreign invasion. Thiers put Marshal MacMahon in charge of the Government forces (some 150,000 men) with which to recapture the capital. So Paris underwent the miseries of a second siege: not this time one of mere starvation or long-range bombardment, but like the fighting of 1830 and 1848, barrier by barrier, and street by street, although both attack and defense were now more sustained, elaborate, and desperate. The Germans from their forts in the outskirts looked on with sardonic neutrality while their late foes slaughtered one another. MacMahon had on his side numbers, equipment, better leadership, and discipline, as well as the moral asset of the better cause. It took him several weeks to storm the outer forts and make a breach in the inner "girdle" of Paris. Then on the 21st of May these were forced, and the fighting began for actual possession of the city.

It was hellish, utterly destructive warfare. The Government troops were madly exasperated at the action of their foes who would thus add to the agonies of France while the victorious alien was still upon their soil.[1] Quarter was seldom asked and more seldom given. In brutal desperation the Communists finally set fire with kerosene to many of the most magnificent edifices in the city. The Tuileries Palace was burned. The Louvre barely escaped. Many other buildings were destroyed or scathed. "The Seine ran down between two walls of fire." Various prominent personages, whom the Communists had seized in April as "hostages," were put to death in cold blood. So perished the Archbishop of Paris, Monseigneur Darboy, and several other prominent churchmen, and the president of the High Court of Cassation.

The victorious troops on their part fought their way forward without mercy. The last stand of the Communists was around the desecrated tombs of the great cemetery of Père-Lachaise. By the 28th of May "the Bloody Week" was over, and the last barricade was forced. After that Paris was to have respite from

[1] Four decades afterward the responsible historian Lavisse, after confessing that the Parisian populace were not without serious grievances in 1871, records as his solemn judgment, "Of all the insurrections whereof history keeps record, undoubtedly the most criminal was that of March, 1871, made under the eyes of the victorious enemy."

actual warfare until Prussian shells dropped again from gigantic cannon and aeroplanes in 1914–18. According to official figures 6500 persons perished in the fighting or were shot upon being taken with arms in their hands. The actual number, however, was probably fully 17,000. At least 36,000 prisoners were marched out to Versailles to be tried by court martial. Of these fully 10,000 were condemned to transportation; often to the desolate Pacific island of New Caledonia. The severity and recklessness of the punishment corresponded with the anger and horror of the victors. And so at length "the torment passed." Thiers and his colleagues could devote themselves to the rebuilding of France.

The Franco-Prussian War, followed as it was by the Commune, inflicted on France a downfall, a sudden humiliation, and an enormous physical loss almost unparalleled prior to 1914. At one blow the country seemed stricken from the list of great nations and its very existence threatened. The disaster had appeared to point to something inherently rotten in the whole foundation of French society, and to be proof positive that here was a decadent and tottering state. The world for the instant lost confidence in France, and took her at her coarsest critic's measure, and France almost lost confidence in herself. No longer the "first Power of Europe" the issue now was whether she was about to sink to the level of decrepit Spain, forever overshadowed and coerced by her mail-clad Hohenzollern neighbor.

The mere physical loss was great. Between the economic prostration of the war, the destruction of property in battle, and the great indemnity due Germany, the nation was at least three billion dollars the poorer; a sum esteemed colossal before 1914, and that loss coming too with 4300 square miles of territory and over 1,500,000 citizens violently wrenched away. As for the seizure of Alsace-Lorraine, it fixed a great gulf of enmity between Frenchman and Teuton which, in the words of a distin-

THE LOSS OF ALSACE-LORRAINE 517

guished American, was "to unsettle the peace of the world for nearly fifty years." [1]

"*Think of it always, speak of it never,*" was the advice Gambetta gave his countrymen concerning the national loss; but such heroic counsel could hardly be followed. The question of "revanche" thrust itself into almost every political discussion directly or indirectly. It was the phantom behind every act of French diplomacy, and behind every act of German diplomacy plotting to keep the snatched plunder and to render its former possessor helpless forever. The duty of "revenge" was taught as a bitter gospel to the next generation, who grew up without the personal memories of seeing the Prussian spiked helmets going down the village streets. In the decade before the Great War it was pretended that the memory was gradually seeming less acute, that the mourning over Strasbourg was becoming more perfunctory. The call to arms, at the threat of the new German invasion, evoked all the old agonies and yearnings of 1871, and to the sons of France the war was not merely a new defense of the beloved *patrie*, it was a crusade to undo an intolerable wrong.

The following is from the most popular textbook upon French history, used by the children of France during the two decades before 1914, its author one of the most distinguished historians of his day and a member of the famous Academy: [2]

After speaking of the great prosperity of France under the Third Republic, the author goes on to say that "this must not suffer us to

---

[1] Speech of President Wilson before Congress, January 8, 1918.

The economic consequences of the loss of this territory to France were very serious. The value of the iron and coal mines was not realized until later, but in 1871 France was deprived of one quarter of her cotton spindles, as well as of a large fraction of all her other textile industries.

[2] *La Deuxième Année d'Histoire de France* (pp. 404-06), by Ernest Lavisse, a book intended for use of boys and girls of eleven to thirteen. The words italicized were printed in heavy type in the original. A certain amount of patriotic exhortation is here omitted: it is entirely along the lines of the material that is reproduced.

The lesson inculcated in this manual was one calculated to burn deep into

forget the disasters of 1870 and 1871, following the peace of Frankfort which humiliated and diminished France. *Our old-time military honor has been wounded.*

"*We were beaten*, because our army was too small, was badly organized, badly commanded, and because our fortresses were not in a proper condition for defense.

"The Imperial Government failed in its duty to maintain the army and the fortresses. Our disasters impose upon us the obligation to watch ourselves, through the deputies which we elect, over the safety of our native land, and *never to entrust our destinies to the power of only one man.*

"*We were beaten*, because many Frenchmen loved too well the pleasures of peace, the tranquillity which it gives, and the riches which it enables them to procure. They said that an army cost heavily, and that it was better to use the money to build machines for industry than to cast cannon. But war came. Our losses, added to the war indemnity, amounted to at least fifteen billion francs [$3,000,000,000]. Our disasters teach us that all economy practiced upon the army costs too dearly, and that *France, which has formidable armed neighbors, must place and keep herself in a state to resist them.*

"*We were beaten*, because very many Frenchmen believed there was no need for them to learn the art of being a soldier.

"*We were beaten*, because very many Frenchmen believed the time for wars was passed. They said that men ought to love one another, and that a war was a barbarism which dishonored humanity. But the Germans were writing and teaching that war is an honor for humanity, and they hated France and never lost an occasion to treat us as 'hereditary enemies.' For a long time they were preparing to make war on France and THEY ARE PREPARING AGAIN. *Our disasters teach us that it is needful to love France above everything else, and then, in the second place only, 'humanity.'* "

"All war begun without just cause is a crime, and so is the conquest of lands belonging to others. France must renounce all ideas of wars of conquest. But at the peace of Frankfort France had to cede provinces inhabited by 1,500,000 Frenchmen. The Germans have never asked the inhabitants of Alsace-Lorraine if they wish to become Germans. Since 1871 they have governed our fellow citizens with extreme forms

---

the memories of the most backward lad of the rearmost bench in all the little communal schools from Calais to Bayonne. The passage shows clearly how the iron had entered into the soul of France.

This textbook had extremely wide use in the schools.

DUTY TO REMEMBER THE LOST PROVINCES 519

of severity. Every time they have had a chance the Alsatians have proved that their sentiments have not changed. When they have elected deputies to the German parliament they have charged them to protest against the treaty of Frankfort, which has delivered them over to Germany.

"They have proved that they have kept faithfully their attachment to France. *The first duty of France is not to forget Alsace-Lorraine which does not forget her.*"

www.ingramcontent.com/pod-product-compliance
Lightning Source LLC
Chambersburg PA
CBHW020344170426
43200CB00005B/42